MANAGING CROSS-CULTURAL COMMUNICATION

Managing Cross-Cultural Communication

Principles and Practice

Barry Maude

First published 2011 by
PALGRAVE MACMILLAN

Palgrave Macmillan in the UK is an imprint of Macmillan Publishers Limited,
registered in England, company number 785998, of Houndmills, Basingstoke,
Hampshire RG21 6XS.

Palgrave Macmillan in the US is a division of St Martin's Press LLC,
175 Fifth Avenue, New York, NY 10010.

Palgrave Macmillan is the global academic imprint of the above companies
and has companies and representatives throughout the world.

Palgrave® and Macmillan® are registered trademarks in the United States,
the United Kingdom, Europe and other countries.

ISBN 978-0-230-24953-0

This book is printed on paper suitable for recycling and made from fully
managed and sustained forest sources. Logging, pulping and manufacturing
processes are expected to conform to the environmental regulations of the
country of origin.

A catalogue record for this book is available from the British Library.

A catalog record for this book is available from the Library of Congress.

10   9   8   7   6   5   4   3   2   1
20 19 18 17 16 15 14 13 12 11

Printed and bound in Great Britain by
CPI Antony Rowe, Chippenham and Eastbourne

Contents

Part 2 Practice

List of figures

Preface

CAREERS AND CROSS-CULTURAL COMMUNICATION

Managing Cross-cultural Communication: Principles and Practice has been written at a time when growing business opportunities in foreign markets are creating more and more demand for managers, business people, and professional staff who have acquired an international outlook and cross-cultural communication ability. For many people, acquiring an international outlook and developing cross-cultural communication skills is a process that begins at college/university level.

Increasingly, managers and business people need to communicate with organisations abroad or with foreign business partners. Growing numbers of expatriate managers, carrying out assignments around the world need to become adept at communicating effectively with the local colleagues and employees. Technical and professional staff who move to other countries for jobs, and students spending some time studying abroad, need to develop cross-cultural communication skills so that they can interact with local people and, through that, learn more about the culture. Managers and professional staff who concentrate on building their careers at home increasingly need cross-cultural communication ability to function effectively in their jobs. In the multicultural workplace, for instance, managers are judged and rewarded by their ability to manage and motivate a diverse workforce.

An international outlook and cross-cultural communication ability contribute to career success, and these attributes are prerequisites for functioning effectively in a world characterized by permeable borders. That is why the topic of cross-cultural communication is already incorporated into numerous academic, professional, management, and international management courses offered by universities and colleges around the world.

READERSHIP

Managing Cross-cultural Communication: Principles and Practice has been written for students on business, management, and international management courses, and also for students on other courses, such as international relations, which study cross-cultural communication in a wider context. The book will also be read by:

- Managers, business people, and professional and technical specialists who are involved in cross-cultural communication because of their jobs – for instance, HR managers in multicultural organisations.

- Expatriate managers and international project personnel.
- People who travel abroad on business.
- Professional people who work with members of other cultures in educational institution or in multicultural workplaces.

These readers will buy the book because it is a readable but serious treatment of the subject, referring to appropriate theories and research.

For many students *Managing Cross-cultural Communication: Principles and Practice* is the only book on the subject they will need to buy. The book covers themes and topics that they need to know about from the point of view of examinations and written assignments. Students majoring in cross-cultural communication studies will use the book as a supplementary text.

AIM OF THE BOOK

Managing Cross-cultural Communication: Principles and Practice sets out the principles and practice of cross-cultural communication in a global context. The book aims to provide a clear and readable introduction to the main problems and issues of cross-cultural communication. Relevant theories and research findings are examined; and important points are illustrated with examples and cases drawn from real life that readers will readily relate to.

Drawing on the author's extensive experience of carrying out consultancy assignments in countries around the world, the book offers practical and realistic guidelines for improving communication practice in a wide range of international and cross-cultural contexts. Situations examined include the multicultural workplace, where the ability to effectively manage cross-cultural communication is a key determinant of managerial success.

HOW THE BOOK IS ORGANISED

The book comes in two parts – Principles and Practice.

Part 1: Principles

Part 1: Principles contains five chapters.

Chapter 1 examines the concept of culture as a logical starting point for understanding the process of cross-cultural communication.

Chapter 2 shows how values are a major source of differences in attitudes and behaviour across cultures, and describes the impact that a culture's values makes on organisations.

Chapter 3 discusses how language differences impede communication when people from different cultures interact and how the barriers can be overcome.

Chapter 4 argues that many aspects of nonverbal communication are cultural products and so liable to be misunderstood by members of other cultures.

Chapter 5 shows how culturally influenced prejudices distorts perception and communication, and thus account for many of the tensions and conflicts in cross-cultural relationships.

Part 2: Practice

Part 2: Practice contains seven chapters.

Chapter 6 explains how the success of expatriate assignments often depends on effectively transferring business and technological knowledge to the host organisation.

Chapter 7 argues that adjustment to a new culture depends on such factors as family situation, personality variables, and cross-cultural communication ability.

Chapter 8 shows how cross-cultural business skills can be developed through formal training programmes – or by using a range of alternative development methods.

Chapter 9 presents the concept of cultural distance, and explains why running a business operation in a culturally distant country can be expensive and risky.

Chapter 10 explains how multicultural teams bring many advantages to their organisations, including creativity and new approaches to problem-solving – but also problems that spring from cultural difference.

Chapter 11 shows how in cross-cultural meetings differences of approach among participants who come from different national cultures are inevitable and have to be dealt with.

Chapter 12 argues that to reap the many benefits of a diverse workforce an organisation must first ensure that its selection procedures are fair and efficient.

KEY FEATURES OF THE BOOK

Summary of key points

Each chapter ends with a summary of key points made in the chapter.

Points for Discussion

Points for Discussion are listed at the end of each chapter, for use in classroom or small-group discussions, or to provide topics for written assignments.

Graphical illustrations

Many of the concepts, theories, and processes discussed in the text are also presented in graphical form. To facilitate classroom discussion, graphical illustrations included in the text could be presented by means of PowerPoint or overhead transparencies.

Mini-cases

Various cross-cultural situations and difficulties drawn from real life are presented in the form of mini-cases. Each mini-case is followed by questions for individual or classroom discussion.

Small-group exercises

Working in pairs or small groups, students discuss key questions posed by each chapter and develop answers that can then be compared with the answers of other groups.

Acknowledgements

Many people contributed to make this book possible. I should particularly like to thank the following people for their interest, help and support:

Dr Jan Schermer helped me to clarify in my own mind the aims of the book and the various approaches that might be taken. Eulla Nasho carried out a survey of intergroup attitudes in Harare and has allowed me to summarise the results. Arthur Shears has kept me aware over a long period of the numerous cross-cultural communication hazards facing international agency staff in crisis and disaster areas around the world. Dr Zhung-zen helped me to understand how cross-cultural interaction theory affects cross-cultural communication practice. Dr Mony Fathy provided illuminating insights into the role of women in modern Islamic societies. Faith and Martin Chiketa gave many examples of the communication dilemmas facing diplomats in culturally distant societies. John Barraclough described the difficulties of running large-scale financial training programmes in developing countries. Dr Silviya Slavova explained how she used nonverbal signals to overcome communication problems with Russian patients. Jessica Mathabatha made many helpful suggestions about content and presentation while I was writing the book. Peter Mountain helped me to understand the wide difference between domestic and international marketing activities. Josephatz Massawe showed me, by example, how to obtain timely and reliable information from individuals and organisations in East Africa.

I should also like to thank Palgrave Macmillan's editorial staff – particularly Ursula Gavin and Ceri Griffiths – for their valuable guidance and support throughout the project. I also owe thanks to Priya Venkat and the copy editing team at Integra for their care and patience. Thanks also to Janice Board and librarians at Staffordshire University, and to library staff at Keele University for all their help and advice.

Every effort has been made to trace all copyright holders, but if any have been inadvertently overlooked the publishers will be pleased to make the necessary arrangements at the first opportunity.

Part 1
Principles

What is culture?

INTRODUCTION

Whenever people from different cultures meet and communicate, cultural norms and expectations surround the participants and guide their thoughts and the way they communicate. That is why examining the concept of culture is a logical starting point for understanding the process of cross-cultural communication since people do not communicate in a vacuum but are imbued by the values, beliefs, and practices of their cultures.

Most definitions of 'culture' are based on the concept of culture as a system of beliefs, values, and practices which enables each culture to solve universal problems in its own unique way. Hofstede's (1980a) landmark survey of 40 national cultures provided the first theoretical basis for understanding national cultural differences. Since then other large-scale surveys, including the GLOBE survey and Schwartz's Value Survey, have provided further evidence about national cultural differences.

Chapter 1 points out that in an increasingly global world, national cultures continue to be extremely important, giving people a sense of identity and uniqueness and providing the legal framework within which multinational firms operate and international trade is carried out. But in all national cultures *subcultures* exist with their own distinctive values. Often effective cross-cultural communication depends on being aware of the characteristics of particular subcultures and how they differ from the dominant majority culture in values, communicative conventions, and norms. Some subcultures are, in effect, countercultures in the sense that they oppose prevailing cultural norms and practices.

Among important cultural questions examined in the chapter is the issue of cultural change. The causes and effects of cultural change are considered, including the impact the change makes on people. Cultural change makes a great impact on organisations (an important component of culture) and the way organisations operate (House et al., 2004). It underlies recent trends away from traditional organisation structures such as functional structures, towards alternative forms such as temporary goal-directed *networks* of organisations.

The chapter refers to relevant theories such as meme theory and cultural evolution theory. These theories explain cultural change by adapting and applying the methods and concepts of biologists studying genetic evolution.

THE MEANING OF CULTURE

Definitions and concepts

Culture is like a kaleidoscope. You look through the eye-piece and if you're a socio-linguist you see that culture is indistinguishable from language and that no two languages can mirror the same reality. If you're a social psychologist you perceive culture as a lens determining what people see in a situation and how they respond to it. For the anthropologist, culture is an engine driving a society's beliefs and traditions forward from generation to generation. As Schein (2004) points out culture, like role, lies at the intersection of several social sciences and reflects some of the biases of each.

More than half a century ago, 64 definitions of 'culture' were identified (Kroeber and Kluckhohn, 1952). Since then the number has expanded exponentially but still no universally acceptable definition has emerged. Recent attempts to define 'culture' include:

- A meaning and information system that is transmitted across generations (Matsumoto et al., 2008).
- Sets of taken-for-granted assumptions (Thompson, 2003).
- Adaptive interactions between humans and environments which are transmitted across time periods (Triandis, 2007).
- A set of basic assumptions – shared solutions to universal problems (Schein, 2004).
- A set of knowledge, beliefs, values, religion, customs, acquired by a group of people and passed on from generation to generation (Harris and Moran, 1996).
- A collective programming of the mind that distinguishes the members of one culture from another (Hofstede, 1994).
- All of the accepted and patterned ways of behaviour of a given people, their ways of thinking, feeling, and acting (Ricard, 1993).

Underpinning most definitions is the concept of culture as a *system of beliefs, values, and practices* which enable particular cultures to solve universal problems (Figure 1.1).

How men and women should relate to each other, how children should be raised, how the aged should be looked after – these are examples of universal

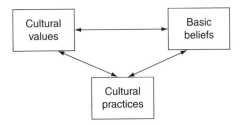

Figure 1.1 Culture as a closed system

problems which each culture solves in its own unique way. Thus the basic functions of culture are universal, although the ways in which the functions play out are localized. In spite of its imprecise nature the concept of culture is a useful tool for understanding the nature of cross-cultural communication. The concept helps us to recognize, for instance, that cross-cultural interactions do not take place in a vacuum – that culture is the hidden hand guiding people's words and behaviour.

Categorizations of culture

Attempts to categorize cultures by alternative classification systems – by religion, for instance – always produce numerous exceptions and anomalies. Thus Iran, Iraq, and Indonesia are all Muslim countries but the countries have distinct, contrasting cultures. Similarly, attempts to categorize cultures by geographic location, historical similarity, and so on invariably lead to many groups protesting about the category in which they have been placed. Perhaps no classification system is capable of fitting the complexity and variety of actual cultural forms.

Although culture remains an imprecise concept, a few helpful generalizations can be made:

- People who share a culture often have the same racial or ethnic background.
- Members of a culture often live in the same geographic region.
- Members of a culture generally share the same value system (which may clash with the value systems of other cultures).
- Cultural conditioning is part of the human condition. Nobody is extra-cultural.
- A person's way of communicating is largely determined by the person's cultural background.

Emic and etic approaches

Cultures are studied by using the 'emic approach' or the 'etic approach' (Peterson and Pike, 2002). An etic approach is the scientific view, while the emic approach is the 'Native' view, the view of the insider. The etic/emic distinction is necessary because the explanations of cultural behaviour are not always those expressed by members of the culture, who may offer spurious reasons for their conduct. The emic approach studies behaviour from within and focuses on the varied ways the culture operates in terms of *its own* beliefs and assumptions. The etic approach, the scientific view, examines beliefs, values, and behaviours that are common to people across many varied cultures. Berry (1969) was the first to present the emic and etic approaches as recommended approaches for studying cultures.

Either approach by itself is restricted in scope and leads to a kind of distortion. That explains why a combination of etic and emic approaches is needed for a methodologically sound assessment of a culture. Cultures are complex. They are more than what appears on the surface. Cuisine, dress, ways of greeting, and so on make an immediate impression on foreign visitors and stick in the memory, but the hidden parts of a culture – the values, beliefs, ways of thinking – are more important for understanding a culture.

Surface and deep-level aspects of a culture

Van Vianen et al. (2004) distinguish between surface and deep-level cultural differences. Surface-level differences are obvious and immediately visible aspects and include climate, housing and transport arrangements, leisure possibilities, and so on. Deep-level cultural differences, on the other hand, relate to values and beliefs that are not immediately visible to a foreign business visitor, tourist, or temporary worker. Deep-level differences might include values such as tolerance, conformity, or acceptance of change. Foreign business visitors who make the effort to discover what a culture is like below the surface often find that they can deal confidently with most of the business and social situations that occur when they visit the country.

VARIETIES OF CULTURE

National cultures

In the nineteenth century, new countries were created when representatives of colonial powers drew lines on a map. Peoples of widely differing cultures, languages, and social systems were yoked together and called a country. An example is Nigeria, with its numerous different languages and cultural traditions. Today, most national cultures are composites of several or many separate cultures.

National boundaries rarely coincide with the boundaries of a culture. Japan is a notable exception as it has retained a single homogeneous culture. Iran, by contrast, is a multicultural state where Fars, Kurds, Arabs, Turks, Azaris, Turkemans, and Baluchis live with their different linguistic, ethnic, and cultural characteristics (Soltani, 2010). Canada, another multicultural state, has distinct Anglophone and Francophone cultures. In Switzerland, there are French Swiss, German Swiss, Italian Swiss, and Romansch Swiss, each group retaining its own cultural identity and speaking its own first language. In a single country there are often major cultural differences between different ethnic groups. In the former Yugoslavia, for instance, although different ethnic groups occupied the same space they were widely separated by differences of religion, tradition, custom, and history.

National cultures differ from each other in numerous ways – for instance, in their *perceptions of time*. In East Asian cultures, time goes more slowly than in Western countries, as Tung (1996: 238) explains:

> There are several reasons why the East Asian pace is slower. One is the focus on the long-term implications of actions. A second reason is the importance attached to the development and nurturing of human relationships.

Zweifel (2003) notes that the rhythm of a typical Swedish movie is much slower than Hollywood but much too fast for Indian viewers. Ji et al. (2001) make the point that a culture's characteristic attitudes towards time may be linked to deep-rooted philosophical tradition in the culture. Thus belief in linear, progressive change is emphasized in American analytic thought, whereas belief in circular, recursive changes is a feature of Chinese dialecticism.

Importance of national culture

In an increasingly global, transnational world, national cultures continue to be extremely important for many reasons. For instance, a national culture

- gives people a sense of identity and uniqueness;
- provides the legal framework within which multinational firms operate and international trade is carried out;
- provides restraints on the conduct of international projects and the practice of cross-cultural business.

In spite of their present importance, it may be that national cultures are destined to be replaced by various forms of *supranational culture*. A study of Italian and British university students found that while British students had a strong sense of British national culture and saw themselves as members of it, Italian students had a much weaker sense of national identity (Cinnirella, 1997). The Italians' sense of European cultural identity was stronger than their sense of Italian national identity.

Hierarchy of national cultures

Are there leagues of national cultures, with membership of the premier league reserved for countries with the highest status and power? A country's status among a hierarchy of national cultures is easier to sense than to prove but, according to Thomas (2002), a generally accepted hierarchy of nationalities does exist, with some national cultures commonly perceived as inferior to others while some others are perceived as superior. Thomas argues that the hierarchy is based on *status and power*.

Often in cross-cultural meetings, international conferences, and other international gatherings it sometimes happens that various countries' relative status and power become perfectly visible. Each country's standing in the international stock exchange is translated into patterns of dominance or submission of its nationals that can be clearly observed as the event unfolds.

HOFSTEDE'S SURVEY OF NATIONAL CULTURES

Comparisons between cultures

Hofstede's landmark survey, which measured the values of IBM employees in 40 countries, provided the first theoretical basis for understanding national cultural differences (Hofstede, 1980a). The results allowed broad comparisons to be made between different national cultures. Further countries and regions were surveyed later, leading to a total data set derived from 50 countries and three multicountry regions. The original survey found four dimensions on which national cultures differ: power–distance, uncertainty–avoidance, masculinity–femininity, and individualism–collectivism. A fifth dimension, Confucian Dynamism/Long-term Orientation, was added after the original study was replicated in China (Hofstede, 1997).

In the original study, each country could be given a score on each of the four dimensions, positioning it relative to other countries. Country scores were extensively validated against conceptually related external data from many different sources. Hofstede et al. (2010: 337) state that 'recent correlations show no loss of validity, indicating that the country differences are indeed basic and long-term.'

Individualism–collectivism

Individualist countries, such as those in North America, Europe and Australia, emphasize the individual over the social group. Individualists see themselves as independent, self-contained, autonomous. Managers, who are high on individualism and achievement, tend to take a tough, results-oriented approach to boss–subordinate relations. By contrast, the collectivist countries of Asia, Africa, South America, and the Middle East are characterized by tight social networks. Family cohesiveness is very strong: Arab families in Israel often vote *en bloc* for the same political party (Dwairy, 1998). In the workplace loyalty is highly valued. Children who grow up in individualistic cultures are expected to develop a critical mind, whereas children growing up in collectivistic cultures are expected to develop a receptive mind. As a result, their world views are different. In collectivistic cultures, the group, family, or tribe comes first. It constitutes a person's identity.

Power–distance

High power–distance countries such as India, Russia, or France value hierarchy and inequality. Managers tend not to communicate easily or on equal terms with employees and use autocratic management methods. High power–distance generally inhibits communication, leads to low levels of disclosure, openness, and informality. Subordinates' communication style conveys deference, while managers' style conveys condescension or paternalism (Gudykunst et al., 1996). Members of high power–distance cultures avoid conflict with their superiors (Bazerman et al., 2000).

In small power–distance cultures, such as Denmark, Israel, and the Scandinavian countries, people feel more equal and employees expect to be consulted by their managers. Communication in the workplace is often marked by high levels of informality.

Uncertainty–avoidance

In strong uncertainty–avoidance countries such as Greece, Portugal, and Japan, people dislike ambiguity and uncertainty. Cultures high in uncertainty–avoidance have high levels of anxiety, and a strong need for formal rules. At work, people fear failure, take fewer risks, resist change, want job security, career planning, retirement pensions, and so on.

People feel the need for rules, formal procedures, and clearly defined 'codes of behaviour'.

Nations with low scores on uncertainty–avoidance can be successful because of their innovativeness (Britain, China) and nations with high scores can be successful because of their expertise in precision technology (Germany, Japan, South Korea).

Masculinity–femininity

'Masculine' countries such as Japan and Italy value achievement, acquisitiveness, and competitiveness, and strongly distinguish between male and female roles. 'Feminine' societies, such as the Scandinavian countries, stress concern for people, quality of life, and sexual equality. In masculine cultures traditional masculine values prevail such as achievement and the effective exercise of power, and men tend to be assertive and competitive. Japan is the most masculine culture and the Scandinavian cultures are the least.

Confucian dynamism

In Confucianism there is a strong emphasis on harmony and order in relationships. People with high scores in Confucian dynamism value thrift, hard work, and respect hierarchy within the family and in society.

Hofstede's contribution

Hofstede's findings provided the first theoretical basis for understanding significant differences between national cultures and provide a map on which countries can be located and compared. The map displays differences between the *value systems* of cultures which directly affect international business persons, expatriate managers, international students, and other migrants who move from one culture to another. Furthermore, Hofstede's findings give a valuable starting point for organising ideas about how and why countries differ from each other. Hofstede's investigation has shaped the themes and controversies of cross-cultural research for several decades.

The different dimensions help to explain features of cross-cultural communication and cross-cultural management that would otherwise be puzzling – for instance:

- why individuals in some countries are reluctant to step out of line or to give their own personal opinions;
- why bosses are easy to get on with in some countries but not in others;
- why people in some countries fire many personal questions at persons they are meeting for the first time.

Shortcomings of the Hofstede model

In spite of its landmark status, Hofstede's model has frequently been criticized for flaws and shortcomings. The most important of these criticisms are:

Biased sample. All participants in the survey were highly educated white-collar professionals employed by a multinational company, IBM. They are therefore not representative of their societies and may hold values different from those of the wider population. In multilanguage nations the data may reflect the attitudes of only one language group. McSweeney (2002) argues that data obtained from IBM employees cannot represent national cultural values. Numerous groups in the countries sampled hold values which do not reflect those of the national culture.

Not comprehensive. Hofstede's model is not comprehensive. For example, an Attitude to Change dimension, a Context dimension, and various other dimensions have been proposed. Moreover, in all cultures both ends of each dimension can exist at the same time. For instance, both individualist and collectivist tendencies exist in any one country (although one may predominate). Thus Sinha and Tripathi (1994) found that Indian culture is neither predominantly individualist nor predominantly collectivist but incorporates elements of both.

Concerns about individualism/collectivism dimension. The individualism/collectivism distinction has been labelled the catchall default explanation for cultural differences in behaviour (Voronov and Singer, 2002). Some authorities question the utility of the dimension as an explanatory tool for cultural variations in behaviour, citing lack of reliability and insufficient conceptual clarity. A review of 15 empirical studies comparing Japan and United States on individualism/collectivism found that there was no difference between the two countries in 9 studies, and that 14 of the 15 did not support the common view; while in 5 studies the Japanese were actually more individualistic than the Americans (Takan and Osaka, 1999).

Overlapping dimensions. The robustness of the Confucian Dynamism/Long-term Orientation concept is frequently questioned, and Confucian dynamism/Long-term Orientation appears to be highly interrelated with individualism/collectivism (Yeh and Lawrence, 1995). Fang (2003) points out that while Hofstede's original four dimensions are based on contrasting or opposed alternatives, this does not apply to the fifth dimension of Confucian Dynamism/Long-term orientation.

Groups of cultures

In spite of their obvious relevance to business and management practice, Hofstede's findings about national cultures have not been extensively used by organisations.

Perhaps organisations and international business people would have been more eager to find ways of using Hofstede's results if they had been presented in the form of *groups of cultures* with members of each group possessing important common characteristics. The groupings would have helped firms intending to expand their foreign operations to make informed decisions about which region to choose. Such a grouping has now been carried out by Ronen (2006) who presents a set of 10 country clusters based on measures of the countries' general life and work values. The country clusters are: Anglo, Nordic, Eastern European, Germanic, Latin European, Latin American, Near Eastern, Far Eastern, Confucian Asian, and African.

GLOBE and Schwartz surveys

Evidence for the general validity of Hofstede's findings has come from other large-scale studies, including the GLOBE survey (House et al., 2004) and Schwartz's Value Survey (Schwartz, 1994) which uses similar but more up-to-date value measures and also assesses China and the former Soviet Republics. The massive GLOBE (Global Leadership and Organisational Behaviour Effectiveness) research programme, carried out in 62 societies, expands Hofstede's framework by identifying nine dimensions of national values. The programme surveyed over 18,000 managers in three industries: food, telecommunications, and banking.

For business and management students, the main significance of the GLOBE survey is that it is a long-term programme aiming to develop an integrated theory regarding the relationship between culture and organisational/managerial effectiveness. Results of the first phases of the project found that *national culture* made an impact on *organisational culture* in the dimensions being investigated. These dimensions are power–distance; uncertainty–avoidance; humane orientation; collectivism; assertiveness; gender egalitarianism; future orientation; and performance orientation. Ways in which national culture makes an impact on organisational culture are examined in Chapter 2.

OTHER TYPES OF CULTURE

Regional cultures

Many cultures do not limit their geographic coverage to the borders of a particular country. To accurately 'map' a given culture, cultural *regions* may need to be identified. In China, for instance, at least three discrete regional cultures exist (Ralston et al., 1996). Regional cultures in many large countries differ to a greater or lesser extent from the national cultures of which they are a part.

For instance, in a recent survey carried out in Brazil Hofstede et al. (2010) found a cultural clustering of Brazil's 27 states that fairly closely followed the administrative division of the country into five regions. The culture profiles for these five regions showed strong cultural differences between the five regions. For instance, there was a remarkable difference between the Northeast region with its Afro-Brazilian roots and the North region with its native Indian roots.

An important inference to be drawn from the findings is that Hofstede's (1980a) national values survey is too coarse a net for catching the cultural nuances between the different regional cultures in a large country such as Brazil. Arguably, an understanding of Brazilian culture requires a multifocal vision capable of simultaneously comprehending similarities and differences between the five regional cultures and their relationship to the national culture.

'Tight' and 'loose' cultures

National cultures can be 'tight' or 'loose' – that is, highly regulated cultures or cultures with few rules governing behaviour. In 'tight' cultures, people tend to agree about what is correct behaviour and severely criticize deviations from cultural norms (Triandis, 1985). Japan is a good example of a tight culture because people are expected to behave according to cultural norms, and deviations from the norms are often punished by various kinds of social sanction, including ostracism. Tight cultures are often based on a largely homogeneous population and a dominant religion. Most Western countries have 'loose' cultures which are based on diverse populations and the encouragement of freedom of thought and speech.

The tight/loose distinction is useful because it gives insights into difficulties that are sometimes experienced in cross-cultural encounters and that otherwise might be difficult to explain or understand – for instance, the sense of unease and suppressed conflict that may be caused by clashing values when members of 'tight' and 'loose' cultures meet and interact. Cultures differ regarding the kind of communication style that should be used in various situations. That is why international business people, expatriate managers, and others who regularly communicate with members of other cultures should aim to develop a flexible communication style repertoire that will enable them to meet the other person's communicative expectations.

High-context/low-context cultures

The concept of high-context and low-context cultures, popularized by Hall (1976), is not based on empirical research but is nevertheless a useful heurism for explaining some of the problems that people from diverse cultural backgrounds experience when they interact. In Arabic, Chinese, Japanese, and other high-context cultures of Asia, Africa, and Latin America, communication is full of *implicit* meaning. Relatively little information is contained in the explicit, transmitted part of the message. The information needed for understanding is already present in the context and in the other person. Thus the Japanese convey meaning through penetrating stares, casual glances, occasional grunts, and meaningful silences (Barnlund, 1989).

By contrast, people in low-context cultures do not assume that there is shared background knowledge and understanding. Everything tends to be explained in words. Meaning depends on the clarity and explanatory power of the communicator and no inside knowledge on the part of the listener is assumed. The high- and low-context distinction helps to convey understanding of the differences between explicit and implicit speech patterns that constantly occur in cross-cultural communication.

High-context communication tends to be relationship-centred so time must be spent building trust. People from low-context cultures, on the other hand, tend to be task-centred, and may not be disposed to spend time on relationship-building. In cross-cultural encounters low-context participants may give the impression of being glib and offensively outspoken. Equally, the lack of clarity and focus of Arabs, Japanese, and other high-context participants can be exasperating for low-context people. Effective cross-cultural communication partly depends on the foreign business visitor being aware of the high-context/low-context distinction and, during any particular business trip, accommodating to the high-context or low-context characteristics of the hosts.

Hall's low-context/high-context distinction is somewhat similar to Bernstein's (1971) distinction between restricted and elaborated codes. Elaborated codes rely on verbal amplification, while restricted codes use shortened words, phrases, and sentences, and use nonverbal communication and other implicit, contextual cues to convey meaning. Restricted code works better for situations where there is much shared or taken-for-granted knowledge in the group. According to Ferraro (1998), both restricted and elaborated codes are found in any speech community, although one or the other code tends to predominate.

Ethnic cultures

Ethnicity is generally taken to refer to all those groups who share a culture, a religion, historical origins, and a language – the most salient feature of ethnicity.

Fisher (1997) describes ethnicity as a mindset which creates a common system of meanings for a group.

An ethnic group is one which adheres over several generations to a set of values and behaviours (Leigh, 1998). Laroche et al. (2009) define 'ethnic identity' as the retention of features from the individual's culture of origin and expressed through language, attitudes, values, or behaviours. The concept of ethnic culture is used by corporate strategists, marketing managers, and professionals in a variety of sectors including education, counselling, and health behaviour.

Although researchers generally see language as the most prominent aspect of ethnic identity, occasionally this is found not to be the case. Thus Ioffe (2003) showed that the native Belarusian language did not rally citizens and that ethnic identity was built on other features. Other widely used dimensions of ethnic identity are religion, participation in clubs, and food preferences (Laroche et al., 1998). A tool used to measure ethnic identity is the Multigroup Ethnic Identity Measure (Phinney and Ong, 2007). The measure incorporates attitudes, behavioural features, and groups to which the respondent belongs.

In many countries, several distinct ethnic groups co-exist within national frontiers. Some countries, such as the United States and Russia, contain hundreds of ethnic groups. A few ethnic groups, such as the Jews and the Arabs, are extremely large and scattered across many countries. There are some 5000 ethnic groups in the world and each of them has its own culture within national cultures (Stavenhagen, 1986).

Collectivist cultures

Just as mutual obligations between group members in pre-industrial societies created the strong bonds and cohesive relationships now associated with collectivist cultures, so does a lack of interdependency in modern industrial society underlie individualism (Durkheim, 1933). Today, most of the world's population subscribes to some kind of collectivist outlook which takes group conformity for granted and sees rejection of group or family norms as shameful (Triandis, 1988).

In traditional collectivist societies, people from birth onwards are integrated into strong, cohesive in-groups which protect them in exchange for total loyalty (Hofstede, 1994). In collectivist cultures family cohesiveness is extremely strong. Analysis of voting trends among Arabs in Israel, for example, shows that families tend to vote *en bloc* for the same political party (Dwairy, 1998).

Some collectivist cultures use social sanctions to maintain community-approved standards of behaviour. The Igbo culture of Nigeria, for instance, uses shame and guilt to achieve the social control of individuals. Shame and ridicule are effective methods to use in collectivist societies where there is close and continual communication between all members. Such mechanisms have been described as 'the means par excellence of social control in small towns and primitive societies' (Murphy, 1980: 137).

Subcultures

Like a pointilliste painting, like cells under the microscope, the more closely a culture is examined, the more it splits into its component elements – its sub-cultures. These are based on social class, ethnicity, lifestyle, geographic region, among others. Gay men, for instance, form a distinct subculture in Cuban society (Arguelles and Rich, 1984). Members of the deaf community in the United States are a distinct and assertive subculture (Dolnick, 1993). More-over, subcultures can be further subdivided by age-group, education level, social class, gender, occupation, and so on, each subdivision having its own particular characteristics and values.

To a greater or lesser extent, members of subcultures think, speak, and behave in ways that fail to reflect central, average values of the national culture. Sub-cultures have their own distinct values and often they have their own specialized vocabulary and communication style. In many countries, for instance, a 'Youth' subculture exists with its own distinctive slang ('yoof-speak'). Managers in many countries, also use their own distinctive managerial jargon. Some subcultures, such as the dissident subcultures of China in recent decades, are in effect *coun-tercultures* opposing prevailing norms and practices and threatening established authority.

If foreign visitors to a country are unaware of subcultural differences, they may communicate in inappropriate and embarrassing ways when they meet indi-viduals or groups whose values differ from those of the majority. The risk of this happening can be reduced by talking to people who know the country well so that a more rounded, realistic picture of the culture and its various subcultures can be obtained. Effective cross-cultural communication is more likely when a foreign business visitor is sufficiently aware of subcultural differences to be able to make appropriate responses to members of various subcultural groups.

Central tendencies

Sweeping generalizations which are often made about a culture on the basis of survey findings are usually unreliable or inaccurate. The reasons are:

- survey respondents constitute only a proportion of a culture's population and may be atypical;
- within a culture numerous subcultures have their own values, behaviour, and ways of communicating;
- survey findings usually describe only the central parts of a tendency and may not capture subcultural characteristics.

Nevertheless, for a business person about to visit a foreign country a knowhow of the central tendencies revealed by official survey findings is extremely useful since the findings usually reveal the values, ideas, and behaviour that are *acceptable* in the culture and that should be conformed to in public.

SMALL-GROUP EXERCISE: Discussion Questions

Working in small groups, discuss each of the following questions and write down the group's agreed answer. At the end of the exercise, each group may present its answers to the other groups for comment.

1. *What is culture? How does culture affect communication?*
2. *Why is national culture so important (a) to individual members of the culture (b) to multicultural companies?*
3. *Give examples of ways in which national cultures typically differ from each other.*
4. *Critics have frequently pointed out flaws in Hofstede's (1980) survey findings. Outline three of the criticisms.*
5. *Explain the difference between high-context and low-context cultures, and the effect the difference can have in cross-cultural encounters.*
6. *Explain why it is important for business visitors to be aware of the main subcultures of a foreign country.*

MULTICULTURAL SOCIETIES

Assimilation or multiculturalism?

Shen et al. (2009) make the point that multiculturalism has always been seen as the most important dimension of diversity in the majority of developed countries. Many developed countries have, indeed, adopted multicultural social policies as a result of large-scale immigration since the end of the Second World War. Multiculturalist policies graft customs, celebrations, and other aspects of the cultures of immigrant communities onto the majority. In countries where multiculturalism has been adopted as a social policy tool, services geared to meet the special needs (linguistic, religious, etc.) of these communities are funded by central government (Yuval-Davis, 1994).

Australia, New Zealand, Canada, and Britain are examples of modern multicultural societies. In Canada, immigrants have accounted for 70 per cent of workforce growth since 2000 (Ng and Sears, 2010). In New Zealand, a typical large manufacturing company might employ 20 per cent Pakeha (New Zealand Europeans), 15 per cent Maori, 15 per cent Samoan, 10 per cent Cook Islanders, 10 per cent Tongans,10 per cent Chinese, 10 per cent Malaysian, 5 per cent Korean, and 5 per cent Indian (Metge, 2001). In Melbourne, more than a hundred languages are spoken on a regular basis, and non-English speakers comprise 40 per cent of the workforce in manufacturing industries (Clyne, 1994).

The main policy alternative to multiculturalism is *assimilation* – a policy that France has always followed. A frequent objection to assimilation as a policy is that it has the effect of suppressing minority cultures. What assimilation means in practice is that immigrants are encouraged to become French in the expectation that they will relinquish their cultural identity and adopt French culture. However, France's assimilation policy is only partly successful when measured against such aims. For example, of 6211 adult immigrants who participated in a 2006 study 44.4 per cent saw themselves as belonging to France, while 30.6 per cent maintained a home culture affiliation (Schleyer-Lindemann, 2006). The less educated and more religiously committed immigrants were the main categories who tended to maintain a home culture affiliation.

Communication problems of minority groups

An important consequence of the cultural diversity within multicultural societies is that constant cross-cultural communication problems occur in the workplace, educational institutions, and in the wider society. In a multicultural workplace, for instance, immigrants and minority-group employees may misunderstand instructions given by supervisors. Or they may fail to observe procedures already agreed in a shop floor meeting because they did not fully understand the procedures that were discussed. Interactions with co-workers from the majority culture may become strained and marked by frequent misunderstandings.

Much anecdotal evidence indicates that problems frequently encountered in multicultural societies range from the relatively simple, such as the different requirements of diverse cultural groups for physical and personal space, to the more complex problems involved in different cultural groups trying to understand and accommodate to each other's values and behaviour. Even when members of a minority group speak the same language as members of the mainstream majority culture, their rules of politeness and etiquette may be very different and lead to misunderstanding or resentment.

In a given multicultural society each ethnic group may occupy its own neighbourhood and maintain its own informal local institutions and religious organisations. In their own neighbourhood group members are surrounded by friends and family and can use their own native tongue so that communication problems are minimized. But communication skills that are effective among friends may be less effective in public or official contexts such as schools and colleges, government offices, the law courts. In such places the communicative norms of the majority culture prevail. To cope with official and public communication, immigrants are forced to learn the language of the majority culture. But the unfamiliar linguistic features of the language create difficulties. Adler (1977), for instance, notes the high incidence of stuttering among bilinguals and attributes this to psychological difficulties caused by linguistic insecurity.

Oscillation between cultures

In multicultural societies immigrants and minority group members have to cope with the stresses of living in two cultures simultaneously – the majority culture and their own original culture. As they move between home and work, the college and the supermarket, they in effect shuttle between old and new cultural identities (Hegde, 1998). Temporary members of multicultural societies – foreign students, short-term contract workers, and so on – are in a different position from permanent immigrants. It is less important for them to fit in and so they may be less motivated to communicate with members of the majority culture. But avoidance of communication with local people may lead to new-comers not coping with the demands of everyday social life and cause stress and psychological disturbance (Furnham and Bochner, 1982).

In the foreseeable future the ethnic and cultural diversity of multicultural societies is likely to increase because of continuing migration flows, more inter-marriage, and differential rates of natural increase. Such tendencies will need to be matched by increased efforts to improve communication and cooperation between the different cultural groups. But the general lack of appreciation for diversity will first have to be overcome.

'INTERNATIONAL' CULTURE

Industrialization link

Several authorities, including Hofstede (1997) and Fukuyama (1992), have argued that as countries develop economically they converge towards com-mon values and patterns of behaviour. According to Fukuyama, there is no real alternative for modern industrialized societies to Western values and lifestyles – to the global marketplace as the primary form of economic organisation; to 'democracy' as the main form of political organisation. The implication is that *economic development* is the hidden hand scattering the seed of a standardized 'international' culture around the globe.

The creation of a common international culture is linked to economic growth and increasing industrialization worldwide. Created by such forces, international culture is already well-established in most parts of the world and no doubt the process will continue. According to Kymlicka (1995), 'modernization' is a functional requirement of a modern economy with its need for a mobile, educated work force; it involves the diffusion through society of a common culture (which is embodied in common economic, political, and educational institutions).

Traditional v liberal

Many industrialized societies have 'modern' features – for instance, egalitarian attitudes, sex equality, high achievement motivation, and a preference for urban life (Yang, 1988). Even strongly traditional societies, such as Iran, have subver-sive, modernizing groups which challenge authority and fight for change. As Yang points out, in conservative societies the traditionalists tend to be rural, less educated people, while those who promote modernization tend to be liberal, urban, well-educated, and non-traditional in lifestyle.

Modern 'international' culture is in many developing countries opposed by nationalist groups who see the danger of a soulless international culture eventually supplanting their own traditional cultures. But according to Yang (1988), there is no clear evidence that this is happening. At the same time, as international culture increases its influence, people continue to demonstrate their commitment to their own ethnic and geographical cultures. In the Cook Islands, for instance, traditional cooperative conduct and modern competitive, self-oriented behaviour have been found to exist in tandem with traditional ethnic cultures.

Language and cultural imperialism

'International' culture is strongly associated with the rise of English. The leaders of some developing countries resist the spread of English because, in their eyes, it is a tool of cultural imperialism and may lead to cultural domination by Britain and the United States. Phillipson (1992) sees the dominance of English as a global tool of power and one of the six interlocking types of imperialism: cultural, economic, political, military, communicative, and social.

Nevertheless, in many parts of the world English is the status language, the 'international' language for technology, commerce, finance, and computers, the language of access to modern life. Choice of English by a young Japanese or a young Russian demonstrates a desire to be perceived as more international, less traditional, on the move. Some French companies choose English because they do most of their business outside of France and because of an increased foreign presence on their boards (*Financial Times*, 25 March 2006: 8). Meetings at Total regularly take place in English even if only French managers are present – because English is the language of the oil industry.

English similarly dominates international communication. Israeli-Palestinian communication is conducted in English. English is now the basic international language for technology, commerce, computers, finance, science, and travel. French and German scientists often choose to publish their work first in English. Pilots on international routes must learn English so that they can speak to the control towers around the world. English has become the most important foreign language in all three Baltic countries where, as elsewhere in Europe, it is a symbol of progress and status (Phillipson, 1992). English, rather than Russian, is today used as a trans-Baltic lingua franca. In the Baltic states, as in many other countries, the ability to speak English seems to be a given among educated young people.

WHY CULTURES CHANGE

Pace of cultural change

No culture remains completely static year after year. Cultures change through absorption, incorporation, translation, invention, indigenization, synthesis (Asante and Gudykunst, 1989). Tourism, migration, and global communications media are part of the mix of influences producing new cultural forms and identities.

Cultures change. However, the extent to which they have changed in the past is uncertain because the great majority of extant cultures have no written records – or at least no records going back much more than a century. According to Berry et al. (1992), preliterate societies tend to be more traditional and change more slowly than modern, developed societies. Historically, Berry argues, cultures have evolved in an identifiable sequence from small hunting and gathering bands to farming societies, and later to industrial and now post-industrial societies. In pre-industrial societies mutual obligations between group members created the strong bonds and cohesive relationships now associated with collectivist cultures. (By contrast, as Durkheim (1933) points out, the *lack* of interdependency in industrial society has led to the emergence of individualist cultures.)

Present-day culture must itself have evolved from simpler forms – as may be the case with the cultures of certain animal species. For instance, the song dialects of birds and whales are known to vary and change over time. Chimpanzees have local foraging traditions, such as cracking nuts or fishing for ants, which vary across Africa, and it is possible that some of these traditions are evolved forms. The implication is that human and animal cultures change in accordance with some over-arching or universal law of change.

Examples of types of cultural change

When cultures change it is often because of technological innovations or contact with other cultures. The changes that occur can range from changes in personal values and customs to the wholesale adoption of a new religion or ideology. In exceptional cases old ideologies are challenged and give way to new ideologies, as in Russia before the Russian Revolution or in Nazi Germany in the 1930s.

As these examples suggest, cultural change is not a uniform process. Component parts of a culture change in different ways and at different speeds. According to Leroi-Gourhan (1968), weapons change very often, tools change less often, while social institutions change very infrequently.

As an example of rapid cultural change brought about by technological developments, consider the change in traditional British reserve brought about by the mobile phone. Use of the mobile phone had to be open and usually in public. At first most British people used mobile phones in public with considerable embarrassment. Often their embarrassment was accompanied by strong negative reactions from those unfortunate enough to be within earshot – fellow-passengers on a train, for instance. Within a surprisingly short time, however, these culturally influenced reactions became blunted and a permanent behaviour change set in – a change towards more openness, more assertiveness, less reserve.

As a culture changes, individual members of the culture also change – and vice versa.

Changes in the culture bring about changes in individuals, but equally individuals strive to change the culture – as in Tiananmen Square, for instance, when the Chinese military suppressed popular demonstrations by students who were, in effect, pushing Chinese society towards more openness. Klapp (1978) argues that cultures tend to alternate between openness and closure, this natural cyclical alternation being a basic survival strategy of cultures and other living systems against entropy.

Human agency: triggers of cultural change

Nawal El Sadaawi was one of the first Egyptian writers to deal with the theme of women in traditional societies. In the 1970s, she denounced female circumcision at a time when speaking about virginity or sex or female circumcision in the Arab world was very difficult. She lost her job as Egypt's Director of Public Health as a result. But her stand helped to bring about cultural change in Arab countries. 'People began to think about these issues,' she told a journalist. 'Now quite a lot of people question female circumcision and quite a lot of families, particularly in the cities, have given up the practice altogether.'

The example shows how cultural change can be brought about by *human agency*. Equally potent drivers of cultural change are economic development, technological advance, and military conquest. These are the forces that often trigger major changes in lifestyle, family ties, population mobility, and numerous other aspects of culture. As change is introduced, cultures move away from their traditional values. Each Asian country, for instance, used to have its own distinctive culture, language, politics, and religion. But in the present day nearly all Asian countries exhibit such 'Western' characteristics as individualism, family planning, social mobility, marital disruption, and divorce (Rogers, 1971). Cultural values in China are presently undergoing radical change as a result of the dramatic economic and social restructuring that has occurred since the introduction of new economic policies which have had the effect of changing many basic, traditional values and assumptions (Mills et al., 2008).

The former communist countries of east Europe and the former Soviet Union have also undergone radical cultural change in recent decades, becoming more individualist in their value-orientations as a result of economic success. Some traditional cultures, however, still exert powerful pressures to resist change. For instance, shame and ridicule are used against individuals who violate cultural values in some African countries (Murphy, 1980). Such sanctions are particularly effective in collectivist societies where there is close and continual communication between members of the culture.

Personal value-change

Some cultural changes are brought about simply as a result of some members of a culture changing their personal values and customs. In Japan, for instance, young people seem to be abandoning traditional Japanese values relating to love and marriage, with a growing preference for free partner choice together with idealized notions of love and companionship similar to those held in the West. Yet paradoxically, even brand-new practices in Japanese society are often underpinned by traditional values. An example is the *wakarasase-ya,* or professional separators, who are employed to end other people's relationships with minimum embarrassment and avoidance of confrontation (Whymant, 2001). The separators use varying approaches but typically make a phone call to the target and warn him – it is usually a 'him' – that the relationship has now terminated: does he agree?

Job mobility and changing norms

The impact that cultural change has on people's lives can be most clearly seen in collectivist countries undergoing rapid globalization and economic transformation, and where increased *job mobility* is becoming the norm (Chen et al., 2009). Job mobility refers to the degree to which people can move between jobs and professions. Countries vary in the extent of job mobility, with individualist Western countries having much higher levels than most Eastern countries. In the United States, for instance, average job duration in 1997 was 7.4 years compared to 11.3 years in Japan and 19.9 years in China (OECD, 1997).

Chen et al. (2009) point out that in traditional Eastern cultures rapidly increasing levels of job mobility are directly related to changes in cultural values. In a high job mobility context, people need to adapt to new job situations, to new organisational cultures, to new normative structures. As a result of individuals changing their jobs and moving to new locations, old social networks and the old, traditional norms tend to disintegrate (Bian and Ang, 1997).

With low job mobility, people tend to remain in the same working environment with stable normative structures. They identify more strongly with their community and its norms than do frequent movers. They have more unconditional support for their community and participate more frequently in community activities (Oishi et al., 2007b). Such findings suggest that a clear link exists between low job mobility and *collectivist norms* and identity. The implication is the effect of increasing job mobility in countries throughout the world is to weaken collectivist values and to gradually strengthen individualist values.

Cultural change generates new organisational forms

Cultural change affects the structure of organisations and the way they operate. Equally, evolving organisation structures encourage further cultural change. In recent decades a number of new organisational forms – such as networks and strategic alliances with other firms – have emerged in response to the pressures and opportunities brought about by increasing globalization (Jarillo, 1988). Increasingly, strategic alliances, joint ventures, and mergers and acquisitions occur across national and cultural boundaries, with cultural differences among the partner firms providing new capabilities, resources, and learning opportunities.

As organisations change, the products they produce also change. Products today are so sophisticated and incorporate so many technologies that not even a General Electric or a Sony can maintain cutting edge expertise in all of them. That explains why a *network* of partners is sometimes needed and cooperative alliances with foreign firms have emerged as a contemporary organisational form. It is a form favoured by firms such as Siemens and Fujitsu and is based on the complementarity of the partners' strengths (Thomas, 2008).

Another new organisation form is that identified by Raab and Kenis (2009): the trend towards international *goal-directed networks* of organisations. Increasingly these networks are being formed in construction, health care, and other sectors in countries around the world. Networks ('keiretsu') are already well-established in Japanese industry, and international networking alliances have already become essential mechanisms for the internationalization of higher education (Teather, 2004).

An example of a temporary, goal-directed network in the banking sector is the network of three medium-size banks established in 2008 as a temporary organisational form to buy the Dutch multinational bank, ABN AMRO. Once the takeover had gone through the bank was carved up and parts dealt out to the network participants. The network was then dissolved. Raab and Kenis (2009) predict that networks will become the dominant organisational form of the future, replacing the formal, vertically integrated organisation that dominated the twentieth century.

Meme theory

The meme concept offers a useful perspective from which to view cultural change. The proponents of meme theory argue that just as biological evolution occurs through selection of adaptive genes, so cultural change occurs by selection of adaptive memes. A meme is 'a unit of cultural transmission, a unit of imitation' (Dawkins, 1989: 352) which is transmitted from one mind to another by means of speech, gestures, or other imitable phenomena. Many cultural entities – new ideas, fashions, pop songs, learned skills – are replicated in this way. Sometimes a group of memes (a 'meme complex') replicate together so that a new ideology or even a new religion is born.

Memes, like genes, are units of information that pass through generations and in this way might be seen as cultural analogues to genes. Memes, like genes, self-replicate. They replicate by exposure to human beings (efficient copiers of information and behaviour). As the process of replication goes on and new memes are introduced, culture itself gradually changes.

However, as Blackmore (1999) notes, there is no precise understanding of what makes up one unit of cultural transmission, and critics question whether a culture can be categorized in terms of discrete units. Nevertheless, meme theory provides a new perspective for understanding cultural change and other aspects of culture that are puzzling. Inexplicable phenomena occur in cultures from time to time – copycat suicides, for instance, or mass hysteria – and these have been represented as memes seen as 'thought contagion' (Lynch, 1996). Other 'thought contagion' memes include pop songs, which can spread like infections, and alternative therapies that don't work but which nevertheless root themselves in a culture. Balkin (1998) describes racist beliefs as 'fantasy' memes; and the internet can be seen as a vast realm of memes growing rapidly by a process of mimetic evolution and not under human control.

Cultural evolution theory

Cultural evolution theory is a logical extension of meme theory. Like meme theorists, cultural evolution theorists adapt the methods and theories of biologists studying genetic evolution in order to study cultural change. According to cultural evolution theory, human culture is the body of information that is passed from individual to individual through social learning processes such as imitation, teaching, and language (Boyd and Richerson, 2005). The theory's proponents argue that cultures change – or, rather, evolve – in a Darwinian manner that resembles biological evolution.

Cultural evolution theory moves past isolated memes to encompass selection processes and the complexity of overall cultural change. Social psychology provides the theory with accurate assumptions regarding social information processing and the mechanisms through which cultural evolution operates (Mesoudi, 2009).

KEY POINTS

1. Examining the concept of culture is a logical starting point for understanding the process of cross-cultural communication since people do not communicate in a vacuum but are imbued by the values, beliefs, and practices of their cultures. Thus, whenever people from different cultures meet and communicate, cultural norms and expectation surround the participants and guide their thoughts and behaviour.
2. Culture is a system of values, beliefs, practices, and communicative norms. There are surface- and deep-level differences between cultures. Deep-level differences relate to aspects which are not immediately visible and relate to a culture's prevailing values and beliefs such as tolerance/intolerance, and attitudes to change and to other cultures. The basic functions of culture are universal, although the ways in which the functions play out are localized.
3. Hofstede's model provides the first sound theoretical basis for understanding differences between national cultures. Hofstede's four dimensions explain many features of intercultural communication that would otherwise be puzzling, such as why bosses are easy to get on with in some countries but not in others.
4. In any culture subcultures exist whose members share a world view, common values, and often a specialized vocabulary and communication style. Some subcultures are, in effect, countercultures, opposing prevailing cultural norms and practices. Effective cross-cultural business communication sometimes depends on a visiting business person being aware of the characteristics of particular subcultures and how they differ from the dominant majority culture in values and communication style.

5. Culture is constantly changing. Change can be brought about by human agency, by economic and technological development, or as a result of military conquest. Cyclical change in culture occurs as a strategy of a living organism against entropy. The effect of change being introduced is to move cultures away from their traditional values.

6. Millions of people throughout the world participate in a quasi-Western, 'international' culture, and increasingly subscribe to 'Western' values. But 'international' culture is at odds with traditional societies. It introduces tensions, for instance, into Islamic societies by giving Islamic youth access to Western values and lifestyles.

7. Cultural change affects the structure of organisations and the way they operate. Thus, there is a trend away from traditional organisation structures towards alternative forms, such as temporary goal-directed networks of organisation. Meme theory and cultural evolution theory adapt the methods and theories of biologists studying genetic evolution to explain cultural change.

QUESTIONS FOR DISCUSSION AND WRITTEN ASSIGNMENTS

1. Describe three subcultures that exist in your own national culture. To what extent do their members have a view of life that differs from that of the majority culture? To what extent does each of these subcultures has its own distinctive vocabulary and communication style?

2. What are the influences that bring about cultural change? To what extent have the values and norms of your own culture changed in your lifetime? What are the reasons for the change?

3. In multicultural societies assimilation is the main policy alternative to multiculturalism. What kind of results and changes is each policy trying to achieve?

4. Is it likely that national cultures will eventually be replaced by various forms of supranational culture?

BIBLIOGRAPHY

Adler, MK. *Collective and Individual Bilingualism: A Sociolinguistic Study.* Buske, 1977, p. 146.

Ali, AJ. Cultural discontinuity and Arab management thought. *International Studies of Management and Organisation*, 25 (3), 1995, 7–30.

Arguelles, L and Rich, R. Homosexuality, homophobia and revolution. *Signs*, 9, 1984, 683–699.

Asante, MK and Gudykunst, WB. (eds), *Handbook of International and Intercultural Communication*. Sage, 1989.

Balkin, JM. *Cultural Software: A Theory of Ideology.* Yale UP, 1998.

Barnlund, D. *Communicative Styles of Japanese and Americans: Images and Realities*. Wadsworth, 1989.

Bazerman, MH. et al., Negotiation. *Annual Review of Psychology*, 51, 2000, 279–314.

Beal, C. Keeping the peace. *Multilingua*, 13 (1–2), 1994.

Bernstein, B. *Class, Codes and Control* (Vol. 1). Routledge and Kegan Paul, 1971.

Berry, JW. On cross-cultural comparability. *International Journal of Psychology*, 4, 1969, 119–128.

Berry, JW. et al., *Cross-cultural Psychology: Research and Applications*. CUP, 1992, p. 168.

Bian, Y-J and Ang, S. Guanxi networks and job mobility in China and Singapore. *Social Forces*, 75, 1997, 981–1005.

Blackmore, S. *The Meme Machine*. OUP, 1999.

Boyd, R and Richerson, PJ. *The Origin and Evolution of Cultures*. OUP, 2005.

Brett, JM. *Negotiating Globally*. Jossey-Bass, 2001.

Buss, DM. et al., International preferences in selecting mates. *Journal of Cross-cultural Psychology*, 21, 1990, 2–47.

Chen, J. et al., The cultural effect of job mobility and the belief in a fixed world: evidence from performance forecast. *Journal of Personality and Social Psychology*, 97 (5), 2009, 851–865.

Cinnirella, M. Towards a European identity? Interactions between the national and European social identities manifested by university students in Britain and Italy. *The British Journal of Social Psychology*, 36, 1997, p. 19.

Clyne, M. *Intercultural Communication at Work*. CUP, 1994.

Dawkins, R. *The Selfish Gene*, 2nd ed. OUP, 1989.

Despharde, R. et al., *Factors Affecting Organisation Performance: A Five-country Comparison*. MSI Report no. 98–100, 1998.

Doktor, RH. Asian and American CEOs: a comparative study. *Organisational Dynamics*, 19 (3), 1990, 46–56.

Dolnick, E. Deafness as a Culture. *Atlantic*, 272, 1993, 37–53.

Durkheim, E. *The Division of Labour in Society*. Free Press, 1933.

Dwairy, MA. *Cross-cultural Counselling: The Arab-Palestinian Case*. Haworth, 1998, p. 35.

Fang, T. A critique of Hofstede's fifth national culture dimension. *International Journal of Cross Cultural Management*, 3 (3), 2003, 347–368, p. 354.

Ferraro, GP. *The Cultural Dimension of International Business*, 3rd ed. Prentice Hall, 1998.

Fisher, G. *Mindsets: The Role of Culture and Perception in International Relations*, 2nd ed. Intercultural Press, 1997.

Fontaine, JRJ, Poortinga, YH, Delbeke, L and Schwartz, SH. Structural equivalence of the values domain across cultures. *Journal of Cross-cultural Psychology*, 39 (4), 2008, 345–365.

Fukuyama, F. *The End of History and the Last Man*. Penguin, 1992.

Fu, H-y, Morris, MW, Lee, SL, Chao, M, Chiu, CY and Hong, YY. Epistemic motives and cultural conformity. *Journal of Personality and Social psychology*, 92, 2007, 191–207.

Furnham, A and Bochner, S. Social difficulty in a foreign culture: an empirical analysis of culture shock. In S Bochner (ed.), *Cultures in Contact*. Pergamon, 1982.

Gudykunst, WB. et al., The influence of cultural individualism-collectivism, self-construals and individual styles on communication styles across cultures. *Human Communication Research*, 22, 1996, 507–534.

Gunthner, S. Argumentation and resultant problems in the negotiation of rapport in a German-Chinese conversation. In H Spencer-Oatey (ed.), *Culturally Speaking*. Continuum, 2000, pp. 218–239.

Hall, ET. *Beyond Culture*. Anchor, 1976.

Hamilton, JB. et al., Google in China: a manager-friendly heuristic model for resolving cross-cultural ethical conflicts. *Journal of Business Ethics*, 86, 2009, 143–157.

Harris, P. and Moran, R. *Managing Cultural Differences*, 4th ed. Gulf Publishing Company, 1996.

Hegde, RS. Swinging the trapeze. In DV Tanno and A Gonzalez (eds), *Communication and Identity across Cultures*. Sage, 1998, pp. 34–55.

Hofstede, G. *Culture's Consequences: International Differences in Work-related Values*. Sage, 1980a.

Hofstede, G. Motivation, leadership and organisation: do American theories apply abroad. *Organisational Dynamics*, 75, 1980b, 42–63.

Hofstede, G. *Cultures and Organisations*. HarperCollins, London, 1994, p. 5.

Hofstede, G. *Cultures and Organisations: Software of the Mind*, Revised ed. McGraw Hill, 1997.

Hofstede, G. et al., Comparing regional cultures within a country: lessons from Brazil. *Journal of Cross-cultural Psychology*, 41 (3), 2010, 336–352.

House, RJ. et al. (eds), *Culture, Leadership and Organisations. The GLOBE Study of 62 Societies*. Sage, 2004.

Ioffe, G. Understanding Belarus: Belarusian identity. *Europe-Asia Studies*, 55, 2003, 1241–1272.

Jarillo, J. On strategic networks. *Strategic Management Journal*, 9, 1988, 31–41.

Ji, L-J. et al., Culture, change and prediction. *Psychological Science*, 12, 2001, 450–456.

Kazakov, AY. et al., Business ethics and civil society in Russia. *International Studies of Management and Organisation*, 27 (1), 1997, 5–18.

Klapp, OE. *Opening and Closing: Strategies and Information Adaptation in Society*. CUP, 1978.

Kohn, ML. *Class and Conformity: A Study in Values*. Dorsey, 1969.

Kroeber, AL and Kluckhohn, C. *Culture: A Critical Review of Concepts and Definitions*. Harvard UP, 1952.

Kymlicka, W. *Multicultural Citizenship*. OUP, 1995.

Laroche, M. et al., A test of nonlinear relationship between linguistic acculturation and ethnic identification. *Journal of Cross-cultural Psychology*, 29, 1998, 418–433.

Laroche, M. et al., The role of language in ethnic identity measurement. *Journal of Social Psychology*, 149 (4), 2009, 513–539.

Leigh, JW. *Communicating for Cultural Competence*. Allyn & Bacon, 1998, p. 176.

Leroi-Gourhan, A. *The Art of Prehistoric Man in Western Europe*. Thames & Hudson, 1968.

Le Vine, R. *Culture, Behaviour and Personality*. Aldine, 1973, p. 26.

Levi-Strauss, C. *Les structures elementaires de la parente*. Presses Universitaires de France, Paris, 1949.

Liebes, T. Cultural differences in the retelling of television fiction. *Critical Studies in Mass Communication*, 5, 1988, 277–292.

Lynch, A. *Thought Contagion*. Basic Books, 1996.

Martin, JN and Nakayama, T. *Intercultural Communication in Contexts*. Mayfield, 1997.

Martin, JN. et al., Conversation improvement strategies for inter-ethnic communication. *Communication Monographs*, 61 (3), 1994, 236–255.

Matsumoto, D. et al., Mapping expressive differences across the world: the relationship between emotional display rules and individualism versus collectivism. *Journal of Cross-cultural Psychology*, 39 (1), 2008, 58.

McSweeney, B. Hofstede's model of national cultural differences and their consequences: a triumph of faith – a failure of analysis. *Human Relations*, 55 (1), 2002, 89–118.

Mesoudi, A. How cultural evolutionary theory can inform social psychology and vice versa. *Psychological Review*, 116 (4), 2009, 929–952.

Metge, J. *Talking Together*. Auckland U Press, 2001.

Mills, M. et al., Converging divergences? *International Sociology*, 23, 2008, 561–595.

Murphy, R. *An Overture to Social Anthropology*. Prentice-Hall, 1980.

Ng, ESW and Sears, GJ. What women and ethnic minorities want. Work values and labour market confidence: a self-determination perspective. *International Journal of Human Resource Management*, 21 (5), 2010, 676–698.

OECD, Employment outlook. Organisation for Economic Cooperation and Development, 1997.

Oishi, S. Lun, J. and Sherman, GD. Residential mobility, self-concept, and positive effects in social interactions. *Journal of Personality and Social Psychology*, 93, 2007a, 131–141.

Oishi, S. et al., The socioecological model of procommunity action: the benefits of residential stability. *Journal of Personality and Social Psychology*, 93, 2007b, 831–844.

Oyserman, D. et al., Rethinking individualism and collectivism: evaluation of theoretical assumptions and meta-analyses. *Psychological Bulletin*, 128, 2002, 3–72.

Peterson, MF and Pike, KL. Emics and etics for organisational study: a lesson in contrast from linguistics. *International Journal of Cross-cultural Management*, 2, 2002, 5–19.

Peterson, MF and Smith, PB. Social structures and processes in cross-cultural management. In PB Smith, MF Peterson and DC Thomas (eds), *Handbook of Cross-cultural Management Research*. Sage, 2008, 35–58.

Phillipson, R. *Linguistic Imperialism*. OUP, 1992.

Phinney, JS and Ong, AD. Conceptualisation and measurement of ethnic identity: current status and future direction. *Journal of Counselling Psychology*, 54, 2007, 271–281.

Raab, J and Kenis, P. Heading toward a society of networks: empirical developments and theoretical challenges. *Journal of Management Enquiry*, 18 (3), 2009, 198–210.

Ralston, DA. et al., The cosmopolitan Chinese manager: findings of a study on managerial values across the six regions of China. *Journal of International Management*, 2, 1996, 79–109.

Ricard, VB. *Developing Intercultural Communication Skills*. Krieger, 1993.

Robie, C. Johnson, KM. Nilsen, D. and Hazucha, JF. The right stuff: understanding cultural differences in leadership performance. *Journal of Management Development*, 20, 2001, 639–649.

Rogers, E. *Communication of Innovations: A Cross-cultural Approach*. Free Press, 1971.

Ronen, S. The new cultural geography: a meta-analysis of country clusters. Address to International Association for Applied Psychology, 26th Congress, 2006.

Rosenthal, D., Ranieri, N. and Klimidis, S.Vietnamese adolescents in Australia. *International Journal of Psychology*, 31, 1996, 81–91.

Sabogal, F. et al., Hispanic familialism and acculturation: what changes and what doesn't? *Hispanic Journal of Behavioural Sciences*, 9, 1987, 397–412.

Schein, EH. *Organisational Culture and Leadership*, 3rd ed. Jossey-Bass, 2004.

Schleyer-Lindemann, A. Developmental tasks of adolescents of native or foreign origin in France and Germany. *Journal of Cross-cultural Psychology*, 37, 2006, 85–99.

Schwartz, SH. Beyond individualism/collectivism: new cultural dimensions of values. In U Kim, HC Triandis, C Kagitcibasis, SC Choi and G Yoon (eds), *Individualism and Collectivism: Theory, Method, and Applications*. Sage, 1994, pp. 85–119.

Schwartz, SH. Mapping and interpreting cultural differences around the world. In V Vinken, J Soeters and P Ester (eds), *Comparing Cultures. Dimensions of Culture in a Comparative Perspective*. Brill, 2004, pp. 43–73.

Shekshnia, SV. et al., Russ Wane equipment: joint venture in Russia. In DC Thomas (ed.), *Readings and Cases in International Management: A Cross-cultural Perspective*. Sage, 2003.

Shen, J. et al., Managing diversity through human resource management: an international perspective and conceptual framework. *International Journal of Human Resource Management*, 20 (2), 2009, 235–251.

Sinha, D and Tripathi, RC. Individualism in a collectivist culture: a case of coexistence of opposites. In U Kim, HC Triandis, C Kagitcibasis, SC Choi and G Yoon (eds), *Individualism and Collectivism: Theory, Methods, and applications.* Sage, 1994, pp. 123–136.

Smith, PB and Schwartz, SH. Values. In JW Berry et al. (eds), *Social Behaviour and Applications: Handbook of Cross-cultural Psychology* (Vol. 3), 2nd ed. Allyn and Bacon, 1997, pp. 78–118.

Soltani, E. The overlooked variable in managing human resources of Iranian organisations: workforce diversity – some evidence. *International Journal of Human Resources Management*, 21 (1), 2010, 84–108.

Stavenhagen, R. *Problems and Prospects of Multi-ethnic States.* United Nations University Press, Tokyo, 1986.

Stewart, R. et al., *Managing in Britain and Germany.* Macmillan, 1994.

Sullivan, J and Taylor, S. A cross-cultural test of compliance-gaining theory. *Management Communication Quarterly*, 5 (2), 1991, 220–239.

Takano, Y and Osaka, E. An unsupported common view: comparing Japan and the US on individualism-collectivism. *Asian Journal of Social Psychology*, 2, 1999, 311–341.

Teather, D. The networking alliance: a mechanism for the internationalisation of higher education? *Managing Education Matters*, 7 (2), 2004, 3.

Thomas, DC.*Essentials of International Management: A Cross-cultural Perspective.* Sage, 2002.

Thomas, DC. *Cross-cultural Management: Cross-cultural Concepts*, 2nd ed. Sage, 2008.

Thompson, N. *Communication and Language: A Handbook of Theory and Practice.* Palgrave Macmillan, 2003, p. 29.

Triandis, H. Some major dimensions of cultural variation in client populations. In P Pedersen (ed.), *Handbook of Cross-cultural Counselling and Therapy.* Greenwood Press, 1985.

Triandis, HC. Collectivism vs. individualism. In G Verma and C Bagley (eds), *Cross-cultural Studies of Personality, Attitudes, and Cognition.* Macmillan, 1988.

Triandis, HC. The psychological measurement of cultural syndromes. *American Psychologist*, 51, 1996, 407–415.

Triandis, HC. Culture and psychology. In S Kitayame and D Cohen (eds), *Handbook of Cultural Psychology.* Guilford Press, 2007, 59–76.

Tung, RL. Managing in Asia: cross-cultural dimensions. In P Joynt and M Warner (eds), *Managing Across Cultures: Issues and Perspectives.* International Thomson Business Press, 1996.

Van Oudenhoven, JP. et al., Asymmetrical international attitudes. *European Journal of Social Psychology*, 32 (2), 2002, 275–289.

Van Vianen, AEM. et al., Fitting in: surface and deep-level cultural differences and expatriate adjustment. *Academy of Management Journal*, 47 (5), 2004, 697–709.

Velasquez, ML. International business ethics. *Business Ethics Quarterly*, 5, 1995, 865–882.

Voronov, M and Singer, JA. The myth of individualism-collectivism: a critical review. *Journal of Social Psychology*, 142 (4), 2002, 461–480, p. 462.

Whymant, R. Japanese lovers pay dear for reluctance to end the affair. *Times*, 4 August 2001, p. 13.

Yagmurlu, B and Sanson, A. Acculturation and parenting among Turkish mothers in Australia. *Journal of Cross-cultural Psychology*, 40 (3), 2009, 361–380.

Yang, K-S. Will societal modernisation eventually eliminate cross-cultural psychological differences? In MH Bond (ed.), *The Cross-cultural Challenge to Social Psychology*. Sage, 1988.

Yeh, R-S and Lawrence, JJ. Individualism and Confucian dynamism: a note on Hof's cultural root to economic growth. *Journal of International Business Studies*, 26 (3), 1995, 655–669.

Yuval-Davis, N. Identity politics and women's ethnicity. In VM Moghadam (ed.), *Identity Politics and Women*. Westview Press, 1994.

Zweifel, TD. *Culture Clash: Managing the Global High-performance Team*. Swiss Consulting Group, 2003.

Cultural values in business and society

2

INTRODUCTION

Cultures vary in their values. Values and practices that are acceptable in one culture are less acceptable in another. That is why foreign business visitors to a country often find themselves confronted by values and practices that are entirely normal in the country they are visiting but that would definitely be unacceptable at home. Can it be right, for instance, to have to pay a government official for assistance in securing a lucrative sales contract? Or, to give an over-generous tip to a telephone operator to obtain an early connection? Difficult questions for international business people to answer! No international consensus exists on standards of international business conduct that would help a foreign business visitor to answer such questions definitively.

Hofstede's (1980a) survey of national cultures found that cultures differ from each other on four main value dimensions – individualism/collectivism, power/distance, uncertainty/avoidance, and masculinity/femininity. The GLOBE survey identifies nine dimensions of national value differences. The values of a country can also be inferred from what is rewarded and punished in families, schools, and other social structures. A society's social, political, and economic institutions carry the culture's values in their ideologies. Once learned, a culture's values are generally resistant to change.

For an expatriate manager or a business person about to visit a foreign country, a knowledge of national values as revealed by these and other surveys is extremely useful since survey findings reveal the values, ideas, and behaviour that are *acceptable* in a particular country and that should be conformed to so as to avoid offending the local people. Ethnocentric people repeatedly offend members of other cultures since they use their own culture's values as the standard when viewing other groups (Baldwin and Hecht, 1995). Ethnocentric people tend to be intolerant and closed-minded and ethnocentric values prevent effective cross-cultural communication and impede cross-cultural relationships.

To a greater or lesser extent, an organisation's values reflect the values of the national culture. For example, Japanese organisations, whose values are derived from Japanese culture, reward their managers for being workgroup-minded and for developing the abilities and skills of their subordinates (Van Oudenhoven et al., 2002). In the United States and western Europe, on the other hand, organisations tend to value and reward managers for being conscientious and effective – for knowing how to get work out of their employees and achieve good bottom-line results.

Increasingly, multinational companies are responding to international pressures urging them to demonstrate their commitment to the values of corporate social responsibility (CSR). Many companies have demonstrated their commitment through membership of the Global Compact and other international initiatives; by weighing in advance the environmental impact of their foreign operations; and by ensuring that their overseas activities are contributing to *poverty alleviation* in the regions where they are established.

HOW VALUES DEFINE CULTURE

What are values?

Values are emotion-linked beliefs about what is good, right, fair, and just, and they are a major source of differences in human behaviour across cultures (Smith and Schwartz, 1997). A culture's values are deep-rooted attitudes that express what most members of a culture believe in and that influence their behaviour. Parsons (1975) asserts, for instance, that most Americans share the common value of the American work ethic, which encourages hard work.

Milgram's classic (1963) experiments in the United States illustrate the strong hold that certain values – in this case respect for authority – have over individuals. Volunteers, who believed they were participating in a study of memory and learning, stood in front of a row of 30 switches labelled from 30 to 450 volts:

> The volunteers were told by the stern, authoritative 'experimenter' in his white coat to give increasingly severe 'shocks' to a 'learner', who was strapped in a chair, if he answered questions wrongly. The victim gave incorrect answers to 3 out of every 4 questions. When the shock reached (as the volunteer believed) the 300-volt level, the learner–victim, as prearranged, kicked on the wall of his room next door. When the volunteer asked the experimenter for guidance he was told authoritatively to carry on right up to the maximum voltage and to ignore the pounding. Two-thirds of the volunteers went on to administer 450 volts to the victim although in many cases they were sweating, laughing nervously, stuttering and showing other signs of severe emotional disturbance.

In following up the initial experiments Milgram found less conformity among French and Norwegian volunteers, and subsequently gathered evidence to show that the French and Norwegians have values that allow people to step out of line.

Values provide the standards by which behaviour and activities in a culture are evaluated. However, the evaluation process is complicated by the fact that a culture may contain *conflicting values*. In a given culture, for instance, the value of material success may conflict with the value of compassion and charity. In another culture the value of equality may conflict with the value of individualism; or the value of reserved communication conflict with the value of openness.

Resistant to change

Establishing a set of values in people's minds is an important function of culture. Indeed, Matsumoto et al. (2008) point out that a society's values are what it relies on to prevent social chaos and maintain social order. The importance of values helps to explain why, once absorbed from the culture in the process of socialization, values tend to be resistant to change. Sabogal et al. (1987) note that Indian migrants in the United States have retained their cultural values concerning family and marriage; and that Mexican Americans put a high value on family cohesion.

Values guide and strongly influence attitudes and behaviour and, once learned, are extremely difficult to unlearn (Roland, 1988). For instance, planes produced by Airbus and Boeing are supposed to be flown by two pilots of approximately equal status, without a significant power–distance between them. One pilot corrects any mistakes made by the other when necessary.

> But South Korea is a large power distance culture, and more than once – according to Korean newspaper reports – a co-pilot working for South Korean Airlines would not correct mistakes made by the other pilot.

People tend to hold onto their values consciously, but sometimes values operate unconsciously – on automatic pilot – and are not visible to an outside observer. Roland (1988) gives the example of Indian men who *at work* may dress in Western clothes and disregard inter-caste rules in eating and other rituals, but who unthinkingly observe traditional codes and dress traditionally *at home*.

How values are weakened

Values may remain stable through many generations (as is the case with individual freedoms in the United States), yet may be weakened when individuals leave their culture of origin and settle in another country. For instance, traditional gender values of Vietnamese adolescents have been found to be progressively undermined when they move to Australia (Rosenthal et al., 1996).

Yagmurlu and Sanson (2009) compare parenting patterns in Turkey and Australia and note that Turkey is a collectivist country where traditional parenting values prevail and where punishment is more common than verbal reasoning among parents. Australia, on the other hand, is predominantly individualistic and parenting goals in that country emphasize independence over obedience and discipline over punishment. Each set of values works well in its own cultural context. However, when Turkish families migrate to Australia traditional parenting values come into conflict with Australian values and are weakened. Other factors that influence the extent and the pace of value-change when individuals move to a foreign country are examined in Chapter 7.

For Levi-Strauss (1949: 10), values are acquired from a person's culture – as opposed to human nature, which is universal. 'All that is universal in humankind arises from the order of nature and is characterised by spontaneity; all that is held to a norm belongs to culture and possesses the attributes of the relative and the particular.'

Different value systems

Different cultures have different value systems. The differences can usually be inferred from what is rewarded and punished in families, schools, and other social structures. In a given culture, some values are given a higher priority than other values. For example, in North America individual happiness is a value of very high priority, but in some Asian countries personal happiness has a lower priority – lower, say, than harmony.

Cultural values are used to identify cultural groups and differentiate among them, and disparities in cultural values are at the root of many cross-cultural misunderstandings. For instance, most Westerners are low-context communicators and value clarity and outspokenness when communicating (Hall, 1976). By contrast, most collectivists are high-context communicators and avoid disharmony by suppressing their opinions, by *not* being outspoken.

Different value systems can lead to resentment and misunderstandings between people from different cultures. Clyne (1994), for instance, studied a multinational workforce in a manufacturing company in Australia and found that Asian employees, in accordance with their culturally derived value system, made little effort to contribute to discussions on the shop floor, never complained, never 'answered back' to workmates and supervisors. But this self-effacing behaviour degraded the Asians in the eyes of employees from cultures that had different values and undermined cross-cultural understanding.

A Western sales manager who made a sales tour of the Middle East soon became aware that values in the Arab world were very different from those of his own culture. He later explained to a business colleague that one prospective client pointedly ignored a polite enquiry about the client's wife. Another abruptly interrupted discussions about the possibility of establishing a partnership so that he could go to pray. The manager said that by observing his hosts' behaviour it soon became clear to him that major value differences separated societies in the Middle East from Western culture; and that one major difference was values relating to sex roles.

As such examples suggest, Western cultural values are often different from those held in other parts of the world. That was also one of the implications of a survey carried out by United Nations Development Programme workers in South America in 2004 (UNDP, 2004). The survey revealed that more than half of Latin American citizens would gladly opt for an authoritarian regime in preference to a democratic government if that would solve their economic problems.

Clashing communicative values

Tensions caused by clashing communicative values were revealed by a study of Australian and French employees of a French-owned company in Australia (Beal, 1994). French managers, following French communicative values, gave very direct, very clear-cut instructions to employees. Australian managers, by contrast, gave instructions in a characteristically indirect, 'democratic' manner, which the French equated with lack of confidence and poor leadership.

Guided by their communicative values, the French tended to focus on the topic rather than on the person they were speaking to. This, together with their habit of beginning remarks with 'Mais', made their speech sound offensively blunt and belligerent to the Australians.

> Even when the French spoke to Australians in English they transferred several linguistic habits from French into English. For instance, they made requests by using imperatives and 'il faut' ('you must...'). This made them seem authoritarian to the Australians who preferred 'Would you mind?'

The French managers' difficulties in dealing with employees and Australian colleagues derived not from poor communication skills but from French communicative values, which stress directness and assertiveness.

A similar clash of communicative values occurred when a Canadian IT consultant, visiting France for the first time, went into a baker's shop in Paris and asked the price of a gateau. The shopkeeper told her in French: 'The price is on the gateau. It's there in front of you.' Later the consultant complained to a French colleague about the shopkeeper's rude behaviour but the friend was puzzled: 'What's the problem? She was just trying to be clear and helpful.'

Values and perception

The powerful influence exerted by culturally derived values over perception and judgment was seen when members of five cultural subgroups in the United States and Israel were assembled to watch the same episode of the television soap series, *Dallas* (Liebes, 1988). The subgroups included Americans, Arabs, Jews, Moroccans, and Russians. After watching the episode, each group was asked to retell the story.

The various cultures interpreted the episode in widely differing ways. The Arabs focused on kinship. Arabs and Moroccans were shocked at the way in which the role of women was portrayed. The Americans and Israelis had a more accepting, amused and tongue-in-cheek attitude towards the events and characters. The Russians interpreted the story in a political way, as giving a false picture of reality regarding the prosperity of Americans.

The example illustrates how people from different cultures tend to perceive and interpret particular situations and events that occur in a particular culture to fit in with their pre-existing, culturally derived value systems.

VALUE VARIATIONS

Culture-specific values

Surveys carried out by Hofstede (1980a), Schwartz (2004), and other researchers reveal that the great majority of values are specific to a particular culture. Indeed, according to Brett (2001), a society's social, political, and economic institutions carry the culture's values in their ideologies. Fontaine et al. (2008) argue that the unique linguistic and historical evolution of each cultural group in a given national culture endow the values of that group with unique meaning. Such evidence helps to explain why the values of different national cultures often differ dramatically in spite of close geographic proximity. Thus Le Vine (1973: 26) notes that the neighbouring Yoruba and Hausa peoples of Nigeria have very different norms regarding the public expression of feelings:

> The Yoruba engaged in a great deal of jovial public conversation with many different persons, often accompanied by laughter and other indications of friendliness. The Hausa ... were much more restrained in their expressions of friendly interest .... Physicians and nurses in the local hospital reported that Yoruba women cried out and moaned freely during childbirth, while Hausa women hardly ever made any sound even during difficult deliveries.

Universal values

Cultures differ on many values. American culture, for instance, places great value on individual political and economic rights. But many Muslims, in ordinary conversation, will point out that Muslim values are linked to the social thinking embodied in the Koran, placing more value on the group than on the individual. Within a given culture, subcultures also differ on values. Different social classes, for instance, tend to have different values systems. Kohn (1969) found that less educated and lower-status employees in various Western countries tend to have more authoritarian values than their higher status co-workers; and that working class parents demand more obedience from their children than middle class parents.

However, a few values seem to be held by virtually all cultures and such values may be universal. All societies, for instance, demonstrate revulsion for child-molesting, and most prohibit sexual relations between blood kin. Values governing politeness seem to exist in all cultures. Buss et al. (1990) make the point that in all cultures men seem to prefer younger women while women tend to prefer older men. Arguably, ethnocentric values are universal in the sense that they are generated by all cultures.

Ethnocentric values

The term 'ethnocentrism', which was coined by Sumner (1906), describes the habit that people have of using their own culture's values as the standard when viewing other groups. That is, they place their own group/society at the top of a hierarchy and rank all other groups/societies as inferior. Later studies have shown that people holding ethnocentric values tend to be *intolerant* and *closed-minded* when they communicate with people from other cultures (e.g. Baldwin and Hecht, 1995). That explains why ethnocentric values prevent effective cross-cultural communication and therefore impede the building and maintenance of healthy cross-cultural relationships.

Everybody is born into a particular culture and grows up absorbing the values of the culture, thereby developing patterns of thought reflecting the culture as 'normal' (Seidner, 1982). Other cultures' values and behaviours are instinctively seen as being – in varying degrees – 'abnormal'. People are therefore conditioned by the culture into which they are born and it is difficult for them to see the values and behaviours of people from a different culture from the viewpoint of that culture rather than from their own.

Cultural imperialism

Language is the fundamental vehicle for expressing a culture and its values and so can be regarded as the main weapon of cultural imperialism – an extreme, militant expression of ethnocentrism. 'Cultural imperialism' can be defined as imposing a culture's values, ideology, or civilization on an unwilling society, with the consequence that much of that society's original culture is destroyed (Ziring et al., 1995). Cultural attributes that can be expressed only in the original language are changed or disappeared.

However, cultural imperialism as a policy by which a government *imposes* its values on other societies needs to be distinguished from the spread of alien cultural influences as a result of international trade, travel, and communication.

MANAGERIAL VALUES

National culture and management style

Studies have revealed the link that exists between national values and management behaviour. For example, Triandis's (1994) review of some 400 studies found that a country's cultural values orientation will determine the optimum leadership/management profile for a particular country. Although there are some universal attributes of effective management that apply across virtually all cultures – taking responsibility for results, for instance – many national cultures have a distinct management style that is directly influenced by that culture.

In some societies a strong directive approach by managers and supervisors is important. In Iran, for instance, managerial appointments and directive management styles are based primarily on the manager's strong ties and allegiance to the government's revolutionary values and the tenets of Islam (Soltani, 2010). As Javidan and Carl (2004: 685) observe, in some countries there are strong pressures on managers urging them *not* to try to change or improve things. The reason is that in such countries, breaking the *status quo* might lead to a change in the balance of power in an organisation.

How managers perform their jobs

Culturally derived values greatly influence the way that people do their jobs, how they relate to bosses and subordinates, how they spend their time at work. The Meaning of Working study, for example, investigated the value of work centrality in various national cultures (MOW, 1987). The study found that countries vary in the extent to which employees regard work as central to their lives. Employees in the United States, for instance, see work as more central to their lives than do employees in the former West Germany but less central than do Japanese employees.

Much evidence shows how national cultural values influence the ways in which managers perform their jobs. Chinese managers, for instance, are limited in the kind of managerial actions that are open to them because of the pressure of Chinese cultural values. Boisot and Xing (1992) point out that the great emphasis that is placed on *hierarchy* in Chinese society means, in a managerial context, that higher levels in the organisation must approve a manager's actions. A practical consequence of this constraint is that Chinese managers spend up to four times as much time communicating up the line as American managers (Doktor, 1990).

Japanese managerial values

Studies have found that managers in the United States and the countries of western Europe use mainly reasoning and friendliness to influence and motivate their subordinates – as opposed to sanctions or appeals to higher authority which are frequently used in other parts of the world (Sullivan and Taylor, 1991). Thus Japanese managers tend to be more assertive than, say, British or Australian managers. They frequently tell subordinates that they must comply with instructions, remind them repeatedly what the instructions are, set frequent deadlines, and hold employees accountable for observing them (Sullivan and Taylor, 1991).

A notable aspect of Japanese organisations is that managers are rewarded for being workgroup-minded. Van Oudenhoven et al. (2002) found that the status of Japanese managers comes mainly from successfully developing their subordinates. The inference is that to be effective Japanese managers must demonstrate both task-centred and relationship-centred leadership behaviour.

In one cross-cultural study of managerial value orientations Japanese managers were found to have a very pragmatic orientation whereas Indian managers were the opposite (England, 1974). The Japanese managers valued achievement, creativity, and autonomy and attached great importance to organisational goals such as profitability and productivity. The Indians, by contrast, were much less concerned about profit maximization or profitability and instead valued organisational stability, job satisfaction, security, and status.

Fujisawa, co-founder of the Honda Motor Corporation, reportedly told a management seminar: 'Japanese and western management is 95 per cent the same and differs in all important respects.' Authentic or not, the comment reflects important differences that separate the mindsets of Western managers from those of their counterparts in Japan and elsewhere in Asia.

Comparative studies of national management styles are often based on the *perfect translation assumption* – the assumption that all concepts and roles generated in one language can be fully rendered in another language (Winch et al., 2000). This, however, is not always the case. For instance, a comparative study by Western researchers of American and Egyptian management styles would be greatly constrained by the fact that few Westerners understand colloquial Egyptian Arabic or even the written script.

Managerial values in European countries

Studies have revealed great differences in the way that managers from different European countries do their jobs and organise their time. For example, Thorpe and Paclica's (1996) study of British and Czech managers revealed great differences between British and Czech management values and practice – differences which, according to the authors, were predictable in view of national cultural differences on Hofstede's dimensions:

- Power distance index: Cz = 47 GB = 15
- Masculinity index: Cz = 90 GB = 5
- Uncertainty index: Cz = 49 GB = 4
- Individualism index: Cz = 50 GB = 101

The British responses stressed the importance of interactions with colleagues and of the achievement of good communication throughout the organisation. More specifically, British managers participating in the survey saw good relationships with their bosses as being very important, whereas this was not the case with Czech managers. Similarly, being consulted about decisions made by superiors was seen as more important by British managers than by Czech managers. According to the researchers, this important difference is due to the hierarchical nature of Czech organisations where there is relatively poor communication between different levels of management.

German and British managers

Stewart et al. (1994) studied German and British managers and found that in both countries telephone calls and enquiries or requests took up most of the managers' time. However, time spent in meetings and informal communication varied greatly. British managers had frequent coordination meetings, but German managers, in accordance with their culturally derived managerial values, relied on structure, rules, and routines to resolve work-related issues. Another notable difference was that British managers were keen to distance themselves from technical involvement, but German managers saw technical duties and managerial responsibilities as inseparable, and they relied on their technical expertise when supervising others. Stewart et al.'s (1994) study is notable for the fact that the researchers found it impossible to compare managers' jobs directly, because jobs in the British and German companies they studied were socially constructed in different ways.

Further striking differences in managerial values and perceptions were revealed when French, British, and German management students were given a case study to solve (Hofstede, 1980b). The three national groups interpreted the problem in completely different ways. The French saw the chief executive as the cause of the problem, the Germans saw lack of written policy as the cause, while the British were sure that the cause was poor face-to-face communication.

Studies suggest that managers in North America hold similar managerial values to those prevailing in western Europe. One study comparing the characteristics of effective managers in the United States and seven European countries found that intelligence, conscientiousness, and ability to motivate subordinates were reported as important qualities of effective managers in all of the countries (Robie et al., 2001). Despharde et al. (1998) compared the way that multinational companies operated. The companies, which were based in the United States, England, France, Germany, and Japan, operated in many different ways but the most successful companies used a similar organisational strategy of encouraging and rewarding innovation and competitive, entrepreneurial managerial values.

French and British managerial values

Writers as diverse as Hofstede (1997), Fukuyama (1995), and Barsoux and Lawrence (1990) have characterized the French as relatively bureaucratic and hierarchical. Guirdham (2005) makes the point that French managers, who are the products of a high power–distance culture, view organisations as a pyramid of differentiated levels of power and think that success is linked to their ability to 'work the system' by managing power relationships effectively.

British managers see things differently, tending to see an organisation as a network of relationships between individuals who get things done by influencing each other through informal communication and meetings (Stewart et al., 1994). No doubt, attempts to install MBO systems in France have been unsuccessful because the idea that boss and subordinate should jointly reach decisions about the subordinate's performance do not fit in with French ideas about the importance of hierarchy and status in organisations.

Graves' (1973) studied managers in French and British electronics factories and found evidence to suggest that the French need a hierarchical structure within which they are able to work efficiently, whereas the British are more flexible and do not need such a structure. Campagnac's (1996) case study of an Anglo-French joint venture – the Second Severn Bridge project – found that in the French organisation authority was centralized and hierarchical, while British management structure was more decentralized with authority being diffused horizontally. The British relied more on communication and procedures, while French managers relied more on clear managerial decision.

Channel Tunnel study

Winch et al. (2000) studied the behaviour of British and French managers who constructed the Channel Tunnel between 1987 and 1993. The managers, mostly engineers, worked for Transmanche-Link, a consortium of British and French construction organisations who built the tunnel on behalf of the tunnel concessionaire, Eurotunnel.

The two groups were similar in terms of specialization of tasks and hierarchy since Transmanche-Link had a relatively flat common organisation structure. Nevertheless, there were notable differences. French managers, for instance, were more competitive, individualistic, and more highly stressed. The French competed with each other, tried to get ahead of each other, and had relatively low unit cohesion. The British managers, by contrast, were collegial in approach, relying on their colleagues for motivation and ideas, and were always ready to communicate and cooperate with each other.

Both French and British managers handled conflict by avoiding the issue or 'working it out', but the French often handed the dispute to higher level management for a resolution. The problem that was most frequently mentioned by the managers was that of language. Cross-cultural communication on the project was overwhelmingly in English simply because of the inability of the British managers to communicate in French.

ORGANISATIONAL VALUES

Organisational culture

As Hofstede (1997) shows, organisations develop organisational cultures that reflect, to a greater or lesser extent, the values and practices of the national culture. National culture makes an impact on business both through the organisational cultures that develop in a country and the management styles that are practised.

Organisational values tend to reflect the values of the national culture. When one company purchases a company in a different country the clash of organisational values may prevent a smooth, effective integration. The poor performance of DaimlerChrysler, for instance, is often blamed on a culture clash that led to major integration problems and affected overall performance (Epstein, 2004).

Korean company values often lead company employees to follow strict rules which show respect to higher levels of status and authority (a national characteristic). Elashmawi and Harris (1998) make the point that conservative values and relationships prevail both in the national culture and in Korean organisations: business is conducted conservatively in Korean companies and is characterized by strong internal ties among family members.

Sitkin and Roth (1993: 368) maintain that within any organisation *trusting relationships* are rooted in 'value congruence' (i.e. the compatibility of individuals' values with the collective values of the organisation). When individual employees share the goals and values of the organisation they are more likely to trust one another since they know that all are working for collective goals and will not be hurt by any other member's opportunistic pursuit of self-interest.

Hawkins' (1997) review found evidence to show that higher levels of organisational performance can be attained through the astute management of organisational culture. Peters and Waterman (1982) linked being an excellent company to management's ability to create a strong unifying organisational culture with a shared vision.

Measuring organisational culture

Organisational culture has been defined as 'the dynamic set of assumptions, values and artefacts whose meanings are collectively shared in a given social unit at a particular point in time' (Ogbonna and Harris, 2002: 674). Attempts to measure organisational culture generally focus on identifying the *prevailing values* of the organisation. For example:

1. Whether the organisation values *flexibility* or *control* with regard to organisation structure, reporting arrangements, and other key aspects of organisation.
2. Whether the organisation values *loyalty* more than it values *capability* among employees.
3. Whether *customer satisfaction* is more important to the organisation than *profits*.
4. Whether individuals are expected to innovate or conform.
5. Whether the organisation values *formal* or *informal communication* practices.

Organisations which favour informal communication are easily identified. They are usually characterized, for instance, by an almost total absence of formal cross-divisional or cross-functional meetings. In these companies virtually all lateral communication is carried out through informal social networks.

Three-dimensional model of organisational culture

Schein's (1990) three-dimensional model of organisational culture consists of values, artefacts, and assumptions:

> *Values* are the shared beliefs and rules that govern the attitudes and behaviours of employees and that influence the ways in which people feel and think. (A usual way of getting at the prevailing values of an organisation is through open-ended interviews with employees and managers.)
>
> *Artefacts* are everything from physical layout, dress code, the way in which people address each other, and key documents – such as statements of mission and the annual report.
>
> *Assumptions* are the taken-for-granted beliefs about human nature and the organisational environment. The perceptions, thought processes, feelings, and behaviour of members of the organisation are based on these assumptions, many of them operating at the unconscious level.

Schein points out that assumptions often start out as values. Gradually some of the organisation's values are taken for granted, and at that stage they take on the character of assumptions – that is they are no longer questioned and become less and less open to discussion.

Clashing organisational cultures

Kanter (2009) looks at a dozen successful international acquisitions ranging from global deals such as Proctor & Gamble's purchase of Gillette, to regional acquisitions such as Shinhan Bank's acquisition of Chohung Bank in South Korea. Kanter discovered that the organisational cultures of acquirer and acquired frequently clash. Thus Shinhan Bank's strong corporate culture was very different from Chohung Bank's culture – so much so that it led to strong initial resistance from Chohung employees. About 3500 Chohung employees and managers shaved their heads and piled their hair in front of Shinhan headquarters. To quieten the labour union Shinhan had to agree to delay formal integration for 3 years – although, before then, *de facto* integration was achieved through integrated task forces and various other integration events including sing-alongs and mountain climbing.

Organisational values reflect the cultural norms that help them survive within their own business environments. That, essentially, is why large and successful companies have strong corporate cultures. The corporate culture relates to the national business environment. Thus, Hofstede (1980a) found that within a single multinational, IBM, there were wide variations of corporate culture *depending on the national location*. IBM's organisational culture had, in effect, adjusted to the national culture in each country.

Organisational subcultures

Schein (1990: 115) explains how, as an organisation develops and grows, two processes occur simultaneously:

- *a process of differentiation* into various kinds of subcultures that will create diversity;
- *a process of integration* – a tendency for the various deeper elements of the culture to become congruent with each other because of the human need for consistency.

Large organisations contain many subcultures. Subcultures exist at different levels of the organisation, in different departments, and in different geographical locations. Each of these organisational subcultures develops its own values – that is, values that are perceived as being important for the group's success in that particular business environment. Thus, when Elashmawi and Harris (1998) asked *engineers* from Petronas to list the cultural values of the engineering division the values that were perceived as important were risk-taking, good project management, and keeping abreast of current technology. By contrast, the *marketing group* at Petronas felt that their functional responsibility required them to focus most of all on maximizing revenue and minimizing costs.

As the example demonstrates, the values held by a particular departmental subculture differ, to a greater or lesser extent, from the values of other subcultures in the same firm as well as deviating from the 'official' company values (i.e. those held and promoted by top management). In any large organisation, accordingly, Schein (1990) argues, overall organisational culture becomes a negotiated outcome of the interaction of the various subcultures.

ETHICAL VALUES

Standards of conduct in international business

Culture is widely regarded as one of the important elements influencing ethical decision-making in business organisations and accounting for variations in international business practices (Su, 2006). Indeed, establishing a set of moral rules in the minds of all members is an essential function of culture – although there are important differences in the moral rules produced by different cultures (Miller and Bersoff, 1992). However, no published scale exists to measure the validity of different moral values produced by different societies (Guerra and Giner-Sorolla, 2010).

Thus business visitors to foreign countries are often confronted with values and practices that are entirely normal in the foreign culture but which would definitely be unacceptable at home. Examples are child labour in India and China and some African countries, and discrimination against women in some countries in the Middle East. Another example is payments for services rendered that would be seen as bribes in the visitor's own country but which are common practices in some countries, where the payments are not regarded as unethical. Ali (1995) found that in Syria, for instance, it is impossible to get a request processed in any government agency without paying bribes; and that the payment of money for services rendered is considered normal business practice. In Russia, corruption and bribery in business affairs have been widespread since the collapse of the Soviet Union. Kazakov et al. (1997) argue that commissions, bribes, and creative ways of cutting corners have to be tolerated by foreign business executives in Russia who are anxious to sign a contract or clinch a deal.

Clashing ethical values and practices

Ethical practices and the underlying values vary across cultures. Values and practices that are acceptable in one culture are less acceptable in another. Americans, for instance, are more unwilling than Brazilians to visit a sick friend if that would mean foregoing personal financial benefit (Shekshnia et al., 2003). In the absence of any clear and uncontested code of business conduct, international business executives and expatriate managers can never be certain that the way they go about dealing with ethical dilemmas encountered abroad is the right way. Is it right or wrong, for instance, to give a generous tip to a foreign telephone operator to obtain an immediate overseas connection? Is it right or wrong to pay a foreign government official for assistance in securing a lucrative overseas contract? Should international business practice, in all situations and in all cultures, adhere to clear-cut and absolute moral standards – or is international business practice necessarily relative and situational?

Expatriate managers working in Chinese organisations frequently encounter employee discipline problems. For example, an expatriate manager who worked in a Chinese manufacturing company dealt with such problems in a simplistic way by suppressing personal judgment and conforming to the Chinese company's rules and practices. The strategy worked well at first but then unravelled. When the manager caught a local employee stealing he simply followed the rules and handed the employee over to the provincial authorities, who executed him. Today in China death sentences must receive final approval from the Supreme People's Court in Beijing, after which most executions are carried out by lethal injection.

Case study

MINI-CASE: The director's dilemma

An international sales executive employed by a machine tool company in Europe came face-to-face with a serious ethical dilemma when he made a business trip to a country in the Middle East.

Payments to lubricate the decision-making machinery in the country were reputed to be common practice. Nevertheless, the sales executive was stunned when, after a short courtesy meeting with government officials, a junior minister approached him and asked for a $100,000 consulting fee. In return for the fee the minister promised special assistance in obtaining a lucrative contract for the European company.

Without his assistance, the minister added, the contract would definitely go to one of the company's competitors.

Questions:

1. *How should the director respond to the minister's offer?*
2. *Should international business people try to maintain 'absolute' moral standards of business conduct in all countries at all times?*
3. *Could 'absolute' standards of business conduct be enforced?*

Honest and dishonest communication

An important component of international business ethics is *honest communication* – honest advertising, honest information provided to foreign customers, honest answers to foreign government officials. But there are many examples of *dishonest* communication in international business, including:

- *numbers manipulation,* which can make the difference between winning and failing to win a lucrative contract;
- *'talking up'* a product or service and deliberately misrepresenting its features or performance;
- *misleading product descriptions* on labels which prevent the prospective client from making an informed choice.

In Israeli settlements across the West Bank, polythene tunnels house rows of herbs which are exported to Europe. European supermarkets sell the herbs, which are often misleadingly labelled as 'West Bank produce'. The label does not tell consumers whether they are buying from a Palestinian farmer or an Israeli settler. (Israeli settlements in the West Bank are illegal under international law).

The fact that no consensus exists on standards of international business conduct helps to explain why executives sometimes regard dishonest communication as part of what it takes to do business abroad. For example, a sales manager from a computer company attended a meeting with the directors of a new publishing company in eastern Europe.

During the meeting the sales manager tried to convince the directors that the product he was trying to sell them, computer software, would correspond to what the company said it needed. The sales manager, however, knew that this was not really true.

Expatriate business conduct

International business people who resort to unethical practices often do so in response to strong pressures and influences such as:

- pressures from the board to achieve good bottom-line results, even if this means taking actions that could be perceived as questionable;
- pressures from shareholders and the stock market for quick returns on investment.

Similar pressures help to explain why managers posted to expatriate jobs abroad are sometimes criticized by local management for their apparent obsession with profits. In China during the go-go years of rapid economic development, foreign firms invested heavily in guanxi (connections) with the authorities (often through the use of bribery) in order to secure commercial deals or to obtain favourable loans from state banks.

In China today expatriate managers continue to need guanxi to be managerially effective, as explained in Chapter 6. But in China, as elsewhere, they also need to demonstrate *ethical leadership*. Harzing (2001) notes that expatriate managers who fail to demonstrate ethical leadership have been criticized in recent years for such activities as:

- making payoffs to local business people or officials so as to achieve increased sales revenue;
- ordering local production staff to use inferior or contaminated raw materials in an effort to reduce costs;
- employing unqualified production staff leading to such problems as poor quality control;
- transferring unsuitable auditing and other compliance systems from their company at home to the local operation, where they sometimes cause major control problems.

Ethical leadership

Expatriate managers and international project managers can demonstrate ethical leadership by setting clear standards, using fair and balanced rewards and punishments, and building trusting relationship with their team (Brown et al., 2005). Walumbwa and Schaubroeck (2009), who define 'ethical leadership' as the demonstration of *normatively appropriate conduct*, found that an important effect of ethical leadership was its impact on boss–subordinate communication. The researchers found that employees with ethical managers trust the managers and tend to communicate with them in a constructive manner. For instance, they are willing to reveal job problems to them as they arise and tend to make innovative suggestions for change. Such characteristics of manager–employee communication no doubt reflect an increased sense of psychological security.

Such evidence suggests that ethical managers breed ethical employees. Readers of the Harvard Business Review, for instance, have identified their managers' behaviour as the most important influence when establishing personal ethical standards (Brenner and Molander, 1977). Another study found that accountants commit fewer unethical acts if their senior managers actively discourage unethical behaviour (Finn et al., 1988). Reviewing all the evidence, Posner and Schmidt (1984) concluded that it is individual managers rather than companies who drive the ethical behaviour of their subordinates. Corporate policies and statements stressing the importance of ethical behaviour in conducting international business have much less effect on employees' behaviour than the influence exerted by the employee's immediate boss. The inference is that although organisations may have some influence on employee values, they actually *change* them much less profoundly than do motivated and determined individual managers, who act as role models.

CORPORATE SOCIAL RESPONSIBILITY

Responsibility of multinational companies

Social responsibility is a popular topic in business journals. However, its meaning is too imprecise to make it a useful guide as to how international business should be conducted. Many multinational companies demonstrate their social responsibility not by issuing mission statements but by taking appropriate action. According to Maak and Pless (2009), multinational companies may *demonstrate* their commitment to social responsibility by such actions as:

- assessing and weighing, in advance, the *environmental impact* of their foreign operations;
- ensuring that their foreign operations are contributing to *poverty alleviation* in the countries or regions concerned;
- proactively finding ways to increase the global *sustainability of resources*.

There is no doubt that many multinational companies have the means and power to make a positive impact in each of these areas in the countries in which they operate. UNCTAD data show that 51 of the world's largest economies are now global corporations – only 49 are countries. Even relatively small firms operating abroad can make an impact by showing social responsibility by such actions as being efficient users of energy and natural resources; and by assessing the environmental effects likely to flow from any of the company's technological developments.

International solutions

Kapur has the largest concentration of leather tanneries in Pakistan, many of them employing child labour. Moreover, workers and local residents are exposed to life-threatening substances as a result of tanning pollution. Since the early 1980s local residents and NGOs have been calling for international support to change the way the industry operates, and results are being achieved. Thus Lund-Thomsen (2009) describes how in the soccer ball industry a Public–Private Partnership between UNICEF, ILO, NGOs, Pakistani manufacturers, and multinational companies has been established and how the international effort has largely succeeded in eliminating child labour from the industry.

The world is becoming increasingly connected and interdependent, and global problems – such as global warming or access to clean drinking water – require *international* solutions. International efforts which are already being made to address such problems include:

- United Nations Norms on the responsibilities of MNEs and other business enterprises with regard to human rights.
- The OECD Declaration of International Investment and Multinational Enterprises.
- The Global Compact.

The Global Compact

The Global Compact is a commitment by business worldwide to *important ethical values.* Conceived by former UN Secretary-General Kofi Annan and launched in 2000, the Global Compact has more than 4500 participating businesses in 120 countries worldwide. Its activities are funded by governments and by company subscriptions. Participating companies agree to implement the Global Compact's ten principles in the areas of human rights, labour, the environment, and anti-corruption and universal principles.

In effect, the Global Compact offers a strategic and operational framework for exercising CSR. Companies which fail to communicate progress in implementing the ten universal principles are removed from the list of signatories. In 2006, more than 400 companies were removed from the list, including Air India, Ernst and Young Brazil, and China Petroleum.

According to the CEO of one participating company, Coca-Cola Company: 'As a global initiative with local networks around the world, the Global Compact allows us to act consistently wherever we operate.'

China's CSR initiative

China's recent CSR initiative can be seen as a response to global concerns about international business ethics (Ip, 2009). CSR, inspired by the Global Compact, lists ten principles which provide clear guidelines for corporate ethics. Besides including norms aimed at preventing forced labour and child labour, CSR spells out the specific responsibilities of firms in the financial, social, and environmental spheres. However, it has yet to be demonstrated that transporting CSR as practised by many Western MNEs to Chinese companies will produce a good cultural fit.

Ip (2009) argues that the *tradition of virtue*, as prescribed by Confucianism, could become a more culturally appropriate basis for Chinese business practice. A Confucian firm would accept morality-constrained profit-seeking; do good for the community and society; and provide fair salaries and a healthy work environment. The goals and practices of a Confucian firm would be defined by the principles of *ren* (benevolence towards others), *yi* (moral rightness), and *li* (the many etiquettes, norms, and protocols in both personal and institutional lives). People's moral character, not rules and regulations, would be the main driver of their actions and decisions.

Case study

MINI-CASE: International business conduct

For an example of an international business deal that went wrong, consider the case of the uncontrolled dumping in 2006 of hundreds of tonnes of highly toxic oil waste around Abidjan, capital of Ivory Coast. The disaster appears to have been caused by oil traders' search for profit at all costs. Traders at Trafigura, the London-based oil trader, hoped to make large profits by buying up cargoes of sulphur-contaminated Mexican gasoline. The fuel was processed on board a tanker anchored off Gibraltar – in spite of the process being banned in Western countries. As a result, toxic waste 'slops' were created.

The tanker finally sailed to Ivory Coast for the waste to be dumped by a local contractor who hired a tanker truck to take away the black slurry and dump it in landfill sites all around Abidjan. According to a report in the Guardian newspaper (17 September, 2009: 1), those living and working nearby subsequently suffered respiratory and eye problems, nose-bleeding, nausea, diarrhoea, loss of consciousness, and death. Thousands of people were forced to leave their homes. Autopsy reports appeared to show fatal levels of the poisonous gas hydrogen sulphide, one of the waste's lethal by-products.

Trafigura issued statements saying that victims' claims to have been poisoned were imaginary, and a Trafigura director told BBC Newsnight that his firm's waste was 'absolutely not dangerous to human beings'. However, a UN human rights special rapporteur reported that according to official estimates there were 15 deaths, 69 persons hospitalized, and more than 108,000 medical consultations. He believed there was strong *prima facie* evidence that the reported deaths and adverse health consequences were related to the dumping.

For 3 years the company insisted that its waste was not dangerous. However, in September 2009 it finally agreed to pay compensation to 31,000 victims when emails came to light that showed that it was fully aware from the outset. Lawyers representing 31,000 people against Trafigura reached a settlement for a reported £28m, which means that each person should receive about £950.

Case study

Continued

Questions:

1. *Who should be held accountable for such abuses? The company? The Ivory Coast government? Both? Neither?*
2. *If there had been in existence a clear code of conduct relating to ethical international business practices would that have prevented the disaster? If not, why not?*

KEY POINTS

1. A culture's values are deep-rooted attitudes that express what most members of a culture believe in and that influence their behaviour. Values are absorbed from the culture in the process of socialization and, once learned, tend to be resistant to change. A society's institutions carry the culture's values in their ideologies. Value differences can lead to resentment and misunderstandings between people from different cultures.
2. Ethnocentric values impede cross-cultural relationships and prevent effective cross-cultural communication. Ethnocentrism describes the habit that people have of placing their own culture at the top of a hierarchy and ranking all others as inferior. People with ethnocentric values tend to be intolerant and closed-minded when they communicate with people from other cultures.
3. Communication between people from diverse cultures is often handicapped by incompatible communicative norms. Communicative norms prescribe, for instance, the kind of communication desirable when men and women interact in public, the kind of topics that may be discussed in public, and the extent to which feelings should be expressed in everyday communication. People from Western countries generally put a high value on clarity and directness and try to put these values into practice during cross-cultural situations. People from collectivist countries, on the other hand, often hide or soften their opinions in order to maintain harmony.
4. Cultural imperialism (with language as its main tool) involves imposing a country's values, ideology, or civilization on an unwilling society, causing many aspects of that society's original culture to be destroyed. Cultural imperialism as a deliberate policy aimed at imposing a country's values on other countries must be distinguished from alien cultural influences as a result of international trade, travel, and communication.
5. Culture makes an impact on organisations through the corporate values they develop and the management styles they encourage. Values influence the way that managers do their jobs and how they relate to their employees. Japanese

managers, for instance, tend to have a very pragmatic orientation and attach great importance to organisational goals such as profitability and productivity. Indian managers, by contrast, tend to be less concerned with profit maximization than they are with organisational stability, job satisfaction, and status.

6. Establishing a set of moral rules in the minds of all members is an essential function of culture, but there are important differences in the moral rules produced by different cultures. For instance, commission payments for services rendered are regarded as bribes in some countries but are common practice in other countries where such payments are not regarded as unethical. Multinational companies are increasingly expected to demonstrate corporate responsibility by avoiding damage to the environment as a result of their foreign activities, and by ensuring that their foreign operations are contributing to poverty alleviation.

7. Organisational values tend to reflect the values of the national culture. Attempts to measure organisational culture usually focus on identifying the prevailing values of the organisation (such as whether an organisation values flexibility or control with regard to reporting arrangements and organisation structure). Organisational *subcultures* develop their own values – that is, values that are perceived as being important for the success of the department or unit concerned.

QUESTIONS FOR DISCUSSION AND WRITTEN ASSIGNMENTS

1. a) Are values learned or innate? b) To what extent are values culture-specific? Illustrate with examples from particular cultures.
2. Give examples of problems that are caused when the practices of a multinational company ignore the values and interests of the host society?
3. 'During cross-cultural encounters people's words and behaviour are guided by their culturally derived norms of communicative behaviour.' Give examples from your own experience of the kind of problems that can occur as a result?
4. Why do the values of the various subcultures of an organisation differ from each other?

BIBLIOGRAPHY

Ali, AJ. Cultural discontinuity and Arab management thought. *International Studies of Management and Organisation*, 25 (3), 1995, 7–30.

Baldwin, JR and Hecht, ML. The layered perspective of cultural (in)tolerance(s): the roots of a multidisciplinary approach. In RL Wiseman (ed.), *Intercultural Communication Theory*. Sage, 1995, p. 65.

Barsoux, J-L and Lawrence, P. *Management in France*. Cassell, 1990.

Beal, C. Keeping the Peace. *Multilingua*, 13 (1–2), 1994.

Boisot, M and Xing, GL. The nature of managerial work in the Chinese enterprise reforms: a study of six directors. *Organisational Studies*, 13 (2), 1992, 161–184.

Brenner, SN and Molander, E. Is the ethics of business changing? *HBR*, 55, 1977, 57–71.

Brett, JM. *Negotiating Globally*. Jossey-Bass, 2001.

Brown, ME et al., Ethical leadership: a social learning perspective for construct development and testing. *Organisational Behaviour and Human Decision Processes*, 97, 2005, 117–134.

Buss, DM et al., International preferences in selecting mates. *Journal of Cross-cultural Psychology*, 21, 1990, 2–47.

Campagnac, E. La maitrise du risqué entre differences et cooperation: le cas du Severn Bridge. Groupe Bagnolet Working Paper 12, 1996.

Clyne, M. *Intercultural Communication at Work*. CUP, 1994.

Despharde, R et al., Factors affecting organisation performance: a five-country comparison. MSI Report no. 98–100, 1998.

Doktor, RH. Asian and American CEOs: a comparative study. *Organisational Dynamics*, 19 (3), 1990, 46–56.

Elashmawi, F and Harris, PR. *Multicultural Management 2000*. Gulf Publishing, 1998.

England, GW. *The Manager and the Man*. Kent State University, 1974.

Epstein, MJ. The drivers of success in post-merger integration. *Organisational Dynamics*, 33, 2004, 174–189.

Finn, DW et al., Ethical problems in public accounting. *Journal of Business Ethics*, 7, 1988, 605–615.

Fontaine, JRJ et al., Structural equivalence of the values domain across cultures. *Journal of Cross-cultural Psychology*, 39 (4), 2008, 345–365.

Fukuyama, F. *Trust: The Social Virtues and the Creation of Prosperity*. Hamish Hamilton, 1995.

Graves, D. The impact of culture on management attitudes, beliefs, and behaviour in England and France. In D Graves (ed.), *Management Research: A Cross-cultural Perspective*. Elsevier Scientific, 1973.

Guerra, VM and Giner-Sorolla, R. The community, autonomy, and divinity scale (CADS): a new tool for the cross-cultural study of morality. *Journal of Cross-cultural Psychology* 41 (1), 2010, 35–50.

Guirdham, M. *Communicating Across Cultures at Work*, 2nd ed. Palgrave Macmillan, 2005.

Hall, ET. *Beyond Culture*, Anchor, 1976.

Harzing, A-W. Of bears, bumble-bees, and spiders: the role of expatriates in controlling foreign subsidiaries. *Journal of World Business*, 36, 2001, 366–379.

Hawkins, P. Organisational culture: sailing between evangelism and complexity. *Human Relations*, 50 (4), 1997, 417–440.

Hofstede, G. *Culture's Consequences: International Differences in Work-related Values.* Sage, 1980a.

Hofstede, G. *Cultures and Organisations: Software of the Mind,* Revised ed., McGraw Hill, 1997.

Hofstede, G. Motivation, leadership and organisation: do American theories apply abroad. *Organisational Dynamics,* 75, 1980b, 42–63.

Ip, PK. Is Confucianism good for business ethics in China? *Journal of Business Ethics,* 88, 2009, 463–476.

Javidan, M and Carl, DE. East meets west: a cross-cultural comparison of charismatic leadership among Canadian and Iranian executives. *Journal of Management Studies,* 41 (4), 2004, 665–691.

Kanter, RM. *Mergers that Stick.* HBR, October 2009, 121–125.

Kazakov, AY et al., Business ethics and civil society in Russia. *International Studies of Management and Organisation,* 27 (1), 1997, 5–18.

Kohn, ML. *Class and Conformity: A Study in Values.* Dorsey, 1969.

Levi-Strauss, C. *Les structures elementaires de la parente.* Presses Universitaires de France, Paris 1949.

Liebes, T. Cultural differences in the retelling of television fiction. *Critical Studies in Mass Communication,* 5, 1988, 277–292.

Le Vine, R. *Culture, Behaviour and Personality.* Aldine, 1973, p. 26.

Lund-Thomsen, P. Assessing the impact of public-private partnerships in the Global South. *Journal of Business Ethics,* 90, 2009, 57–78.

Maak, T and Pless, NM. Business leaders as citizens of the world. *Journal of Business Ethics,* 88 (3), 2009, 537–550.

Matsumoto, D et al., Mapping expressive differences across the world: the relationship between emotional display rules and individualism versus collectivism. *Journal of Cross-cultural Psychology,* 39 (1), 2008, 58.

Milgram, S. Behavioural study of obedience. *Journal of Abnormal and Social Psychology,* 67 (4), 1963, 371–378.

Miller, J and Bersoff, D. Culture and moral judgment. *Journal of Personality and Social Psychology,* 62, 1992, 541–554.

MOW International Research Team, *The Meaning of Working.* Academic Press, 1987.

Ogbonna, E and Harris, LC. Organisational culture: a ten year, two-phase study of change in the UK food retailing sector. *Journal of Management Studies,* 39 (5), 2002, 673–706.

Parsons, T. *Social Systems and The Evolution of Action Theory.* Free Press, 1975.

Peters, TJ and Waterman, R. *In Search of Excellence.* Harper & Row, 1982.

Posner, BZ and Schmidt, WH. Values and the American manager: an update. *California Management Review,* 26 (3), 1984, 202–216.

Robie, C et al., The right stuff: understanding cultural differences in leadership performance. *Journal of Management Development,* 20, 2001, 639–649.

Roland, A. *In Search of Self in India and Japan*. Princeton University Press, 1988, p. 94.

Rosenthal, D et al., Vietnamese adolescents in Australia. *International Journal of Psychology*, 31, 1996, 81–91.

Sabogal, F et al., Hispanic familialism and acculturation: what changes and what doesn't? *Hispanic Journal of Behavioural Sciences*, 9, 1987, 397–412.

Schein, EH. Organisational culture. *American Psychologist*, 45 (2), 1990, 109–119.

Schwartz, SH. Mapping and interpreting cultural differences around the world. In Vinken, V. Soeters, J. and P Ester (eds), *Comparing Cultures. Dimensions of Culture in a Comparative Perspective*. Brill, 2004, pp. 43–73.

Seidner, S. *Ethnicity, Language, and Power from a Psycholinguistic Perspective*. Centre de recherche sur le pluralinguisme, Bruxelles, 1982.

Shekshnia, SV et al., Russ Wane equipment: joint venture in Russia. In DC Thomas (ed.), *Readings and Cases in International Management: A Cross-cultural Perspective*. Sage, 2003.

Sitkin, SB and Roth, NL. Explaining the limited effectiveness of legalistic 'remedies' for trust/distrust. *Organisation Science*, 4, 1993, 367–392.

Smith, PB and Schwartz, SH. Values. In JW Berry et al. (eds), *Social Behaviour and Applications: Handbook of Cross-cultural Psychology* (Vol. 3), 2nd ed. Allyn & Bacon, 1997, pp. 78–118.

Soltani, E. The overlooked variable in managing human resources of Iranian organisations: workforce diversity – some evidence. *International Journal of Human Resources Management*, 21 (1), 2010, 84–108.

Stewart, R et al., *Managing in Britain and Germany*. Macmillan, 1994.

Su, S. Cultural differences in determining the ethical perception and decision-making of future accounting professionals. *The Journal of American Academy of Business*, 9 (1), 2006, 147–158.

Sullivan, J and Taylor, S. A cross-cultural test of compliance-gaining theory. *Management Communication Quarterly*, 5 (2), 1991, 220–239.

Sumner, WG. *Folkways*. Ginn, 1906.

Thorpe, R and Paclica, K. Management development: contradictions and dilemmas arising from in-depth study of British and Czech managers. In P Joynt and M Warner (eds), *Managing Across Cultures: Issues and Perspectives*. International Thomson Business Press, 1996, 212–232.

Triandis, HC. Cross-cultural industrial and organisational psychology. In HC Triandis et al. (eds), *Handbook of Industrial and Organisational Psychology* (Vol 4). Consulting Psychologist Press, 1994, pp. 103–172.

UNDP, Human Development Report, 2004.

Van Oudenhoven, JP et al., Asymmetrical international attitudes. *European Journal of Social Psychology*, 32 (2), 2002, 275–289.

Walumbwa, FO and Schaubroeck, J. Leader personality traits and employee voice behaviour: mediating roles of ethical leadership and work group psychological safety. *Journal of Applied Psychology*, 94 (5), 2009, 1275–1286.

Winch, GM et al., Organisation and management in an Anglo-French consortium: the case of Transmanche-link. *Journal of Management Studies*, 37 (5), 2000, 663–685.

Yagmurlu, B and Sanson, A. Acculturation and parenting among Turkish mothers in Australia. *Journal of Cross-cultural Psychology*, 40 (3), 2009, 361–380.

Ziring, L et al., International Relations: A Political Dictionary, 5th ed. ABC-CLIO, 1995.

Language matters 3

INTRODUCTION

There are approximately 6000 languages in use in the world today, most of them existing only in spoken form (Aitchison, 2001). The words, grammar, and expressions of each language reflect the perceptions and biases of the underlying culture, and each language has its own strengths and weaknesses. A weakness of the Arabic language, for instance, is its paucity of vocabulary in fields such as medicine and some areas of scientific research. For example, Arabic lacks a vocabulary that would allow psychiatric patients to accurately describe their symptoms – the patients would be more likely to use metaphors and images in which the language is rich. People from other cultures who wish to improve communication with Arab people should perhaps learn to communicate on the metaphoric and imaginative level.

Languages differ in the information they convey. The German and French languages, for instance, give much information about the relative status and power of speaker and listener, reflecting the formality and hierarchical nature of social relations in German and French cultures (Muir, 1959). Japanese people put a higher value on communicating subtle aspects of feeling and relationship than on communicating information. In contrast to Japanese, English tends to be functional and unemotional, splitting feeling and thought into separate, abstract categories.

Cultural noise – impediments to communication that occur when people from different cultures interact (O'Connell, 1997) – often leads people to misunderstand each others' intentions and meanings in cross-cultural situations. Words such as 'democratic' or 'free', for instance, have different meanings for people from different cultures. The ideal situation in cross-cultural encounters is communication that is free from cultural noise and from other sources of distortion, such as power distortion or strategic distortion.

The high risk of misunderstanding is a problem that lies at the core of cross-cultural communication. Miscommunications and misinterpretations occur because people from different cultural backgrounds have different ways of sending and receiving messages, different communicative norms. Miscommunications occur when there is a mismatch between what the speaker intends his words to mean and how the hearer interprets them (Coupland et al., 1991). Miscommunication is a common feature of cross-cultural communication because people from different cultures send and interpret messages in different, culturally influenced ways.

Many foreign and minority group employees lack proficiency in the language used in workplace. As a result they have difficulty becoming involved in social interaction and networking activities which, in many organisations, are activities which are essential for career success. Moreover, lack of language skills may trigger workplace discrimination, leading to lower levels of job commitment.

LANGUAGE CHOICE

Impact on attitudes and behaviour

Using a particular language in preference to another language not only influences what can be said and not said, it also influences the attitudes and behaviour of the people who use it. De Zulueta (1990) describes a Colombian couple, both of whom speak English fluently. When the husband uses English while speaking to his wife, he comes across as unassuming, tolerant, and gentle. But as soon as he starts to use Spanish he becomes macho and starts to bully and dominate his wife.

Laitin (1977) observed a group of Somali students who were participating in a role-play exercise. The Somalis used either English or Somali in the role-plays.

> The researcher notes that the Somalis are much more diplomatic when using Somali, much more confrontational when using English. Using English seems to have the effect of making them see the other person as an adversary with whom future dealings are unimportant. When they speak Somali, on the other hand, they see each other as equals, reflecting Somali cultural values.

A Japanese manager explained to a Canadian colleague in Japan that when he spoke Japanese in business meetings he found it a struggle to use impolite, abrasive words – but not when he spoke English. Hofstede (1994: 216) noted that at INSEAD, the European Business School, whenever a case study was discussed in French

> it led to highly stimulating intellectual discussion but few practical conclusions. When the same case was discussed in English, it would not be long before someone asked 'So what?' and the class tried to become pragmatic.

When a researcher asked French-American bilinguals to do the Thematic Apperception Test in both languages, the 'narratives', or descriptions of what was perceived, were much more romantic and emotional in French than in English (Ervin, 2002).

English expression tends to be more succinct and pointed than French, and succinct, precise expression has at least the advantage of being easy to understand – and sometimes it makes monetary sense. After *The Times* reported that Rudyard Kipling was being paid £1 a word for an article he was writing, some Oxford students sent him a £1 note with the request: 'Please send us one of your best words.' Kipling replied by postcard: 'Thanks.'

Effects on perception

Languages differ in what it is possible to say and what it is impossible to say when using them. Some Asian languages reflect the extended-family kinships common in collectivist cultures, thus Hindi speakers can use separate words for your mother's sister and brother-in-law, and your mother's brother and sister-in-law. The same is true for your father's relatives. A family lawyer working only in English would find it extremely difficult to understand the subtlety of a Hindi client's family relationships since in English there are only the words aunt and uncle (d'Ardenne and Mahtani, 1989).

The language a person speaks encourages habitual patterns of perception. As Bennett (1998: 16) points out, English speakers cannot easily distinguish coconuts in their different stages but Tongans can because their perception has been guided by the vocabulary of the Tongan language. A given language offers a perceptual window on to the world, presents reality in a distinctive culture-influenced way. Whorf (1956: 207) argued that culture is encoded into language and that the language a person learns structures and organises how the person perceives the world:

> the background linguistic system (in other words, the grammar) of each language is not merely a reproducing instrument for voicing ideas but rather is itself the shaper of ideas, the programme and guide for people's mental activity, for their analysis of impressions.... Formulation of ideas is not an independent process, strictly rational in the old sense, but is part of a particular grammar and differs, from slightly to greatly, among different grammars. We dissect nature along lines laid down by our native languages... the world is presented in a kaleidoscopic flux of impressions which has to be organised by our minds – and this means largely by the linguistic systems in our minds.

Perceptual relativity

This assumption of perceptual relativity lies at the core of cross-cultural communication. It accounts for numerous cross-cultural miscommunications, and explains why constant cross-cultural misunderstandings occur in multicultural societies such as those of the United States, Canada, Australia, and New Zealand. Business people in these countries follow their own cultural norms when communicating with foreign business prospects. For instance, a Canadian sales manager making a sales tour in Europe is likely to use an informal communication style with the people he meets and to move onto first-name terms immediately. But an informal, first-name approach is not favoured in many European countries, including Germany, Russia, and France. In these countries, distancing or deferment strategies are used when interacting with people from other countries, and an informal communication style by foreign business visitors would strike them as offensively over-familiar (Gudykunst and Ting-Toomey, 1988).

STRENGTHS AND WEAKNESSES OF A LANGUAGE

Uniqueness of each language

Each language is a lens which offers a unique world view. English has only one way to count things, but Japanese has many different counting systems classifying the different appearance of objects – long things, for instance, are counted with different words from flat things (Bennett, 1998). The Tiwi language of Australia specifies more than a dozen seasons in its vocabulary. Yolngu, another Australian language, has a taboo attached to mentioning the name of a deceased person or words similar to that name.

There are approximately 6000 languages in use in the world today, most of them existing only in spoken form (Aitchison, 2001). The words, grammar and expressions of each language together reflect the strengths and weaknesses, the perceptions and biases, of the underlying culture. For example, a particular weakness of *Yoruba*, a language widely used in Nigeria, is that it lacks words that give the meaning of senility, neurosis, depression, and other classifications of mental illness as understood in most parts of the world. On the other hand, a strength of the language is the richness of its metaphorical expressions and imagery and, as Murphy (1976) points out, the Yorubas do have words for 'unrest of mind which prevents sleep', 'terror at night', 'intense shame', 'fear of being among people'.

French and German languages

Culture includes language and language is the most clearly recognisable part of culture, as Hofstede (1980) pointed out. Because they reflect culture, languages differ in the information and perceptions they convey. For instance, when the German or the French language is used, much information is given about the relative *status and power* of speaker and listener, reflecting the formality and hierarchical nature of social relations in German and French cultures. Forms of address are more formalized in these languages than in English.

Much information is given about the authority and power of speakers and listeners when German is used – which helps to explain why German speakers may be perceived by a non-German audience as somewhat rigid or intransigent. A professional translator noted how the very shape and sound of the German language predisposes its speakers to overvalue power, authoritative statement, and purposive drive (Muir, 1959). She pointed out that a German sentence is not like an English sentence, that the thought which flows into it controlled and directed in a different way. The meaning of a typical German sentence is controlled until the verb at the end clinches the statement.

Japanese language

The Japanese language reflects Japanese culture in displaying a keen perception of *status differences*. The language has complicated systems of second person singular (*you*) words that indicate the speaker's status relative to the listener. Honorifics are used when speaking to or about a superior (Morsbach, 1982). Yoshimura and Anderson (1997) note that when two Japanese people converse they can hardly avoid implicitly defining the reference groups to which they think each of them belongs.

Cross-cultural business discussions conducted in Japanese have a distinctive, status-conscious flavour that comes across to native English-speakers even when an interpreter is used. According to Nakata (2009), Japanese managers use language in a purposive way to direct and motivate their staff, including:

- frequent use of impersonal verbs so as to avoid casting direct blame;
- use of the passive voice for extra politeness;
- use of silence on certain issues so as to convey to employees what the manager's own view is.

Relational emphasis

Japanese people generally put a much higher value than native English-speakers on communicating subtle aspects of feeling and relationship, and a correspondingly lower value on communicating information. In contrast to Japanese, English tends to be functional and unemotional, splitting feeling and thought into separate, abstract categories (Stewart, 1985). A European sales manager based in Tokyo told a business visitor that after learning Japanese he found that using the language helped him quickly to establish cordial relations with his Japanese customers: 'With an interpreter it's difficult to chat. You can't talk about the weather or ask about the daughter. The nuances are lost.'

A defining quality of the Japanese language is its relational emphasis. There are many Japanese words for 'I' but these words are frequently omitted both in writing and speech. Nakata (2009) points out that Japanese people often refer to themselves not as 'I' but by a word that expresses their relation to person they are speaking to – they will call themselves 'teacher' during a conversation with a student or 'doctor' in a conversation with a patient. Nakata (2009) explains how a Japanese boy with muscular dystrophy wrote a poem in which he described his feeling about life, but using 'we' not 'I'. This made it sound as if he was just one member of a group of children with the same disorder and therefore he was not lonely.

Arabic language

A weakness of the Arabic language is its relative paucity of vocabulary in fields such as medicine and some areas of scientific research. It lacks a vocabulary, for instance, that would allow psychiatric patients to accurately describe their symptoms – they would be more likely to use metaphors and images, in which the language is rich (Dwairy, 1998). They might, for instance, describe their fear by saying 'My heart fell down', or their astonishment and anger by saying 'My mind flew up'.

Dwairy believes that this kind of metaphoric language is an imaginative and creative way of talking about subjective feelings and personal experience, and that better cross-cultural communication with Arab people could be achieved by learning to communicate on the metaphoric and imaginative level. Metaphors, sayings, and parables are ways of gaining insights into another person's culture and of gaining a better understanding what the other person means. Accepting and working with this kind of language, Dwairy argues, would enable technical expert, counsellors, and therapists to work within the world view of Arab culture and to find solutions that fit the culture.

Culture-relevant solutions are certainly needed since patients from Arab countries (and from other collectivist cultures) often describe their symptoms in ways that confuse or mislead health professionals in Western countries (Spencer et al., 2005). Thus collectivist patients often substitute vague physical symptoms for anxiety or depression, which can lead to inaccurate diagnosis and ineffective treatment. Indeed, the very format of the medical interview can limit the ability of these patients to tell their stories coherently – the doctor's careful questioning disrupts the patient's attempts to tell her story in her own way (McTear and King, 1991).

Cross-cultural communication breaks down even more when doctors and nurses use technical terms that are unintelligible to the patient. The names of common illnesses such as arthritis or stomach ulcer or diabetes may mean something different to a patient from a Middle Eastern or Asian country than they do to a Western health professional. When a British doctor asked a Pakistani woman if there was any history of cardiac arrest in her family the woman angrily protested that she had never been in trouble with the police.

Use of a lingua franca

Cultural boundaries can sometimes be crossed and effective cross-cultural communication achieved by using a lingua franca. For example, Nigeria has numerous different languages and cultural traditions but some Nigerian playwrights successfully communicate with many of them at the same time by using

Pidgin as a lingua franca. Pidgins are hybrid or compromise languages, used to establish rapport between people who have no other language in common. Swahili, widely used throughout East Africa, and Melanesian Pidgin in the South Pacific, are examples of a compromise language. Most compromise languages are based on a European language that has been simplified in pronunciation and grammar.

According to Pavis (1996), 'transcultural theatre' is a form of lingua franca, in that it crosses boundaries and connects people worldwide. It does so by using a universal theatre language that presents basic human experience as revealed in human sounds and gestures. According to Pavis, these *universal sounds* make the same chords vibrate in people from virtually all cultural backgrounds.

SMALL-GROUP EXERCISE: Discussion Questions

Working in small groups, discuss each of the following questions and write down the group's agreed answer. At the end of the exercise, each group may present its answers to the other groups for comment.

1. *'Some Asian languages reflect the extended-family kinships common in collectivist cultures.' Support this statement by giving relevant examples.*
2. *'Languages differ in the information they convey.' What kind of information is typically conveyed if German or French is the language used for communication?*
3. *Identify some of the main strengths and weaknesses of Arabic language. Give examples of how specific weaknesses of the language can affect cross-cultural communication.*
4. *Explain how notable characteristics of the Japanese language reflect Japanese culture.*
5. *What is a lingua franca? Give one or more examples of a lingua franca and explain how using a lingua franca can facilitate cross-cultural communication.*

MISCOMMUNICATION

Misinterpretations in cross-cultural interactions

In same-culture communication, participants speak the same mother tongue, have a common cultural background, and tend to think and reason in similar ways. Each speaker uses language in much the same way as the other speakers (Scollon and Scollon, 2001). Through their knowledge of context, culture, and typical speech patterns in the culture, people can accurately interpret each other's meanings, leading to effective interpersonal communication.

But this is not the case with cross-cultural communication. People from dissimilar cultural backgrounds often misinterpret each other's meanings. Blacks and whites in the United States, for instance, have been found to assign dissimilar meanings to nonverbal behaviours such as length of gaze or body postures

(Kochman, 1983). In many cross-cultural interactions, the cultural origins, beliefs, and attitudes of the participants are different, and miscommunication can safely be predicted: differences in both language use and nonverbal behaviour lead to misinterpretations and mutual misunderstandings.

For cross-cultural communication to be successful the participants must share at least some *common ground* – shared knowledge and beliefs, for instance, or similar ways of reasoning and thinking (McTear and King, 1991). When there is common ground the quality of communication is raised and the risk of miscommunications is reduced.

Miscommunication: causes and effects

Miscommunication occurs when there is a mismatch between what the speaker intends his words to mean and how the hearer interprets them. The mismatch stems from misunderstanding by the hearer and/or from the communicative incompetence of the speaker (Coupland et al., 1991). Miscommunication occurs very frequently in cross-cultural interactions because people from different cultures send and interpret messages in different, culturally influenced ways. For example, Saville-Troika (1982) has described the miscommunication that occurred when Egyptian pilots radioed their intention to land at an airbase on Cyprus and the Greek traffic controllers responded with silence.

> The Greeks intended silence to indicate *refusal* of permission. But the Egyptian pilots, not understanding the Greeks' intention, interpreted silence as assent. The miscommunication caused the loss of several lives since the Greeks fired at the planes as they approached the runway.

Miscommunication leads to numerous misunderstandings in cross-cultural business discussions. If, for instance, a cross-cultural business meeting which is held in Moscow is conducted in Russian, participants whose first language is not Russian may have difficulty presenting their ideas and proposals clearly and so miscommunications are likely.

Goffman's (1956) model of social behaviour as dramatic performance implies that miscommunication is likely to occur as a result of people playing various theatrical roles during social interactions. Thus when a participant in a cross-cultural conversation successfully presents herself in a deliberately misleading way – for instance, as having a higher social status in her own country than is actually the case – the result is that miscommunication occurs.

Miscommunication repair

Miscommunications often occur in cross-cultural business discussions and other cross-cultural situations and, as a general rule, once a miscommunication has occurred and been detected it should be quickly 'repaired'. For instance, if a senior manager is leading the discussion, she could ask the speaker to clarify or expand on the point he has just made. This gives the speaker the opportunity to 'repair' his miscommunication – for instance, by:

- repeating the original point but using simpler words;
- using different illustrations and examples;
- providing extra information so as to set the message in a wider, more comprehensible context.

In a cross-cultural context, 'repair' of a miscommunication works well when participants are encouraged to interrupt the discussion, draw attention to any unclear points, and to ask for clarification. When this is done, any uncertainties and misinterpretations of meaning can then be dealt with immediately. Drummond and Hopper (1991) point out that although repair interventions violate the 'let it pass' principle which is widely practised in normal everyday conversation, in cross-cultural discussions, corrections and clarifications are usually welcomed by all participants.

'Repair' activities are an important condition of effective cross-cultural communication. The repairs are needed because people from dissimilar cultural backgrounds are often ignorant of each others' communicative conventions. This leads to frequent miscommunications and misinterpretations of the other person's meaning – a feature which is widely perceived as being one of the most fundamental problems of cross-cultural communication.

Miscommunication in the workplace

In multicultural organisations employees from minority groups who are not fluent in the language used in the organisation – often the language of the majority culture – may fail to make progress in their jobs. Their relative lack of language proficiency means that they may find it difficult to become involved in social interaction and *networking* – activities which in many large organisations are essential for career success. Moreover, their relative lack of language skills may lead to minority-group employees experiencing communication problems at work. This, in turn, may trigger workplace discrimination and lead to lower levels of job commitment from the employees concerned.

Diversity policies

When workplace discrimination occurs against groups of employees based on their race, ethnicity, or minority-group status, it often needs to be countered by the introduction and implementation of diversity policies which aim to strengthen norms of acceptance and equality in multicultural companies. For example, Colgate–Palmolive's diversity policy is based on equal treatment and opportunity across gender, race, sexual orientation, and disability, and is implemented internationally. Although the policy does not translate easily in countries such as Saudi Arabia where gender divisions are clear and rigid, the company insists that senior managers in all overseas operations keep to the essential policies of banning discrimination and sexual harassment.

Case study

MINI-CASE: Communication at work

A US manufacturing company employs English-speaking supervisors and a largely Spanish-speaking workforce. But this volatile mix leads to poor shop floor communication and high labour turnover and accident rates. Many companies with a multicultural workforce experience similar problems, but management in this company declines to be fatalistic about the situation. They reason that training is needed to improve understanding between shop floor workers and their supervisors.

As a result, training sessions are arranged to teach the work force basic English and the supervisors basic Spanish. All sessions are firmly anchored to job needs. Thus Spanish-speaking employees learn the English words for various shop floor activities and the meaning of terms such as 'seniority' and 'incentive' in the Union contract while the English-speaking supervisors learn how to give important instructions in Spanish – for instance, phrases such as 'Don't put your hand near the blade' and 'Keep your goggles on at all times'.

The training sessions also unearth a number of problems that have a cultural background and which prove easy to put right. These include workers' resentment about the 20-minute lunch break. The workers, like many other Spanish-speakers, eat their main meal in the middle of the day and need more than 20 minutes.

The company sees a quick return on its training investment. Supervisors are better understood by operatives; and at the end of the year the accident rate has gone down substantially and shop floor output had increased by 20%. Management assumes that the improvements have been triggered by the training programme.

Questions:

1. *Is management right to assume that output and accident rate improvements have been brought about by the training? What other factors might explain the improvements?*
2. *What further management actions would increase levels of morale and job commitment in the workforce?*
3. *To what extent are mutual misunderstandings inevitable in a multicultural workplace?*

COMMUNICATION DISTORTIONS

Types of distortion in cross-cultural communication

The ideal situation in cross-cultural interactions is communication which is free from sources of distortion. The aim of this section is to describe common kinds of distortions that occur in cross-cultural communication, to increase understanding of what causes them, and to outline strategies to counter them. Common types of distortion that affect cross-cultural interactions are:

- Power distortion
- Entrenched distortion
- Strategic distortion
- Systematic distortion
- Arrested communication

Power distortion

Power imbalances can distort communication during cross-cultural exchanges according to the degree of power displayed. For instance, an immigrant interviewed by a Social Security official may feel unable to express his opinions freely if he senses that they would clash with those of the powerful official who is interviewing him. The immigrant might well be inhibited by the difference in status from raising the issue with the interviewer. Young (1996) points out that in such an event the distortion could not be rectified until the politics of the communicative relationship had been addressed.

In Germany, an example of distorted communication is the behaviour of foreign workers, many of them Turkish, who deliberately distort their communication by using a pidginized German rather than a more acceptable form. Hinnenkamp (1980) argues that their behaviour stems from anger and frustration about always having to communicate with high-status Germans in ways that the Germans require and expect. The foreign workers' frustration leads them to refuse linguistic integration into German society and generates distorted cross-cultural communication.

Power distortions occur in those Asian cultures in which the higher-status person has the right to introduce the topic of conversation and where that right supersedes the question of who speaks first (Scollon and Scollon, 2001). Power distortions stemming from status differences also occur in Western societies. Low-status employees, for instance, may be inhibited from speaking freely and expressing their opinions in meetings because of the threat of possible sanctions or its effect on their careers. Milgram's (1963) famous experiments, carried out in the United States, provide a graphic demonstration of the impact that displays of power and authority have on individuals, irrespective of their cultural background.

Entrenched distortion

Some kinds of distorted communication are so deeply entrenched in a social system, so institutionalized, that attempts to rectify the distortion are strongly resisted. The use of 'foreigner talk', between Japanese and foreign visitors is an example of entrenched distortion. This form of distorted communication is based on the entrenched attitude in Japan that it is impossible for foreigners to be really fluent in Japanese. The language is endowed with numerous 'honorifics' implying degrees and kinds of mutual obligation and, according to many Japanese, such cultural loading makes the language impossible for foreigners to use correctly. As a result, Ross and Shortreed (1990) point out, Japanese people feel confused when faced with a foreigner who speaks Japanese fluently. Accordingly, even if a foreigner speaks Japanese fluently the Japanese may distort the communication by resorting to crudely over-simplified 'foreigner-talk'.

Strategic distortion

Strategic distortion is based on conscious deception or trickery. It occurs when a person uses language in a 'strategic' or manipulative way with the aim of concealing her real purpose. Deliberate deception is difficult to detect in cross-cultural interactions – as when a member of a distant culture claims to have very high social status in his own country. Goffman's (1956) model of social behaviour as dramatic performance implies that distorted communication may result from people playing various theatrical roles and thereby deliberately misleading others. *Self-presentation* efforts usually involve greater or lesser degrees of deception or concealment and, to that extent, almost everybody is guilty of practising the strategic distortion of communication.

Systematic distortion

Systematically distorted communication stems from people's repressed motives and intentions. According to Freud's (1923) structural model of the mind:

- The *id* is the unconscious part of the mind and the reservoir of primitive instincts. It is dominated by the pleasure principle.
- The *super-ego* suppresses unacceptable thoughts and feelings.
- The *ego* relates to external reality and tries to mediate between the demands of the id and the authority of the super-ego.

Tensions between the id, ego, and super-ego are battled out within the person, and the implication is that communication can be distorted at source. Kim (1995) notes that extreme stress reactions in the form of escapism, neurosis, and psychosis are most frequently witnessed among those whose native culture radically differs from that of the society in which they live and work.

Systematically distorted communication may cause an individual to communicate with members of other racial groups in a hostile manner, even if the hostile feelings are expressed indirectly. If, for instance, a black participant in a cross-cultural discussion has suppressed feelings of aggression towards white participants he may express his feelings nonverbally – through body language or a sarcastic tone of voice. It may be that at one level of his mind the individual hates racial prejudice, yet he communicates a very different message – and he is not aware of the contradiction because, as Giddens (1984) points out, such awareness would depend on three distinct levels of awareness being attained:

1. Awareness of his 'unconscious motivations' which, by definition, are not available to the individual.
2. Awareness of motivations at the level of consciousness but below the level of active awareness.
3. Awareness of motivations at the level of discursive consciousness. Only at this level of consciousness could the individual talk about the reasons and provide justifications for his attitudes.

Freeing a person's communication from this kind of systematic, 'at-source' distortion might be achievable only through long-term psychoanalysis (Bernstein, 1995).

Arrested communication

When important information is prevented by outside forces from being disseminated and discussed, arrested communication is the result. Arrested communication occurs, for instance, when state-controlled propaganda is used to control the vocabulary and arguments used in political debate – thus limiting the individual's capacity to participate effectively in the debate. Minority groups and permanent immigrants who are forced to use an alien language in the society where they live and work are often victims of arrested communication. These groups tend to be restricted in access to information which has a practical value to them, as well as being restricted in expression because of linguistic difficulties. As a result, they are effectively barred from cross-cultural communication with native speakers about important public issues (Tsuda, 1986).

Arrested communication also occurs when people are swamped by continuous media-generated information and misinformation about celebrities and trivial aspects of popular culture. As a result, their attention is deflected from real-life concerns and their ability to discuss them is weakened. This danger recalls Bernstein's (1971) argument that the *restricted code* of working class people – as opposed to the *elaborated code* of the middle classes – greatly limits their ability to articulate ideas and defend their own interests.

'NOISE' IN CROSS-CULTURAL COMMUNICATION

Information theory and noise

Shannon's (1948) information theory deals with the engineering problem of transmitting information electronically over a noisy channel. *Noise* on the channel (crackling, fading etc.) blocks, distorts, or interferes with the meaning of the message. Film grain is a source of 'noise' because it interferes with the impact made by the film on an audience. Whatever method of communication is used to transmit a message, when ways are found to reduce the noise the quality of the communication increases (Figure 3.1).

Since its inception, information theory has been applied to many other areas, including business and management communication. In business discussions a speaker's strange accent and poor pronunciation are sources of 'noise' – that is, they deflect attention from the speaker's argument and interfere with the listener's comprehension. In cross-cultural encounters a person's physical appearance or unusual speech or behaviour are further examples of 'noise' because they divert attention from the information that the person tries to convey.

Cultural noise

Cultural noise refers to impediments to communication that occur when people from different cultures interact (O'Connell, 1997). In cross-cultural encounters language differences are a potent source of cultural noise. For example, some of the words used in cross-cultural discussions (e.g. fair, free, and adequate) often have different meanings for people from different cultural backgrounds, thus contributing to the cultural noise that impedes the communication.

Cultural noise leads people from different cultures to misunderstand each others' intentions and meanings. D'Ardenne and Mahtani (1989) give the example of an American visitor to England who speaks effusively with the owner of a wine bar with the intention of expressing appreciation for excellent service. But the English owner, locked into the communicative norms of her own culture, interprets the American's behaviour as flirtatious and offensive.

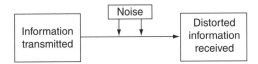

Figure 3.1   Effect of 'noise' on communication

Source: Based on Shannon (1949).

The comments of a Kenyan teacher (Ojore, 2003: 50) illustrate how different cultures have different values and expectations and how these expectations are often violated by various kinds of cultural noise:

> I come from a Luo community where elderly people do not sit down and speak with young people as if they were equals. Neither do we address our elders by their first name.... Americans have no problems using expressions such as 'guys', 'hey man', 'get the hell out of here', 'bull shit' or 'you piss me off'! Africans find these shocking and unacceptable....

Noise-free communication

Clyne (1994: 206) develops a convincing model of communication in multicultural societies, based on a continuum of cultural groups, all with 'ingroup' or 'outgroup' features and all interacting with one another both within the mainstream culture and outside it. A simpler model would be of a majority mainstream culture interacting with varying degrees of frequency and success with many minority groups. Many of these inter-group communication efforts would inevitably be impeded by varying degrees of cultural noise.

In a multicultural society acculturation processes produce a diversification of the majority language into many non-native varieties. Successful communication with minority group members often depends on understanding the group's jargon and the variety of language that is used by the group, and then using speech accommodation to achieve communication. Well-educated people tend to utter complete thoughts or statements using grammatically correct phrases and clear enunciation, and this is a form of a language that members of minority groups and foreigners often say they find easiest to understand. By contrast, the everyday informal language that people use presents them with problems of comprehension. Kelly (1981) notes that everyday informal language is not concerned with uttering complete statements. It communicates by leaving things unsaid, sentences unfinished. There are exclamations and pregnant silences. Constructions are changed in mid-sentence. Slang and regional dialects are used.

The benefits of popular speech forms are in their immediacy and spontaneity but foreigners and members of minority groups are baffled by them. The kind of language that non-native speakers find easiest to understand is language free from noise. From the viewpoint of a foreigner, noise-free language consists of short, complete statements, with simple vocabulary, grammatically correct phrases, and clear enunciation (Trudgill, 1986).

Exchange relationships

Exchange relationships introduce additional layers of complication into cross-cultural communication. Exchange relationships occur in cross-cultural situations when individuals behave in ways they calculate to be in their own best interest. They may, for instance, try to build relationships with members of another culture – in spite of formidable cultural differences – if they calculate that such relationships are potentially rewarding to themselves. In the world of international business, exchange relationships are a fact of life.

Exchange theory (Homans, 1958) improves understanding of the social behaviour of people in firms and also gives insights into the calculated self-interest underlying many cross-cultural relationships. According to Homans (1958: 606):

> Social behaviour is an exchange of goods, material goods but also non-material ones, such as the symbols of approval or prestige. Persons that give much to others try to get much from them, and persons that get much from others are under pressure to give much to them. This process of influence tends to work out at equilibrium to a balance in the exchanges.

Exchange theory views individuals as communicating not with other individuals but with a market. As Griffin (1994) points out, we live in an interpersonal, cross-cultural economy and constantly take stock of the *relational value* of others we meet. When we establish a relationship with someone from another culture it may be at least partly an exchange relationship – in the sense that benefits are given in exchange for benefits expected in the future.

AMBIGUITY IN CROSS-CULTURAL COMMUNICATION

Conversational inference

Linguistic ambiguity is responsible for many of the miscommunications and mis-understandings that occur in cross-cultural exchanges. 'After the women came they found some old coins and rings'? What is the precise meaning of this state-ment? Were the coins found by the women or by somebody else ('they') Were only the coins old or were both coins and rings old? There is nothing in the words themselves that makes the meaning totally clear and unambiguous. The intended meaning must be inferred through *conversational inference.*

But for foreigners conversational inference is much more difficult than for native-speaking members of a culture (Levinson, 1990). That explains why mis-understandings caused by linguistic ambiguity occur much more frequently in cross-cultural communication than in same-culture communication. In same-culture communication people can infer the speaker's meaning from their intimate knowledge of the culture and the language. If a statement remains unclear they recognize this and can ask for clarification. But in cross-cultural conversations people often fail to identify statements that are ambiguous because of their inadequate understanding of the language and the culture. Even if they recognize that a statement is ambiguous they may blame *themselves* for failing to understand the precise meaning and stay silent.

Grammar and vocabulary problems

Immigrants, refugees, international students, and other foreign visitors often find it difficult to communicate on equal terms with members of the majority culture and the most common reason is lack of proficiency in the language of the culture. Studies show that linguistic barriers make it difficult for them to communicate with local people and thus to become familiar with the culture (Furnham and Bochner, 1986; Peltokorpi, 2008). Highly skilled immigrants who, however, are not proficient in the language of the host culture often find it extremely difficult to find suitable employment (Syed and Murray, 2009).

When non-native speakers communicate with members of the culture, weaknesses of grammar and vocabulary are quickly exposed. For instance, if they consult a doctor non-native speakers may misunderstand common medical terms that the doctor uses. Eight per cent of patients from minority groups participating in one study thought that 'heartburn' meant 'passage of wind through the mouth' (Boyle, 1975).

Misunderstanding of common terms used in a foreign culture can have unpleasant practical consequences – as a British visitor to France discovered:

> The woman spent the night locked in a French town hall after mistakenly assuming that L'Hotel de Ville was the town's main hotel. According to newspaper reports, the woman entered the building on Friday evening but officials locked up and left while she was using the lavatory. She was released the following morning by the mayor.

CROSS-CULTURAL COMMUNICATION COMPETENCE

What is it?

For Ruben (1976), cross-cultural communication competence involves several distinct dimensions, including:

- Demonstrating respect for members of other cultures.
- Responding to members of other cultures in a non-judgmental way.
- Taking turns appropriately in intercultural conversations.
- Seeing the world through the other person's eyes – empathy.

Cross-cultural communication competence requires both *linguistic competence* and *interactional competence* (Eerdmans, 2003). Interactional competence is acquired by becoming familiar with the interactive conventions and rhetorical strategies that members of a culture use when communicating with each other (including greeting, turn-taking, and politeness conventions).

Cross-cultural communication competence has been linked to various personality traits such as honesty, flexibility, empathy, and displaying respect (Kealey and Ruben, 1983). Conscious competence is demonstrated when a person consciously works out ways of improving cross-cultural communication – for

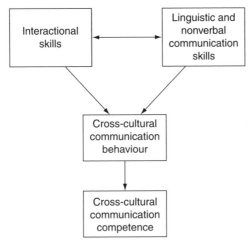

Linguistic skills, interactional skills, and cultural awareness come together and lead to appropriate behaviour and cross-cultural communication competence.

Figure 3.2   Cross-cultural communication competence

instance, by using speech accommodation or feedback and clarification strategies. Unconscious competence is demonstrated when people's cross-cultural communication skills are sufficiently effective for them not to have to think about them (Figure 3.2).

Cross-cultural communication competence also requires the ability to use *appropriate* communication. It would not be appropriate, for instance, to use a clear and direct style of communication or to ask direct questions in a collectivist country. People from many collectivist countries do not say exactly what they think at all times. They tend to use *indirectness* as a conversational strategy with the aim of avoiding friction and antagonism. As Trudgill (2000) notes, they avoid asking direct questions which impose an obligation on the other person to provide an answer whereas indirectness leaves them with a choice.

According to Prensky (2001), cross-cultural business success increasingly requires the ability to understand and use a wide range of *technology-based* communication methods, and users must learn the accompanying competences. Computers, emails, and other kinds of electronic communication have resulted in a new technical jargon, common abbreviations, and appropriate levels of protocol and formality. The ability to use the jargon and become familiar with the protocol is rapidly becoming an essential requirement for effective cross-cultural business competence.

Speech accommodation

Being willing and able to accommodate to the communicative needs of people from other cultures is an important indicator of cross-cultural communication competence. Studies show that speech accommodation is very often used by people who interact with members of other cultures (Gallois et al., 1995). In cross-cultural gatherings, for instance, native-speakers may accommodate to foreigners by speaking slowly and deliberately.

Giles and Coupland's (1991) *speech accommodation theory* deals with two communication tendencies:

> *Convergence* reduces social distance. The speaker adjusts aspects of her speech – rate, volume, vocabulary, tone, intensity, and so on – to match those of the other person. The intention is usually to win approval and make communication more effective.
>
> *Divergence* accentuates distinctiveness or disengagement from the other person or from the other person's culture. The speaker makes her speech deliberately different from the other person's speech. Members of ethnic minorities, for instance, may deliberately exaggerate their own speech codes when talking to members of the majority culture as a symbolic act of resistance.
>
> (Ylanne-McEwen and Coupland, 2000)

People who practise positive speech accommodation – convergence – often accommodate nonverbally too, using gestures and facial expressions that match those of the other person. Kim (1986) refer to a study which found that when a social worker visited a poor person's home he would make himself comfortable and sit down, not stand in the doorway as if feeling ill at ease: this would have made the client apprehensive. The social worker would dress in a clean and casual fashion but not wear a suit and tie because that would make the client feel at a disadvantage. In cross-cultural situations, nonverbal accommodation strategies have the effect of making the parties feel closer and more equal.

LANGUAGE AND POWER

Unequal communication

According to Thomas (2002), a generally accepted hierarchy of nationalities exists which leads to some national cultures and their languages being perceived as superior to others. In international forums and conferences, for instance, this perception produces *inequality of communication,* with the debates and cross-cultural discussions being conducted in the language of a high-prestige country. Power relations come into play because people from high-status countries are able to use their own native language to control proceedings – for instance, by determining topics that should be discussed, by controlling the turn-taking, interrupting or ignoring low-status speakers, and so on (Schirato and Yell, 2000). By such means a pattern of domination and submission is often established. Low-status groups, moreover, often *accept* domination by deferring to what they see as the superior knowledge, judgment, and communicative competence of the high-status, dominating group.

A more fundamental kind of unequal communication is established when an alien, non-indigenous language is imposed on a country's population – for instance, when the language of the former colonial power becomes the official language. The measure leads to inequality of communication because it favours a small elite who already know the language. Speakers of the indigenous languages become marginalized. Pugh (1996: 112) argues that this particular form of language imposition is a kind of cultural hegemony that enables the most powerful groups in the society to exert their control:

> This hegemony assumes and promotes the dominance of one language at the expense of others, and thus not only derogates the relatively powerless minority language groups but also operates at the personal level too, so that the personal identity of individuals who are members of the linguistic minorities may also be compromised.

In such countries, equality of communication would only be restored if one of the indigenous languages became the official language.

Cultural aggression

The close connection between language and other forms of power has been described by Thomas (1999). French colonial rule in North Africa and the integration of most of central Asia into the Soviet Empire were both examples of overt cultural aggression against the populations of these regions, with political and military power being used to promote French and Russian, respectively, over the indigenous languages.

For Bourdieu (1984: 461) language domination is indistinguishable from political repression:

> The dominant language discredits and destroys the spontaneous political discourse of the dominated. It leaves them only silence or a borrowed language, whose logic departs from that of popular usage… . It forces recourse to spokesmen, who are themselves condemned to use the dominant language.

The political resonance of a language was demonstrated in Corsica in the nineteenth century. Establishing a Corsican written language was synonymous with the establishment of a Corsican nationality, and was interpreted by neighbouring European powers as a dangerous political move that had to be stopped. According to Knudsen (1997), the mere writing of Corsican became impossible for political reasons (except in private, non-political domains such as poetry).

Position of indigenous languages

Language is a core aspect of cultural identity, and when alien languages are imposed on populations indigenous languages may fall into disuse and the cultures they represent may disintegrate. More than 230 indigenous languages in Africa have, indeed, already been obliterated. A United Nations body, Pro-gramme International, estimates that at least half the world's languages – together with the knowledge, customs, and culture embedded in them – could disappear over the next century unless effective policies are developed to pro-tect them. An example is the Council of Europe's Charter of Regional and/or Minority Languages. The Charter requires undertakings from European states to promote and support endangered languages.

In some countries different languages are used for different purposes. In Morocco, for instance, French is usually chosen for scientific and technical discussions but Arabic is used for personal, cultural, and religious topics. In Singapore there are four official languages – Malaysian, Tamil, Chinese, and English – with English often being used as a lingua franca when different eth-nic groups communicate. Studies of immigrants in the United States reveal that English is generally used by the immigrants in public or formal settings, whereas they use their own first language for informal, non-public communication (Ryan and Carranza, 1977).

Rise of the English language

A prime example of language domination on a world-wide scale is the ubiquitous use of English. English is now the basic international language for technology, commerce, finance, science, and diplomacy; and, increasingly, English is seen as the corporate language of big business. Israeli-Palestinian communications are conducted in English. Scientists in France, Germany, Spain, and other European countries often choose to publish their work first in English. The internet is overwhelmingly an English language medium. The result of this language dom-ination is that the global flow of information is mainly one way – from the English-speaking countries to the rest of the world.

KEY POINTS

1. Language reflects the underlying culture, each language is a lens offering a unique world view. The Japanese language, for instance, has complicated systems of second person singular (*you*) words that indicate the speaker's sta-tus relative to the listener. Honorifics are used when speaking to or about a superior. Cross-cultural business discussions conducted in Japanese have a distinctive, status-conscious flavour that comes across even when an inter-preter is used. In cross-cultural interactions, using a particular language for communication greatly influences the attitudes and behaviour of the people who use it.
2. Miscommunication occurs in cross-cultural interactions when there is a mis-match between what the speaker intends his words to mean and how the hearer interprets them. Miscommunication often occurs in cross-cultural communication because people from different cultures send and interpret

messages in different, culturally influenced ways. In a cross-cultural discussion, once a miscommunication has occurred and has been detected, it should be quickly 'repaired'.

3. The high risk of mutual misunderstanding is a problem that lies at the core of cross-cultural communication. People from different cultural backgrounds have different communicative norms, different ways of sending and receiving messages. Thus errors of interpretation and understanding are inevitable. Linguistic ambiguity contributes to the problem as the words themselves often contain insufficient information to give a clear, unambiguous meaning, and *conversational inference* is much more difficult for foreigners than for native-speaking members of a culture.

4. In cross-cultural encounters language differences are a potent source of cultural noise – that is impediments to communication that occur when people from different cultures interact. For instance, some of the words used in cross-cultural discussions (e.g. fair, free, and adequate) have different meanings for people from different cultures.

    Cultural noise leads to people from different cultures misunderstanding each others' intentions and meanings.

5. The ideal situation in cross-cultural discussions is communication which is free from cultural noise and sources of distortion. Common kinds of distortion that affect cross-cultural discussions are power distortion, entrenched distortion, strategic distortion, systematic distortion, and arrested communication.

6. In some cross-cultural gatherings, powerful, high-prestige individuals and groups control and constrain the contributions of the less powerful. They do so by determining the topics to be discussed, determining the terms of address, and controlling the turn-taking. The contributions of members of low-status groups may be dismissed as trivial.

7. Cross-cultural communication competence requires both *linguistic competence* and *interactional competence,* and involves such behaviours as

   • Demonstrating respect for members of other cultures.
   • Responding to members of other cultures in a non-judgmental way.
   • Taking turns appropriately in intercultural conversations.
   • Seeing the world through the other person's eyes – empathy.

People who speak a language imperfectly tend to have difficulty not only with the linguistic aspects but also with the interactional aspects of communication (e.g. turn-taking, use of appropriate politeness strategies, use of appropriate communication styles).

8. Unequal communication is established when an alien, non-indigenous language is imposed on a country's population. This happens when, for instance, the language of the former colonial power is imposed on the population and becomes the official language. The measure leads to unequal communication because it favours a small elite who already know the language. Speakers of the indigenous languages may be relegated to a marginal position.

QUESTIONS FOR DISCUSSION AND WRITTEN ASSIGNMENTS

1. Why is there such a high risk of miscommunication and mutual misunderstanding in cross-cultural discussions? Give examples from your own experience of cross-cultural interactions.
2. Describe typical language problems experienced by immigrants, members of minority groups, and others for whom the language of the majority culture is a foreign language. How could the problems be reduced?
3. 'People from different cultural backgrounds have different communicative norms, different ways of sending and receiving messages.' From your own experience of cross-cultural situations, give examples of the confusions and misunderstandings that are caused by differing communicative norms.

BIBLIOGRAPHY

Aitchison, J. Language change. In P Cobley (ed.), *The Routledge Companion to Semiotics and Linguistics*. Routledge, 2001.

Bennett, MJ (ed.), *Basic Concepts of Intercultural Communication*. Intercultural Press, 1998.

Bernstein, B. *Class, Codes and Control* (Vol. 1). Paladin, 1971.

Bernstein, JM. *Recovering Ethical Life: Jurgen Habermas and the Future of Critical Theory*. Routledge, 1995, p. 51.

Bourdieu, P. *Distinction*. Harvard U Press, 1984, pp. 461–462.

Boyle, CM. Differences between patients' and doctors' interpretations of some common medical terms. In C Cox and A Meads (eds), *A Sociology of Medical Practice*. Collier-Macmillan, 1975.

Clyne, M. Inter-cultural Commn at Work. CUP, 1994.

Coupland, N, Giles, H and Wiemann, JM. (eds), *'Miscommunication' and problem talk*. Sage, 1991.

d'Ardenne, P and Mahtani, A. *Transcultural Counselling in Action*. Sage, 1989.

de Zulueta, F. Bilingualism and family therapy. *Journal of Family Therapy*, 12, 1990, 225–265.

Drummond, K and Hopper, R. Misunderstanding and its remedies: telephone miscommunication. In N Coupland, H Giles, and JM Wiemann (eds), *'Miscommunication' and Problem Talk*. Sage, 1991, p. 306.

Dwairy, MA. *Cross-cultural Counselling: The Arab-Palestinian Case*. Haworth Press, 1998, p 168.

Eerdmans, SL. A review of John J Gumperz's current contributions to interactional sociolinguistics. In SL Eerdmans, CL Prevignano and PJ Thibault (eds), *Language and Interaction*. Jorn Benjamins Publishing, 2003, pp. 85–103.

Ervin, SM. Language and TAT content in bilinguals. *Journal of Abnormal and Social Psychology*, 68, 2002, 500–567.

Freud, S. *The Ego and the Id. Standard Edition* (Vol. 19). Hogarth Press, 1923.

Furnham, A and Bochner, S. *Culture Shock: Psychological Reactions to Unfamiliar Environments*. Methuen, 1986.

Gallois, C, Giles, H, Jones, E, Cargile, AC and Ota, H. Accommodating intercultural encounters: elaborations and extensions. In RL Wiseman (ed.), *Intercultural Communication Theory*. Sage, 1995, pp. 115–147.

Giddens, A. *The Constitution of Society: Outline of the Theory of Structuration*. Polity, 1984.

Giles, H and Coupland, N. *Language: Contexts and Consequences*. Brooks/Cole, Pacific, 1991.

Goffman, E. *Presentation of Self in Everyday Life*. Edinburgh University Press, 1956.

Griffin, E. *A First Look at Communication Theory*, 2nd ed. McGraw-Hill, 1994, p. 88.

Gudykunst, WB and Ting-Toomey, S. *Culture and Interpersonal Communication*. Sage, 1988, p. 109.

Hinnenkamp, V. The refusal of second language learning in interethnic context. In H Giles et al. (eds), *Language: Social Psychological Perspectives*. Pergamon, 1980, p. 180.

Hofstede, G. *Culture's Consequences: International Differences in Work-related Values*. Sage, 1980.

Hofstede, G. *Cultures and Organisations: Software of the Mind*. HarperCollins, 1994, p. 216.

Homans, GC. Social Behaviour as Exchange. *American Journal of Sociology*, 63 (6), 1958, 597–606.

Kealey, DJ and Ruben, BD. Cross-cultural personnel selection criteria, issues and methods. In D Landis and RW Brislin (eds), *Handbook of Intercultural Training* (Vol. 1). Pergamon, 1983, pp. 155–175.

Kelly, JC. *A Philosophy of Communication. Centre for the Study of Comms & Culture*. London, 1981, p. 66.

Kim, YY. *Interethnic Communication: Recent Research*. Sage, 1986.

Kim, YY. Cross-cultural adaptation: an integrative theory. In RL Wiseman (ed.), *Intercultural Communication Theory*. Sage, 1995, 170–193.

Knudsen, A. Identity in writing. In D Palumbo-Liu and HU Gumbrecht (eds), *Streams of Cultural Capital*, Stanford University Press, 1997.

Kochman, T. *Black and White: Styles in Conflict*. University of Illinois Press, 1983.

Laitin, DD. *Politics, Language and Thought: The Somali Experience*. University of Chicago Press, 1977, p. 214.

Levinson, SC. *Interactional Biases in Human Thinking*. Max-Planck-Gesellschaft, 1990.

McTear, MF and King, F. Miscommunication in clinical contexts: the speech therapy interview. In N Coupland, H Giles, and JM Wiemann (eds), *'Miscommunication' and Problem Talk*. Sage, 1991, pp. 195–214.

Milgram, S. Behavioural study of obedience. Journal of Abnormal and Social Psychology, 67 (4), 1963, 371–378.

Morsbach, H. Aspects of nonverbal communication in Japan. In LA Samovar and RE Porter (eds), *Intercultural Communication: A Reader*. Wadsworth, 1982, pp. 300–316.

Muir, W. Translating from the German. In RA Brower (ed.), *On Translation*. Harvard UP, 1959, pp. 94–95.

Murphy, J. Psychiatric labelling in cross-cultural perspective. *Science*, 191, 1976, 1019–1028.

Nakata, Y. We-feeling for the Japanese. *Journal of Critical Psychology, Counselling and Psychotherapy*, 9 (3), 2009, 153–157.

JO'Connell (ed.), *The Blackwell Encyclopaedic Dictionary of International Management*. Blackwell, 1997, p. 67.

Ojore, A. Cross-cultural living. In L Brennan (ed.), *Intercultural Living: Gift or Chaos?* Paulines Publications Africa, 2003, p. 50.

Pavis, P (ed.) *The Intercultural Performance Reader*, Routledge, 1996.

Peltokorpi, V. Cross-cultural adjustment of expatriates in Japan. *International Journal of Human Resource Management*, 19 (9), 2008, 1588–1606.

Prensky, M. Digital natives, digital immigrants. *On the Horizon*, 9 (5), 2001.

Pugh, R. *Effective Language in Health and Social Work*. Chapman and Hall, 1996, pp. 112–113.

Ross, S and Shortreed, IM. Japanese foreigner talk: convergence or divergence. *Journal of Asian Pacific Communication*, 1 (1), 1990, 135–146.

Ruben, B. Assessing communication competency for intercultural adaptation. *Group and Organisational Studies*, 1, 1976, 344.

Ryan, B and Carranza, MA. Ingroup and outgroup reactions to Mexican-American language varieties. In H Giles (ed.), *Language, Ethnicity and Intergroup Relations*. Academic Press, 1977.

Saville-Troike, M. *The Ethnography of Communication: An Introduction*, Blackwell, 1982.

Schirato, T and Yell, S. *Communication and Culture: An Introduction*. Sage, 2000.

Scollon, R and Scollon, SW. *Intercultural Communication: A Discourse Approach*, 2nd ed. Blackwell, 2001.

Shannon, C. A mathematical theory of communication. *Bell System Technical Journal*, 27, 1948, 623–656.

Shannon, C. Communication in the presence of noise. *Proceedings of the IRE*, 37 (1), 1949, 10–21.

Spencer, MS et al., The equivalence of the behaviour problem index across US ethnic groups. *Journal of Cross-cultural Psychology*, 36 (5), 2005, p. 573.

Stewart, EC. Culture and decision-making. In WB Gudykunst et al. (eds), *Communication, Culture, and Organisational Processes*. Sage, 1985, p. 178.

Syed, J and Murray, P. Combating the English language deficit: the labour market experiences of migrant women in Australia. *Human Resource Management Journal*, 19 (4), 2009, 413–432.

Thomas, DC. *Essentials of International Management: A Cross-cultural Perspective*. Sage, 2002.

Thomas, EH. The politics of language in former colonial lands. *Journal of North African Studies*, 4 (1), 1999, 1–44.

Trudgill, P. *Dialects in Contact*. Blackwell, 1986.

Trudgill, P. *Sociolinguistics: An Introduction to Language and Society*, 4th ed. Penguin, 2000, p. 116.

Tsuda, Y. *Language Inequality and Distortion in Intercultural Communication: A Critical Theory Approach*. John Benjamins, 1986, p. 86.

Whorf, BL. Science and linguistics. In JB Carroll (ed.), *Language, Thought, and Reality: The Selected Writings of Benjamin Lee Whorf*. MIT Press, 1956, pp. 207–219.

Ylanne-McEwen, V and Coupland, N. Accommodation theory: a conceptual resource for intercultural linguistics. In H Spencer-Oatey (ed.), *Culturally Speaking: Managing Rapport Through Talk Across Cultures*. Continuum, London, 2000, pp. 191–216.

Yoshimura, N and Anderson, P. *Inside the Kaisha: Demystifying Japanese Business Behaviour*. Harvard Business School Press, 1997, p. 59.

Young, R. Intercultural communication: pragmatics, genealogy, deconstruction. *Multilingual Matters*, 1996, p. 125.

Nonverbal aspects of cross-cultural communication

4

INTRODUCTION

In international business, verbal communication is often used in a misleading way. In cross-cultural business discussions and sales negotiations, for instance, people can and do use words to mislead. Sometimes signals are sent nonverbally that cast doubt on the reliability of what is said. Sometimes the meaning of words uttered in a foreign language in a cross-cultural meeting gets lost in translation. In the world of international business, verbal communication used alone is unreliable. In cross-cultural interactions it is often the nonverbal behaviour – in the context of the words spoken – that communicates the meaning.

A major advantage of nonverbal communication is that it is so versatile. For instance, even if some participants in a cross-cultural business discussion cannot express themselves clearly in what to them is a foreign language, they can usually make themselves understood by communicating nonverbally through the use of gestures and facial expressions.

Nonverbal communication is harder to control than verbal messages and so is a more reliable indicator of feelings and attitudes. In many cross-cultural situations people's attitudes and emotions are communicated nonverbally without their conscious awareness (DePaulo and Friedman, 1998). For instance, during a social function two people from different ethnic or cultural groups may unconsciously convey their dislike of each other by avoiding eye contact, or by standing at a great distance from each other. In cross-cultural business negotiations, nonverbal signals such as these can give valuable insights into the attitudes and priorities of the participants. In the tense atmosphere of a cross-cultural negotiation, posture, facial expression, and body-tension are harder to control than verbal communication and are more reliable indicators of feeling and intention.

But since much nonverbal communication is culturally conditioned, a person's nonverbal behaviour is sometimes misinterpreted by members of other cultural groups. Nonverbal behaviours learned and accepted in one culture – such as spitting in public – may be totally unacceptable in another cultural setting. Misinterpretation is particularly likely when a nonverbal behaviour has a specific meaning in one culture but a different meaning in other cultures. In the multicultural workplace, for example, an employee's frank, direct gaze might be interpreted by an American supervisor as a sign of honesty, but by an Asian supervisor as aggressive behaviour that lacks respect.

Many nonverbal behaviours are cultural products and so liable to be misunderstood in a cross-cultural context (Elfenbein and Ambady, 2002). The Chinese method of apologizing by bowing and smiling might be seen by someone from another culture as a sign of insincerity and untrustworthiness. Africans often smile when they are embarrassed, while Japanese people are more likely to smile to mask distress or anger. Many misunderstandings occur in cross-cultural interactions because people misinterpret other people's nonverbal communication.

Some nonverbal messages, however, appear to have the same meaning in all cultures. Standing up straight, for instance, indicates respect and formality in virtually all cultures whereas slouching indicates the opposite. Flushing, panting, trembling, and twitching are triggered unconsciously and possibly express universal biological or psychological states. Thus the messages they send are the same in all cases irrespective of the person's cultural origins.

NONVERBAL COMMUNICATION IN BUSINESS

Cross-cultural business communication

Nonverbal communication is important in international business. For example, market researchers assess consumers' attitudes towards certain imported goods – imported flowers, say – by watching and assessing the nonverbal behaviours of a focus group which is discussing the products. By paying close attention to the nonverbal communication of the group – the participants' body language, facial expressions, gestures, eye contact, and other nonverbal behaviours – the market researchers are able to accurately evaluate the subjects' *real* feelings about imported flowers as opposed to what they say they feel.

Nonverbal communication is so important in business contexts because verbal communication is often misleading or unreliable. In cross-cultural business discussions, verbal communication may not accurately convey what participants mean since people from different cultures have different native tongues and different communicative norms. Consequently, meaning gets lost in translation. In focus groups and numerous other business contexts people can and do lie, can and do deliberately mislead. But nonverbal communication usually tells the truth, and conveys feelings and attitudes accurately.

Common elements

The most common elements in nonverbal communication in a business context are:

- facial expression
- touch
- eye contact
- gestures
- movement (e.g. pacing)
- posture (e.g. tense or relaxed)
- position (e.g. close to or distant from the other person)

Effective cross-cultural business communication tends to be a mix of verbal and nonverbal behaviours. However, Gallois and Callan (1997) argue that in cross-cultural encounters it is nonverbal behaviour – in the context of the words spoken – that communicates the meaning.

Nonverbal communication is an important component of cross-cultural business communication. The nonverbal messages communicated by an international business person during a sales negotiation – signals expressing sincerity or determination, for instance – can help her to get her message across to foreign business prospects. But, equally, nonverbal communication can also send messages that could be misinterpreted by members of foreign business cultures, or that could cause uncertainty and confusion. This happens especially when nonverbal messages contradict the verbal.

Function of nonverbal communication

Nonverbal behaviour is more effective than speech for communicating in certain situations – in a noisy steel works, for instance. Equally, in cross-cultural business discussions nonverbal communication plays an essential role. Even if some of the participants have inadequate linguistic skills and cannot express themselves clearly in words, they can usually make themselves understood by means of nonverbal communication. An Irish sales manager explained to others attending a management seminar how lack of fluency in Italian had prevented him expressing himself clearly in a cross-cultural meeting in Rome – but how he had been able to get his point across eventually with the help of miming and gestures and facial expressions.

As the example suggests, a key function of nonverbal communication in cross-cultural discussions is to clarify the speaker's meaning by elaborating or correcting his words. Indeed, people from all cultures consciously or unconsciously use gestures, facial expressions, eye contact, and other nonverbal behaviours to hold the listener's attention, and to emphasize, elaborate, or modify the verbal communication. One researcher, for instance, found that in conversations between spouses only about 30 per cent of the language could be categorized as emotionally positive or negative, but that this became 70 per cent when nonverbal communication was taken into account (Noller, 1984).

Spontaneous, believable

Much of the impact made by nonverbal behaviour during cross-cultural interactions comes from its *spontaneous* nature. Studies have found that people in all cultures send spontaneous nonverbal messages that reveal their emotions, attitudes, and state of mind (e.g. Burgoon et al., 1989). Indeed, when there is a discrepancy between verbal and nonverbal messages sent during a cross-cultural business meeting, it is usually the nonverbal messages that will be believed – the main reason being that nonverbal signals are usually sent unthinkingly, without calculation, without 'spin'.

Although systematic study of nonverbal communication has been hampered by lack of an underlying integrated theory, valuable insights have come from numerous specific studies. A study conducted by DePaulo and Friedman (1998), for instance, found that the attitudes and emotions of people are often communicated nonverbally *without their conscious awareness*. Thus, in a cross-cultural business meeting, even if a business person tries to hide his dislike of participants from a particular country, his negative feelings may still seep through in spite of himself. He may, for instance, unconsciously avoid eye contact with the disliked group.

Communicating dislike

According to Burgoon et al. (1989), many spontaneous nonverbal behaviours originate in the unconscious and are sent without calculation – a characteristic which helps to explain why nonverbal messages are generally more believable than verbal communication. Trail et al. (2009) make the point that two people from different countries or from different ethnic groups may unconsciously but very clearly convey their distrust or dislike of each other through various kinds of nonverbal behaviour, such as:

- standing or sitting at a large physical distance from each other;
- answering the other person's questions in an awkward and embarrassed way;
- avoiding eye contact;
- demonstrating other distancing behaviours associated with prejudice and dislike.

Conversely, people tend to communicate mutual liking by such nonverbal behaviours as smiling, mutual gaze, and forward lean (Guerrero and Floyd, 2006).

The impact made by nonverbal communication has been confirmed by various survey results. For instance, surveys conducted in the United States by PR consultants who advise business leaders and politicians have reportedly revealed that while only 10 per cent of impressions of a candidate's eligibility are based on the candidate's verbal communication, 90 per cent is nonverbal communication (including voice quality).

Clear messages

Nonverbal behaviours tend to be believable – indeed, certain nonverbal responses cannot lie. For instance, when a heterosexual man sees a picture of a nude woman or when a homosexual man looks at a picture of a nude male, the pupil becomes much larger (Fast, 1971). Much nonverbal communication is spontaneous and only partly controllable – key features, which help to explain its impact in cross-cultural business meetings, where it is important to correctly interpret the participants' words and to understand their intentions.

Nonverbal communication tends to tell the truth about a person's attitudes and emotions. In cross-cultural encounters between whites and blacks, for instance, white participants' blinking and eye contact with black interaction partners are more consistent with their actual attitudes towards black Americans than are their stated evaluations (Dovidio et al., 1997). In Germany during the Nazi years, Jews trying to pass as non-Jews often betrayed themselves through nonverbal communication. For instance, their hand movements were freer than the Germans' hand movements.

In cross-cultural business discussions, unconscious expressions of emotion through nonverbal behaviour signal the importance placed by participants – whatever their cultural origins – on the various issues being discussed, whether these are price, delivery dates, guarantees of quality, or the possibility of further orders. The ability to detect and interpret such signals can give valuable insights into the attitudes and priorities of the diverse participants. In the tense atmosphere of a cross-cultural sales negotiation, posture, facial expression, body-tension, gaze, and other nonverbal behaviours are harder to control than verbal messages and so are more reliable indicators of feeling than are opening remarks or carefully prepared verbal statements.

Mehrabian's (1981) theory of implicit communication postulates three basic dimensions of emotional response: arousal, attraction, and dominance. All three kinds of response are communicated nonverbally and spontaneously:

- *facial expression* shows arousal;
- choice of *spatial distance* communicates liking or disliking;
- *body posture/tension* shows if an individual considers the other persons round the negotiating table to be more powerful and to have higher status than himself.

Micromessages in the workplace

One kind of nonverbal communication – the micromessage – sends a very clear message to the recipient. Micromessages are the subtle and often subconscious nonverbal messages that people in all organisations in all cultures transmit to each other, either consciously and unconsciously. In a ten-minute conversation, two people may send each other more than 50 micromessages by looks, gestures, tone of voice, or other small nonverbal signals (Guirdham, 2005).

In the multicultural workplace negative micromessages may be sent to employees who do not see eye-to-eye with their manager, or to individuals who are perceived to be *different* – such as foreigners or members of ethnic minority groups (Pierce, 1992). In Germany, for instance, Turkish 'guest-workers' may be perceived as different and so may receive negative micromessages. In New Zealand, Maoris employed by traditionally white firms may be perceived as different. Consequently, they may receive more negative micromessages than do the pakehas. Pierce (1992) maintains that in countries around the world, employees who stand out in some way are at risk of being sent negative micromessages ('microinsults') by supervisors and co-workers on a daily basis.

> For instance, a supervisor in an assembly plant regards black employees as lazy and unreliable. He avoids criticizing the employees verbally but is less careful about his nonverbal communication, and he constantly sends micromessages to black employees conveying a negative stereotype. During the annual appraisal, this supervisor is criticised for his department's high rates of labour turnover and absenteeism.

Young (2006) argues that sending continual *negative* micromessages to employees not only complicates cross-cultural communication in the workplace, it also discourages and impairs employee performance. *Positive* micromessages, by contrast, boost employees' morale and encourage employees' commitment to organisational goals.

Case study

MINI-CASE: Impact of micromessages

The sensitivity and skills required to send positive micromessages and avoid sending negative micromessages to employees are topics which are sometimes included in cross-cultural communication programmes for managers. The aim is to equip the managers with motivational skills which are effective with employees from diverse cultural backgrounds.

When a young IT expert employed by manufacturing company attended a management training course on communication in the multicultural workplace, one of the sessions focused on the impact made by various forms of nonverbal communication, including the way in which micromessages are conveyed in the workplace and the effect they can have on employee motivation.

A few days after attending the course the IT expert experienced the effects of negative micromessaging. This happened when he handed a stock turnover report to the CEO – who mispronounced the expert's name. Later in the day he

Case study

Continued

attended a progress meeting called by the production manager, but each time he started to make a point the manager glanced at his watch. After leaving the progress meeting the expert tried to discuss a network problem with a colleague, who immediately started to send a text message to somebody. By the end of the day the young expert felt demoralized and demotivated – but he was not sure why.

Questions:

1. *Why did the IT expert feel demotivated?*
2. *How do employees typically respond to receiving (a) negative micromessages (b) positive micromessages.*
3. *What actions could be taken by management in the company to reduce negative micromessaging and increase positive micromessaging?*

Nonverbal communication competence

Nonverbal communication competence helps a foreign business person or an expatriate manager to 'fit in' to a foreign culture. Because nonverbal communication is largely the product of a particular culture, expatriate managers, immigrants, international students, and others who live for an extended period in a foreign culture are faced with the challenge of accurately interpreting the nonverbal behaviours which they observe in members of the culture. They also need to become aware of how their own culturally derived nonverbal behaviours will be perceived. Such self-awareness will give them early warning of which of their own nonverbal behaviours they need to adjust in order to 'fit in' to the culture.

Expatriate managers and international business personnel need to be aware of the impact that their nonverbal communication is making on colleagues and business prospects in other cultures. Part of the process of arriving at that level of awareness is to build nonverbal communication competence, using the cross-cultural training tool.

For example, a simple but effective training technique to increase an expatriate manager's nonverbal communication competence is to show a video of the manager's 'normal', pre-training nonverbal behaviour, then to discuss with the manager her reasons for making *that* gesture or exhibiting *that* facial expression or body posture at a particular point, before inviting the manager to speculate on how employees in the host organisation might interpret those behaviours.

Culturally appropriate behaviour

An important aspect of nonverbal communication competence is the ability to use *culturally appropriate* nonverbal behaviours when living and working in a foreign culture. That was the assumption when expatriate staff working in a Middle Eastern country attended a cross-cultural training programme. One of the objectives of the programme was to provide opportunities for the expatriates to learn nonverbal behaviours that were appropriate to the culture of the country.

> Typical nonverbal behaviours were demonstrated by a member of the culture. These included standing very close to the conversational partner, smiling and looking intently at the other person while speaking. These behaviours were then practised by the trainees and feedback given. Typical gestures used in the country were also demonstrated and practised. These included showing both open palms to indicate enthusiasm and patting the chest after a meal to indicate 'I've had enough'.

At the end of the course, the expatriates returned to their jobs in the country and, in the following weeks, put into practice what they had learned. Several trainees later reported that their communication with local people had become more effective as a result of the training.

UNDERSTANDING CULTURAL DIFFERENCE

Cultural factors

Effective cross-cultural business communication depends on acquiring an understanding of basic cultural differences and the various patterns of verbal and nonverbal behaviour among members of different cultures. It is essential, for instance, for international business people and expatriate managers to have a good understanding of cultural differences in communicative preferences.

An expatriate manager needs an understanding of cultural preferences when deciding, for example, *which media* to use in support of a particular commercial strategy in a particular market. Albers-Miller (1996) posited links between various advertising appeals and Hofstede's cultural dimensions. Such links need to be understood before any effective international advertising plan can be constructed. General or 'universal' advertising approaches tend to be ineffective (Mortimer and Grierson, 2010). In individualist countries, for instance, people read more than in collectivist cultures and consequently a manager working in an individualist country might decide to rely on newspapers, journals, and other verbal media to provide suitable channels of communication. In collectivist countries, on the other hand, people tend to be more visually oriented and consequently television, posters, and other media which depend, essentially, on *nonverbal communication* would be considered to be the prime channels of communication and influence.

Local brands

As these examples suggest, to be effective cross-cultural business communication needs to be adapted to the communicative preferences and characteristics of the local culture. Accordingly, in order to be successful expatriate managers need to demonstrate awareness of the preferences. A few ubiquitous global brands are often used as examples of global business success but – as international business people soon come to realize – in most countries *local brands* are the most trusted and the most frequently purchased. Thus the most popular car in France is Renault; in Germany and Austria it is Volkswagen; in the Czech Republic, Skoda; in India, Maruti; in most of East Asia, Toyota or Honda; and so on.

The implication is that cross-cultural business communication often needs to be calculated and differentiated. There are no universal models of cross-cultural business communication which can be applied at all times in all countries. Prior knowledge about cultural differences and preferences must be factored into an international sales manager's calculations about markets that should be pursued and the kind of communication that should be adopted (verbal, nonverbal, multimedia) in each market.

Potential pitfalls

Nonverbal communication is a key component of cross-cultural business communication and its relative importance varies across cultures. Therefore international business persons, firms intending to expand their overseas operations, expatriate managers, and others need to be aware of important variations.

> In 2002, England football fans attending World Cup matches in Japan and South Korea were warned by the British Foreign Office to keep their shirts on and their tattoos hidden. The warnings were necessary because the baring of chests is considered highly offensive in Japan and South Korea, while in Japan tattoos are associated with criminal gangs.

The example illustrates how nonverbal behaviours learned and accepted in one culture may be totally unacceptable in another cultural setting. That is why foreign business visitors to a country need to be aware that their own 'natural' nonverbal communication may well make a negative impact on potential business partners if it deviates too greatly from local norms. That is precisely what happened when an American sales manager held a business meeting with a sales prospect in Brazil. At the end of the meeting the salesman made an 'O.K.' symbol with his hand, intending it to express satisfaction with a good first meeting. But in Brazil this is seen as an obscene gesture. Needless to say, there was no follow-up meeting.

Foreign business visitors to Arab countries need to be aware of the many differences that exist between social events held in these countries from those they are used to at home. The most obvious difference that strikes most foreign visitors is that no women are present. Another difference is the seating arrangements – carpet-level seating with cushions is usual at mealtimes. When entering the room the foreign visitor needs to quickly decide who are the oldest people and/or the highest status individuals in the room and to make a point of greeting these individuals first.

When people from different countries interact they do not have the advantage of a common cultural background hence their respective communicative conventions naturally differ. Some of the most basic difficulties of cross-cultural communication derive from this simple fact.

Misinterpretation risk

When people have the same cultural background and the same native language they can correctly interpret each others' nonverbal behaviour in the context of the words spoken. From their experience of being in everyday social situations in that particular culture they know which nonverbal signals go with which words. The skills that tell them which emotions and attitudes are being expressed have been learned since childhood. Thus, it is not surprising that studies show that people quickly and accurately interpret nonverbal expressions of emotion by others from the same culture (Anderson et al., 2003; Elfenbein and Ambady, 2002).

But the same does not apply in cross-cultural situations. In cross-cultural encounters people tend to be much less adept at *accurately* interpreting the nonverbal behaviours of individuals who belong to other ethnic, racial, and cultural groups. Fast (1971) explains how black shop floor workers in a US manufacturing company were judged lazy by their white managers. But when research was carried out it revealed that the managers' unfavourable judgments stemmed from their interpretation of the workers' *nonverbal behaviours* – their typically relaxed stance and their casual, swinging movement when walking.

The example shows how people's nonverbal behaviours can be grossly misinterpreted by members of other racial, ethnic, or cultural groups. Misinterpretation is likely when a particular nonverbal behaviour has a specific meaning in one culture but a different meaning in other cultures. For example, a slight down-turning of the corners of the mouth might be interpreted by a New Yorker as anger but by a Muscovite as nausea. In the multicultural workplace an employee's frank, direct gaze might be interpreted by an American supervisor as a sign of honesty but by an Asian supervisor as aggressive behaviour that lacks respect.

The simple act of smiling has different meanings in different cultures. For example, Africans often smile when they are embarrassed but Japanese people are more likely to smile to mask distress or anger. In a cross-cultural context, numerous nonverbal messages are likely to be misinterpreted. Pall and McGrath (2009) suggest that the next frontier to be crossed in the field of cross-cultural nonverbal recognition is technology capable of unambiguously interpreting gestures and expressions across cultures.

National variations

Business visitors to Brazil often comment that in parties and other informal social events Brazilians like to stand very close together, with strong levels of eye contact and frequent touching between members of the same sex. These characteristics are very different from those of Asian cultures and North European cultures where nonverbal behaviours tend to be much more restrained. When two male friends in Brazil greet each other after a short absence they may hug and backslap and shake hands warmly. When women talk they sometimes tug at the buttons or sleeve of the person they are talking to. Foreign business visitors to Brazil need to be prepared for these typical nonverbal behaviours in Brazil (and perhaps to make adjustments to their own nonverbal communication during their visits).

Every culture has a language of nonverbal behaviour that can confuse people from other cultures. The Shona people of Zimbabwe silently clap hands to express thanks, and they express refusal or lack of interest by a slight shrug of the shoulders. Italians run the thumb down the cheek to indicate a woman's physical attractiveness. Indians greet a foreign visitor by placing both hands together and making a slight bow. All these gestures have a stable, well-defined meaning *within* their cultures. Foreign business visitors, however, are often baffled by them. In one study participants were asked to interpret gestures made by members of various cultures: people from cultures that were 'distant' from the cultures providing the gestures made many inaccurate interpretations (Rosenthal et al., 1979).

Many aspects of nonverbal communication are cultural products and so liable to be misunderstood by members of other cultures. To someone from another culture the Chinese method of apologizing by bowing and smiling may appear to be insincere and an early warning signal of untrustworthiness. Japanese smiling is another culturally influenced behaviour which can be misinterpreted by foreign visitors. Quite often, Japanese people smile to mask pain or distress since it is culturally unacceptable to inflict the unpleasantness of grief on others. (Albright et al., 1997).

In some cultures, women may be required to be silent under certain circumstances while in other cultures silence is expected in the presence of high-status persons.

In Western societies, close physical distance between two women is acceptable in public, but in some countries in the Middle East it is just as acceptable for two men to walk down the street hand in hand. Foreign business visitors may misinterpret such aspects of everyday conduct, jump to the wrong conclusions, and offend potential business partners or sales prospects in the process.

Only when foreign visitors learn the basic social and *communicative rules* of a culture can they hope to interpret its nonverbal behaviours with reasonable accuracy.

Universal nonverbal behaviours

Perhaps people are born carrying within themselves the basic elements of a nonverbal communication system. In spite of the cultural variability of many nonverbal behaviours, a few nonverbal messages seem to have the same meaning in all cultures. For example, in almost all cultures standing up straight signifies respect and formality, while slouching signifies the opposite. There are some expressions of feeling that may be universal – for instance, smiling, crying, facial expressions showing pain, and certain other gestures. Trembling, twitching, panting, flushing and several other kinds of nonverbal communication which are triggered spontaneously may express universal biological or psychological states. Accordingly, the messages they send are the same in all cases irrespective of the person's racial or ethnic group.

According to Gallois and Callan (1997) three nonverbal dimensions have been found by researchers to be universal across cultures:

- expressing affiliation/solidarity
- expressing dominance–submission
- expressing arousal/involvement

One or more of these dimensions of nonverbal expression are found in every cross-cultural communication situation.

Darwin (1872) believed that facial expressions of emotion are similar among all humans, regardless of culture. Basing his belief on man's evolutionary origin, Darwin argued that various facial expressions derive from movements that were at one time functional. Raising the lips in anger, for instance, he interpreted as a biting response to attack. The inference is that a number of facial expressions and some other nonverbal behaviours are innate, not acquired in the process of socialisation.

FUNCTIONS OF NONVERBAL COMMUNICATION

Range of functions

Expressing emotions is an important function of nonverbal communication but different cultures have different rules governing the extent to which emotions may be expressed in public (Thomas, 2002). The public expression of anger, for instance, is a cultural performance and defined within specific cultural boundaries. Thus in a cross-cultural business meeting the nonverbal expression of emotions by people from other cultures can easily be misinterpreted. As a result, the interaction and even the outcomes of the meeting may be affected.

Argyle (1988) argues that different types of nonverbal communication are linked to personality, and that the expression of emotion is just one of the primary functions of nonverbal communication. Other important functions are:

- Facilitating social interaction
- Managing the cues of interaction
- Expressing emotions
- Expressing interpersonal attitudes
- Self-presentation
- Ritual-performance (e.g. greetings)

Facilitating social interaction

Like same-culture interactions, cross-cultural interactions have to be coordinated and regulated and in all cultures nonverbal signals are used for this purpose. For instance, nods, facial expressions, uh-huhs, gestures, and so on are used to control turn-taking. Making or breaking eye contact communicates the speaker's intention to speak or to finish speaking – typically, a speaker breaks eye contact as he finishes speaking then gives a sustained gaze which helps the speaker assess the other person's reaction.

Nonverbal signals which are used to hold people's attention and to motivate them to communicate, include smiling, nodding, looking interested and leaning forward. According to Findlay (1998), nonverbal signals such as 'hm', head nodding, and gestures are used to encourage people to continue speaking or to facilitate the continuation of one-sided conversations.

In business meetings and other forms of social interaction, *paralinguistic features* such as intonation, stress, rhythm, and sentence speed are used to control the flow and temper of the discussion. A fall in tune, for instance, generally signals in Western cultures that the speaker has completed her turn. This particular paralinguistic cue is often used in interviews and informal discussions – although the precise ways in which it is used varies across cultures. Thus according to Eerdmans (2003), one researcher found that English-speaking Indians tend to increase loudness and pitch to get back into a discussion after being interrupted. Native English speakers, by contrast, tend to use more direct verbal means – for instance, saying 'I didn't finish.' or 'Can I go on?' The effect of such cultural variations is that in cross-cultural discussions participants sometimes appear to be blind and deaf to each others' culturally influenced attempts to regulate the interaction.

Managing the cues of interaction

Many nonverbal signals can only be understood in the context of the words that accompany them. Novinger (2001) points out that English, like other languages, has a set of body motions that are closely tied to the linguistic structure. There is a systematic relationship between verbal and nonverbal communication – indeed, the two can be seen as interdependent language systems. This helps to explain why observers studying a silent film of an American speaking Italian, Yiddish, and English could tell immediately from his nonverbal behaviour which language he was speaking (Birdwhistell, 1970). One study found that during ordinary conversations verbal and nonverbal points of emphasis (such as pitch, loudness; gesture, shifts in posture) were closely connected and marked a regular pattern of rhythm that could be measured by a metronome (Erickson and Shultz, 1982).

Many of the nonverbal signals that people use to manage and regulate interaction in meetings, interviews, discussions, and other forms of social interaction are culture-specific and may not be effective in cross-cultural situations. The European and American pattern of eye contact to control turns, for instance, involves the speaker ending with her eyes in contact with the next speaker, but this is not the pattern used in some Asian cultures, which require averted eyes and a period of silence between speakers (Bennett, 1998). One consequence of this particular cultural variation is that in cross-cultural discussions Asian participants may find it difficult to get a turn.

Expressing emotions

Bijlstra et al. (2010: 657) point out that fast and correct recognition of emotional expressions in cross-cultural encounters is a prerequisite for fluent social interaction. The researchers make the point that 'a face carries a wealth of informative cues and can say more than a thousand words'.

Even when people try to disguise their feelings, the emotions tend to leak through in the form of conscious or unconscious facial expressions and other nonverbal signals. That was the conclusion reached by an international aid worker when he asked a Palestinian doctor to describe an Israeli air raid that had led to buildings being destroyed and the loss of civilian lives.

> The aid worker noticed that the doctor deliberately avoided using emotive words in describing what happened and instead expressed his feelings through nonverbal communication. This included tense body-posture and strained facial expression.

The doctor's nonverbal communication sent a very clear message to somebody from a completely different cultural background.

People express emotions through facial expressions, posture, vocal qualities, and other kinds of nonverbal communication (Ekman, 1993). *Anxiety and fear*, for example, may be expressed through tense body posture, strained facial expression, and vocal characteristics such as intonation, rapidity, loudness, and breathlessness (Juslin and Laukka, 2003). *Anger* is conveyed by fast speech rate, high voice intensity, and much high-frequency energy. *Sadness*, on the other hand, is conveyed by slow speech rate, low voice intensity, and little high-frequency energy.

Research in many cultures shows that people have the ability to recognize emotion which is expressed nonverbally by individuals from their own cultures (Thomas, 2002). While emotions are recognized at above chance levels across cultural boundaries, members of the same culture achieve much higher levels of accurate recognition (Izard, 1971). However, in some situations the expression of emotions by members of other cultures is capable of accurate recognition – as demonstrated by the following case:

Case study

MINI-CASE: The Russian Patient

When the wife of a Russian manager assigned to an expatriate post in Bulgaria complained to a Bulgarian doctor about depression, it was difficult to make

Case study

Continued

an accurate diagnosis. The patient spoke no Bulgarian and the doctor spoke very little Russian. However, the doctor was able to establish the severity of the patient's depression by using *nonverbal communication*:

'I let the patient know that I was interested and involved in her problem not by words but by nonverbal signals – by smiling and maintaining eye-contact and a relaxed body posture. I spoke to her quietly in Bulgarian, with occasional Russian words interspersed – the purpose was not to give information but to suggest that there was no need to be anxious or alarmed.

'The patient's own nonverbal behaviour, especially her facial expressions, gestures and body posture, supplied much of the information I needed for my diagnosis. Her face was sad, almost tearful, her body movements were sluggish and retarded. She spoke very quietly, in Russian, with long pauses between the phrases – a sign of nervous exhaustion.

'I read these nonverbal signals as indications of a chronic depressive disorder, and this was confirmed when she showed me some old prescriptions for drugs. The class of drugs on the prescription and the sheer number of them made it clear that I should refer the patient to a psychiatrist. Subsequently the psychiatrist found that the lady was suffering from a major depressive disorder that required treatment based on a combination of pharmacotherapy and psychotherapy.'

Questions:

1. *To what extent was the doctor right to put so much emphasis on nonverbal communication during the consultation?*
2. *Is it likely that the doctor would have reached similar conclusions if an interpreter had been used?*
3. *What would have been the advantages and disadvantages of using an interpreter in this particular situation?*

Rules of emotional display

Darwin (1872) considered the universal occurrence of the same facial expressions as important evidence that emotions are innate, but many later researchers (e.g. Birdwhistell, 1970) have found that different cultures have different rules governing emotional display. Although anger, for instance, is a basic human emotion with biological components that are the same in all cultures, the way that anger is expressed is culture-specific. In Japan, for instance, norms of self-control require a person not to show anger at all (Morsbach, 1982).

Some rules relating to the expression of emotion seem to be specific to social roles so that an awareness of the rules facilitates communication with the role-players. In the United States, for instance, men are expected to control their emotions. In European countries, solicitors dress soberly and communicate with their clients in a restrained and sober fashion. Prior knowledge of such unspoken rules facilitates communication with the role-player and also allows correct deductions to be drawn from the role-player's behaviour.

Expressing interpersonal attitudes

Argyle (1988) argues that spoken language is normally used for communicating information about events external to the speakers, but that nonverbal communication is used to establish and maintain interpersonal relationships and to express interpersonal attitudes. According to Aguinis et al. (1998), a key function of nonverbal communication is to transmit information about the social relationships of individuals.

People who share a common culture can easily and accurately assess each others' attitudes from nonverbal behaviours. They have learned to recognize over many years the meanings of the attitudes and feelings which the nonverbal behaviours express. For example, within a culture various body movements and body postures send very clear signals about the attitude held by an individual regarding another person's social status and importance. In a US hospital, for instance, the people with the highest status at a meeting were those who adopted the most relaxed postures (Goffman, 1961b).

However, as many nonverbal behaviours used to express attitude are culturally derived, interpretation problems arise in cross-cultural interactions. Does the fact that two people are standing in very close proximity to each other indicate the existence of an intimate relationship between them? Not necessarily, since people from different cultures have differing needs for personal space.

Arabs tend to stand much closer to one another than North Americans, touch each other more often, maintain a high degree of eye contact, and face each other more squarely (Watson and Graves, 1966). Watson (1970) found that Arabs require very little personal space, closely followed by Indians and Pakistanis, while Europeans and Americans require considerably more personal space in order to feel comfortable. In Japan, the relative status of people when they meet is indicated by the depth of their bows, but people from other cultures usually have difficulty in understanding this behaviour (Beaupre and Hess, 2006).

Self-presentation

Some nonverbal behaviours are used in a calculated way for purposes of self-presentation, impression-management, or deception. Frequent, animated gestures and body movements, for instance, may be consciously used to indicate to observers the possession of a dynamic personality. In many Asian countries a frank, open gaze can be considered aggressive or shameless. In most Western countries, on the other hand, a frank, open gaze is used to suggest honesty and reliability. Physical appearance is an important aspect of self-presentation. Studies show that people consistently attribute more desirable attributes to physically attractive persons than to less attractive persons (Shaffer et al., 2000).

People tend to deliberately build a repertoire of nonverbal behaviours that they use to present themselves as they wish to be seen by others (although others may react in unforeseen ways). People communicate high status, for instance, by means of dress, facial expression, body posture, and gaze. Goffman (1961a) states that in Western societies high status is signalled by looking more while speaking and looking less while listening; and that high-status people in the United States tend to sit in relaxed positions, often with their arms flung over the back of the chair – as opposed to low-status people who sit more formally and straight in their chairs. In Japanese society, the relative status of people when they meet is indicated by the depth of their bows (Morsbach, 1988).

Scollon and Scollon (2001: 48) make the point that because any communication is a risk to one's own face and, the same time, a risk to the other person's, we 'have to carefully project a face for ourselves and to respect the face rights and claims of other participants'.

Rituals

Ritual communication relates to how people create and express meaning through verbal and nonverbal rituals. It applies to more than collective religious expression, and is an intrinsic part of everyday interactions, ceremonies, theatrical performances, political demonstrations, coming-of-age ceremonies, and so on.

All cultures have their nonverbal rituals. In India, for instance, 'byth namaste' involves placing both hands together while at the same time making a slight bow and lowering the gaze. It is widely used and shows respect for Indian customs. Many of the nonverbal behaviours used in ritual communication in various cultures are formulaic and repetitive, as in religious services, public ceremonies of thanksgiving, coronation ceremonies, weddings, and so on. Ritual communication tends to be highly participative. The ritual is shaped by time, space, and the individual body as well as by aesthetic considerations.

SMALL-GROUP EXERCISE: Discussion Questions

Working in small groups, discuss each of the following questions and write down the group's agreed answer. At the end of the exercise, each group may present its answers to the other groups for comment.

1. *Identify five important functions of nonverbal communication.*
2. *In cross-cultural business discussions why are the nonverbal messages sent by participants often more believable than verbal communication? Give examples.*
3. *Give examples of how dislike of people from a particular ethnic group may unconsciously be expressed through nonverbal signals.*
4. *Why is it important to try to use culturally appropriate nonverbal behaviour when living and working in a foreign country?*
5. *Give examples of how high social status can be communicated by nonverbal signals.*

6. *'Every culture has a language of nonverbal behaviour that can confuse people from other cultures.' Give examples of nonverbal behaviours in Zimbabwe, China, and the Middle East that can have this effect.*
7. *Explain the impact – positive or negative – that micromessages can have on employee morale.*

TYPES OF NONVERBAL BEHAVIOUR

Proxemics (spatial distance)

Hall (1955) pioneered the study of proxemics, which includes the spatial distances that people choose when they communicate with each other. According to Hall, there are at least four zones of interpersonal distance that are related to various types of social interaction:

- Intimate distance.
- Personal distance, when chatting with friends.
- Social distance, in formal and semi-formal social and business situations.
- Public distance, for official and ceremonial occasions.

Hall found that every culture has a language of spatial distance. For example, Arabs at a social function feel comfortable when they are standing or sitting very close to other guests. In marked contrast, Europeans and Americans feel comfortable when they have much personal space. Hall observed what happened when Arabs interact with Westerners. A kind of dance is performed in which the Westerners continually back away from the Arabs who, in keeping with their cultural norms, keep trying to get closer. Social regulation of personal space is apparent in India, where unspoken rules determine how closely members of a particular caste may approach other castes.

Business persons' individual space requirements may be violated when they attend a cross-cultural meeting and are forced – by the seating arrangements or the layout of the conference room – to sit too close to the other participants, or too far from them. When this happens a whole series of nonverbal signals such as rocking, leg swinging, foot tapping, and high blinking rate often conveys their unease. However, such effects tend to be short-lasting. If individuals from different cultures with varying space requirements are thrown together in, say, a multicultural project team they quickly learn to compromise to colleagues' requirements and adjust their own spatial norms.

Facial expressions

Researchers surveyed display rules across cultures in 32 countries and found several universal effects, including greater expressiveness shown towards *ingroups* in all cultures than towards *outgroups* (Matsumoto et al., 2008). A few nonverbal behaviours may be universal, including smiling, crying, and facial expressions showing pain, but most other facial expressions have no fixed meaning across cultures. In China, for instance, smiling is associated with a lack of calmness and self-control while in some African countries laughter and smiling may express surprise or embarrassment.

Japanese display rules require a person not to show anger or other negative feelings when shocked or upset (Morsbach, 1982). Consequently, in Japan a controlled expressionless face is the ideal – so much so that business visitors to Japan often report that during their visits they find it difficult to communicate with Japanese managers because of the lack of visual clues about what they are feeling.

Darwin believed that facial expressions of emotion are similar among humans regardless of culture, and later researchers have found that the basic emotions – anger, fear, sadness, disgust, happiness, surprise – are evident in facial expressions in all cultures from a very early age (Levensen et al., 1992). According to Fast (1971), the custom of women wearing veils in Muslim countries is primarily to allow them to conceal their true emotions, written on their faces, and so protect them from any male aggression.

Interpreting facial expressions accurately is not an easy task. One reason is that the face often shows a mixture of two or more emotions at the same time, in accordance with the blend of conflicting emotions that a person may be experiencing internally. In cross-cultural interactions the facial expressions of persons from a particular culture may be misinterpreted and may even become the basis for dangerous stereotyping. A Japanese woman who smiled when told that her friend has died shocked her American hosts who immediately perceived her as superficial and unfeeling. The Americans were unaware that in Japan smiling is a customary way of concealing painful emotions.

Gestures

Gestures alone can be very eloquent. Deaf and dumb people communicate efficiently using a combination of gestures and facial expressions. Studies have found that men use gestures more frequently than women, and the uneducated use gestures more frequently than the educated (Brault, 1990).

A repertoire of gestures is common to a broad range of cultures. Within a particular culture, conventional gestures have an accepted, stable, and well-defined meaning, but gestures often have different meanings in different countries. For instance, it is usual and acceptable to point in Western societies, whereas in many Asian societies pointing is considered impolite.

There are few if any universal gestures. As Kelly (1981) points out, some gestures are used on the spur of the moment for some immediate expressive purpose. Others, such as a raised fist, may be used unconsciously and reveal invisible biological or psychological states.

Gaze

Eye-to-eye contact is one of the most direct and powerful ways in which people communicate nonverbally in all cultures. We like others who gaze at us relative to those who gaze away (Mason et al., 2005) – possibly because we infer that those who gaze at us may be interested in interacting with us.

While eye gaze is often a signal of interest, averting one's gaze from an individual is the most frequently used nonverbal cue to indicate the silent treatment, a form of ostracism (Wirth et al., 2010). Participants in Wirth et al.'s (2010) study who received averted eye gaze felt ostracized, and experienced feelings of reduced self-esteem and increased temptation to act aggressively towards the interaction partner.

However, as Thomas and Inkson (2004) point out, in a given culture the pattern of eye contact is subject to different rules depending on gender, status, age, situation, and other variables. Different racial groups have different norms about patterns of eye contact. If a white American looks away while the other person is speaking it usually indicates lack of attention, whereas for African Americans or Latinos looking away does not necessarily have that meaning (McCaskey, 1979). In English-speaking countries, long eye contact is often perceived as an aggressive challenge or as a response to looking at a physically attractive person.

Thus, like other aspects of nonverbal communication, gaze and gaze avoidance are strongly influenced by cultural background. For instance, high-gaze levels are usual for Arabs and people from Latin America, and low-gaze levels are typical for people from northern Europe and India (Watson and Graves, 1966). In some parts of Africa direct eye contact must be avoided when addressing a higher status person (Gallois and Callan, 1997). The Chinese consider a general lack of eye contact as social courtesy (Joy, 1989).

In cross-cultural situations the cultural variability of gaze behaviour can lead to awkwardness and tension. People from low-gaze cultures may be perceived as impolite and inattentive. People from high-gaze cultures, on the other hand, are likely to give the impression of being pushy or threatening.

Touch

In encounters between strangers the participants are usually careful to avoid physical contact, taking care not to touch each other or to stand too close to each other (Finnegan, 2002). Close friends, on the other hand, often touch each other: the contact reinforces their relationship. In cross-cultural as in same-culture interactions, touching is used to emphasize, clarify, modify, or contradict verbal messages, but sometimes it is used as a sign of status or dominance. Henley and LaFrance (1992) found that in the United States touching the other person's arm or body often signals the toucher's dominance and power.

Like most other types of nonverbal communication, touching behaviour varies cross-culturally. Arabs, for instance, touch each other frequently, maintain a high degree of eye contact, and face each other squarely (Watson and Graves, 1966). In most social situations Americans tend to avoid physical contact and stand at a distance from the other person. In some Arab countries all-male touching is considered normal while male-female touching is discouraged. Male-female greeting between close relatives and friends is usually limited to handshakes. Business visitors to India often notice that Indians use their right hand only to touch somebody, to pass money, or to pick up an item in a shop. The left hand is widely considered to be unclean.

In a foreign culture, knowing when and on what part of the body one is permitted to touch another person requires a good level of cultural awareness. A Maori greeting, for instance, requires a firm pressing together of noses. Not surprisingly, differences in touching behaviour can lead to discomfort and tension when members of different cultures meet, and often an adjustment of the participants' own touching behaviour is required.

Dress

The connections between dress and identity are so intimate that for some theorists the self does not exist independently of the clothes one wears (Negrin, 1999). Dress is the key to understanding how people represent themselves both as individuals and as group members (e.g. Rafaeli and Pratt, 1993). Dress is an important symbol that conveys information about a person and the person's collective identity, as Humphreys and Brown (2002) found when they examined the role of the Islamic headscarf in collective identity maintenance and challenge in an all-female Turkish University department.

In cross-cultural business, choice of dress has important practical implications. A business person's dress and grooming makes it easier to 'fit in' when visiting a foreign country. If it is badly chosen, however, it will make the visitor feel uncomfortable and out of place, adding an additional layer of difficulty to cross-cultural business discussions. In a cross-cultural context each particular situation has an appropriate type of dress that goes with it. In a cross-cultural meeting, for instance, a foreign business visitor's dress will make the other participants feel comfortable or uncomfortable, and will influence the extent to which the others trust and like the person. The mechanism involved may be that by choosing to dress in a certain way the visitor helps the people he communicates with to feel comfortable, and they repay the kindness with feelings of trust and liking.

Handshake

Although the handshake may appear to be a formality, it is a potent form of communication and influence in many cross-cultural business situations, including cross-cultural interviews. According to Stewart et al. (2008), a firm handshake is a form of nonverbal communication that has an immediate effect on impressions formed during an interview.

For Western interviewers, a desirable handshake is a firm handshake with strong and complete grip, vigorous shaking for lasting duration, and eye contact while hands are clasped (Chaplin et al., 2000). According to the researchers, such a handshake communicates sociability, friendliness, and dominance. A poor handshake, on the other hand, may communicate introversion, shyness, and neuroticism. Other nonverbal behaviours, such as smiling, eye contact, and posture, have also been found to have a strong influence on the way that interviewees are assessed during job interviews.

Posture/body movements

Postures communicate conscious or unconscious messages about the assumed relative status of people. Thus the most important people at meetings in a mental hospital were those who adopted the most relaxed postures (Goffman, 1961b). According to Argyle (1988), a confident, high-status person behaves like a confident, high-status animal – sprawling in a relaxed position or striding about in a relaxed way. A posture that salesmen and other business people are sometimes observed to adopt is to stand close to the other person, with a square orientation and leaning forward. The posture may be used as part of an attempt to reduce psychological distance between the parties.

Bowing in Japan is a complicated process determined by the relative status of the parties. It is possible to tell the relative status of two people who meet and communicate by the depth of their bows (Ferraro, 1998). Some female store employees in Japan have the sole function of bowing to customers (Morsbach, 1982).

Synchronized movements

In cross-cultural conversations people sometimes synchronize their body rhythms. As one person speaks and moves the other person moves with a matching rhythm. The movements may be of the whole body or movements of the hands, head, and eyes (Kendon, 1970). The unconscious purpose of this coordinated behaviour seems to be to increase social rapport. Lakin and Chartrand (2003) make the point that in interpersonal interactions performing actions that are similar to and coordinated with those of another person is a critical determinant of successful social exchange.

Movement-matching behaviour in cross-cultural encounters can be a sign that the participants feel comfortable speaking to each other. According to von Raffler-Engel (1988), its occurrence in cross-cultural encounters may indicate mutual empathy and be a sign that successful communication has been achieved. Synchronized movements can also be observed among very young children, which suggest that the behaviour may be a basic element of communication.

Silence

Silence, like smiling, is an ambiguous behaviour and can have a range of meanings in various cultural contexts. In Japan and some other Asian countries, silence may signal the rejection of a business proposition or a sales offer. In cross-cultural negotiations silence is sometimes used as a tactic used to put pressure on the other side to make a concession or to modify a proposal. At other times silence may simply be a sign that a speaker 'is still in the business of completing a reply' (Goffman, 1974: 543) and perhaps is considering the best line of action to take.

Paralanguage

The nonverbal elements of speech – paralanguage – include voice quality, emotion, rhythm, intonation, and stress. These elements give to the human voice a fascination quite distinct from the meaning of the words. Doob (1961) refers to an African man who listened to BBC News every night without being able to understand a word of it, but he remained fascinated by the voice of the newsreaders. According to Raffler-Engel (1988), studies show that 80 per cent of radio audiences tend to attribute temperamental and physical traits to radio speakers on the basis of the sound of the voice alone.

But the paralinguistic aspects of speech are not mere adjuncts to communication. Sometimes they are the message. Even in the absence of visual cues (as in a telephone conversation, say) the paralinguistic aspects of speech adequately convey the speaker's thoughts and feelings and sometimes convey a message which totally contradicts the words uttered.

Cultural norms ascribe different meanings to various paralinguistic features, such as tone of voice, loudness, and intensity. In the United States dominance tends to be indicated by loud, low-pitched, and rapid speech, but in Germany by soft, low-pitched, and breathy speech (Scherer, 1979). In some cultures, rapid intense bursts of speech indicate anger, but not in some Arab or Chinese societies where they constantly occur in normal conversation.

The matching of paralinguistic features of speech is very common (Raffler-Engel, 1988). During a cross-cultural conversation, for instance, if a person from one culture lowers her voice her conversational partner from another culture is likely to respond by also lowering her voice. If one participant begins to speak faster the other person also begins to speak faster. This matching behaviour may occur because of mutual liking or empathy between the individuals. An alternative explanation is that one of the individuals is recognized as dominant and is allowed to dictate the rhythm and emphasis pattern of the conversation (Raffler-Engel, 1988).

KEY POINTS

1. Nonverbal communication is important in international business. In cross-cultural business discussions, attitudes to a product or a business proposal can be accurately assessed by observing the nonverbal behaviours of participants. Body posture, facial expressions, gestures, eye contact, and other nonverbal behaviours reveal participants' real feelings about the proposal as opposed to

what they *say* they feel. In cross-cultural business meetings, even if participants try to hide their dislike of someone their negative feelings may seep through in spite of themselves.

2. In cross-cultural business discussions verbal communication may not accurately convey what participants mean. One reason is that people from different cultures have different native tongues and different communicative norms and meaning gets diluted in translation. Another reason is that in business discussions people can and do lie, can and do deliberately mislead. But nonverbal communication usually tells the truth, and conveys feelings and attitudes more accurately than words alone. At other times nonverbal behaviours clarify a speaker's meaning by clarifying or correcting his words.

3. Micromessages are the subtle and often subconscious nonverbal messages that people in all cultures transmit to each other. When managers send negative micromessages to employees the effect is to discourage and impair employee performance. *Positive* micromessages, by contrast, have the effect of boosting employees' morale and encourage employees' commitment to organisational goals. Managers who learn the skills of sending positive micromessages have been found to be successful in motivating employees from a wide range of cultures.

4. Cross-cultural business communication has to be adapted to the communication preferences and characteristics of particular cultures and local markets. Global brands are often cited as examples of global business success, but in the great majority of countries *local brands* are the most trusted and the most frequently purchased. Thus the most popular car in France is Renault; in Germany and Austria it is Volkswagen; in the Czech Republic, Skoda; in India, Maruti; and in most of East Asia, Toyota or Honda. Thus cross-cultural business communication needs to be calculated and differentiated. There is no universal model of cross-cultural business communication which can be applied at all times in all countries.

5. The paralinguistic aspects of speech, such as tone of voice, loudness, and intensity, are not mere adjuncts to communication: sometimes they *are* the message. Even in the absence of visual cues (as in a telephone conversation, say) the paralinguistic aspects of speech adequately convey the speaker's thoughts and feelings. Sometimes they totally contradict the words uttered and convey the true message. However, cultural norms ascribe different meanings to various paralinguistic features. In the United States, for instance, dominance tends to be indicated by loud, low-pitched, and rapid speech whereas in Germany it is indicated by soft, low-pitched, and breathy speech.

6. Many aspects of nonverbal communication are cultural products and so liable to be misunderstood by members of other cultures. The Chinese method of apologizing by bowing and smiling, for instance, may be interpreted by foreign visitors as a sign of insincerity and untrustworthiness. Japanese smiling is another culturally influenced behaviour which is frequently misunderstood by foreign visitors. Japanese people often smile to mask pain or distress since it is culturally unacceptable to inflict the unpleasantness of grief on others.

QUESTIONS FOR DISCUSSION AND WRITTEN ASSIGNMENTS

1. Why is nonverbal communication liable to be misinterpreted in cross-cultural encounters? Give examples of misinterpretation from your own experience.
2. Give examples from your own experience and observation of the cultural variability of gestures and facial expressions. Explain how this variability can lead to misunderstanding in cross-cultural interactions.
3. Give examples of positive and negative micromessages. Why can the practice of habitually sending negative micromessages to some employees undermine morale?

BIBLIOGRAPHY

Aguinis, H, Simonsen, MM and Pierce, CA. Effects of nonverbal behaviour on perceptions of power bases. *Journal of Social Psychology*, 138 (4), 1998, pp. 455–469.

Albers-Miller, ND. Designing cross-cultural advertising research: a closer look at paired comparisons. *International Marketing Review*, 13 (5), 1996, 59–75.

Albright, L et al., Cross-cultural consensus in personality judgments. *Journal of Personality and Social Psychology*, 73, 1997, 270–280.

Anderson, C et al., Emotional convergence between people over time. *Journal of Personality and Social Psychology*, 85 (5), 2003, pp. 1054–1068.

Argyle, M. *Bodily Communication*, 2nd ed., International Universities Press, 1988.

Beaupre, MG and Hess, U. An ingroup advantage for confidence in emotion recognition judgments. *Personality and Social Psychology Bulleting*, 32 (1), 2006, 16–26.

Bennett, MJ (ed.), *Basic Concepts of Intercultural Communication*. Intercultural Press, 1998.

Birdwhistell, RL. *Kinesics and Context: Essays on Body Motion Communication*. University of Pennsylvania Press, 1970.

Bijlstra, G et al., The social face of emotion recognition: evaluations versus stereotypes. *Journal of Experimental Social Psychology*, 46 (4), 2010, 657–663.

Brault, GJ. Kinesics and the classroom: some typical French gestures. *French Review* 36, 1990, 374–382.

Burgoon, JK. Buller, DB and Woodall, WG. *Nonverbal Communication: The Unspoken Dialogue*. Harper & Row, 1989, p. 9–10.

Chaplin, WF et al., Handshaking, gender, personality and firdst impressions. *Journal of Personality and Social Psychology*, 79, 2000, 110–117.

Darwin, C. *Expression of the Emotions in Man and Animals*. John Murray, 1872.

DePaulo, BM and Friedman, HS. Nonverbal communication. In Gilbert, DT et al. (eds), *Handbook of Social Psychology* (Vol. 2), 4th ed. McGraw-Hill, 1998, pp. 3–40.

Doob, LW. *Communication in Africa*. Yale UP, 1961.

Dovidio, JF et al., On the nature of prejudice: automatic and controlled processes. *Journal of Experimental Social Psychology*, 33, 1997, 510–540.

Eerdmans, SL. A review of John J Gumperz's current contributions to interactional sociolinguistics. In SL Eerdmans et al. (eds), *Language and Interaction*. Jorn Benjamins Publishing, 2003, 85–103.

Elfenbein, HA and Ambady, N. On the universality and cultural specificity of emotion recognition: a meta-analysis. *Psychological Bulletin*, 128, 2002, 203–235.

Ekman, P. Facial expression and emotion. *American Psychologist*, 48, 1993, 384–392.

Erickson, F and Shultz, J. *The Counsellor as Gatekeeper: Social Interaction in Interviews*. Academic Press, 1982.

Fast, J. *Body Language*. Pan Books, London, 1971.

Ferraro, GP. *The Cultural Dimension of International Business*, 3rd ed. Prentice Hall, 1998, p. 69.

Findlay, MS. *Language and Communication: A Cross-cultural Encyclopedia*, ABC-CLIO, 1998.

Finnegan, R. *Communication: The Multiple Methods of Human Interconnection*. Routledge, 2002.

Gallois, C and Callan, V. *Communication and Culture: A Guide for Practice*. Wiley, 1997.

Goffman, E. *Encounters*. Bobbs-Merrill, 1961a.

Goffman, E. *Asylums*. Anchor, 1961b.

Goffman, E. *Frame Analysis*. Harper & Row, 1974, p. 543.

Guerrero, LK and Floyd, K. *Nonverbal Communication in Close Relationships*. Erlbaum, 2006.

Guirdham, M. *Communicating Across Cultures at Work*, 2nd ed. Palgrave Macmillan, 2005.

Hall, ET. *The Anthropology of Manners*, Scic Aman, 192, 1955, 84–90.

Henley, NM and LaFrance, M. Gender as culture: difference and dominance in nonverbal behaviour. In A Wolfgang (ed.), *Nonverbal Behaviour: Perspectives, Applications, Intercultural Insights*. Hogrefe, 1992, pp. 351–371.

Humphreys, M and Brown, AD. Dress and identity: a Turkish case study. *Journal of Management Studies*, 39 (7), 2002, 927–952.

Izard, CE. *The Face of Emotion*. Appleton-Century-Crofts, 1971.

Joy, RO. Cultural and procedural difficulties that influence business strategies and operations in the People's R of C. *Advanced Management Journal*, 29, 1989, 30.

Juslin, PN and Laukka, P. Communication of emotions in vocal expression and musical performance: different channels, same code? *Psychological Bulletin*, 129, 2003, 770–814.

Kelly, JC. *A Philosophy of Communication*. Centre for the study of communications and culture, 1981.

Kendon, A. Movement coordination in social interaction. *Acta Psychologica*, 32, 1970, 100–125.

Lakin, JL and Chartrand, TL. Using unconscious behavioural mimicry to create affiliation and rapport. *Psychological Science*, 14, 2003, 334–338.

Levensen, RW et al., Emotion and autonomic nervous system activity in the Minangkabau of West Sumatra. *Journal of Personality and Social Psychology*, 62, 972–988, 1992.

Mason, MF et al., The look of love: gaze shifts and person perception. *Psychological Science*, 16, 2005, 236–239.

Matsumoto, D et al., Mapping expressive differences across the world: the relationship between emotional display rules and individualism versus collectivism. *Journal of Cross-cultural Psychology*, 39 (1), 2008, 55–74.

McCaskey, MB. The hidden messages mans send. *Harvard Business Review*, November–December 1979, 135–148.

Mehrabian, A. *Silent Messages*, 2nd ed. Wadsworth, 1981.

Morsbach, H. Aspects of nonverbal communication in Japan. In LA Samovar and RE Porter (eds), *Intercultural Communication: A Reader*. Wadsworth, 1982, pp. 300–316.

Morsbach, H. Nonverbal communication and hierarchical relationships: the case of bowing in Japan. In Poyatos, F. (ed.), *Cross-cultural Perspectives in Nonverbal Communication*. Hogrefe, 1988, pp. 189–199.

Mortimer, K and Grierson, S. The relationship between culture and advertising appeals for services. *Journal of Marketing Communications*, 16 (3), 2010, 149–162.

Negrin, L. The self as image: a critical appraisal of postmodern theories of fashion. *Theory, Culture and Society*, 16 (3) 1999, 99–118.

Noller, P. *Nonverbal Communication and Marital Interaction*, Pergamon, 1984.

Novinger, T. *Intercultural Communication: A Practical Guide*. University of Texas Press, 2001.

Pall, GS and McGrath, RG. *Institutional Memory Goes Digital*. HBR, February 2009, p. 27.

Pierce, CM. Contemporary psychiatry: Racial perspectives on the past and future. In A Kales et al. (eds), *The Mosaic of Contemporary Psychiatry in Perspective*. Springer-Verlag, 1992, pp. 99–109.

Rafaeli, A and Pratt, MG. Tailored meanings: on the meaning and impact of organisational dress. *Academy of Management Review*, 18, 1993, 32–55.

von Raffler-Engel, W. The impact of covert factors in cross-cultural communication. In F Poyatos (ed.), *Cross-cultural Perspectives in Nonverbal Communication*. Hogrefe, 1988, pp. 80–90.

Rosenthal, R et al., Measuring sensitivity to nonverbal communication. In A Wolfgang (ed.), *Nonverbal Behaviour: Applications and Cultural Implications*. Academic Press, 1979, 159–174.

Scherer, KR. Personality markers in speech. In KR Scherer and H Giles (eds), *Social Markers in Speech*, CUP, 1979, pp. 147–209.

Scollon, R and Scollon, SW. *Intercultural Communication: A Discourse Approach*, 2nd ed. Blackwell, 2001.

Shaffer, DR, Crepaz, N and Chien-Ru Sun, Physical attractiveness stereotyping in cross-cultural perspective. *C-c Psychy*, 31 (5), September 2000, 557.

Stewart, GL et al., Exploring the handshake in employment interviews. *Journal of Applied Psychology*, 93 (5), 2008, 1139–1146.

Thomas, DC. *Essentials of International Management: A Cross-cultural Perspective*. Sage, 2002.

Thomas, DC and Inkson, K. *Cultural Intelligence: People Skills for Global Business*. Berrett-Koehler, 2004.

Trail, TE et al., Interracial roommate relationships: negotiating daily interactions. *Personality and Social Psychology Bulleting*, 35 (6), 2009, 671–684.

Watson, OM and Graves, TD. Quantitative research in proxemic behaviour. *American Anthropologist*, 68, 1966, 971–985.

Watson, OM. *Proxemic Behaviour*. Mouton, 1970.

Wirth, JH et al., Eye gaze as relational attribution: averted eye gaze leads to feelings of ostracism and relational devaluation. *Personality and Social Psychology Bulletin*, 36 (7), 2010, 869–882.

Young, S. Micromessaging: Why Great Leadership Is Beyond Words. McGraw-Hill, 2006.

Prejudice and stereotypes

5

INTRODUCTION

Prejudice is dislike or hatred of a person or group formed without reason. It is culturally conditioned since it is rooted in a person's early socialization. It distorts perception and communication and creates tensions and conflict in cross-cultural exchanges. People may become prejudiced to find an outlet for their aggressive feelings. Prejudice and conflict between groups occurs when they compete for housing, welfare, education, space, or other scare resources. Prejudice towards immigrants commonly takes the form of blaming them for job shortages, inadequate health and education provision, crime, and various other social ills.

Ethnocentric individuals believe in the general superiority of their own cultural group and the inferiority of most others and thus tend to be prejudiced towards many other groups. Ethnocentric speech, which belittles or disparages the other person or the other person's culture, sometimes occurs in cross-cultural inter-actions. Xenophobia, based on a strong and irrational fear of most other ethnic and cultural groups, is the extreme form of ethnocentrism.

According to modern racism theory, traditional blatant racism is being replaced by 'modern racism'. This is typically expressed through discrimination with regard to school admission criteria, housing eligibility, access to health and other services, but especially with regard to employment. In the work-place, employees perceived as 'different' is some way often become the targets of prejudice and discrimination and may be excluded from informal networks of co-workers, receive poor and inaccurate performance appraisals, and suffer from lack of constructive feedback from their supervisors. Absenteeism is a common form of escape behaviour for victims of workplace discrimination.

Both in the workplace and in the wider society stereotypes may be used to jus-tify prejudice and discrimination on the assumption that the stereotype reflects inherent characteristics of the stereotyped group reflects reality. When used in cross-cultural interactions stereotypes distort the communication and damage cross-cultural relationships. Stereotypes also play a more positive role by facilitating initial communication between people from different cultural backgrounds. Often the only framework they have for initial interactions is the stereotype each person holds about the other person's culture.

Hostile national stereotypes may influence relationships between governments. Neither parliaments nor electors may realize that the mental images they hold of another country are biased and inaccurate. By stereotyping a country serious errors of judgment can be made, leading to hostile relations or worse between governments.

WHAT IS PREJUDICE?

Prejudice in business

A frequent dilemma for consultants carrying out assignments in a foreign country is whether to give the client the right advice or acceptable advice. But acceptable advice often turns out to be advice that echoes the client's own fixed prejudices. That was the conclusion reached by consultants who had been called into a textile plant in South Africa that was losing money.

> After examining all the evidence they were convinced that the correct solution was for the company to go into liquidation and they said so when they presented their report to the CEO. The CEO reacted angrily, threw the report across the table and said a management buyout was the obvious answer to the company's problems. The consultants had not given him what he wanted, and he ordered them to leave the building.

As the example shows, impartial advice may be seen as a threat when it counters a person's fixed prejudices. Farley (2000) identifies three distinct kinds of prejudice:

- *cognitive prejudice* refers to what people strongly believe is true;
- *affective prejudice* springs from feelings and emotions and refers to people's likes and dislikes;
- *conative prejudice* refers to how people are inclined to behave.

The three types of prejudice don't all have to be present in a particular individual – but in the South African company they possibly were.

Prejudice in everyday life

Prejudice can be defined as 'dislike' or 'hatred' of a person or group formed without reason. Usually prejudice is rooted in a person's early socialization and reinforced by contact with other prejudiced people. It passes from person to person like a contagious disease. For instance, people exposed to racist opinions themselves develop racist opinions (Blanchard et al., 1991). Prejudice distorts perception and communication and accounts for many of the tensions and conflicts that occur in cross-cultural exchanges.

Guerrero and Floyd (2006) note that prejudice can influence a person's *speech* and typically is characterized by awkward and disjointed speech patterns and unwillingness to self-disclose; and that prejudice also influences a person's *nonverbal* behaviour. Nonverbal expressions of prejudice include standing well back from the target of the prejudice, avoiding eye contact, and other distancing behaviours associated with dislike.

But not all prejudiced feeling is negative. *Positive* prejudice is communicated through affability, willingness to self-disclose, showing sympathetic interest in the other person, and is expressed by such nonverbal behaviours as smiling, mutual gaze, and leaning towards the other person, and other signals associated with liking (Guerrero and Floyd, 2006). Physically attractive people may benefit from positive prejudice because people consistently attribute more desirable qualities to physically attractive persons than to unattractive persons (Shaffer et al., 2000).

Targets of prejudice

In a classic text, Allport (1954) described prejudice as *general attitude,* thus obscuring the great variety of negative emotions that prejudiced individuals direct at their targets. The emotions include *anger* (e.g. directed at foreigners who criticize a country's conventions and institutions); *fear* (e.g. directed at members of minority groups and their distinctive lifestyles); *disgust* (e.g. directed homosexuals, alcoholics, Rastafarians, and others); and *resentment* (directed at new immigrants who will compete for scarce jobs (Cottrell and Neuberg, 2005).

Ethnic and racial minorities, religious minorities, the disabled, sexual minorities, and other minority groups are frequent targets of prejudice in many countries. Prejudice against immigrants and even the children of immigrants occurs frequently. For instance, von Grunigen et al. (2010) investigated peer acceptance and victimization of both immigrant and Swiss children in kindergarten classes in various German-speaking parts of Switzerland. Immigrant children – that is children with parents of foreign nationality – were less accepted by peers and were more often victimized than Swiss children. An important reason for non-acceptance of immigrant children was their lack of competence in using the German language.

Opposition to prejudice takes various forms in different cultures. In Western countries, for instance, feminists denounce male domination and stress the need for sexual freedom. This, however, is not necessarily the stance taken by feminists in developing countries. Nawal El Sadaawi, one of the first Egyptian writers to deal with the theme of women in traditional societies, told a British journalist: 'When you hear shooting every day, when you're bombed by Israeli planes, when you might be killed at any time, how can you bother whether you have an orgasm or not?'

Blatant and subtle prejudice

Prejudice can be blatant or subtle (Pettigrew and Mertens, 1995). Mimicry, staring, avoiding communication are examples of subtle prejudice. Blatant prejudice is more openly hostile or insulting. When prejudice is both blatant and organised, as in Nazi Germany or South Africa in the apartheid years, propaganda and the media may be used to whip up hate campaigns against targeted groups – often with disastrous results. For instance, victims of blatant prejudice and hate campaigns often suffer various painful emotional and physiological reactions, including lowered self-esteem (Nielsen, 2002). Mullen and Smyth (2004) note that ethnic immigrants to the United States who are subjected to hate-speech have higher suicide rates than other immigrants.

Stigma

Stigmatization is a blatant form of prejudice that consists of discrediting people because they are racially different or different in some other way (Goffman, 1963). One of the burdens carried by stigmatized people is that they are never sure whether they will be accepted or rejected by 'normal' people. Stigmatized interracial couples have revealed to researchers the pain and distress caused by being unable to discuss their problems with family members (Donovan, 2004).

Victims of stigmatization often seek the company of similar others, such as members of the same racial group with the same stigmatized background. Simply being with similar others increases the value of the shared and undervalued racial identity and leads to greater self-esteem (Postmes and Branscombe, 2002). An important coping strategy for stigmatized people is to talk about the stigma and the problems it causes with supportive friends or relatives. Thus male and female homosexuals in one study reported greater well-being on days when they disclosed – as opposed to concealed – their sexual orientation to others (Beals et al., 2009). When stigmatized people choose to conceal their stigma the consequences can be disastrous. For example, gay men who concealed their sexual identity had poorer immune function, progressed more rapidly to an AIDS diagnosis, and died sooner than men who disclosed their sexual orientation more widely (Cole et al., 1996).

Victims of stigmatization may sometimes inflict on others the treatment they themselves receive (Shapiro and Neuberg, 2008). Perhaps one of the few ways in which a stigmatized person is able to experience feelings of power and status is through persecuting others. In one study black participants were more likely than white participants to recommend committing to a mental institution an individual described as depressed and emotionally disturbed (Galanis and Jones, 1986).

Ethnocentrism

'Ethnocentrism' (culture-centred) is the term used to describe people's habit of using their own culture's values as the standard when viewing other groups (Triandis, 1994). Ethnocentric individuals perceive their own cultural or ethnic group as superior to most other cultural or ethnic groups. The greater the cultural difference between their own cultural group and another group, the greater the potential for prejudice towards the other group (Bennett, 1998). As can be gathered from the history of Jews in Europe or from the apartheid years in South Africa, extreme forms of ethnocentrism lead to prejudice, discrimination, and suppression.

Ethnocentric people tend to feel scorn or hostility towards members of other national and ethnic groups. They believe that the ideas and beliefs of their own culture are rational and correct and that people from other cultures who do things differently are obviously wrong. It is 'obviously' wrong for men to wear make-up or earrings, for instance. Muslim women who wear the veil are 'obviously' oppressed. People who do not conform to normal behaviour are 'obviously' strange and contact with them should be avoided. As an example of ethnocentric attitudes, Pell (1997) cites Americans who evaluate other countries by how closely they resemble the United States – not only in their social institutions but also with regard to kitchens, plumbers, dress, eating conventions, and other details.

Ethnocentric communication

Ethnocentric people tend to be intolerant and closed-minded when communicating with people from other cultures (Baldwin and Hecht, 1995). According to social identity theory (Tajfel and Turner, 1986), ethnocentrism is a means of increasing self-esteem. Individuals strive for a positive social identity by comparing their own ingroups with outgroups, and ethnocentrism is the consequence.

Common types of ethnocentric speech used when communicating with members of other cultures, identified by Lukens (1978), include:

- speech conveying indifference or lack of concern for the other person or the person's culture;
- disparaging, derisive, or belittling speech;
- speech aimed at avoiding or limiting future interaction with the person.

Ethnocentric people tend to disapprove of foreigners and to hold negative stereotypes of other cultures. They often feel uncomfortable and anxious during cross-cultural interactions causing communication blockages to occur (Stephan et al., 1999). Merely hearing a foreign accent may trigger negative feelings and judgments about the ability or character of a person from another culture.

Patronizing speech

For effective cross-cultural communication it is important not to sound superior, to communicate on terms of equality, but ethnocentric individuals find it difficult to communicate in this way. In cross-situations, ethnocentric attitudes lead to misunderstanding and conflict because assumptions are made about the other person and the other person's culture that are inaccurate and insulting and that lead to patronizing or demeaning speech forms.

Research shows that ethnocentric people tend to disapprove of the speaking styles of members of other cultures. For instance, a person with a foreign accent is often perceived as less competent and harder to understand than a person with a native accent using exactly the same words (Giles and Coupland, 1991). In cross-cultural interactions a foreign accent may trigger critical judgments and stereotyped reactions that lead to the other person losing status and prestige (Bdzinski, 1992). In ways such as these, ethnocentric attitudes sour relations with members of other cultures.

Communicating with ethnocentric individuals can be an uncomfortable experience for members of other cultures, and ethnocentric individuals themselves may find cross-cultural contact uncomfortable. Ethnocentric Dutch people, for instance, experience anxiety and irritation when communicating with members of various immigrant groups (Dijker, 1987).

Xenophobia

Xenophobia is the extreme form of ethnocentrism and it causes people to fear most of other ethnic and cultural groups (in the same way as a contagious disease is feared). Some political parties in several European countries appeal to xenophobic sentiments in the electorate – calling, for instance, for the repatriation of immigrants. In Japan the strong cultural and religious concentration on conformity and tradition generates suspicion of foreigners (Ross and Shortreed, 1990). The 700,000 persons of Korean origin who live in Japan are reportedly the objects of deeply entrenched social discrimination. According to various newspaper reports, there are an estimated 100,000 camouflage-wearing, xenophobic right-wingers in Japan. They are fiercely conservative and committed to violence to press an agenda they equate with patriotism. The groups believe that Japan has apologized too much for the Second World War.

Cultural relativism: antidote to ethnocentrism

Hofstede (1994) presents a strong case for cultural relativism. The cultural relativist approach is based on the assumption that no one approach to basic cultural questions can be considered the best. The best approach to the question of how children should be raised, for instance, or to the issue of role of women in society, depends on the particular cultural context. There is no absolute right or wrong. As the classical anthropologists have shown, each culture has its own unique way of seeing the world and that one culture is not generally superior to another.

Unlike ethnocentrism, cultural relativism encourages an accepting and under-standing attitude towards other cultures, and thus creates the conditions for successful cross-cultural communication and healthy cross-cultural relationships. It frees us from being locked up in our cultural cages, enables us to view the world differently (Kabagarama, 1993). Instead of rushing to pass judgment on members of other cultures – the way they speak and dress, their eating habits, and so on – cultural relativists suspend judgment and try to understand people by their own standards.

Although some cultural practices are easier to accept than others, for cultural relativists no culture is better or worse than another in a general, overall sense. The practice of widespread tree-felling in parts of Africa, for example, simply reflects a level of economic development and it is easy to understand the prac-tice. On the other hand, practices that violate fundamental human rights, such as female circumcision, or putting to death by stoning women who commit adul-tery, are less easy to accept. Ruth Benedict, the American anthropologist and early supporter of cultural relativism, was forced to change her relativist stance during the Second World War. She could not bring herself to believe that Nazi culture was just as valid as any other, and eventually came to believe that any culture that works against basic human goals is antihuman and evil.

RELEVANT THEORIES

Range of approaches

Several theories have been developed which help to explain the nature of prejudice, why it occurs, and the negative impact it makes in cross-cultural interactions. Relevant theories include:

- Authoritarian personality theory
- Scapegoat theory
- Social identity theory
- Realistic conflict theory

Authoritarian personality theory

Adorno et al. (1950) argue that certain personality traits predispose some indi-viduals to be open to totalitarian and antidemocratic ideas and therefore to be prone to many kinds of prejudice. Authoritarian personality types tend to be rigid in their opinions and beliefs; hostile to people of inferior status, and obedient to those of higher status. The researchers reported the results of psychometric test-ing and clinical interviews that revealed aspects of the childhood of participants in the study. Many participants with authoritarian personalities had been brought up by very strict parents or guardians.

A weakness of authoritarian personality theory is that a harsh parenting style does not always produce prejudiced offspring. More important, many prejudiced people do not conform to the authoritarian personality type. Moreover, the theory fails to explain why prejudiced people target certain groups (e.g. immigrants) and not others.

Scapegoat theory

Scapegoat theory (Weatherly, 1961) explains the phenomenon of racial prejudice and other kinds of prejudice by linking the expression of prejudice to a person's frustration and aggression.

> Weatherly generated a sense of frustration in students then asked them to write stories based on given pictures. When the people in the pictures were given Jewish names, students with anti-Semitic tendencies wrote stories that included aggression towards the Jewish characters.

The theory assumes that people become prejudiced towards a person or group – the scapegoat – to find an outlet for their anxiety and aggression. The scapegoats selected are usually those who cannot, for whatever reason, immediately resist or retaliate. It is therefore safe to pick on them. Minority groups and immigrants are often selected as scapegoats. The Nazis, for instance, used Jews as scapegoats for all of their country's economic and political problems. Szasz (1997) uses the practice of scapegoating to explain the hostility directed towards the mentally ill.

The practice of scapegoating increases when people are seeking an outlet for their upset and anger. It is an effective, if temporary, means of achieving group solidarity and it can become a powerful propaganda tool – as the scapegoating of whites in Zimbabwe demonstrates.

Social identity theory

According to social identity theory (Tajfel and Turner, 1986), people see their own groups (ingroups) in a positive light, and groups they don't belong to (outgroups) in a negative, prejudiced way. Positive prejudice tends to be felt towards ingroups while negative prejudice tends to be felt towards outgroups. In everyday life, membership of outgroups may be based on race, nationality, religion, language spoken, and so on. It is widely recognized that the tendency of people to be prejudiced against members of outgroups is one of the most basic problems of cross-cultural communication.

Merely dividing people into groups generates ingroup/outgroup prejudices, as training consultants demonstrated by splitting delegates attending a management training course into two groups.

> Red name tags are given to one group, green to the other. The groups then complete questionnaires in sight of each other. There is no interaction, yet within minutes each group experiences hostile feelings towards the other group. When one group comprises only black members and the other only whites, the prejudiced feelings are intensified.

Realistic conflict theory

According to realistic conflict theory (Stephan et al., 1999), conflict occurs between different racial, ethnic, or national groups when they compete for housing, welfare, education, space, or other scarce resources, or pose any other kind of real threat to each other.

Sherif et al. (1961) placed 22 boys into two groups which competed with each other for medals, knives, and other rewards. Each group regarded its own members *positively* (e.g. as friendly, courageous) but perceived members of the other group *negatively* (e.g. as untrustworthy, liars). The study demonstrated that competition between groups for the same goal generates intergroup prejudice and conflict.

Where immigrants are perceived as a threat, prejudice commonly takes the form of blaming them for job shortages, inadequate health and education provision, crime, and various other social ills (Florack et al., 2003). Thus, Europeans who compete with non-European immigrants in the labour market hold the strongest anti-immigrant prejudices (Gang et al., 2002). The security needs of members of the majority culture who feel under threat often lead them to stress their own cultural identity in an attempt to protect their own cultural values. They may, for instance, adopt a minimum-contact strategy with immigrant groups, or support political campaigns aimed at forcing immigrants to adopt the majority group's language and culture.

One of the weaknesses of realistic conflict theory is that it fails to explain why people can be deeply prejudiced against people from groups they have never met and with whom they are not in competition for scarce resources.

PREJUDICE IN A CROSS-CULTURAL CONTEXT

Types of prejudice

Common types of prejudice that affect the interaction and outcomes of cross-cultural communication are:

- Prejudice towards foreigners
- Prejudice towards minority groups
- Prejudice in the workplace
- Racial prejudice
- Religious prejudice

Prejudice towards foreigners

Cultural difference is at the root of anti-foreigner prejudice. Foreigners have different eating habits and they may dress differently. They react differently – they may smile when they hear painful news, for instance. Such differences help to explain why communicating with foreigners can be stressful – indeed, people have experienced threat-like cardiac responses as a result of stress brought on by cross-cultural interaction (Blascovich et al., 2001). Some people avoid communicating with foreigners altogether in order to stave off the anxiety that face-to-face contact would arouse (Plant and Devine, 2003).

Simply hearing a foreign accent can generate prejudice. For instance, persons with a foreign accent may be perceived as less competent and harder to understand than a person with a native accent using exactly the same words (Giles and Coupland, 1991).

Another common source of anti-foreigner prejudice is ignorance of foreign cultures. When a Canadian IT consultant, visiting France for the first time, went to see a French doctor in his clinic she noticed that the receptionist always used the imperative form of the verb when showing patients to the waiting room.

> The receptionist would say in an authoritative tone without smiling: 'You will wait here'. The Canadian perceived the receptionist as unfriendly and aggressive, although if she had known a little more about French communication styles she would have realised that in France using the imperative is a normal way of making a request.

Any French observer would have felt that the secretary was taking good care of the patients.

Ignorance of a foreign culture was a major factor contributing to the prejudice and discrimination experienced by Malay students in Britain, as described by Swami (2009). However, all of the students were Muslims and this may have been a contributing cause, together with English language difficulties and the resulting minimal contact with British people.

Ironically, Malaysians in Malaysia are themselves not free from anti-foreigner prejudice. According to The Asia Times (3 March 2007), politicians, the general public, and the state-controlled media blame foreign workers for recent crime waves. Their strident demands for 'tough' new measures include confining foreign workers to their ramshackle quarters, even during their days off. Anti-foreigner prejudice underpins the demands since, in reality, only about 2 per cent of criminal incidents in Malaysia are directly attributable to foreign workers.

Prejudice towards minority groups

In many countries minority groups become the targets of prejudice (Gardikiotis et al., 2004). Anti-immigrant prejudice can be seen as a specific form of bias against minority group members. A 2003 survey of about 30,000 people from across Europe revealed that 38 per cent were opposed to normal civil rights for legally established immigrants (EUAFR, 2005: 12). Older adults tend to show greater prejudice than younger adults towards a variety of minority and immigrant groups (Herek, 2000). According to Radvansky et al. (2010), this may be because older people have difficulty inhibiting their unintentionally activated *negative stereotypes*.

People who strongly agree with the Protestant work ethic tend to be prejudiced towards racial minorities in the United States; and in Australia support tough-minded solutions to unemployment, including reducing unemployment benefits (West and Levy, 2002). The 1948 Universal Declaration of Human Rights has nothing at all to say about minority group *rights* – it recognizes only individual and not collective or group rights (Fottrell and Bowring, 1999). An example of a minority right which, in numerous cases is denied, is the right of a minority group to have publicly funded education in its mother tongue.

Prejudice in the workplace

Employees who are perceived as 'different' is some obvious way such as speech or skin colour or dress are often the targets of prejudice and discrimination in the workplace (Ogbonna and Harris, 2006). For example, co-workers may form negative stereotypes of Muslim female employees because the headscarf is a visible marker of difference.

Employees who are perceived as different – perhaps because of skin colour or inadequate language skills – may be excluded from conversations and job-related information, and barred from entry to certain job categories (Larkey, 1996). They are often segregated from informal networks of co-workers, suffer from lack of constructive feedback from supervisors, and receive poor or inaccurate performance evaluations (Stangor and Thompson, 2002). For victims of workplace discrimination, absenteeism becomes a common form of escape behaviour.

Much anecdotal evidence suggests that in many large organisations, the effective management of culturally diverse employees has low priority; and certainly appropriate effective anti-discrimination policies are rarely implemented. In some Australian workplaces, discrimination towards Asian employees takes the form of not adequately recognizing Asian qualifications (Parr and Guo, 2005).

Exclusion from decisions

Managers form stronger relationships with some employees than with others, and in many firms an inner circle of trusted subordinates often takes shape whose members often come from the same ethnic or cultural background as the manager (Burris et al., 2009). When this is the case, employees from cultures and ethnic groups that are different from the manager's find themselves in an outer circle where they may experience lower levels of interaction and support from their manager – and receive lower performance ratings – than do members of the inner circle (Stauffer and Buckley, 2005).

The multicultural nature of the modern workforce makes an inclusive style of management essential for the successful motivation of diverse human capital. Managers with an inclusive style of management signal their acceptance of employees from diverse backgrounds by establishing good relationships with them and insisting on norms of equality and inclusion (Nishii and Mayer, 2009).

Inclusive, non-discriminatory management consists of ensuring that all employees (not just the inner circle) participate in decision-making and have access to sensitive work information (O'Hara et al., 1994). Treating employees in even-handed way regardless of race or cultural background is at the core of effective leadership in a multicultural workplace.

Case study

MINI-CASE: Problems with the decision-making process

Employees in some organisations may be excluded from the decision-making process because they are not members of the boss's inner circle. The result of this kind of discrimination is that suboptimum decisions are sometimes taken. That was the case at a cereals-processing company in a Baltic Republic.

The company's workforce comprised both Russian and local employees. When a two-man committee, consisting of the general manager and a fellow-Latvian, was set up to select capital investment proposals for funding, the two managers felt they knew instinctively which were the most urgent projects. And sometimes they supported their gut-feeling with a rough payback calculation.

So the managers were surprised when the Financial Controller, a Russian, complained that the selection procedure for investment projects needed to be refined, and that he thought it was essential that more managers should participate in the process.

Questions:

1. *Was the Financial Controller right? Why should the capital project selection process be refined?*
2. *Should more managers be involved in the selection process? In what other ways could the process be improved?*
3. *What effect would improved selection procedures have on the capital investment programme?*

Racial prejudice

Racial prejudice, which is based on belief in the superiority of a particular race and the inferiority of other races, seems to exist in most, if not all, societies.

- The European Commission (1997) admits that racism, xenophobia, and anti-Semitism exist throughout Europe. The European Social Survey of 2002 found that 52 per cent of European citizens oppose immigration of people of a different racial or ethnic group, and that 27 per cent would mind if somebody from a different ethnic group married a close relative.

- Racism is endemic to US institutions which, according to Feagin (2006), reflect the racial hierarchy created in the seventeenth century. All black participants in a US study had experienced numerous expressions of overt racism (Rosenblatt et al., 1995).
- A study carried out in Britain found widespread prejudice towards blacks and minority groups (Dustmann and Preston, 2001). Men were more prejudiced than women, and the less well educated were more prejudiced than people with more education. Older people tended to be the most prejudiced and strongly opposed race relations legislation.
- In a US study people expressed harsher anti-immigrant prejudice when the immigrant was of Mexican descent and had accumulated several parking tickets than when the immigrant was of English-Canadian descent – irrespective of the number of parking tickets accumulated (Short and Magana, 2002).

Conspicuous difference

The scientific journal *Science* (July 2005) notes the ease with which people learn to fear people from other racial groups and concludes that everybody has an inbuilt tendency to fear people who are conspicuously different from themselves. Such fears translate easily into racial prejudice – and blacks can be as racially prejudiced as other racial groups. When a 'wall of shame' appeared overnight on an American university campus it attracted considerable media attention. The wall, which named and shamed interracial couples in the university, was the work of a group of African Americans who strongly disapproved of interracial relationships.

Unconscious racism is a potent barrier to cross-cultural friendships. When tens of thousands of people tested themselves for prejudice on a web site set up by US researchers, more than half of white respondents found that they were unconsciously prejudiced towards blacks (Nosek et al., 2002). In one study white French people, who were sure they had no kind of prejudice towards Arabs, were shown pictures of Arabs and responded by increased heartbeat rate. Researchers interpreted the increase rate as indicating unconscious prejudice towards Arabs (Dambrun et al., 2003).

Modern racism theory

Surveys reveal a trend in public opinion towards less overt racial prejudice, reflecting the social stigma now attached to blatant racism (Blair et al., 2004). In developed countries explicit racial barriers have been dismantled. Virtually every major employer in North America and Europe has adopted equal opportunities policies; and many organisations have implemented affirmative action programmes to remedy prejudice and discrimination against ethnic minorities.

However, according to modern racism theory (Kinder and Sears, 1981; McConahay, 1986), traditional, blatant racism is being replaced by 'modern racism' which is typically expressed through discrimination with regard to school admission criteria, housing eligibility, access to health and other services, but especially with regard to employment (DeVries, 2000):

> Jobs at all levels in New York City administration are widely advertised and applications are welcomed by members of all ethnic groups. Yet when black, white and Hispanic applicants with the same qualifications applied for entry-level positions in New York City, whites with criminal records were often preferred over Hispanics, who in turn were chosen over blacks.

Employment discrimination

Employment discrimination exists worldwide. According to the ILO (1996), substantial wage differences exist in Brazil to the detriment of women and blacks. Although nearly half the population has some African ancestry, there are very few blacks in senior positions in the government, armed forces, or the private sector.

Syed and Murray (2009) found that qualified migrant women from Pakistan, Iran, and Afghanistan who entered the labour market in Australia were particularly disadvantaged under the combined influence of sexism and racism – occupational 'double jeopardy'. These women, like other non-English speaking women in Australia, were employed in lower-status and lower-paying jobs relative to Australian-born women – a situation which partly reflects an English language deficit.

The British Social Attitudes Survey (2001) found that 20 per cent of the British public believed employers discriminated against job applicants on grounds of race. In the United States, promotion decisions in all sectors tend to be biased in favour of white employees and against black employees and minorities (Rosette et al., 2008). In some English-speaking countries, foreign-sounding names may have an adverse impact on the employment prospects of migrant workers. University of Chicago researchers have found widespread selection discrimination against job applicants whose names merely *sound* black, and black-sounding applicants are 50 per cent less likely than candidates with white-sounding names to receive invitations to second interviews (Arai and Skogman Thoursie, 2006).

Religious prejudice

Religious prejudice occurs when a society or groups within society are intolerant of practices, persons, or beliefs on religious grounds. The constitutions of some countries contain provisions expressly forbidding the state from engaging in certain acts of religious intolerance or preference within its own borders. Examples include The First Amendment of the United States Constitution. Article 2 of the United Nations Universal Declaration of Human Rights forbids discrimination on the basis of religion.

However, such official declarations have not succeeded in eliminating religious prejudice. In some Western countries, for instance, conspicuous cultural differences, such as Muslim dress, arranged marriages, demands for *halal* meat (from animals killed according to Muslim law), and the subordinate role of women in Muslim communities, arouse prejudices towards Muslims. Argyle (2000) finds high correlations between prejudice and *religious fundamentalism* among Christians, Jews, Muslims, and Hindus, and argues that fundamentalism is a predisposing factor for religious prejudice.

A South African sociologist working on an international project in Sudan reported to colleagues that most of the local Muslim women she interviewed resented being forced to wear the burkha. However, the women blamed male domination for this rather than religious fundamentalism. The sociologist (herself a Muslim) told colleagues that although Islam is often seen as a major element oppressing women, most other religions (including Judaism, Christianity, and Asian religions) have had similar attitudes towards women at certain times in their history. The sociologist explained that Islam is not one Islam. 'There is the Islam of Saudi Arabia, the Islam of Morocco, the Islam of Indonesia ... Islam is used by patriarchal systems to justify their repressive character.'

In China religion has long been considered by CCP to be an obstacle to national integration, so that some cases of apparent religious prejudice and discrimination have strong political overtones. Reny (2009) points to the central Chinese government's severe monitoring of religious activities in Xinjiang, a Muslim-majority autonomous region. For example, young members of the Uyghur population are not allowed to receive any kind of religious instruction, Islamic texts are all under state control, and public sector employees are not allowed to wear clothing marked as religious such as coverings for women (Fuller and Lipman, 2004). Uyghurs who practice Islam cannot find a job in the state sector of the Xinjiang economy.

SMALL-GROUP EXERCISE: Discussion questions

Working in small groups, discuss each of the following questions and write down the group's agreed answer. At the end of the exercise, each group may present its answers to the other groups for comment.

1. *What is prejudice?*
2. *Which of the theories outlined in the chapter provides the most convincing explanation of why people feel prejudice towards members of other racial or national groups?*
3. *Explain the difference between blatant and subtle prejudice.*
4. *What effect does ethnocentrism have on cross-cultural communication? What is the extreme form of ethnocentrism?*
5. *What actions can be taken to reduce prejudice and discrimination in the multicultural workplace?*
6. *What effect can prejudice have in international business discussions? Give examples.*
7. *What is 'modern racism'? Why has it developed?*

CAN PREJUDICE BE UNLEARNED?

Just as prejudice is learned so it can be unlearned. According to Brewer and Miller (1988), an effective method is to learn to gradually replace prejudiced responses with non-prejudiced responses. Before that can happen one needs to become aware of one's own prejudices – an important pre-requisite for success in the unlearning process (Monteith et al., 2002).

The unlearning process begins by a person first admitting that there is a gap between her actual prejudiced behaviour and her conscious ideals. Once this step has been successfully taken the prejudice and the associated stereotypes should become more clearly visible. The next step is to bring *mindfulness* – heightened self-awareness – into actual, face-to-face cross-cultural interactions where prejudiced responses are likely to come into play. As the conversation proceeds the prejudiced person consciously appraises her own communication performance by asking herself such questions as:

- How am I reacting to this person?
- Are my feelings and thoughts negative and prejudiced?
- Am I being patronizing or demeaning?
- Am I communicating to my stereotype of the person's culture?

By constantly monitoring her own communication performance in this way – and by noting and correcting any lapses – the prejudiced person sets about unlearning her prejudice.

The final step in the unlearning process is to develop strategies for removing prejudiced responses from *future* cross-cultural encounters. A relevant strategy for achieving this goal when talking to people from other ethnic groups might be:

- to consciously avoid patronizing comments or questions;
- to adopt a more open and friendly manner, as opposed to being reserved or over-correct.

Replacing prejudiced with non-prejudiced responses is difficult but possible – in the same way that breaking a bad habit is difficult but possible.

INTERGROUP CONFLICT

Realistic conflict in Australia

Intergroup prejudices are sometimes so intense that they develop into outright conflict – as in the case of Catholics and Protestants in Northern Ireland. But not all intergroup conflict is bad. Some kinds of conflict are necessary for the healthy functioning of different social groups as it provides a way for interests to be balanced. However, many conflict situations are destructive. According to *realistic conflict theory* (Stephan et al., 1999), intergroup conflict stems from different groups competing for scarce resources such as housing and education, or from posing some other kind of 'realistic' threat to each other.

In Perth and other Australian cities competition generates intense intergroup prejudice and rivalry between urban Aborigines and recently settled African refugees escaping from civil wars at home. Aborigines resent the refugees being given priority to public housing and say that African immigrants are getting special treatment whereas they, the original owners of the country, are getting nothing (Colic-Peisker and Tilbury, 2008). Intergroup tensions sometimes translate into brawls at railway stations, bus stops, and on the streets. Name-calling is common. Bricks are thrown at houses. There are incidents of screwdriver stabbing. A young Aboriginal girl attacked a Sudanese youth with a broken bottle. The fighting is linked mainly to jobs and housing but an underlying issue is each group's symbolic position in Australian society and the unresolved problem of which of the two groups has the higher status.

Realistic conflict in southern Africa

Zimbabwe

In Zimbabwe, four distinct racial groups – blacks, whites, Asians, and 'Coloureds' (mixed race) – compete for limited resources, especially housing and jobs. The groups tend to move in segregated primary communities, drawing on their personal networks of relatives and friends within their own communities to supply social relationships. An attitude survey carried out in Harare (CCM, 2003) revealed that each group perceived the other groups in a prejudiced, predominantly negative way.

- Asians were perceived by all other groups as unsociable and untrustworthy.
- Blacks were untrustworthy and unreliable.
- Coloureds were untrustworthy, disloyal, and lazy.
- Whites were cold, selfish, and unsociable.

Younger people in all four communities were as stereotype-ridden as older respondents, and women were as stereotype-ridden as men.

The intergroup conflict revealed by the survey can be explained by continuing economic inequalities and unequal educational and job opportunities in Zimbabwe, which have led to extremely high unemployment among the black and Coloured communities. Moreover, the white and black communities opposed each other during the liberation war that ended in 1980 with the defeat of the white settler government, and some of the prejudiced intergroup attitudes and resentments formed at that time persist today.

South Africa

In South Africa, 'Amakwerekwere' is the derogatory term used for foreigners who have come to South Africa to escape political strife and economic hardship in Zimbabwe, Angola, Democratic Republic of Congo, and other African countries. According to Warner and Finchilescu (2003), native South Africans sometimes refuse to communicate with the refugees. A Congolese refugee told the researchers: 'They don't want to communicate with us because we're foreigners. They think we want to take their jobs.'

Many of the refugees claim that being a foreigner in South Africa is an instant barrier to employment. A Zimbabwean who went to the Home Affairs Ministry to change his papers was told: 'Why don't you go back to your own country?' A well-qualified Angolan applied for admission to a medical school but was told bluntly: 'Don't waste your time. It's only for South Africans.' Hatred of the 'Amakwerekwere' sometimes erupts in the streets of Johannesburg in the form of violent clashes between local street traders and competing foreign vendors.

Reducing intergroup prejudice

Jackman and Crane's (1986) *contact theory of prejudice* explains how increased intergroup contact can reduce intergroup prejudice as a result of accurate information being gained about the other group through sustained, informal face-to-face contact between group members. Support for the theory has come from several subsequent studies (e.g. Pettigrew, 1998). The implication is that cross-cultural exchange schemes, school visits, and other forms of intergroup contact lead to improved intergroup communication and reduce intergroup prejudice by providing opportunities for members of the groups to break through the stereotypes and to get to know each other as real people.

Joint projects and other forms of *cooperative activity* are particularly effective in improving intergroup attitudes, and one-to-one friendships can be even more effective (Pettigrew and Tropp, 2006). Archbishop Desmond Tutu recalls, from the hearings of the Truth and Reconciliation Commission in South Africa, the warm relationship that developed following sustained contact between two former enemies – a black political prisoner and her white wardress (Tutu, 2000). In the words of the prisoner: 'We met as human beings, there was such communication there.'

Crisp and Turner (2009) argue that prejudices held towards other groups can be reduced simply by *imagining* contact. People who imagined talking to a homosexual man on a train, for instance, subsequently regarded homosexual men in general with less prejudice (Turner et al., 2007). Perhaps the mechanism involved is that repeatedly imagining contact eventually prompts people to engage in actual face-to-face contact, and that it is this actual contact which reduces the prejudice.

Conflict resolution mechanisms

Mechanisms can be developed of resolving serious intergroup prejudice and conflict in a controlled, constructive way. Examples of mechanisms which have been found to be effective are:

- intergroup dialogue;
- external interventions;
- truth commissions;
- mediation.

In *intergroup dialogue* the parties engage in meaningful conversations for the purpose of developing a better understanding of their opponents. According to Williams (1994), intergroup dialogue proceeds through a sequence of distinct stages:

1. The parties describe what they find offensive in each other's behaviour.
2. By carefully listening to each other they get an understanding of each others' cultural perceptions.
3. By listening, each side learns how the problem would be handled in the opponent's culture.
4. At the end of the discussion, the parties have a much better understanding of each other's position and are often able to agree on a method of reaching a conflict resolution.

When intergroup conflict is severe, however – as was formerly the case in Northern Ireland, Bosnia, or South Africa – *external interventions* are needed to create structures and processes to institutionalize equality and respect among the groups concerned. For instance, election systems may have to be re-designed to fragment the support of a majority ethnic or religious group (Fisher, 1994).

The worst cases of intergroup conflict involve war crimes and human rights abuses that are so deep-rooted that *truth commissions* may be needed to provide a formal mechanism to publicly account for what happened, apologize, and forgive. This mechanism can be very effective in bringing about reconciliation between previously warring groups. An example is South Africa's Truth and Reconciliation Commission which provided a means of rebuilding trust after decades of violence during the apartheid years. It was effective because it provided the means for those involved in the conflict to engage in the essential psychological process of truth-telling and reconciliation.

Mediation is an important form of external intervention since it can modify the stereotypes that conflicting parties hold of each other. The mediator's starting point is to understand each group's perceptions of the opposing group and the conflict situation. The mediator ensures that the parties understand each other through listening and paraphrasing skills. However, the parties must solve their own problems. The role of the mediator is to be a facilitator of communication, to ensure that the parties listen to each other on a deeper level than previous hostile feelings allowed.

HOW STEREOTYPES AFFECT COMMUNICATION

Function of stereotypes

Stereotypes tend to be both crude and inaccurate, and are often used to justify prejudice and discrimination on the assumption that the stereotype reflects inherent characteristics of the stereotyped group. If stereotypes are used in cross-cultural interactions they distort the communication and may damage relationships. Stereotypes form as a result of cultural influences, including family, friends, education, and the media (Myers, 2005).

Stereotypes are inaccurate because they are limited to just one or two salient dimensions and assume that these are the whole picture, thus blinding us to the differences that exist between members of the group (Scollon and Scollon, 2001). The 'Asian American' stereotype, for instance, is necessarily inaccurate. There are some 30 distinct subgroups of Asian Americans, each of them having its own distinct traditions, customs, and languages. Moreover, each of these subgroups has within-group variations. For example, an American-born Chinese raised in one of the many Chinatown communities in the United States will be less acculturated to Western values than an American-born Chinese who has been raised in, say, Connecticut. The unreliable nature of stereotyping is shown by the fact that people can hold a very negative stereotype of a culture even though they have never met a single member of the culture.

Initial communication

Stereotypes supposedly tell us how members of the stereotyped group behave and in this way they simplify decision-making by overriding the effects of other relevant information. In his classic text on prejudice, Allport (1954: 20) makes the point:

> If I can lump thirteen million of my fellow-citizens under a simple formula, 'Negroes are stupid, dirty, and inferior,' I simplify my life enormously. I simply avoid them.

Stereotypes, however, can play a more positive role by facilitating initial communication efforts. For example, when people from different cultures meet for the first time they often know very little about each other – the only framework they have for initial interaction is the stereotype each person holds about the other person's culture. The stereotype may be crude and inaccurate but at least it allows assumptions to be made about the other person – the sort of person she is, her preferences, and so on – thus providing a basis for initial communication.

Follow-up communication

Although stereotypes facilitate initial cross-cultural communication, subsequent interactions are more successful when the participants no longer have to rely on stereotypes to predict and understand each other's behaviour (Gudykunst et al., 1987). International business people who travel to many countries and come into contact with many people necessarily rely on *cultural stereotypes* to facilitate initial communication, but in follow-up interactions usually have to refine their stereotypes.

> A European sales manager making his first business trip to Brazil relies on a crude 'Latin American' stereotype and a few phrases of Portuguese to see him through initial meetings with prospective clients. But in follow-up meetings the stereotype collides with reality and has to be adjusted. One client, for instance, a soft-spoken book-lover, fails to fit the 'macho' part of the stereotype.

Ratui (1983) found that international managers rated the most internationally effective by their peers use crude stereotypes of various national groups as a starting point for communication. However, as the conversation proceeds they learn more about the other person and, consciously or unconsciously, alter and refine their initial stereotypes. Individuals rated the least internationally effective are those who stick to their initial stereotypes and fail to adjust.

Distorting effect of stereotypes

Stereotypes distort cross-cultural communication by making false assumptions about other persons and other cultures. Stereotyped individuals generally feel under pressure to communicate and to behave in accordance with the stereotype. When, for instance, a 'black' stereotype (musical, athletic, attitude) is projected onto someone the person often reacts by adjusting her behaviour to match the stereotype (Detweiler, 1986). Individuals often underperform in situations that remind them that they are stereotyped to do poorly (Schmader, 2010). Thus white men tend to perform more poorly when solving mathematical problems if told they will be compared to Asian men (Aronson et al., 1999).

A similar distortion effect is produced when an 'elderly' stereotype is projected onto a person – the stereotyped person often begins to speak and move more slowly than is natural, in accordance with the stereotype (Schubert and Hafner, 2003). Awareness of being stereotyped is *a powerful distraction that leads to inhibited responses*. For instance, blacks who become aware of being stereotyped in job interviews often start to behave in a self-conscious, inhibited way (Stangor and Thompson, 2002).

Sometimes a person who senses that she is the object of stereotyping will symbolically withdraw from the conversation, or will deliberately avoid behaviours that would corroborate the stereotype.

A subtler kind of distortion occurs in cross-cultural conversations when a participant consciously monitors his own communication performance for unintentional expressions of racial stereotyping. These self-regulatory efforts are usually accompanied by stress, embarrassment, and social anxiety which have an inhibiting or distorting effect on the communication (Amodio, 2009).

Hostile national stereotypes

People from different national groups often hold negative stereotypes of each other. Finns are silent, Irishmen are thick, white Americans are brash, African Americans have attitude. Tannen (1998) identifies the very negative attitudes that German and American students held of each other: Germans are pigheaded and inclined to humiliate people publicly. Americans are superficial, uncommitted, and ignorant. When students at Princeton selected attributes that they thought were the most characteristic of Germans, English people, Jews, Negroes, Turks, Japanese, Italians, Chinese, Americans, and Irish, predominantly negative or hostile stereotypes emerged for all groups (Gilbert, 1951).

Stereotypes of national groups are often hostiles. That helps to explain why, when persons of a given national culture are confronted with stereotypes of themselves by other nationalities, they fail to recognize themselves in the stereotype (Lipianski, 1992). The national stereotype concerned is usually so hostile that they feel they are being attacked and deny belonging to the group being stereotyped.

According to Ziring et al. (1995), hostile national stereotypes may influence relationships between governments since neither parliaments nor electors realize that the mental images they hold of another country are biased and inaccurate. By stereotyping a country – Iraq harbours terrorists, for instance – serious errors of judgment can be made leading to hostile relations (or worse) between governments.

Hostile racial stereotypes

Racial stereotypes are often used to justify deep-rooted, pre-existing prejudice. A US study, for instance, found that whites saw blacks as irrational, hostile, destructive, and out of control (Alexander et al., 2005). Blacks saw whites as exploitative, dominating, and intentionally oppressive. 76 per cent of African Americans in one survey thought that whites were insensitive to people and did not want to share with people, and 79 per cent thought that whites saw themselves as superior and liked to boss others around (Leonard and Locke, 1993).

During interactions between people from different racial groups, physical appearance and speech characteristics, such as pacing, pausing, volume, and accent, lead to impressions being formed about the person's reliability, personality, and intelligence. These impressions may then become the basis for dangerous racial stereotypes that are used to justify prejudice and discrimination.

Can stereotypes be undermined?

Stereotyping can occur *automatically*, without awareness or intent. Something as simple as a hair style, a foreign accent, skin colour, can automatically trigger the stereotype. Once activated, the stereotype allows conclusions to be reached about the stereotyped person with very little conscious thought since the response is guided by automatic processing (Monteith et al., 2002). Once a 'disabled' stereotype has been activated, for instance, the disabled person is unthinkingly assumed to be easily offended and oversensitive about her disability.

Stereotyping has an obvious effect on cross-cultural communication. The fact that many stereotypes are automatically activated means that it is difficult to reverse their effect on perception during a cross-cultural interaction (Towles-Schwen and Fazio, 2003). Stereotypes can, however, be undermined by a longer-term effort to assess their reliability. This can be done by consciously questioning whether the various members and components of a particular stereotyped group actually 'fit' the group stereotype. How reliable, for instance, is the 'African American' stereotype (athletic, musical, attitude) when applied to the various African American subgroups – the very young, the very old, the richest, the poorest, the unemployed, and so on? This kind of long-term, deliberate, self-questioning examination should eventually have the effect of gradually exposing the unreliability and incompleteness of the original stereotype.

Simply by noting ways in which subgroups deviate from the group stereotype weakens the stereotype and may encourage the holder of the stereotype to take further positive action, such as seeking more contact with members of the stereotyped group.

KEY POINTS

1. Prejudice is dislike or hatred of a person or group formed without reason. Prejudice is rooted in a person's early socialization and reinforced by contact with other prejudiced people. It distorts perception and communication and accounts for many of the tensions and conflict in cross-cultural exchanges. In cross-cultural gatherings, prejudice may be communicated by standing well back from the target of the prejudice, avoiding eye contact, and other distancing behaviours associated with dislike.
2. Ethnic and racial minorities, religious minorities, the disabled, sexual minorities, and other minority groups are frequent targets of prejudice. A variety of negative emotions are directed at such groups, including anger, fear, disgust, and resentment. Victims of prejudice and stigmatization may suffer various painful emotional and physiological reactions, including lowered self-esteem.

3. Ethnocentric people tend to feel scorn or hostility towards members of other national and ethnic groups. They believe in the general superiority of their own cultural or ethnic group, and the inferiority of most other cultural or ethnic groups. Extreme forms of ethnocentrism lead to discrimination and suppression, as shown by the history of Jews in Europe or by the apartheid years in South Africa.

4. Employees who are perceived as *different* (e.g. because of skin colour, dress, accent) may become the targets of prejudice and discrimination in the workplace. They are often excluded from informal networks of co-workers, receive poor or inaccurate performance appraisals, and suffer from lack of constructive feedback from their supervisors. They may be barred from entry to certain job categories. Absenteeism is a common form of escape behaviour for these employees.

5. There is a trend in public opinion towards less overt racial prejudice, reflecting the social stigma now attached to blatant racism. Most employers in developed countries have adopted equal opportunities policies and many have implemented affirmative action programmes to remedy prejudice and discrimination against ethnic minorities. But traditional, blatant racism is being replaced by 'modern racism'. This is expressed through *discrimination* with regard to school admission criteria, housing eligibility, access to health, but especially with regard to employment.

6. Increased intergroup contact can reduce prejudice as a result of accurate information being gained about the other group through sustained, informal face-to-face contact between group members. Exchange schemes, school visits, and other forms of contact lead to improved communication and reduce intergroup prejudice by providing opportunities for members of the groups to break through the stereotypes and to get to know each other as real people. Joint projects and other forms of cooperative activity are particularly effective in improving intergroup attitudes, and one-to-one friendships can be even more effective.

7. Stereotypes tend to be inaccurate and are often used to justify prejudice and discrimination on the assumption that the stereotype reflects inherent characteristics of the stereotyped group. If stereotypes are used in cross-cultural interactions they distort the communication and may damage relationships. But stereotypes also play a positive role by facilitating initial communication. When people from different cultures meet for the first time they often know very little about each other. The only framework they have for initial interactions is the stereotype each person holds about the other person's culture.

8. National and racial stereotypes are often hostile. When persons of a given national culture are confronted with stereotypes of themselves held by other nationalities they fail to recognize themselves in the stereotype. The national stereotype concerned is usually so hostile that they feel they are being attacked and deny belonging to the group being stereotyped. Hostile racial stereotypes are often used to justify deep-rooted, pre-existing prejudice.

QUESTIONS FOR DISCUSSION AND WRITTEN ASSIGNMENTS

1. Xenophobia and violence are often associated with football. What responsibility does the game itself have for addressing nationalism, xenophobia, and violence?
2. Why are immigrants and minority groups the targets of prejudice and discrimination? What are the effects of discrimination against these groups, and how could it be countered?
3. Why are national stereotypes usually hostile – and does it matter? Describe the stereotype that people from other cultures hold of your own national culture?

BIBLIOGRAPHY

Adorno, TW, Frenkel-Brunswick, E, Levinson, DJ and Sandford, RN. *The Authoritarian Personality*. Harper, 1950.

Alexander, MG et al., Putting stereotype content in context: image theory and interethnic stereotypes. *Personality and Social Psychology Bulletin*, 31 (6), 2005, 781–794.

Allport, G. *The Nature of Prejudice*. Anchor Books, 1954.

Amodio, DM. Intergroup anxiety effects on the control of racial stereotypes: a psychoneuroendocrine analysis. *Journal of Experimental Social Psychology*, 45, 2009, 60–67.

Arai, M and Skogman Thoursie, P. Giving up foreign names: an empirical examination of surname change and earnings. Research Papers in Economics, Stockholm University, 2006.

Argyle, M. *Psychology and Religion: An Introduction*. Routledge, 2000.

Aronson, J et al., When white men can't do math: necessary and sufficient factors in stereotype threat. *Journal of Experimental Social Psychology*, 35, 1999, 29–46.

Baldwin, JR and Hecht, ML. The layered perspective of cultural (in)tolerance(s): the roots of a multidisciplinary approach. In RL Wiseman (ed.), *Intercultural Communication Theory*. Sage, 1995, p. 65.

Bdzinski, DM. The impact of accent and status on information recall and perception information. *Communication*, 5, 1992, 99–106.

Beals, KP et al., Stigma management and well-being: the role of perceived social support, emotional processing, and suppression. *Personality and Social Psychology Bulletin*, 35 (7), 2009, 867–879.

Bennett, MJ (ed.), *Basic Concepts of Intercultural Communication*. Intercultural Press, 1998.

Blair, VI, Judd, CM and Fallman, JL. The automaticity of race and Afrocentric facial features in social judgments. *Journal of Personality and Social Psychology*, 87 (6), 2004, 763–778.

Blanchard, FA et al., Reducing the expression of racial prejudice. *Psychological Science*, 2, 1991, 101–105.

Blascovich, J et al., Perceiver threat in social interactions with stigmatised others. *Journal or Personality and Social Psychology*, 80, 2001, 253–267.

Brewer, MB and Miller, N. Contact and cooperation: when do they work? In P Katz and D Taylor (eds), *Eliminating Racism*. Plenum, 1988.

Burris, ER et al., Playing favourites: the influence of leaders' inner circle on group processes and performance. *Personality and Social Psychology Bulletin*, 35 (9), 2009, 1244–1257.

CCM, Intergroup stereotypes in Harare. Unpublished paper. CCM, 2003.

Cole, SW et al., Accelerated course of human immunodeficiency virus infection in gay men who conceal their homosexual identity. *Psychosomatic Medicine*, 58, 1996, 219–231.

Colic-Peisker, V and Tilbury, F. Being black in Australia: a case study of intergroup relations. *Race and Class*, 49 (4), 2008, 38–56.

Cottrell, CA and Neuberg, SL. Different emotional reactions to different groups: a sociofunctional threat-based approach to 'prejudice'. *Journal of Personality and Social Psychology*, 88 (5), 2005, 770–789.

Crisp, RJ and Turner, RN. Can imagined interactions produce positive perceptions? *American Psychologist*, 64 (4), 2009, 231–240.

Dambrun, M et al., On the multifaceted nature of prejudice. *Current Research in Social Psychology*, 8, 2003, 187–206.

Detweiler, R. Categorisation, attribution and intergroup communication. In WB Gudykunst (ed.), *Intergroup Communication*. Edward Allen, 1986, pp. 62–73.

DeVries, R. When leaders have character: need for leadership performance, and the attribution of leadership. *Journal of Social Behaviour and Personality*, 15 (3), 2000, 413–430.

Dijker, AJM. Emotional reactions to ethnic minorities. *European Journal of Social Psychology*, 17, 1987, 305–325.

Donovan, S. *Stress and Coping in Successful Intercultural Marriages*. Virginia State University, 2004.

Dustmann, C and Preston, I. Attitudes to ethnic minorities, ethnic context and location decisions. *Economic Journal*, 111 (470), April 2001, 367.

EUAFR, *Majorities' Attitudes Towards Migrants and Minorities: Key Findings from the Eurobarometer and the European Social Survey*. European Union Agency for Fundamental Rights, 2005.

European Commission, *Developing an intercultural outlook: Directorate-General for Employment*, Industrial Relations and Social Affairs. 1997, p. 17.

Farley, JE. *Majority-Minority Relations*, 4th ed. Prentice-Hall, 2000.

Feagin, JR. *Systemic Racism: A Theory of Oppression*. Routledge, 2006.

Fisher, RJ. Generic principles for resolving intergroup conflict. *Journal of Social Issues*, 50, 1994, 47–66.

Florack, A et al., Perceived intergroup threat and attitudes of host community members toward immigrant acculturation. *Journal of Social Psychology*, 143 (5), 2003, 633–648.

Fottrell, D and Bowring, B. (eds), *Minority and Group Rights in the New Millennium*. Kluwer Law International, 1999.

Fuller, GE and Lipman, JN. Islam in Xinjiang. In F Starr (ed.), *Xinjiang: China's Muslim Borderland*. ME Sharpe, 2004, pp. 320–352.

Galanis, CM and Jones, EE. When stigma confronts stigma: some conditions enhancing a victim's tolerance of other victims. *Personality and Social Psychology Bulletin*, 12, 1986, 169–177.

Gang, IN et al., Economic strain, ethnic concentration and attitudes towards foreigners in the European Union. IZA, Discussion Paper 578, 2002.

Gardikiotis, A et al., The representation of majorities and minorities in the British press: a content analytic approach. *European Journal of Social Psychology*, 34, 2004, 637–643.

Gilbert, GM. Stereotype persistence and change among college students. *Journal of Abnormal and Social Psychology*, 46, 1951, 245–254.

Giles, H and Coupland, N. *Language: Contexts and Consequences*. Open University Press, 1991.

Goffman, E. *Stigma: Notes on the Management of Spoiled Identity*. Prentice-Hall, 1963.

Gudykunst, WB, Chua, E and Gray, A. Cultural dissimilarities and uncertainty reduction processes. In M McClaughlin (ed.), *Communication Yearbook* (Vol. 10). Sage, 1987.

Guerrero, LK and Floyd, K. *Nonverbal Communication in Close Relationships*. Erlbaum, 2006.

Herek, GM. The psychology of sexual prejudice. *Current Directions in Psychological Science*, 9, 2000, 19–22.

Hofstede, G. *Cultures and Organisations: Software of the Mind*. Harper-Collins, 1994.

ILO, *Wage Discrimination in South America*. International Labour Organisation, 1996.

Jackman, MR and Crane, M. 'Some of my best friends are black': interracial friendships and whites' racial attitudes. *Public Opinion Quarterly*, 50, 1986, 459–486.

Kabagarama, D. *Breaking the Ice: A Guide to Understanding People from Other Cultures*. Allyn & Bacon, 1993.

Kinder, DR and Sears, DO. Prejudice and politics: symbolic racism versus racial threats to the good life. *Journal of Personality and Social Psychology*, 40, 1981, 414–431.

Larkey, LK. The development and validation of the workforce diversity questionnaire. *Management Communication Quarterly*, 9 (3), 1996, 296–337.

Leonard, R and Locke, D. Communication stereotypes: is interracial communication possible. *Journal of Black Studies*, 23 (3), 1993, 332–343.

Lipinski, E-M. Identite, communication interculturelle et dynamique des groupes. In *Interculturel: groupe et transition*. Editions Eres, 1992, pp. 59–70.

Lukens, J. Ethnocentric speech. *Ethnic Groups*, 2, 1978, 35–53.

McConahay, JB. Modern racism, ambivalence, and the modern racism scale. In JF Dovidio and SL Gaertner (eds), *Prejudice, Discrimination and Racism.* Academic Press, 1986, pp. 91–125.

Monteith, MJ et al., Putting the brakes on prejudice: on the development and operation of cues for control. *Journal of Personality and Social Psychology*, 83 (5), 2002, 1048.

Mullen, B and Smyth, JM. Immigrant suicide rates as a function of ethnophaulisms: hate speech predicts death. *Psychosomatic Medicine*, 66, 2004, 343–348.

Myers, DG. *Social Psychology*, 8th ed. McGraw-Hill, 2005.

Nielsen, LB. Subtle, pervasive, harmful: racist and sexist remarks in public as hate speech. *Journal of Social Issues*, 58, 2002, 265–280.

Nishii, LH and Mayer, DM. Do inclusive leaders help to reduce turnover in diverse groups? The moderating role of leader-member exchange in the diversity to turnover relationship. *Journal of Applied Psychology*, 94 (6), 2009, 1412–1426.

Nosek, BA et al., Harvesting implicit group attitudes and beliefs from a demonstration website. *Group Dynamics*, 61, 2002, 101–115.

O'Hara, KB et al., Organisational centrality: a third dimension of intraorganisational career movement. *Journal of Applied Behavioural Science*, 30, 1994, 198–216.

Ogbonna, E and Harris, LC. The dynamics of employee relationships in an ethnically diverse workforce. *Human Relations*, 59 (3), 2006, 379–407.

Parr, N and Guo, F. The occupational concentration and mobility of Asian immigrants in Australia. *Asian and Pacific Management Journal*, 14 (3), 2005, 351–380.

Pell, RH. *Not Like Us: How Europeans Have Loved, Hated, and Transformed American Culture Since World War II.* Basic Books, 1997.

Pettigrew, TF. Personality and sociocultural factors in intergroup attitudes: a cross-national comparison. *Journal of Conflict Resolution*, 2, 1998, 29–42.

Pettigrew, TF and Mertens, RW. Subtle and blatant prejudice in western Europe. *European Journal of Social Psychology*, 25, 1995, 57–75.

Pettigrew, TF and Tropp, LR. A meta-analytic test of intergroup contact theory. *Journal of Personality and Social Psychology*, 90, 2006, 751–783.

Plant, EA and Devine, PG. The antecedents and implications of interracial anxiety. *Personality and Social Psychology Bulletin*, 29, 2003, 790–801.

Postmes, T and Branscombe, NR. Influence of long-term racial environmental composition on subjective well-being in African Americans. *Journal of Personality and Social Psychology*, 83, 2002, 735–751.

Radvansky, GA et al., Stereotype activation, inhibition, and aging. *Journal of Experimental Social Psychology*, 46, 2010, 51–60.

Ratui, I. Thinking internationally: a comparison of how international executives learn. *International Studies of Management and Organisation*, X111 (1–2), 1983, 139–150.

Reny, M-E. The political salience of language and religion. *Ethnic and Recial Studies*, 32 (3), 2009, 490–521.

Rosenblatt, PC, Karis, TA and Powell, RD. Multiracial couples: black and white voices. Sage, 1995.

Rosette, AS, Leonardeli, GJ and Phillips, KW. The white standard: racial bias in leader categorisation. *Journal of Applied Psychology*, 93 (4), 2008, 758–777.

Ross, S and Shortreed, IM. Japanese foreigner talk: convergence or divergence? *Journal of Asian Pacific Communication*, 1 (1), 1990, 135–146.

Schmader, T. Stereotype threat deconstructed. *Current Directions in Psychological Science*, 19 (1), 2010, 14–18.

Schubert, TW and Hafner, M. Contrast from social stereotypes in automatic behaviour. *Journal of Experimental Social Psychology*, 39, 2003, 577–584.

Scollon, R and Scollon, SW. *Intercultural Communication*, 2nd ed. Blackwell, 2001.

Shaffer, DR. Crepaz, N and Chien-Ru Sun, Physical attractiveness st/typing in c-c perspective, *C-c Psychy*, 31 (5), September 2000, 557.

Shapiro, JR and Neuberg, SL. When do the stigmatised stigmatise? The ironic effects of being accountable to (perceived) majority group prejudice-expression norms. *Journal of Personality and Social Psychology*, 95 (4), 2008, 877–898.

Sherif, M et al., *The Robbers' Cave Experiment: Intergroup Conflict and Cooperation*. Wesleyan University Press, 1961.

Short, R and Magana, L. Political rhetoric, immigration attitudes, and contemporary prejudice: a Mexican American dilemma. *Journal of Social Psychology*, 142 (6), 2002, 701–712.

Stangor, C and Thompson, EP. Needs for cognitive economy and self-enhancement as unique predictors on intergroup attitudes. *European Journal of Social Psychology*, 32, 2002, 563–575.

Stauffer, JM and Buckley, MR. The existence and nature of racial bias in supervisory ratings. *Journal of Applied Psychology*, 90, 2005, 586–591.

Stephan, W, Stephan, C and Gudykunst, W. Anxiety in intergroup relations. *International Journal of Intercultural Relations*, 23 (6), 1999, 613–828.

Swami, V. Predictors of sociocultural adjustment among sojourning Malaysian students in Britain. *International Journal of Psychology*, 44 (4), 2009, 266–273.

Syed, J and Murray, P. Combating the English language deficit: the labour market experiences of migrant women in Australia. *Human Resource Management Journal*, 19 (4), 2009, 413–432.

Szasz, TS. *The Manufacture of Madness*, paperback edition. Syracuse University Press, 1997.

Tajfel, H and Turner, JC. The social identity theory of intergroup relations. In S Worchel and W Austin (eds), *Psychology on Intergroup Relations*, 2nd ed. Nelson-Hall, 1986, pp. 7–17.

Tannen, D. *The Argument Culture*. Virage, 1998, p. 217.

Towles-Schwen, T and Fazio, RH. Choosing social situations: the relation between automatically activated racial attitudes and anticipated comfort interacting with African-Americans. *Personality and Social Psychology Bulletin*, 29, 2003, 170–182.

Triandis, HC. *Culture and Social Behaviour*. McGraw-Hill, 1994.

Turner, RN, Crisp, RJ and Lambert, E. Imagining intergroup contact can improve intergroup attitudes. *Group Processes and Interegroup Relations*, 10, 2007, 427–441.

Tutu, D. No Future Without Forgiveness. Doubleday, 2000, p. 184.

von Grunigen, R et al., Immigrant children's peer acceptance and victimisation in kindergarten: the role of local language competence. *British Journal of Developmental Psychology*, 28, 2010, 679–697.

Warner, C and Finchilescu, G. Living with prejudice – xenophobia and race. *Agenda*, 55, 2003, 36–44.

Weatherly, D. Anti-Semitism and the expression of fantasy aggression. *Journal of Abnormal and Social Psychology*, 62, 1961, 454–457.

West, T and Levy, SR., Background belief systems and prejudice. In WJ Lonner et al. (eds), *Online Readings in Psychology and Culture*. International Association of Cross-cultural Psychology, 2002, http://www.www.edu/-culture.

Williams, A. Resolving conflict in a multicultural environment. *MCS Conciliation Quarterly*, Summer 1994, 2–6.

Ziring, L et al., *International Relations: A Political Dictionary*, 5th ed. ABC-CLIO, 1995.

Part 2
Practice

Expatriate
performance

6

INTRODUCTION

Expatriates are managerial, professional, and technical staff who live and work in a foreign country, normally for more than 1 year (Richardson and McKenna, 2002). Multinational companies use expatriates in the absence of qualified and effective local staff, and to develop high-potential managers by means of international experience. Expatriate staff who fail to complete their assignments do so for two main reasons – inadequate job performance and failure to adjust to the foreign culture (Black and Gregersen, 1999). The low proportion of female expatriates (about 15 per cent according to one estimate) stems from the reluctance of companies to select female expatriates because of the perceived prejudice against women managers in many foreign countries.

A few decades ago the traffic in expatriate managers was overwhelmingly one-way – from developed to developing countries. However, that pattern is changing. More and more managers from developing countries are being sent to expatriate posts in developed countries. More and more multinational companies based in developing countries are starting operations in the developed world. For example, Tata Industries of India has acquired Tetley Teas and Corus Steel in Europe.

Qualities that contribute to expatriate success generally include cultural sensitivity, openness to change and new experiences, cross-cultural communication skills, and willingness to adapt to local cultural norms. Such qualities enable expatriates to carry out key features of their assignments wherever the assignments are carried out. A key responsibility of many expatriate managers is to oversee the transfer of technology and business knowledge between the parent company at home and the subsidiary or host company abroad (Rosenzweig and Nohria, 1994). Expatriate managers are required to resolve the frequent problems that arise. These include the need to adapt the imported technology so that it meets local needs. Thus when Chinese expatriates implemented a rice seed project in Liberia, they failed to adapt their approach to local conditions and as a result the project failed. Another recurrent problem faced by expatriate managers is the scarcity of local management talent and the inadequacy of other local resources.

Success in carrying out expatriate assignments may depend on the expatriate manager establishing effective formal and informal communication links with the parent firm. Setting up and maintaining these links enable the expatriate manager to facilitate the transfer of technological and business knowledge from the parent firm to the subsidiary. Expatriate manager also needs to build informal communication networks among local colleagues and members of the local community – a task which becomes much easier if the expatriate learns to speak the local language. Expatriates who are unable to speak the local language are often restricted in their social relationships to fellow-expatriates throughout the period of their assignments.

EXPATRIATES

Who are they?

More and more people are living and working abroad, many of them expatriates sent by their organisations to work on overseas assignments. The great majority of expatriate managers worldwide are male and most are employed by multinational enterprises (MNEs). The MNE is a unique organisational form composed of a complex network of differentiated subsidiaries located in various locations around the world (Bartlett and Ghoshal, 1989).

Expatriates are managerial, professional, and technical staff who live and work in a foreign country on a temporary basis but normally for more than 1 year (Richardson and McKenna, 2002). Expatriate managers tend to be young professionals who make two moves before returning to the career structure of their native country – expatriates are transferred more often than other employees in order to round out their experience (Edstrom and Galbraith, 1977). Frequent transfers of expatriate managers updates their knowledge, renews contacts developed earlier, and ensures that each location is linked into the worldwide operations of the parent company.

PricewaterhouseCoopers (2000) has identified a trend in *non-standard* expatriate assignments. These may involve a manager commuting between the home and host country several times a month. Some MNEs have also experimented with *virtual* international assignments for some managers and technical experts. The way in which virtual teams operate is outlined in Chapter 10.

Edstrom and Galbraith (1977) identify three major reasons why MNEs use expatriate managers:

- to fill particular positions in the absence of qualified local staff;
- to develop high-potential managers by means of international experience;

- to develop the parent organisation and its overseas units by establishing social communication networks.

Black and Gregersen (1999) report that nearly 80 per cent of large and mid-size companies in the United States send expatriate managers to work in the firms' overseas subsidiaries at all management levels. According to the researchers, 10–20 per cent of all US managers sent abroad return early from their assignments for two main reasons: failure to adjust to the foreign culture and inadequate job performance.

Female expatriates

Expatriate positions are increasingly viewed as important career steps for women. This is reflected in the number of Western female expatriate managers which increased from 2 to 3 per cent in the 1980s to 15 per cent more recently (Selmer and Leung, 2003). Van der Boon (2003) found that women account for only 14 per cent of expatriate executives posted from the United States and less than 5 per cent of those sent abroad from European companies. But although the number of women expatriate managers has increased it is still small in proportion to men, and much smaller than the proportion of women managers in the domestic environment.

Research evidence suggests that important barriers to women undertaking international assignments include the impact of stereotypes, corporate resistance, foreigner prejudice, women's own disinclination, and lack of family and other support mechanisms. Thus when Hutchings et al. (2010) surveyed female managers in seven Middle Eastern countries, over half the respondents reported that stereotypical perceptions of women managers were a barrier to their international career opportunities. About 40 per cent of the respondents pointed to important limiting factors, including:

- limited training opportunities;
- lack of female role models;
- the business culture of the home country, and antagonism towards women as managers in some host countries;
- family commitments related to child rearing.

Negative attitudes towards women managers

In some countries, negative attitudes towards women managers make success and adjustment for female expatriates difficult to achieve (Owen et al., 2007). In male-dominated societies must learn to deal with more pressures than male expatriate managers encounter. Female expatriates sometimes encounter sexual harassment; for instance, or are forced to perform duties well below their qualifications and capabilities (Napier and Taylor, 1995). In Japan, there have been cases of sexual harassment of female expatriates by Japanese men as well as discriminatory practices against women expatriates who try to get promotion in Japanese organisations (Usui et al., 2003).

In China, negative attitudes towards women as managers – even among Chinese women – make it difficult for women expatriate managers to be successful in their assignments. Aspects of Chinese society that help to explain negative feelings towards women managers include lower levels of education and training, job segregation, and limited access to Communist Party membership for women, a key path to managerial position in China (Hymowitz, 2005). Unfavourable social attitudes help to explain why women have not achieved workplace equality in China. As Wang (2004) shows, lower-level jobs are overwhelmingly occupied by women. Moreover, the relatively small numbers of women managers in China are concentrated in 'soft' rather than 'hard' functional areas – in HR departments, for instance, rather than in Manufacturing, Marketing, or Finance (Hymowitz, 2005).

According to Sinangil and Ones (2003), female expatriates are as successful as their male counterparts, even in male-dominated cultures. Openness to change and new experiences combined with the *ability to adapt* to local cultural norms are qualities which contribute to the success of female expatriate managers (Caligiuri and Cascio, 1998). Companies such as Dell and McDonalds that are planning for extensive expansion in China need to help their women expatriate managers to make a success of their assignments by providing training and information about Chinese cultural and business practices and Chinese attitudes to women managers. The training would need to encourage the women to develop strategies for dealing with local employees whose cultural values make it difficult for them to accept women as managers.

International managers

Globalisation is accelerating the trend towards more expatriate managers and towards more international managers (i.e. specialist managers responsible for managing global diversity). International managers are employed by MNEs in diverse locations around the world. They plan and implement policies and practices aimed at transcending national differences in the global organisation (Ozbilgin, 2008). A quality that international managers must have is *cross-cultural communication competence* since this attribute is widely accepted as being essential for managing diversity worldwide.

The increasingly multicultural and multinational nature of the modern workforce means that managers need to be adept at implementing policies and practices required for effective diversity management. Indeed, the *management of diversity* has become a key strategic business issue for many MNEs, including Shell and Colgate–Palmolive.

Bartlett and Ghoshal (1989) distinguish between multinational industries, where responsiveness to local conditions is all-important, and global industries where scale economies are essential and little account taken of national differences. In multinational firms each overseas subsidiary is usually decentralized and becomes nationally self-sufficient. But global ('transnational') organisations integrate local activities into global operations. These are polycentric organisations – as opposed to organisations coordinated from the centre (Trompenaars and Hampden-Turner, 1997). Differentiated contributions from national units are integrated into worldwide operations. International manager bring this integration about by establishing an integrated network that works essentially through communication linkages and interdependencies (Jackson, 2002).

Even in MNEs pursuing bureaucratic, centralized control strategies and where major decisions are taken by head office, a measure of local discretion is facilitated by using expatriate managers who carry out an overseas assignment. The same objective is achieved by using *international managers* who spend at least half the time travelling from subsidiary to subsidiary (Edstrom and Galbraith, 1977).

The expatriate brand is changing

The demand for expatriates is certain to increase as MNEs establish more bases in the emerging markets of China, Russia, India, Brazil, and South Africa. Half a century ago the traffic in expatriate managers was overwhelmingly one-way – from developed to developing countries. But the pattern has changed. More and more MNEs based in developing countries are starting operations in the developed world. Lenovo, for instance, the largest manufacturer of PCs in China, purchased an IBM division in 2004. Tata Industries of India has taken over Tetley Teas and Corus Steel in Europe.

More managers from developing countries are being posted to expatriate assignments in both developed and developing countries (Tung and Varma, 2008). Thus a Chinese or South American manager may be assigned to a senior expatriate post in France. An Indian manager may be sent by his company to supervise production in an Australian subsidiary. McDonnell et al. (2010) discovered that 56 per cent of foreign MNEs in Ireland (in accordance with the traditional model) had expatriates from their home countries on assignment in their Irish subsidiaries. However, 46 per cent had personnel from the Irish operations on assignment in other parts of their worldwide empires.

Multicultural project teams

The nature of expatriation is changing. Some expatriates – those working on multicultural project teams, for instance – do not necessarily carry out their assignment in a particular foreign country. Multicultural teams may be assembled to construct or maintain offshore oil rigs, for instance. Others build oil or gas pipelines and are constantly on the move, to and fro across national borders. Their work is not carried out in any particular country. In these cases, the expatriate's exposure to any one national culture is low (unless most members of the team have been recruited from a particular country). Expatriates who fall into this category are faced with a new kind of challenge. Not with the traditional problem of adapting to a specific foreign culture, but with the greater challenge of working 24 × 7 with colleagues from many other cultures – and dealing with the inevitable stress and conflicts that this brings.

The 'expatriate' brand is changing in other ways too. Expatriate managers on traditional 1- to 3-year assignments continue to play a very important role in managing today's global organisations. But increasing numbers of people are seeking work abroad not to further their careers in an MNE but for social, recreational, and lifestyle reasons. Sijanen and Lamsa (2009) distinguish between four distinct types of expatriates who have emerged in recent years, namely:

- global careerists;
- balanced experts;
- idealizers;
- drifters.

Only the first two of these categories measure up to the traditional conception of expatriates.

Use of expatriates

Edstrom and Galbraith (1977) found that many MNEs use expatriate managers for two main reasons:

- to fill management positions in subsidiary companies when qualified local individuals not available or not easily trained;
- to facilitate or accelerate organisation development – as a way to modify the MNE's structure and decision processes.

In many cases the appointment of an expatriate manager to a key position in the subsidiary company eventually leads to greater local discretion. For instance, the expatriate may install new, modified procedures, acquired from the parent company, which the subsidiary uses for its own purposes. The problem-solving abilities of the expatriate manager further accelerate the movement towards more local discretion and decentralisation.

Japanese expatriates

Some multinationals make greater use of expatriates than other. Gamble (2010), for instance, found that Japanese retail multinationals in China made greater use of expatriate staff than comparable European and American firms. The Japanese expatriates tend to communicate intensively with head offices in Japan by phone, fax, emails, and visits. Japanese expatriates hold all senior positions, including all store manager posts. Postings of Japanese expatriates are for an average period of 3 years.

The Japanese companies followed a similar pattern for recruiting local staff. The firms preferred to recruit those with no work experience since such recruits could be moulded to fit into the company's approach to customer services. The firms all introduced Japanese-style greetings and farewell ceremonies for the day's first and last customers. Typically, each morning as the store opens, a group of local staff and Japanese expatriates form two phalanxes that bow and repeat 'Good morning, welcome to the store' to customers as they enter (Gamble, 2010: 720).

EXPATRIATE ASSIGNMENTS

Wide-ranging

The assignments of expatriate managers are very wide-ranging and carried out at varying levels of responsibility and seniority in overseas organisations. The host organisations include subsidiaries of MNEs, foreign joint-ventures, foreign government departments or agencies, and state-owned industries. Examples of typical expatriate assignments are:

- Transfer advanced production technology to the subsidiary of an MNE and evaluate local management's ability to oversee its safe use.
- Train accounting and administrative staff in a foreign subsidiary to operate a new IT system.
- Promote the parent company's products in a South American country and penetrate the regional market.
- Manage a new store opened in an Asian country by a multinational retailer.
- Act as adviser to a Ministry in a former Soviet-bloc country.
- Help establish a national management training institution in an African country, and recruit and train local staff.
- Open a new regional office in South America and identify future business partners.

Professional competence, managerial ability

In order to carry out such assignments successfully expatriate managers need to possess *professional competence* – the ability to solve problems in their own functional area of human resource management, production, marketing, finance, and so on – as well as *managerial ability*. Managerial ability requires the ability to motivate and organise employees from other cultures.

Successfully carrying out expatriate assignments in China, for instance, demands market knowledge and cultural awareness – as well as the ability to sense and respond to rapid change (Paine, 2010: 104). Indeed, to be successful in China expatriate managers require a repertoire of skills that goes well beyond the management orthodoxies provided by Western business teaching.

For instance, expatriate success in China almost always depends on government backing. Without it, nothing gets implemented. The implication is that expatriate managers need to communicate and cooperate with Chinese government and Communist Party officials by establishing 'guanxi', and by demonstrating how their particular project is contributing to China's development (Chen and Chen, 2004).

Key roles that expatriate managers in China and other emerging economies need to play are, according to Harzing (2001), those of bumblebee (socialisation), spider (development of informal communication networks), and bear (centralisation of decision-making and replication of corporate practices).

Communication competence, which is a an essential prerequisite for most expatriate assignments, refers to the expatriate's ability to initiate interaction with people from another culture, enter into meaningful conversation with others, and deal effectively with and communication misunderstandings that occur (Holopainen and Bjorkman, 2005).

Technology transfer

Many expatriate assignments involve the *transfer of technology* between the parent company and the host organisation abroad. The expatriate manager is responsible for overseeing the transfer and overcoming the many problems that this entails (Rosenzweig and Nohria, 1994). In developing countries major problems for the expatriate manager sometimes arise from lack of adequate local resources, including local management talent.

A lesson learned by many expatriate managers carrying out assignments in developing countries is that imported technologies will not be successful if they presuppose resources and values that run counter to local values and traditions. Imported manufacturing systems can lead to huge increases in efficiency and quality, but they need sophisticated electronics, systems, and programming skills – resources which are in short supply in most developing countries. Moreover, advanced manufacturing systems rely on precisely timed completion of various operations and intense horizontal information flows, and local managers may be incapable of establishing such conditions or of maintaining the systems when the expatriate managers go home.

The role of appropriate technology

Often technology must be adapted to suit local conditions before it can be used successfully in developing countries. For instance, an expatriate project manager heading an agricultural development project in Zimbabwe was disappointed to find that an imported sorghum mill was too large for the small scattered villages of Zimbabwe. The manager eventually found a local firm which was able to adapt the mill to suit local conditions.

Expatriate managers will have a greater chance of being successful in their assignments if they remember that people in developing countries often resist adopting new technologies that have not been adapted to meet their particular needs. Thus when Chinese expatriates implemented a rice seed project in Liberia, they failed to adapt their approach to local conditions and as a result the project failed. Liberia has almost no irrigation infrastructure and the Chinese methods of tractorized cultivation and neat irrigated paddies had little to do with Liberian farming.

Case study

MINI-CASE: Cultural realities

Expatriate managers need and awareness of local conditions as much as they need professional knowledge. When a company in West Africa which made construction equipment started operating at a loss, the expatriate general manager developed a strategy for dealing with the problem. This was to start making simple agricultural machinery from local components, so as to cut costs and expand the customer base. Subsequently, the general manager successfully sold his strategy to the board.

But making the new equipment turned out to be difficult because of long production delays – mainly caused by unreliable local suppliers. Within a few months, the company was doing only maintenance and clean-up work.

Questions:

1. *To what extent did the strategy fail because it had been developed by only one person, the general manager?*
2. *Which other people should have been involved in developing a strategy?*
3. *Give examples of alternative strategies that could have been considered.*

Managing and motivating local employees

Expatriate managers need to be aware of the cultural values of their employees and to ensure that their management practices are compatible with them. In China and Japan as in most collectivist countries, open criticism of an employee is at odds with the values of the culture and confronting an employee with his failure is perceived as being very tactless. In Japan, instead of criticizing an under-performing employee in an appraisal interview, say, politeness norms call for an apology from other members of the work group for not helping her and for not supporting her need for a positive self-image.

Expatriate managers have to manage and motivate employees from diverse cultures. *Flexibility* is the essential quality required for this task because management methods that worked at home may not produce the same results in Shanghai or Brazilia or Mumbai. Members of different cultures respond in different ways to imported management techniques. They have different performance standards, and they respond in their own culturally influenced ways to various incentives and rewards. Formal rewards signal, for instance, whether collaboration or individual achievement is important, and are an important indicator of the kind of work behaviour the manager values. Expatriate managers need to be aware that employees in many collectivist countries prefer *equality-based* payment systems which reward group effort and efficiency. *Equity-based* systems, on the other hand, which reward individual merit and achievement, may be ineffective in collectivist cultures (Sparrow, 1998).

Organisations in collectivist countries often judge individual employees on their loyalty and team-membership skills more than on their ability to hit production targets. That is why production-chasing expatriate managers often find that they need to adapt their 'natural' managerial approach – which worked well for them at home – to fit in with the realities of the host culture. Early warning signs of the need to do so may come in the form of clear signals sent to the expatriate by local staff. Employees may, for instance, become frigidly distant after being openly criticized by the manager for persistent late-coming or poor performance. During a shop floor meeting they may stubbornly refuse to offer suggestions about how a particular production target might be met or how costs might be cut. These nonverbal signals are ways of telling the manager that he needs to adjust to the cultural realities, needs to change his managerial approach.

Payment systems

Expatriate managers' attempts to boost output by installing some kind of payment-by-results (PBR) system often fail. While PBR works well in competitive, individualistic countries such as the United States, Britain, and Australia, when introduced into organisations in countries with strong collectivist values PBR can have a disastrous effect on morale, absenteeism, and labour turnover. Jackson and Bak's (1998) study of 13 companies in Beijing found that expatriate managers had introduced many inappropriate rules and procedures, reward, and career planning systems that later had to be changed when they proved to be ineffective and inappropriate. Thus flexibility and the willingness to make the adjustments that the unfolding situation requires are the prerequisites for expatriate success.

An expatriate manager's ability to motivate employees in a foreign culture usually depends on using motivational techniques and systems which do not run counter to local values and which are appropriate to the culture. In developing countries people often resist adopting new technology unless it has been adapted to meet their particular needs. The need to ensure that technology is *appropriate* helps to explain why, according to Ghosal and Nohria (1993), most multinational companies emphasize both global integration and local responsiveness. From their experience of operating in a wide range of sectors and countries they know that failing to take local realities into account can have disastrous consequences – as demonstrated by Union Carbide's experience in India (Figure 6.1).

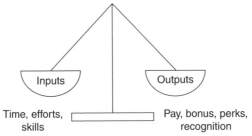

Time, efforts,   Pay, bonus, perks,
skills   recognition
In all cultures employees become demotivated when they feel their inputs
are not fairly rewarded.

Figure 6.1 Reward systems and fairness

MINI-CASE: New bonus scheme

When an American manager is appointed to a senior expatriate post in a Chinese-American joint venture company in Shanghai, he neglects to observe cultural realities and decides to introduce a new bonus scheme with the aim of boosting manufacturing output.

The manager tries to convince local managers that (following the US system) bonus payments should henceforth be based on the performance of individual employees. However, many Chinese managers continue to have doubts about the new scheme. Subsequent events prove them right.

In China *teamworking* is the norm and numerous complaints from employee representatives eventually force the company to withdraw the new scheme. The manager later admits to American colleagues that he had misunderstood the situation and that the introduction of individual bonuses had undermined employees' commitment to their workgroups. The American discovered how an expatriate manager's ability to successfully introduce new methods depends on first winning the consent of the local workforce.

Questions:

1. *To what extent can the failure of the new bonus scheme be attributed to inadequate cross-cultural communication?*
2. *What alternative actions should the manager consider if he wishes to increase manufacturing output?*

Inappropriate management techniques

Can management concepts and techniques that have been developed mainly in one country (the United States) be successfully transferred to very different cultures in the developing world? This is a key question that expatriate managers must answer in order to succeed in their assignments.

The theory of *job enrichment*, for instance, reflects the strong achievement needs of the United States individualistic culture, but may be seen as inappropriate in cultures which downplay individual competition and encourage relationships. In the 'feminine' Scandinavian countries, for instance, self-managed work-groups might be more appropriate than job enrichment schemes because the very act of establishing a self-managed work-group promotes close interpersonal relationships in the workplace.

Maslow's *hierarchy of needs* is a powerful concept that puts self-actualisation and achievement above security and social needs, reflecting the value system of the US middle class to which Maslow belonged. However, most cultures in Asia, South America, and the Middle East are collectivist and, as such, are based on family mutual support and obligations and on a strong sense of social belonging. When transferred to the work environment in these countries, such values mean that security and social needs are far more important than self-actualisation and achievement. As Markus and Kitayama (1991) point out, Western motivation theories fail to match the needs of many countries where the need for self-determination and self-growth is largely absent.

In Western countries, managerial and professional staff respond enthusiastically to increased challenge and responsibility. They *want* to be involved in decisions and to participate in planning activities. Herzberg (1966) found that American accountants and engineers were motivated by *the work itself* rather than by the tangible rewards it brought. Money was a 'hygiene' factor, a mere preventer of dissatisfaction. Western expatriate managers have absorbed such 'obvious' truths in the course of climbing the managerial ladder. But they are often surprised and disappointed when appointed to senior expatriate posts abroad and find that their local colleagues are totally unconvinced by such self-evident truths.

Motivating Egyptian employees

In Arab countries, the relationship between Western expatriate managers and local colleagues and employees is complicated by differences in religion, values, concepts of time, and different attitudes to planning and organisation (Dadfar and Gustavsson, 1992). Problems are particularly likely to occur if expatriate managers fail to find *culturally appropriate* ways of motivating the workforce. Thus when a canning factory in Cairo experienced severe productivity problems the board blamed the American production manager for not knowing how to motivate the poorly educated workforce.

The expatriate blamed the work force and told the board that none of the Egyptian employees had the ability to do managerial-type work. But when a new managing director was appointed his first act was to replace the American with an Egyptian who communicated with employees constantly. Employees welcomed the change and productivity gradually improved.

To be successful expatriate managers must take account of the cultural realities. This means finding ways to meet the expectations of their employees. The American failed to realize that work motivation in an Arab country differs from the Western model because of the great value attached to interpersonal *communication and relationships* in the workplace. In Arab countries, work is done in the service of the family, and doing well at work is valued because it increases the status of the family.

Case study

MINI-CASE: Korean expatriates in China

The rapid rise of Asian MNEs is exemplified by the progress of the Hyundai Motor Company (HMC), a Korean MNE whose expansion strategy includes transplanting assembly operations to newly industrializing countries in Asia. In 2002, when HMC started a joint venture with the Chinese car maker, Beijing Automotive Company, more than 200 expatriate managers and engineers from Korea were assigned to set up and manage HMC's Beijing operation (Zou and Lansbury, 2009). The Korean expatriates were appointed to all senior management positions and controlled production activities and workshop procedures.

However, the Koreans' dominance triggered tensions with the Chinese. The expatriates regarded local managers as inexperienced and unreliable, and criticized the Chinese workforce for lacking discipline and work ethic. The Chinese criticized the Koreans for their authoritarian management style which the Chinese saw as inappropriate for the local workforce. At first HMC relied on standard employment policies and practices transferred directly from its Korean operation but it soon recognized the need to adapt these to Chinese conditions.

In 2005, HMC reduced labour costs by cutting the number of expatriate managers in the Beijing factory from 200 to 60 (Chinese managers are cheaper to hire than Korean expatriates). Since then, Korean managers and engineers have been sent to Beijing for short, focused periods to carry out very specific tasks, such as overseeing the introduction of a new model or training Chinese employees to implement a new procedure.

Small groups of Chinese managers and engineers are periodically sent to Korea not only to be trained in production management skills, but also to learn the company's values of loyalty and strong work ethic. While they are in Korea the Chinese delegates learn how their cross-cultural communication skills could be improved, with the long-term aim of minimizing conflict between Korean and Chinese employees in Beijing.

Questions:

1. *What specific employment policies and practices would have the effect of improving relations between Chinese and Korean managers and employees at HMC's Beijing plant?*

> **Case study**
>
> **Continued**
>
> 2. 'HMC's success in China depends on its ability to effectively manage cross-
>   cultural communication with Chinese managers and employees.' Suggest three
>   specific ways in which cross-cultural communication in the plant could be
>   improved.

EXPATRIATE MANAGEMENT STYLES

Participative style

Many expatriate managers discover that they need to change their 'natural' management styles to be successful in their assignments. They may find, for instance, that their participative management style is counterproductive in a high power–distance culture such as Russia or India, where autocratic styles are expected and are the norm.

A Swedish manager appointed to a job in an Indian textile company assumes that his Indian employees, following the example of his employees in Sweden, will welcome the opportunity to be involved in planning decisions. But his assumption proves to be wrong. The Indian employees ignore his requests to submit their ideas. They regard these requests as a sign of his managerial incompetence.

The Swede was frustrated by his employees' reluctance to become involved in planning decisions, but failed to realize that the true cause of their reluctance lay beyond individual employees and was rooted in Indian culture.

In high power–distance cultures expatriate managers are expected to behave in an autocratic, directive way and to take all necessary decisions. Signalling an intention to use a participative management style when the workforce is looking for firm direction and control only leads to frustration on both sides. Expatriate managers carrying out assignments in countries where firm direction and guidance from managers is expected generally need to demonstrate decisive, clear-cut leadership. They are, as Paine (2010) points out, expected to communicate clear performance standards and behaviour standards to their employees, and to identify a few non-negotiable standards – those that employees will lose their jobs for violating.

But even in high power–distance countries and within authoritarian organisations it is sometimes possible for the expatriate manager to promote flexibility – for instance, by the simple device of allocating some decision rights to a committee of employees and giving the committee access to relevant information. Committees can also be set up to ensure connectivity across departmental boundaries. By such means levels of flexibility and responsiveness in the host organisation can be increased and levels of employee commitment can be raised.

Laissez-faire style

A blatant example of an expatriate manager choosing to use a wholly inappropriate management style occurred in an international research programme, where the manager allowed local staff to spend all their time working only on the projects that interested them. For many of these projects the prospects of commercial application and eventual return-on-investment were minimal. Yet the manager unwisely chose a *laissez-faire* style of leadership that would almost certainly have a negative impact on the research programme's sustainability.

Paternalistic style

Fiedler (1967) compares two opposing styles of leadership:

- psychologically distant and controlling;
- psychologically close and more permissive.

Paternalistic management has some of the characteristics and effects of Fiedler's model of psychologically close leadership. Fiedler argues that a close, liking relationship enables a manager to be more decisive and to obtain the cooperation of subordinates – whatever their cultural background – without resorting to power or status. The manager introduces change by winning the *consent* of employees rather than through *coercion* (Tuckman, 1995).

A paternalistic management style is common and widely preferred in Russia, Taiwan, South America, and other countries where superior–subordinate relationships are hierarchical and interdependent in nature (Aycan, 2008). In such countries bosses are assumed to know what is good for their employees – and employees are expected to show loyalty and deference to their bosses. Employees in these countries have been found to experience high levels of job satisfaction when working in a controlled organisational context (Testa et al., 2003).

National styles

Studies have documented cognitive differences between Westerners and Asians (Varnum et al., 2010). For instance, Westerners tend to be more analytic while Asians tend to be more holistic. These differences are sometimes explained as being due to corresponding differences in social values – Westerners are more independent and Asians are more interdependent. Cognitive differences such as these become obvious when Western managers carry out expatriate assignments in Asian countries.

Managers from diverse countries tend to think in different, culturally influenced ways. For instance, according to Palich et al. (2002), Americans have a decisive, clear-cut logic that excludes contradictory visions of a concept such as human rights or democracy. Human rights is *this* so we won't waste time considering *that*. Chinese managers, by contrast, see the value of considering opposing ideas – possibly because they have been exposed to dialectical logic from childhood.

As these examples demonstrate, expatriate managers display culturally influenced approaches to the way they carry out their assignments. French managers, for instance, tend to focus on grasping complex issues. As Schneider and Barsoux (1997) note, French managers are good at analysing complicated problems and arriving at logical solutions. German expatriate managers, on the other hand, are reputed to be always extremely interested in the technological aspects of their assignments and strive to achieve technically correct solutions to the problems that arise. British expatriate managers, by contrast, often give the impression of regarding their assignments as an extended exercise in cross-cultural communication. For instance, they put much effort into explaining their plans to local managers and staff and to winning their support.

SMALL-GROUP EXERCISE: Discussion questions

Working in small groups, discuss each of the following questions and write down the group's agreed answer. At the end of the exercise, each group may present its answers to the other groups for comment.

1. *What are the main reasons why companies appoint managers to expatriate posts abroad?*
2. *What are the main reasons for the low proportion of female expatriates? What practical policies and actions would have the effect of increasing the numbers of female expatriate managers?*
3. *Identify the various ways in which the expatriate brand is changing.*
4. *An important responsibility of many expatriate managers is the transfer of technology and business knowledge to the host organisation. Describe typical problems encountered in carrying out this responsibility.*
5. *'Expatriate managers need to manage and motivate local employees.' Explain why flexibility is the essential quality required for this task.*

MEASURING EXPATRIATE PERFORMANCE

Success factors

MNEs measure the performance of their expatriate managers by the same yardsticks used to assess home-based managers. These include the contribution that the manager – or the manager's unit – has made to profits. Another measure of success (often used by cross-cultural researchers) is the extent of the expatriate's cross-cultural adjustment by the end of the assignment (Tung and Varma, 2008). Factors influencing expatriate adjustment are examined in Chapter 7.

To a large extent expatriate job performance depends on the expatriate manager's ability to overcome the stresses and conflicts that go with the job. Thus the literature on expatriate management emphasizes the need for expatriates to recover from *culture shock* and adjust to the foreign culture in order to avoid failure of the assignment and the premature return of the manager. One study found that expatriates from Western countries had high dissatisfaction levels with their assignments in Pakistan, India, South East Asia, the Middle East, and North Africa because business incompatibilities and cultural differences in those countries were much greater than in other world regions (Torbiorn, 1982).

Other important factors which contribute to the success of expatriate assignments are:

- knowledge transfer;
- effective training/coaching of local staff;
- establishing communication links with parent company;
- overcoming information difficulties;
- dealing with ethical dilemmas.

These aspects of expatriate success are considered below.

Knowledge transfer

Gupta and Govindarajan (2000) found that the success of many expatriate assignments depends on the expatriate's ability to transfer valuable knowledge to foreign subsidiaries. Two kinds of knowledge are transferred:

- the expatriate manager's own *implicit knowledge* that has been acquired through experience;
- *technological and business knowledge* that has accumulated in the parent company and to which the expatriate manager – often because of his own efforts – has access.

The usual way in which expatriate managers gain these accumulated resources is by establishing *formal and informal communication links* with the parent firm. Successfully establishing these links enables them to play a key role in facilitating the transfer of technological and business knowledge from the parent firm to the subsidiary operation (Rosenzweig and Nohria, 1994). Viewed from this perspective, expatriate managers are, first and foremost, the *carriers of culture*. They initiate practices and procedures in the host organisation that resemble those of the parent organisation at home.

McDonnell et al. (2010) found that MNEs with headquarters in many countries but with operations in Ireland used various means to transfer learning to

Technology transfer mechanisms	MNE's using
1. International informal networks	75%
2. International project groups	70%
3. Expatriate assignments	59%
4. International formal committees	50%
5. External secondments	21%

Figure 6.2   Technology transfer mechanisms used by multinationals

Source: Adapted from McDonnell et al. (2010).

their Irish operations. The main mechanisms used to transfer technological and business knowledge across borders were:

- expatriate management assignments
- international formal committees
- international informal networks
- secondments to external organisations internationally (e.g. suppliers)
- international task forces (considered critically important by some MNEs through developing global integration)

Sixty per cent of MNEs with operations in Ireland used three or more of these learning transfer mechanisms. Large MNEs – those with at least 5000 employees worldwide – were the ones most likely to utilize multiple learning transfer mechanisms.

McDonnell et al. (2010) found that expatriate assignments were a widely used means of transfer (Figure 6.2). Expatriate managers, from their experience of a wide range of different cultures and job situations, acquire valuable skills which can be used to benefit the MNEs in other parts of the world.

Knowledge-transfer and subsidiary performance

Much evidence shows that the successful transfer of knowledge from the parent company to a subsidiary leads to improved subsidiary performance. Fang et al. (2007), for instance, found that the successful transfer of business and technological knowledge leads to:

- improved operational performance in the subsidiary;
- improved bottom-line results in the parent company.

Fang et al. (2010) analysed 1660 foreign subsidiaries of Japanese firms over a 15-year period and concluded that expatriate managers facilitated knowledge transfer from the parent company and that this strengthened the subsidiary's performance *but only in the short term*. The researchers concluded that the expatriate manager's positive influence on subsidiary performance as a result of successful knowledge transfer gradually disappears as the subsidiary builds its own independent experience and expertise – over, say, a 10-year period. The

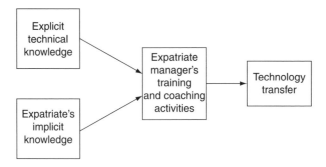

Figure 6.3   Technology transfer process

Based on Fang et al. (2010).

implication is that an expatriate manager's impact on subsidiary performance usually diminishes as the subsidiary becomes more mature (Figure 6.3).

Effective training of local staff

The training of local staff is a key responsibility of many expatriate managers. Typical training responsibilities are:

- to train accounting and administrative staff to operate a computerized administrative system;
- to train shop floor workers to operate computer-controlled machine tools;
- to train local managers to use imported financial control and auditing techniques.

Anecdotal evidence suggests that successful results in carrying out such responsibilities are sometimes achieved by adopting a *training to systems* strategy. The strategy is based on the recognition that training is a finite resource, and that it should therefore focus on equipping local staff with the knowledge and skills needed to efficiently operate and maintain the organisation's *systems and subsystems* – that is those that enable the organisation to function.

'Training to systems' is cost-effective because it protects the capital investments that have already been made in the organisation by the parent company (or by the government, or by an international agency such as the World Bank, Asian Development Bank, or the European Union). The strategy involves training local staff to efficiently operate and maintain the organisation's assets, notably:

- *systems*, such as computerized management control systems;
- *machines*, equipment and structures;
- *procedures*, such as monitoring, accounting, and billing procedures.

Coaching

In addition to such training interventions, one-to-one coaching by an expatriate manager of promising local staff ensures that a local manager is ready to take over at the end of the expatriate's assignment, thus solving the succession problem. Expatriate managers who act as on-the-job coaches *show* subordinates what to do as opposed to merely telling them.

According to Cocks (2009), business leaders in Australia's best-performing companies exhibit coaching styles of leadership as a way of developing winning teams. Managers who use a coaching style of leadership are effective because they make themselves available. They support promising staff by being close to them and constantly explaining and communicating – as opposed to setting targets from afar.

Establishing communication links with parent company

To facilitate knowledge transfer expatriate managers must establish formal and informal *communication links* with senior management in the parent organisation, which gives them access to the parent firm's knowledge resources. They must also become adept at establishing informal *communication networks* that allow them to build cooperative relationships with colleagues and employees in the host organisation. Establishing these networks is a first step to successfully transferring business and technological knowledge. Thus Clouse and Watkins (2009: 118) advise managers facing their first expatriate position abroad to reach out and start building communication networks with local colleagues immediately after starting the job. As a result of doing so word will quickly spread that the new manager means business.

Ability to speak the local language simplifies the task of building of informal communication networks among local colleagues and members of the local community. It enables the expatriate manager to discuss job-related issues with local colleagues and employees, as well as providing access to written and spoken sources of information in the country so that the manager does not have to depend on others for important information. Expatriates who are unable to speak the local language are often restricted in their social relationships to fellow-expatriates throughout the period of their assignments.

Overcoming information difficulties

A recurring problem for expatriate managers in the Middle East, China, Mexico, and other emerging economies is the inaccuracy or inaccessibility of many kinds of information. For instance, an expatriate general manager working for a US company in Mexico was so frustrated by the Mexican subsidiary's inability to collect market-related information from distribution centres that he had to persuade the company to invest in its own costly satellite-based communication system.

Expatriate managers carrying out assignments in developing countries often face cultural and linguistic barriers that cloud perceptions and block access to information. Chinese managers' seemingly roundabout ways of communicating, sudden changes of plan, and 'yeses' that actually mean 'no', are extremely frustrating for Western expatriates – as are the information problems encountered. China has a huge system to collect and analyse data for central planning and business purposes and the State Statistical Bureau has several tens of thousands of employees. Nevertheless, many kinds of information are extremely difficult to extract because they are scattered among various agencies, and often the person responsible for dealing with the information in any one agency is unidentifiable. Yet expatriate success may depend on overcoming such fundamental constraints on effectiveness.

In China an effective approach to overcome such fundamental constraints is to do what the Chinese themselves do – establish 'guanxi' (connections). Guanxi refers to establishing mutually advantageous connections with appropriate individuals and institutions and to a long-lasting exchange of favours (Chen and Chen, 2004). Guanxi is as important for business success in China as networking is in Western countries. It helps managers – both Chinese and expatriate managers – to find ways round numerous bureaucratic snags. Business in China relies heavily on relationships, and 'guanxi' is the all-important method which expatriate managers can use to meet information and other business needs.

'Kankei' in Japan is somewhat similar to 'guanxi', and in Arab countries there is 'wasta', which refers to the how managers get things done through establishing connections with people in influential positions (Cunningham and Sarayrah, 1993).

Dealing with ethical dilemmas

Expatriate managers are sometimes confronted with ethical issues during their assignments. They may be confronted with practices that are entirely normal in the host culture but that would be completely unacceptable in their own country. As a result, they do not know how to act. Typical examples are:

- payment of 'commissions' to obtain contracts;
- discrimination against women in some Arab countries;
- child labour in some Asian countries.

Maintaining ethical standards may require the expatriate manager to create appropriate monitoring mechanisms. For example, the expatriate general manager of a manufacturing company in Chile reportedly set up an approvals committee to assess and approve certain kinds of sales and marketing expenses with the aim of ensuring that they complied with the company's limits on gifts and entertainment.

For an expatriate manager, making a decision about how to act is complicated by the fact that no international consensus on standards of business conduct exists. Consequently, the manager can never be certain that any particular action is the right action. And in many cases, few elements in the manager's earlier education and training may have prepared him to confront important ethical issues. Ghosal (2005) discusses the influence of management education and training on business, and the role of the business schools as breeding grounds for unethical management practices. Velasquez (1995) cuts through the uncertainties by arguing that the right thing for expatriate managers to do when confronted by ethical dilemmas is to stick to *traditional ethical principles* – utility, rights, justice, and so on.

Hamilton et al.'s (2009) approach to reducing the uncertainty involved in such situations is to be logical. They offer six heuristic questions to help expatriate staff and business people to resolve cross-cultural ethical conflicts created when methods of doing business in the host country differ from those used at home. The questions are presented in a decision tree format with 'yes' or 'no' answers, moving the manager down different branches of the tree. By working through the questions the manager becomes clearer about how to deal with the questionable business practices in question.

EXPATRIATE SELECTION

Selection procedures

Maintaining an expatriate workforce can be extremely expensive. For instance, the first-year costs of sending expatriates on foreign assignments are at least three times the base salaries of their domestic counterparts (Shaffer et al., 1999). Moreover, expatriates who are wrongly selected may fail to adjust to the foreign culture and consequently may suffer from high stress levels, underperform in their jobs and, in some cases, have to be replaced. The costs of failed assignments are high both for the expatriate and for the expatriate's employer (Jun and Gentry, 2005).

Such considerations make it essential that the right people are selected for expatriate assignments in the first place. Three multinationals which have worked to overcome the problem of high failure rates for expatriate managers admitted that poor selection was to blame (Blockyn, 1989). The implication is that poor selection procedures sometimes lead to expatriate managers failing to achieve their assignment objectives and, in some cases, having to be replaced.

Global succession planning

Most expatriates are employed by MNEs, and many MNEs have developed global succession planning systems (McDonnell et al., 2010). In companies which have developed these systems, headquarters has the means to identify high-performing and high-potential employees in operations worldwide. These high-performing individuals may then be selected to carry out expatriate assignments in other countries where the MNE operates. In this way, the knowledge and skills possessed by highly effective managers are diffused across the MNE's operations worldwide. McDonnell et al. (2010) report that while 56 per cent of foreign MNEs in Ireland had expatriates from their home countries on assignment in their Irish subsidiaries, 46 per cent of the MNEs had personnel from the Irish operations on assignment in other parts of the world.

However, global succession planning is the exception rather than the rule, and many companies use less sophisticated methods of expatriate selection. Solomon (1994), for instance, found that in up to 90 per cent of cases expatriates were selected on the basis of *technical expertise* alone while other important qualities were ignored. When researchers surveyed 50 CEOs of global companies and executive search consultants, many respondents revealed that they relied on *personal preferences* or unquestioned organisational traditions when selecting people for senior positions at home or abroad (Fernandez-Araoz et al., 2009). Half of the companies relied mainly on the interviewing manager's gut feeling. Little attention was paid to carrying out careful reference checks.

Unsophisticated selection methods

According to Harris and Brewster (1999), expatriate selection methods in some companies are so unsophisticated that they consist mainly of identifying individuals who are willing to go. Moreover, in some companies there is even uncertainty about such fundamentals as:

- Who should be interviewed: only insiders, only outsiders, or both?
- Which assessment instruments should be used – if at all?
- Who should handle expatriate selection – the HR department? The expatriate's present and/or future boss? A selection committee? Recruitment consultants?

In many cases the HR department is responsible for selecting expatriate staff, yet only 11 per cent of HR managers have ever worked abroad themselves and so may have little understanding of the challenges and difficulties involved in carrying out overseas assignments (Black and Gregersen, 1999).

Companies which presently rely on unsophisticated selection procedures could improve expatriate selection by taking the following practical measures:

- ensure that standardized tests and other reliable instruments are routinely used to improve candidate assessment;
- make a thorough review of each candidate's skills and motivations;
- identify ways in which candidates are equipped to contribute to the firm's global expansion strategy;
- carefully assess the extent of the candidate's 'cultural fit' with the host country.

The importance of cultural fit was highlighted by a survey carried out in 2009 of 144 recruitment consultants based in 40 countries (Korn/Ferry, 2009). The survey revealed that most managers are extremely reluctant to be posted to expatriate posts in countries they perceive as insular, very different from home. More than half of the consultants surveyed (51 per cent) thought that the most common reason for failure in expatriate assignments was *lack of cultural fit*. The next most common reason was *family/personal issues* (23 per cent).

Expatriate qualities

Before an expatriate manager is sent to India to fight a competitor who is gaining market share, or to China to keep the computers running in a joint venture company, the qualities required for success in the assignment concerned should be carefully identified. The manager should then be assessed for possession of the required qualities.

Managers with *previous international experience* are able to predict what a new foreign assignment is likely to involve. They will have more realistic expectations than candidates who lack foreign experience (Black et al., 1992). Previous work- or non-work-related experiences abroad give accurate work expectations and so higher levels of adjustment and performance can be expected (Black et al., 1991). However, the positive effects of previous experience – which tend to be great early in an expatriate assignment – disappear later in the assignment (Selmer, 2002; Takeuchi et al., 2002).

Qualities that researchers have identified as contributing to expatriate success include:

- openness to change and new experiences (Huang et al., 2005);
- cross-cultural communication skills and ability to get on with host country nationals (e.g. Tung, 2004);
- willingness to adapt to local cultural norms (Caligiuri and Cascio, 1998);
- likeability and signalling attentiveness to others (Leung and Bond, 2001);
- cultural sensitivity (Puck et al., 2008).

Cultural sensitivity is important because it helps expatriates to cope with the many cultural differences they would be faced with during their assignments. Black and Gregersen (1999) found that companies that successfully manage expatriates usually look for cultural flexibility in candidates (such as liking to eat dal and chapattis for lunch in India; or taking a strong interest in the fortunes of the local jai alai team in Brazil).

Barnham and Oates's (1991) survey of 50 British, American, and Japanese MNEs to discover which qualities of expatriate management they valued the most identified the following:

- strategic awareness
- adaptability
- sensitivity to different cultures
- ability to work in cross-cultural teams
- language skills

- international negotiating skills
- high task orientation

Multicultural personality

Van der Zee and Van Oudenhoven's (2000) assessment instrument for measuring *multicultural personality* is sometimes used as part of the expatriate selection process. According to Van der Zee and Van Oudenhoven (2000), multicultural personality equips managers to become effective leaders of multicultural teams. The five dimensions of multicultural personality are cultural empathy, open-mindedness, social initiative, emotional stability, and flexibility.

According to Puck et al. (2008), *previous experience* of working on multicultural teams facilitates an individual's integration into a diverse team as the individuals would have developed behavioural strategies that would help them to participate effectively in such teams.

Local language skills

Many MNEs recognize the importance of their expatriate employees acquiring proficiency in the host country majority language. When German MNEs, for instance, were asked what attributes they look for when appointing managers to expatriate posts, *language skills* and cross-cultural *communication competence* headed the list of desirable characteristics as these qualities were found to promote good work performance and facilitate cross-cultural adjustment (Marx, 2001). In multinational teams English is often used as the lingua franca and when this is the case proficiency in English becomes a key selection criterion, as this ability helps to ensure effective communication within the team.

Excellent job performance often depends on an expatriate manager demonstrating adequate local language skills. Ability to speak the local language enhances the prestige and effectiveness of the expatriate by increasing communication opportunities with local employees and reducing the need for interpreters. Zimmermann et al. (2003), investigating German expatriates in China, found that inability to speak Chinese was adversely affecting the expatriates' job performance and delaying their adjustment to Chinese society. According to the Germans, ability to speak Chinese would have provided a base for communicating with Chinese colleagues and employees.

> Subsequently, when the Germans started to learn Chinese, they found that it helped both with relationship-building and with understanding Chinese culture. For instance, they learned the cultural importance of 'face' and of not criticising Chinese employees in front of their co-workers.

Generally, migrants' ability to speak the host country language is a strong predictor of their ability to obtain and keep employment and to increase their earning capacity. In Australia, since the ability to speak English is a prerequisite for most jobs, English language proficiency is extremely important for Indians, Chinese, Iraqis, Pakistanis, and other immigrants who seek employment. Syed and Murray (2009) found that female immigrants with previous English language training or experience of using the language face far fewer difficulties in adjusting in the Australian labour market.

Assessment tools

According to Fernandez-Araoz et al. (2009), improving the quality of assessments of candidates for expatriate posts is three times more profitable than increasing the size of the candidate pool. Higher-quality assessments can be achieved by making greater use of the range of instruments that are available to assess candidates' competences and personality attributes. Examples of tried and tested assessment instruments are:

- the *Cross-cultural Adaptability Inventory* (Kelley and Meyers, 1999), which measures personal autonomy, perceptual acuity, emotional resilience, and flexibility and openness;
- the *Multicultural Personality Questionnaire* (Van der Zee and Van Oudenhoven, 2000), which measures personality traits likely to facilitate cross-cultural adjustment, including open-mindedness, cultural empathy, and emotional stability.

Selection of female expatriates

Constantly moving managers around the world to address global business needs is common business practice – less common, however, if the manager is a woman. A persistent barrier for female managers who wish to gain experience overseas is the reluctance of companies to send them. Estimates of the proportion of female expatriates range from 10 per cent (PricewaterhouseCoopers, 2005) to 20 per cent (GMAC, 2007), with strong variations across countries and regions. One reason for the low proportion of female expatriates is the reluctance exhibited by many Western companies to select female staff for expatriate assignments because of the perceived prejudice against women managers in many foreign countries.

Most companies, for instance, would not consider sending a female candidate for an expatriate post in Saudi Arabia, where women are not involved in business negotiations. A letter published in the *Times* (11 July 2006) commented on the selection of two female officers for an assignment in Afghanistan:

To send two female officials for discussions with conservative Afghan leaders is madness. This shows a lack of understanding of the culture. Their own women would not even be allowed in the room with men there. I have known

Afghan commanders refuse to shake hands with women expatriate aid workers and walk out of the room.

Yet female expatriates are found to be as successful as their male counterparts, even in male-dominated cultures (Sinangil and Ones, 2003). But perhaps the quality most needed by women expatriate managers in male-dominated cultures is *mental toughness*, and candidates should be assessed for this attribute during the selection process.

KEY POINTS

1. Expatriates are managerial, professional, and technical staff who live and work in a foreign country on a temporary basis but normally for more than 1 year. Multinational companies use expatriates in the absence of qualified and effective local staff, and to develop high-potential mangers by means of international experience. Nearly 80 per cent of US companies send expatriate managers to work in the companies' overseas subsidiaries. The number of women expatriate managers is still small in proportion to men, and much smaller than the proportion of women managers in home-based posts.

2. The traffic in expatriate managers used to be one-way – from developed to developing countries. But the pattern has changed. More and more multinational companies based in developing countries are starting operations in the developed world. Lenovo, for instance, the largest manufacturer of PCs in China, purchased an IBM division in 2004. Tata Industries of India has acquired Tetley Teas and Corus Steel in Europe. More managers from developing countries are being posted to expatriate assignments in both developed and developing countries.

3. Many expatriate assignments involve transferring of technology from the parent company to an overseas subsidiary. The expatriate manager is responsible for overseeing the transfer – and for overcoming the many problems that this entails. Major problems can arise from lack of adequate local resources. For instance, advanced manufacturing systems rely on precisely timed completion of various operations and intense horizontal information flows. However, local managers may be incapable of establishing such conditions, or of maintaining the systems after the expatriate's departure.

4. Expatriate managers' success depends on their using *appropriate* techniques which do not run counter to local values. Managers who use inappropriate techniques often find themselves confronting employee morale and productivity problems. If, for instance, the manager tries to boost output by installing a payment system based on PBR he may fail. While PBR works well in competitive, individualistic countries, when introduced into organisations in countries with strong collectivist values it can have a disastrous effect on morale, absenteeism, and labour turnover.

5. Managers may need to change their 'natural' management style to be successful abroad. A participative management style, for instance, is likely to be counterproductive in a high power–distance culture such as Russia or India, where autocratic styles are the norm. A paternalistic management style is common and widely preferred in Russia, Taiwan, South America, and other countries where superior–subordinate relationships are hierarchical and interdependent in nature. In such countries bosses are assumed to know what is good for their employees – and employees are expected to show loyalty and deference to their bosses.

6. Ability to transfer business and technological knowledge to the host organisation is a key factor which is central to the success of many expatriate assignments. Access to the necessary knowledge is gained when the expatriate establishes formal and informal communication links with the parent firm. Successful expatriate managers also establish informal communication networks in the host organisation as a first step to transferring this knowledge. In addition to training, one-to-one coaching by an expatriate manager of promising local staff ensures that a local manager is ready to take over at the end of the expatriate's assignment.

7. When expatriate managers can speak the local language this simplifies the task of building of informal communication networks among local colleagues and members of the local community. It enables them to discuss job-related issues with local colleagues and employees, as well as providing access to written and spoken sources of information in the country. Expatriates who cannot speak the local language may be restricted in their social relationships to fellow-expatriates throughout the period of their assignments.

8. In the majority of cases expatriates are selected on the basis of technical expertise alone. Other important qualities are ignored. Many recruitment and executive search consultants rely on personal preference or gut feeling when selecting people for senior positions at home or abroad, and often little attention is paid to carrying out careful reference checks. Ways of improving expatriate selection procedures would be to ensure that reliable instruments are routinely used for candidate assessment, and to identify ways in which candidates would be able to contribute to the firm's global expansion strategy.

QUESTIONS FOR DISCUSSION AND WRITTEN ASSIGNMENTS

1. 'The expatriate manager is responsible for overseeing the transfer of technology and for overcoming the problems that this entails.' What are the problems? How could they be overcome?

2. Which qualities/attributes (e.g. personality, networking skills, cultural awareness, positive approach to other cultures, etc.) enable expatriate managers to succeed in their assignments?

3. Often managers are selected for expatriate assignments on the basis of technical expertise alone while other important qualities are ignored. Which other qualities are important for expatriate success and why?

BIBLIOGRAPHY

Aycan, Z. Cross-cultural approaches to leadership. In PB Smith et al. (eds), *Handbook of Cross-cultural Management Research*. Sage, 2008, pp. 219–238.

Barnham, K and Oates, D. *The International Manager*. Business Books, 1991.

Bartlett, CA and Ghosal, S. *Managing Across Borders: The Transnational Solution*. Hutchinson, 1989.

Black, JS et al., Towards a comprehensive model of international adjustment: an integration of multiple theoretical perspectives. *Academy of Management Review*, 16, 1991, 291–317.

Black, JS, Gregersen, HB and Mendenhall, ME. *Global Assignments: Successfully Expatriating and Repatriating International Manager*. Jossey-Bass, 1992.

Black, JS and Gregersen, H. The right way to manage expats. *HBR*, 77, 1999, 52–62.

Blockyn, P. Developing the international executive. *Personnel*, 66, 1989, 44.

Caligiuri, PM and Cascio, WF. Can we send her there? Maximising the success of Western women on global assignments. *Journal of World Business*, 33, 1998, 394–416.

Chen, X-P and Chen, CC. On the intricacies of the Chinese guanxi. *Asia Pacific Journal of Management*, 21, 2004, 305–324.

Clouse, MA and Watkins, MD. Three keys to getting an overseas assignment right. *HBR*, October 2009, 115–119.

Cocks, G. High performers down under: lessons from Australia's winning companies. *Journal of Business Strategy*, 30 (4), 2009, 17–22.

Cunningham, RB and Sarayrah, YK. *Wasta: The Hidden Force in Middle Eastern Society*. Praeger, 1993.

Dadfar, H and Gustavsson, P. Competition by effective management of cultural diversity: the case of international construction projects. *International Studies of Management and Organisation*, 22 (4), 1992, 81–92.

Edstrom, A and Galbraith, JR. Transfer of managers as a coordination and control strategy in multinational organisations. *Administrative Science Quarterly*, 22, 1977, 248–263.

Fang, Y et al., International diversification, subsidiary performance, and the mobility of knowledge resources. *Strategic Management Journal*, 28, 2007, 1053–1064.

Fang, Y et al., Multinational firm knowledge, use of expatriates, and foreign subsidiary performance. *Journal of Management Studies*, 47 (1), 2010, 27–54.

Fernandez-Araoz, C, Groysberg, B and Nohria, N. The definitive guide to recruiting in good times and bad. *HBR*, May 2009, 74–84.

Fiedler, FE. *A Theory of Leadership Effeciveness*. McGraw-Hill, 1967.

Gamble, J. Transferring organisational practices and the dynamics of hybridisation; Japanese retail multinationals in China. *Journal of Management Studies*, 47 (4), 2010, 705–732.

Ghosal, S. Bad management theories are destroying good management practices. *Academy of Management Learning and Education*, 4, 2005, 75–91.

Ghosal, S and Nohria, N. Horses for courses: organisational forms for multinational organisations. *Sloan Management Review*, 34 (2), 1993, 23–35.

GMAC Global Relocation Services, Global relocation trends: 2006 Survey report. GMAC, 2007.

Gupta, AK and Govindarajan, V. Knowledge flows within multinational corporations. *Strategic Management Journal*, 21, 2000, 473–496.

Hamilton, JB et al., Google in China: a manager-friendly heuristic model for resolving cross-cultural ethical conflicts. *Journal of Business Ethics*, 86, 2009, 143–157.

Harris, H and Brewster, C. The coffee machine system: how international selection really works. *International Journal of Human Resource Management*, 10, 1999, 488–500.

Harzing, A-W. Of bears, bumble-bees, and spiders: the role of expatriates in controlling foreign subsidiaries. *Journal of World Business*, 36, 2001, 366–379.

Herzberg, F. *Work and the Nature of Man*. World Publishing Company, 1966.

Holopainen, J and Bjorkman, I. The personal characteristics of the successful expatriate. *Personnel Review*, 34, 2005, 37–50.

Huang, T-J, Chi, S-C and Lawler, JJ. The relationship between expatriates' personality traits and their adjustment to international assignments. *International Journal of Human Resources Management*, 16, 2005, 1667.

Hutchings, K et al., Exploring Arab Middle eastern women's perceptions of barriers to, and facilitators of, international management opportunities. *International Journal of Human Resource Management*, 21 (1), 2010, 61–83.

Hymowitz, C. Chinese women bosses say long hours on job don't hurt their kids. *Wall Street Journal*, 17 May 2005.

Jackson, T. *International HRM: A Cross-cultural Approach*. Sage, 2002.

Jackson, T and Bak, M. Foreign companies and Chinese workers: employee motivation in the People's Republic of China. *Journal of Organisational Change Management*, 11 (4), 1998, 282–300.

Jun, S and Gentry, JW. An exploratory investigation of the relative importance of cultural similarity and personal fit in the selection and performance of expatriates. *World Business*, 40, 2005, 1–8.

Kelley, C and Meyers, J. The cross-cultural adaptability inventory. In SM Fowler and MG Mumford (eds), *Intercultural Source Book: Cross-cultural Training Methods* (Vol. 2). Intercultural Press, 1999, pp. 53–60.

Korn/Ferry, *Executive Recruiter Index*, 10th ed. Korn/Ferry International, 2009.

Leung, SK and Bond, MH. Interpersonal communication and personality. *Asian Journal of Social Psychology*, 4, 2001, 69–86.

Markus, HR and Kitayama, S. Culture and the self: implications for cognition, emotion, and motivation. *Psychological Review*, 98, 1991, 224–293.

Marx, E. *Breaking Through Culture Shock*. Nicholas Brealey Publishing, 2001.

McDonnell, A et al., Learning transfer in multinational companies: explaining inter-organisation variation. *Human Resource Management Journal*, 20 (1), 2010, 23–43.

Napier, NK and Taylor, S. *Western Women Working in Japan*. Quorum Books, 1995.

Owen, CL et al., Success strategies for expatriate women managers in China. *Review of Business*, March 2007.

Ozbilgin, MF. Global diversity management. PB Smith, MF Peterson and DC Thomas (eds), *Handbook of Cross-cultural Management Research*. Sage, 2008, pp. 379–396.

Paine, LS. The China rule. *HBR*, June 2010, 103–108.

Palich, LE et al., Comparing American and Chinese negotiating styles. *Thunderbird International Review*, 44, 2002, 777–798.

PricewaterhouseCoopers, *Managing a Virtual World: Intrernational Non-standard Assignments Policy and Practices*. PricewaterhouseCoopers, Europe, 2000.

PricewaterhouseCoopers, *International Assignments: Global Policy and Practice, Key Trends*. PricewaterhouseCoopers, 2005.

Puck, JF, Mohr, AT and Rygl, D. An empirical analysis of managers' adjustment to working in multi-national project teams in the pipeline and plant construction sector. *International Journal of Human Resource Management*, 19 (12), 2008, 2252–2267.

Richardson, J and McKenna, S. Leaving and experiencing: why academics expatriate and how they experience expatriation. *Career Development International*, 7 (2), 2002, 67–78.

Rosenzweig, PM and Nohria, N. Influences on human resource management practices in multinational corporations. *Journal of International Business Studies*, 25, 1994, 229–251.

Schneider, SC and Barsoux, J-L. *Managing Across Cultures*. FT Prentice Hall, 1997, p. 193.

Selmer, J. Practice makes perfect: international experience and expatriate adjustment. *Management International Review*, 42, 2002, 71–87.

Selmer, J and Leung, ALM. International adjustment of female vs male business expatriates. *International Journal of Human Resource Management*, 14 (7), 2003, 1117–1131.

Shaffer, MA, Harrison, DA and Gilley, KM. Dimensions, determinants, and differences in the expatriate adjustment process. *Journal of International Business Studies*, 30, 1999, 557–581.

Sijanen, T and Lamsa, A-M. The changing nature of expatriation: exploring cross-cultural adaptation through narrativity. *International Journal of Human Resource Management*, 20 (7), 2009, 1468–1486.

Sinangil, HK and Ones, DS. Gender differences in expatriate job performance. Applied Psychology: *An International Review*, 52, 2003, 461–475.

Solomon, CM. Success abroad depends on more than job skills. *Personnel Journal*, 73 (4), 1994, 51–54.

Sparrow, PR. Reappraising psychological contracting. *International Studies of Management and Organisation*, 28 (1), 1998, 30–63.

Syed, J and Murray, P. Combating the English language deficit: the labour market experiences of migrant women in Australia. *Human Resource Management Journal*, 19 (4), 2009, 413–432.

Takeuchi, R. Yun, S and Tesluk, PE. An examination of crossover and spillover effects of spousal and expatriate cross-cultural adjustment on expatriate outcomes. *Journal of Applied Psychology*, 87, 2002, 655–666.

Testa, MR, Mueller, SL and Thomas, AS. Cultural fit and job satisfaction in a global service environment. *Management International Review*, 43, 2003, 129–148.

Torbiorn, I. *Living Abroad*. Wiley, 1982.

Trompenaars, F and Hampden-Turner, C. *Riding the Waves of Culture*, 2nd ed. Nicholas Brealey, 1997.

Tuckman, A. Ideology, quality and TQM. In A Wilkinson and H Willmott (eds), Making Quality Critical: New Perspectives on *Organisational Change*. Routledge, 1995, pp. 54–81.

Tung, RL. Female expatriates: the model global manager? *Organisational Dynamics*, 33 (3), 2004, 243–253.

Tung, RL and Varma, A. Expatriate selection and evaluation. In PB Smith, MF Peterson and DC Thomas (eds), *Handbook of Cross-cultural Management Research*. Sage, 2008, pp. 367–378.

Usui, C, Rose, S and Kageyama, R. Institutions and leadership in Japan. *Asian Perspective*, 27, 2003, 85–123.

Van der Boon, M. Women in international management. *Women in Management Review*, 18 (3/4), 2003, 132–146.

Van der Zee, KI and Van Oudenhoven, JP. The Multicultural personality: a multidimensional instrument of multicultural effectiveness. *European Journal of Personality*, 14, 2000, 291–309.

Varnum, ME et al., The origin of cultural differences in cognition: the social orientation hypothesis. *Current Directions in Psychological Science*, 19 (1), 2010, 9–13.

Velasquez, ML. International business ethics. *Business Ethics Quarterly*, 5, 1995, 865–882.

Wang, A. *Holding Up Half the Sky*. Fortune, 2004, pp. 170–176.

Zimmermann, A et al., Unravelling adjustment mechanisms: adjustment of German expatriates to intercultural interactions, work, and living conditions in the People's Republic of China. *International Journal of Cross Cultural Management*, 3, 2003, 45–66.

Zou, M and Lansbury, RD. Multinational corporations and employment relations in the People's Republic of China: the case of Beijing Hyundai Motor Company. *International Journal of Human Resource Management*, 20 (11), 2009, 2349–2369.

Cross-cultural adjustment

7

INTRODUCTION

The severe stress experienced by people who are suddenly plunged into a new and unfamiliar culture (often referred to as 'culture shock') has been extensively studied and documented. Typical *causes* of culture shock are difficult job and general living conditions and the absence of family and friends (Tsang, 2001). Typical *symptoms* include psychological disorders such as sleeplessness and irritability, relationship difficulties with local colleagues, and longing to return home. Studies show that the great majority of newcomers shake off the symptoms and gradually adjust to the culture.

A notable trend in cross-cultural adjustment studies has been to replace the classic, recovery-from-shock model of adjustment with a model of adjustment based on *adequate preparation and interaction* with local people (e.g. Kim, 1995). As a result, the psychological distress that accompanies culture shock is today less likely to be seen as pathological and more likely to be seen as a normative response that improves with time. The preparation-and-interaction model is based on the assumption that adjustment depends on the individual's willingness and ability to communicate with members of the culture in accordance with their cultural norms and conventions. A measure of anticipatory adjustment is also possible as a result of the individual's education and training, and the individual's previous experience of living and working in foreign countries.

Kim's (1995) cross-cultural adaptation theory provides strong support for the preparation-and-interaction model of adjustment. According to the theory, when expatriates and other immigrants first arrive in a new culture they struggle to cope with the experience. As a result of their struggles, new learning and growth (acculturation) occurs. Thus although entering a foreign culture for the first time can be a stressful and disorienting experience for the newcomer it is also an opportunity to learn and grow both professionally and emotionally.

A widely accepted approach to adjustment is that three separate dimensions are involved – work adjustment, interaction adjustment, and general living adjustment (Black, 1990). People do not adjust to these different facets of adjustment at the same time or in the same way. Expatriate managers, for instance, often adjust quickly to the work environment but may take longer to make a general living adjustment. Expatriate managers are generally committed to doing their jobs well and achieving that goal requires constant communication with employees and local colleagues. This facilitates work and interaction adjustment but general living adjustment may take longer to achieve.

The cross-cultural adjustment of permanent immigrants is more of a problem. Sometimes the host society is unwilling to collaborate with the immigrants to facilitate their integration. In many cases it is in the host society's interest to collaborate. In the United States, for instance, immigrants already constitute nearly 10 per cent of the population. But people are often unwilling to accept immigrants who are culturally dissimilar from themselves; and sometimes permanent immigrants fail to make a satisfactory cross-cultural adjustment because they are oppressed by feelings that they have lost their *own* culture, their *own* language, and sometimes their *own* family and friends, and that nothing can ever be done to recover them.

The extent to which a newcomer feels psychologically comfortable in a new culture depends on various factors, including family situation, cultural factors, personality factors, and linguistic factors. Adjustment is more difficult in countries where the cultural barriers are greater. For instance, China is the location with the highest rate of failure for expatriate assignments because of the radical differences in living conditions and business environments (Korn/Ferry, 2009). Many of the expatriate managers who fail to complete their contracts return home early because they fail to cope with the complexity of Chinese culture and the Chinese language.

Research suggests that personal qualities which generally facilitate cross-cultural adjustment include communication competence, ability to form relationships with members of the host culture, a non-judgmental approach to new cultures, and the ability to tolerate social and cultural isolation.

CULTURE SHOCK

What is it?

International business people, expatriate staff, international project personnel, exchange students, and others who move to a new culture often experience stress, nervous fatigue, and other unpleasant responses which are associated with *culture shock*. Oberg (1960) defines 'culture shock' as an occupational disease of people who are suddenly transplanted overseas. Culture shock is typically experienced a few weeks after arrival in the country.

The severe stress experienced by people who are suddenly plunged into a new and unfamiliar culture has been extensively studied and documented (e.g. Tsang, 2001).

Typical stress symptoms include:

- psychological disorders (e.g. irritability, depression, sleeplessness);
- relationship difficulties (e.g. with local colleagues);
- uncertainty about job role and status in the host organisation;
- shock and disgust caused by some cultural practices;
- longing to return home.

Only a small minority of newcomers fail to adapt to living and working in their new society. Most successfully shake off the initial symptoms and go on to make a satisfactory adjustment. Some, however, find the effects of culture shock less easy to shake off. The World Bank, for instance, sends thousands of staff every year on overseas missions but when they return one in ten seeks prescription drugs or counselling (Marx, 2001).

Entering a foreign culture for the first time can be stressful and disorienting experience. But – viewed from another perspective – it is also an opportunity to learn new cross-cultural skills and to develop psychologically (Ward et al., 2001). Kim (1995) points out that working in a new organisation and a new culture with colleagues who are members of the culture is an opportunity to learn and grow both professionally and emotionally. A further benefit is that the more people learn about another culture by living and working in it the more they learn about their own culture's strengths and weaknesses and about their own cultural conditioning. Such insights free them from ethnocentric assumptions of superiority that can cripple communication with members of other cultures.

Causes of culture shock

Common causes of culture shock include:

- disturbing cultural practices;
- difficult job conditions;
- absence of family and friends.

Disturbing cultural practices

A frequent cause of stress after arriving in a new country is exposure to shocking and disturbing cultural practices. In some developing countries, for instance, animals are slaughtered on the street or other public places, instant and violent punishment is meted out to bag-snatchers and pickpockets, and so on. Anecdotal evidence suggests that exposure to such practices can trigger the strong negative emotional responses associated with culture shock.

China began to open its retail sector to foreign involvement in the early 1990s, a development reinforced by its accession to the World Trade Organisation in

2001. Before expanding its retail business into China, Wal-Mart conducted market research and discovered that Chinese people dislike food wrapped in plastic. It gives them the impression that the food is old, and they won't buy it. Having obtained this particular insight into Chinese consumer preferences, the company acted on it. Consequently, a foreign business visitor or an expatriate manager who walks into the Shanghai branch of Wal-Mart may be shocked to see a pool filled with live turtles and cages of live chickens. In Western countries there would be protests by consumer or animal rights groups.

> But Wal-Mart conducts its business in China in the Chinese way and western business visitors had better get used to it. The way retail business is conducted in their own country (they have to accept) is not necessarily the best way or the only way.

Difficult job conditions

A common contributor to culture shock is difficult job conditions. Although expatriate adjustment is positively related to performance (Stahl and Caligiuri, 2005), the adjustment of expatriate managers may be delayed because of culture shock. Many expatriate managers – particularly those carrying out assignments in developing countries – often feel intense stress and frustration as a result of performance standards and efficiency levels in the new job being much lower than those prevailing at home. For instance, a French manager working in a Middle Eastern country explained to fellow-trainees attending a management training seminar how business would grind to a halt on Fridays.

> All the men go out for Friday prayers. I'm the only man left in the office. Sometimes a lady walks in with a pile of invoices but I just have to tell her that we can't talk and please can she come back tomorrow.

This same manager was equally frustrated by the over-casual approach adopted by local staff:

> It takes forever for management to make simple decisions. Employees here are different from employees at home – it takes much longer to get things done. In business you have to have a sense of urgency, but there's no urgency here. It's the same thing if you go to Immigration or the Tax Office. They'll do it in their own time . . . .

An Australian expatriate explained how, soon after arriving in the country, he unintentionally insulted a local manager.

> I wanted to find out when some new equipment was expected to arrive so I went to the Goods-In office. That turned out to be a mistake because hierarchy is important here. If you want some information you ask at the top and

the request is relayed down the line. Then the answer is relayed back up. It wastes a lot of time.

Another source of stress derives from the fact that expatriate managers are often accountable to two bosses. They are required to carry out the instructions of top management in the host organisation, but they also need to observe instructions stemming from senior management in their parent company at home (Black and Gregersen, 1992). The resulting *role conflict* can create intense stress and contribute to culture shock. That was the experience of an expatriate adviser to a government organisation in a former Soviet-bloc country. A key responsibility of the adviser was to arrange management training programmes for senior government officials.

> The government wanted the training to take place in western Europe. But the adviser's employer wanted the training to be held in-country because of the big cost-savings. The adviser was left wondering how he should handle the situation. He eventually decided that the client is always right.

Absence of family and friends

Adjusting to a new culture can be a slow and difficult process, especially in the absence of family, friends, and other social support networks that were relied on at home. On the other hand, support networks can be a Trojan horse. As Kim (2004) cautions, over-reliance on support networks can actually delay cross-cultural adjustment. Feldman (1991) produces evidence to show that well-motivated individuals with positive attitudes about their new culture tend to adjust quickly and are more successful than individuals without them.

The adjustment of expatriate staff is a relatively short-term process – as opposed to the adjustment of permanent immigrants, which can be much longer-term. Immigrant adjustment relates to individuals or groups of people who have moved, often permanently, from one culture to another. For permanent immigrants, adjusting to the new culture may seem to be an endless process or even impossible. Many of their problems stem from severe *communication difficulties*. Lim (2009: 1035) reports the words of a refugee from Southern Sudan, a Dinka, after arriving in California:

> Those who have lost friends, language and culture are totally lost. They are nothing. I feel my tie. I know my language. I know I'm Sudanese.

Some permanent immigrants fail to make a satisfactory cross-cultural adjustment because they are oppressed by feelings that they have lost their *own* culture, their *own* language, and sometimes their *own* family and friends – and that nothing can ever be done to recover them. Such strong and painful feelings help to explain, perhaps, why immigrants in most developed countries have a much higher than average risk of suffering from mental illness (Florack, 2003).

MODELS OF CROSS-CULTURAL ADJUSTMENT

U-curve model

Conceptions of cross-cultural adjustment have changed. Early studies on cross-cultural adjustment were based on the idea that people entering a new culture needed to recover from the symptoms of *culture shock* before adjustment was possible. Oberg's (1960) classic U-curve model of the adjustment process comprises an initial honeymoon stage, soon followed by a culture shock stage of disillusion and frustration, and eventually by recovery and adjustment stages.

The U-curve model implies that culture shock is an integral part of the adjustment process and that cross-cultural adjustment comes about as a result of progressing through four distinct stages:

1. After arriving in a new country the newcomer experiences a short period of *euphoria*, the honeymoon stage, which typically lasts for a few weeks.
2. This is followed by a *culture shock* stage of stress and disillusion, based on observed differences between the new culture and the home culture. This stage typically lasts 3–4 months.
3. As the individual gradually becomes more comfortable with the new culture and begins to accept its values and practices a stage of *recovery* begins.
4. The final stage is full adjustment or *integration*, which is marked by the individual's ability to function and feel at home both in the new culture and the original culture.

How valid is the model?

Empirical evidence for the validity of the model is mixed. For instance, Black and Mendenhall's (1991) review of 18 studies found that only 12 studies provide support for a U-shaped curve. However, a recent Israeli study which examined the psychological adjustment of 382 new immigrants from the former Soviet Union during their first 2 years in Israel, found that the pattern of their adjustment to Israeli society could be described as U-shaped (Markovizky and Samid, 2008). The immigrants adjusted to Israeli society in distinct stages:

1. The first stage was *loss of initial euphoria* which occurred from the first days up to 5 months.
2. The second stage was *low well-being* (a culture-shock phase) which occurred between 5 and 11 months. This stage was characterized by such symptoms as disappointment, frustration, homesickness, sleeping difficulties, and over-irritability.
3. The third stage, *recovery and adjustment*, occurred after more than 11 months.

Huang et al. (2005) make the point that people need time to recover from culture shock and to adjust their attitudes and behaviours to a new cultural context. As expatriate personnel normally carry out overseas assignments lasting at least 12 months they should have adequate time to overcome the effects of culture shock and adjust to living and working in the new country. Tung (1998) studied expatriates in 51 countries and found that the majority take from 6 to 12 months to feel psychologically comfortable with their new cultural setting – a prerequisite for cross-cultural adjustment.

Preparation-and-interaction model

A trend in cross-cultural adjustment studies has been to replace the classic recovery-from-shock model with a model of adjustment based on *adequate preparation and interaction* with local people (e.g. Laroche et al., 1998). Today, the psychological distress that accompanies culture shock is less likely to be seen as pathological and more likely to be seen simply as a normative response that improves with time (Ritsner and Ponizovsky, 1999).

Acceptance into any new cultural group depends to a great extent on the individual's ability to demonstrate competent and appropriate communicative behaviour. The preparation-and-interaction model is based on the assumption that adjustment largely depends on the individual's aptitude for cross-cultural communication – on the individual's willingness and ability to communicate with members of the culture in accordance with their cultural norms and conventions. Cross-cultural friendships can be difficult to establish because of the many barriers that have to be overcome, including language differences, different value systems, and different styles of socializing. But cross-cultural adjustment is accelerated when the newcomer makes a conscious effort to communicate regularly with the local people and to become familiar with their beliefs and norms.

Anticipatory adjustment

Black et al. (1991) found that adjustment starts before a person arrives in a new culture (anticipatory adjustment) and continues after arrival. Anticipatory adjustment is possible because of the individual's education and training and previous experience of living and working abroad. Adequate preparation and training is sometimes the key that enables people to adjust to a new culture and avoid the symptoms of culture shock. Even a limited amount of pre-departure information about the new culture and the new job can be extremely helpful in helping the individual to cope with the initial uncertainty and confusion.

Acculturation process

'Acculturation' has been defined as the adoption and retention of a language, identity, behaviour, and values as a result of coming into contact with another culture (Miller et al., 2009). Most of the learning that is involved occurs through communication with members of the host society.

Berry (1992) explains that when people move from their own society to another country whether for career reasons or for business or educational purposes, they tend to adopt a complex pattern of continuity with their old culture combined with new behaviours and practices appropriate to the new culture. Old habits are dropped and new habits are learned. For example, an expatriate manager may continue to read newspapers sent from home but may also change his diet and meal times to match local customs.

This gradual movement away from the old culture towards the new culture is accompanied by psychological and behavioural changes which have the effect of increasing the individual's ability to function effectively in the new society. According to Berry, two distinct dimensions are involved in this gradual process of acculturation:

- maintaining the original cultural identity;
- learning the cultural norms and behaviour patterns of the new culture.

Cross-cultural adaptation theory

Kim's (1995) cross-cultural adaptation theory provides strong support for the interaction-based model of adjustment. Kim argues that when expatriates and other immigrants first arrive in a new culture they often struggle to cope with the experience. But as a result of their struggles, new learning and growth occurs (*acculturation*).

According to Kim, the growth is characterized by cognitive, affective, and behavioural changes which, together:

- facilitate more effective communication with local people;
- prompt more positive attitudes towards the host culture;
- encourage good psychological adjustment.

Cross-cultural adaptation theory is based on the assumption that:

1. Human beings have an inherent drive to adapt and integrate to their environment.
2. They adapt to their social environment through communication.
3. The adaptive process is multifaceted – that is change in one part may cause changes in other parts. Improved local language skills, for instance, bring about better understanding of local cultural practices.

Systems theory

Cross-cultural adaptation theory incorporates elements of systems theory (von Bertanlanffy, 1973). According to systems theory, every organisation is an open system that exists in multiple environments. Changes in any of these environments will produce stresses and strains in the individual or group, forcing new learning and adaptation.

A system is a combination of interdependent parts which has *inputs, outputs,* and *outcomes.* Inputs include resources such as raw materials, money, technologies, and people. Outputs might be a particular product or service. Outcomes might be improved productivity, improved performance, or cross-cultural adjustment. Open systems are constantly reacting to and adapting to environmental changes.

Four adjustment outcomes

Berry (1990) identifies four possible cross-cultural adjustment outcomes for the individual:

1. *Segregation*: Remaining detached from the culture of the new society. Maintaining close ties with the culture of origin.
2. *Marginalization*: Vacillating between the norms and values of the original and new cultures as a result of loss of identification with both the original and new societies.
3. *Assimilation*: Relinquishing the original cultural identity and becoming part of a new society; accepting the mainstream cultural elements of the host society.
4. *Integration*: Complete cross-cultural adjustment – full social participation in the host society but, at the same time, maintaining a positive relationship to the original culture.

Assimilation is a process in which immigrants become full participants in the institutions of the host society and identify completely with that society. As Alba and Nee (1997) point out, it is the most common way for immigrants to gain access to the opportunity structure of a new society. Assimilation generally results in a rise in occupational status and earnings, stemming from a greater awareness and knowledge about the local labour market, acquisition of language skills, and acquisition of host society credentials (Kossoudji, 1989).

Integration is the indicator that shows that full cross-cultural adjustment has been achieved. Examples of integration are those South Africans – black and white – who move easily and constantly between black and white cultures. Such individuals have developed the ability to step into and out of two distinct cultural environments and feel completely at home in either. The adjustment process is complete when the individual's behaviour becomes *socially acceptable* and when the outcomes include successful social interactions and psychological well-being (Aycan, 1997). The fully adjusted, integrated individual is able to:

- manage stress;
- manage everyday social interactions;
- communicate effectively at work and in the wider community;
- maintain cross-cultural relationships.

Expatriate adjustment is important because studies show that adjustment relates positively to expatriate performance (Stahl and Caligiuri, 2005). When expatriates fail to adjust their assignments tend to fail (Caligiuri, 2000).

DIMENSIONS OF ADJUSTMENT

Different approaches

Most researchers see cross-cultural adjustment as a multidimensional process. Studies have identified different kinds of cross-cultural adjustment which need to be independently investigated.

- Searle and Ward (1990), for instance, distinguish *psychological* adjustment from *sociocultural* adjustment.
- Bennett and Bennett (2004) see the adjustment process as a gradual movement from an *ethnocentric* position to an *ethnorelative* stance (an approach adopted by many cross-cultural training providers).

Black et al.'s (1991) three-dimensional model of adjustment has received much empirical support (e.g. Shaffer et al., 1999) and has become the most widely accepted model of adjustment. The model is based on three inter-related dimensions:

1. *work adjustment*;
2. *interaction adjustment* (achieved through communication with members of the culture);
3. *general living adjustment*.

The popularity of this model is based on the perception that people do not adjust to the three different aspects of adjustment at the same time or in the same way. Expatriate managers, for instance, often adjust quickly to the work environment but take longer to make a general living adjustment. A possible explanation is that expatriate managers are generally committed to doing their jobs well, and achieving that goal requires constant communication with employees and local colleagues. The communication has the effect of facilitating interaction adjustment as well as work adjustment.

Most adjustment studies are limited in terms of the number of locations, and the expatriates surveyed usually represent a single national culture. However, Shaffer et al.'s (1999) study was based on a multinational sample of expatriates living and working in 45 countries. Their results provide broad support for Black et al.'s (1991) multidimensional model of expatriate adjustment.

Work adjustment

Poor working conditions, low performance standards, and other work-related stressors very often have the effect of delaying work adjustment. In developing countries, working conditions are often experienced as very difficult by expatriate managers, and difficult to get used to. Tahir and Ismail (2007), for instance, report the complaint made to researchers by an expatriate manager in Malaysia:

> The way we work in Europe is different. We have to work with precise objectives and targets. The pressure is very high in Europe. But people here are not used to this type of pressure and it's not very easy to handle . . . I can't put pressure on them all the time.

Work adjustment takes much longer to attain in some countries than in others. Harrison (1995) studied managers in Singapore and Australia and concluded that job satisfaction was lower, job tension higher, and relations with local employees poorer for managers working in the high power–distance, collectivist culture of Singapore than in the low power–distance, individualist culture of Australia.

Major work-related problems in a foreign country cannot usually be removed easily or quickly. Thus work adjustment may depend on expatriate staff changing their job expectations as well as adjusting their sometimes critical attitudes towards local colleagues and employees.

General living adjustment

General living adjustment relates to the degree of psychological comfort with most aspects of the cultural environment, including food, transport, housing conditions, shopping facilities, educational facilities, and leisure activities. The newcomer's responses to such aspects of the cultural environment influence the extent and pace of general living adjustment. General living adjustment, however, can be a slow and difficult process in 'distant' cultures – that is, in cultures that are very different from the newcomer's own culture.

The existence of social support networks both inside and outside the new society helps expatriates to cope with general living adjustment problems although, as Kim (2004) warns, over-reliance on support networks can actually delay overall adjustment.

Interaction adjustment

Interaction adjustment depends on regular interaction with members of the host culture, thus enabling the newcomer to learn host society habits and customs (Laroche et al., 1998). This kind of cultural learning makes a critical contribution to the overall adjustment process. Through interaction with local people the expatriate learns why members of the culture think and behave in the way they do. The insights gained often lead to constructive changes in the expatriate's own thinking and behaviour and improve relationships with members of the culture (Figure 7.1).

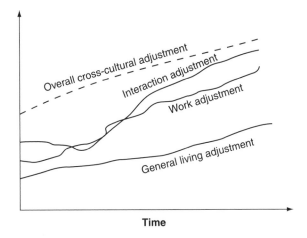

Figure 7.1   Aspects of cross-cultural adjustment

Acquiring *local language skills* is a strong predictor of successful interaction adjustment as well as overall cross-cultural adjustment (Kang, 2006). Ability to speak the local language increases opportunities for interacting with local colleagues and acquaintances, reduces the need for interpreters, and gives access to local media which, in turn, provide further insights into the way members of the culture think and behave. Interactions with members of the host culture can be difficult and embarrassing if the expatriate is unable to speak the local language. In Malaysia, for instance, people are required to acknowledge who they are talking to in terms of the person's title – Tan Sri, Professor, Dato, and so on – a requirement that reflects cultural values of respect for elders and hierarchy in that country.

Impact of trust and distrust on adjustment

Mutual trust facilitates interaction adjustment by influencing levels of disclosure and openness during cross-cultural interactions (Tan and Chee, 2005). When participants *distrust* each other they may fail to listen to each other, withhold important information, or even give misleading information. Trust is an important prerequisite for successful cross-cultural relationships since it provides the lens for interpreting the other person's behaviour and for reaching conclusions about the desirability of continuing the relationship (Dirks and Ferrin, 2002).

The amount of trust that people bring to cross-cultural interactions depends partly on their country of origin. Researchers have found huge differences across nations in the capacity to trust others. One study of trust across 41 countries found that only 5 per cent of Peruvians trusted others compared with 61 per cent of Norwegians and not much less in Sweden, Denmark, and Finland. In

Britain 44 per cent of respondents trusted their fellows, and 36 per cent in the United States (Zak and Knack, 2001).

According to Fukuyama (1995), the ability to trust others is linked to economic prosperity. In rich countries there is trust because deterrents to fraud and malpractices exist in the form of financial services authorities, compliance officers, and contract enforcement. In societies where strangers can trust each other people can trade without formal contracts. One result is that high-trust societies achieve faster growth rates due to lower transaction costs. Distrust of foreigners or strangers, on the other hand, is a characteristic of many poor countries.

IMMIGRANT ADJUSTMENT

Greater adjustment challenge

Permanent immigrants face greater adjustment challenges in a new society than do expatriate staff, business visitors, exchange students, and others who are temporary residents. In multicultural societies such as the United States, United Kingdom, France, Canada, Australia, and New Zealand, there is widespread acceptance of people from different parts of the world. Nevertheless, in these countries some immigrant groups find integration a difficult process. For instance, among men of West Indian origin who were born in Britain, half marry a white woman whereas hardly any Pakistanis and Bangladeshis do.

The adjustment of immigrants can be extremely difficult unless the host society collaborates with immigrants to facilitate their integration. It is in the host society's interest to do so. In the United States, for instance, immigrants already constitute nearly 10 per cent of the population according to the 2000 dicennial census. In Canada, immigrants accounted for 70 per cent of workforce growth over the past decade (Ng and Sears, 2010). However, Canadian organisations may overlook immigrant workers for a variety of reasons including language barriers, unfamiliarity with Canadian lifestyle, a lack of recognition of foreign credentials and work experience, and disparate performance standards (Conference Board of Canada, 2004).

An underlying difficulty is that members of host societies are often unwilling to accept immigrants who are *culturally dissimilar* from themselves (Ho et al., 1994). Such evidence suggests that immigrant adjustment may depend not on the efforts made by the individual immigrant or on efforts made by the host society alone, but on a collaborative effort between the two.

Viewed from the immigrant's viewpoint, host societies which are culturally distant from their own culture of origin are psychologically and linguistically inaccessible to them and therefore extremely difficult to adjust to. Examining the challenges that migrant women from Afghanistan, Iran, and Pakistan face in

Australia, Syed and Murray (2009) found that a major barrier to their adjustment was lack of awareness of their legal rights – as migrant employees or as ordinary citizens.

Most researchers agree that the integration of permanent immigrants is usually a long-term process taking three or four generations. According to Vermeulen (2010), in the case of permanent immigrants integration is not a simple straight-line process, and there are many ways that immigrant groups get integrated. For instance, there is *downward* integration – eventual integration into one of the under-classes that exist in any multicultural society.

Social and cultural capital

In many countries, immigrants from culturally distant societies often encounter discrimination, prejudice, and other barriers to integration. Even so, individuals who possess comparative advantage in terms of skills and *social and cultural capital* can usually overcome the barriers and successfully adjust to their new society (Alba and Nee, 1997). Like physical and human capital, social capital is a productive resource that provides channels for information and resource flows. Cultural capital has been defined as 'culturally valued taste and consumption patterns within a particular cultural field' (Bourdieu, 1990).

However, many immigrants are disappointed when they find that stocks of cultural capital and social capital that brought prestige and influence at home have much less value in the new society, making cross-cultural adjustment more difficult to achieve. Palumbo-Liu (1997: 6) gives the example of Chinese immigrants in the United States who

> cannot easily convert [their] symbolic capital into high social standing in Anglo circles. Their cultural performances as a new faction of the social elite are discredited by a perceived difference in their 'money politics,' their accent, and the colour of their skin.

Social capital is a durable network of more or less institutionalized relationships of mutual acquaintance (Bourdieu, 1983). Immigrants often rely on their social capital to establish themselves in a new country. For instance, they turn to family or 'contacts' for information about job vacancies and recruitment procedures, how they can acquire a driving licence, how they can open a bank account, and so on. But social capital, which was a valuable resource at home for providing business and social opportunities, has much less value in the new country, contributing to the sense of frustration and dissatisfaction that makes adjustment a slow and painful process for many permanent immigrants.

Failures to adjust

At an early stage, permanent immigrants to a new country become aware both of surface-level and deep-level cultural differences between their culture of origin and the new society (Van Vianen et al., 2004). Surface-level differences include food, climate, housing, leisure activities, transport arrangements, and so on, and these are apparent from the start. Deep-level differences, however, include values, beliefs, ideological ideas, convictions about how interpersonal problems should be dealt with, and so on, and such differences only become apparent over a lengthy period.

Deep-level differences are harder to understand than superficial differences. They are less visible, take longer to detect and adjust to, and can make cross-cultural adjustment for immigrants difficult to attain.

Case study

MINI-CASE: Failure to adjust

Deep-level differences between the host society and a person's own country can make cross-cultural adjustment difficult to attain, as a Belgian counsellor discovered when she went to live and work in a Middle Eastern country. The counsellor's inability to deal with deep-level cultural differences caused some of her Arab neighbours to regard her as a member of an alien culture with outlandish attitudes and threatening ideas.

After less than a year in the country the counsellor admits to herself that she has failed to adjust to Arab culture and she decides to move back to Belgium.

'I can't cope with the culture,' she tells an expatriate friend. 'It's suffocating for women. Muslim men don't care about a woman's feelings. If a Muslim man divorces his wife, the children are his.'

Later, however, the counsellor wonders if she contributed to her own problems by being inflexible, by not adjusting to the cultural realities.

Throughout her stay in the country her approach to relationship counselling had been based on Western theories of independence and couple negotiation, and had ignored local cultural imperatives such as the need to involve family networks in mediating marriage problems. Such basic differences – together with language difficulties and gender disparities – eventually lowered her morale and she decided to return to Belgium.

Questions:

1. *Identify three reasons why the counsellor failed to adjust to living and working in the Middle East. Rank these reasons in order of importance.*
2. *What changes of approach would have helped the counsellor to adjust to the country.*

PREDICTORS OF ADJUSTMENT

Relevant factors

Several researchers see cross-cultural adjustment as being the extent to which individuals are *psychologically comfortable* in a new cultural context (e.g. Torbiorn, 1982). Evidence exists that the extent to which a newcomer feels psychologically comfortable in a new culture largely depends on the following:

- Positive response to cultural factors
- Family situation
- Personality factors
- Dispositional and motivational factors
- Previous international experience
- Linguistic factors

Positive response to cultural factors

As the pace of globalization increases more and more people are living and working in foreign countries. Business managers, professional and technical staff, project personnel, aid workers, international students, and expatriate managers – all these people spend varying lengths of time living and working abroad. But not all of them are prepared, emotionally and motivationally, to cope with the experience. Some find that cultural barriers make it particularly difficult to communicate with local people or to understand their behaviour (Peltokorpi, 2008).

Adjusting to the new culture is relatively easy if there are common linguistic and cultural features linking the new society to the newcomer's own culture. But when home and new cultures differ widely in their values and practices adjustment can be much more difficult (Grove and Torbiorn, 1985). For instance, China has become the top destination for Western expatriate managers (Korn/Ferry, 2009). But China is also the location with the highest rate of failure for expatriate assignments because of the radical differences in living conditions and business environments. According to Selmer (2006), many of the expatriate managers who fail to complete their contracts return home early because they fail to cope with the complexity of Chinese culture and the Chinese language.

Adjustment is generally more difficult in countries where the cultural barriers are greater. Thus Torbiorn (1982) found that assignments in Asia, the Middle East, and North Africa are particularly difficult for Western expatriate staff to carry out and often lead to low levels of morale and job satisfaction, because of the many cultural barriers that the expatriates encounter. A failure to adjust to living and working in these countries leads to continuing stress for the expatriate and extra costs for the employer, since expatriates who fail to complete their assignments usually have to be replaced. The first-year costs of sending employees on foreign assignments have been estimated to amount to at least three times the base salaries of their domestic counterparts (Shaffer et al., 1999).

Family situation

MNEs are continuing to send managers to strategically important economies such as China, India, and Brazil. However, Western expatriate managers are not always successful in adjusting to living and working in these countries. A major reason for this failure to adjust was revealed by a survey of international recruitment consultants which found that many expatriate assignments fail because of an unfavourable family situation (Korn/Ferry, 2009). When 338 expatriates from 26 countries and 45 organisations, who were working in a wide range of posts in 43 countries, identified factors contributing to their cross-cultural adjustment, the most important factor identified was favourable family situation (Arthur and Bennett, 1995).

When the family situation is *not* favourable – when the family stays at home while the expatriate lives abroad – the manager's job performance may be affected and cross-cultural adjustment may be delayed. The antidote, according to Clouse and Watkins (2009), is for the expatriate to quickly establish a family foundation in the country. Families provide much social and psychological support for expatriates during their assignments, especially in the early months when demoralization may set in.

Often there are different patterns of adjustment for expatriate and spouse. But when the spouse makes a satisfactory adjustment at an early stage in the assignment this facilitates all forms of the expatriate's cross-cultural adjustment (Bhaskar-Shrinivas et al., 2005).

Over-reliance on fellow-expatriates

Expatriates who are involved in large-scale projects, such as the design and construction of power stations or road and rail systems, often live with their families in expatriate villages or closed expatriate compounds. These provide a comfortable and safe living environment as well as a range of social and sports facilities. However, the close and continuous contact between a group of expatriate families can impede cross-cultural adjustment. When expatriates rely heavily on fellow expatriates for social contacts this situation reinforces their national identity and expatriate status and limits opportunities for communicating with the local people and participating in their social activities (key factors in the cross-cultural adjustment process).

Personality factors

As Bond and Smith (1996) note, the 'Big Five' personality traits are often identified as important factors in the cross-cultural adjustment process because of their importance in directing types of social behaviours, such as subordination

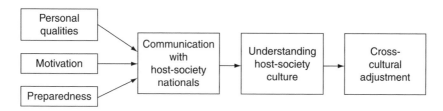

Figure 7.2   Cross-cultural adjustment process
Based on Kim (1995).

and affiliation, which occur in all cultures (Figure 7.2). However, culture asserts its influence in any particular situation by emphasizing some Big Five attributes over others. The Chinese, for instance, emphasize *conscientiousness* more often than Americans do.

Mol (2005) found that four of the 'Big Five' personality traits – *extroversion, emotional stability, agreeableness,* and *conscientiousness* – contribute to expatriate work adjustment. Surprisingly, they found no clear evidence that the fifth trait, *openness to experience,* did so. When Huang et al. (2005) studied expatriate adjustment in a specific cultural context, Taiwan, the personality traits of *extroversion, agreeableness,* and *openness to experience* were found to facilitate general living adjustment. It may be that these particular traits increase expatriates' ability to tolerate stress and frustration during their assignments.

A study of expatriates from 26 different nationalities, found that personal qualities which facilitate cross-cultural adjustment include *job knowledge, openness to other cultures,* and *adaptability* (Albright et al., 1997). Thomas and Ravlin (1995) report that Australian managers and serving expatriates saw *adaptability* as the most important requirement for expatriate success. Asian managers, on the other hand, rated *technical competence* as more important. Mendenhall and Oddou (1985) found that personal qualities facilitating cross-cultural adjustment included;

- communication competence;
- ability to form relationships with members of the host culture;
- ability to tolerate social and cultural isolation;
- non-judgmental approach to new cultures.

Dispositional and motivational factors

When Benish-Weisman (2009) interviewed emigrants from the former Soviet Union who had emigrated to Israel in the 1990s, the interviews revealed the important role of dispositional and motivational factors in facilitating cross-cultural adjustment. The researcher discovered that when immigrants were asked to write about their experiences, some of the narratives were coherent and well-structured, reflecting adjustment and well-being. They contained well-organised episodes, for instance, describing such goals as finding a job or learning Hebrew.

These individuals had made a good adjustment to Israeli society. By contrast, emigrants who had not adjusted to Israeli society produced narratives that were fragmented and lacked coherence.

> Negative emotions destroyed their coherence. Many had a victimisation theme. The storyline was circular and repetitive. The same events occurred again and again. It was as if the individuals concerned lacked the ability to control events.

As these examples suggest, optimistic, hopeful individuals are more likely than pessimistic, confused individuals to make a successful cross-cultural adjustment to a new society.

Well-motivated expatriate managers with positive attitudes towards their assignments tend to adjust more quickly and completely than those with less positive attitudes. Well-motivated individuals find it easier to accept a foreign culture, thus making cross-cultural adjustment easier to attain. 'You've got to accept the culture to get results,' an expatriate manager working in the Middle East told fellow-managers attending a management seminar. 'When I ask my assistant to do a job and he says, "Sorry. Can't do. Must go pray" – well that's ok. It's the culture and you accept it.'

Successful adjustment will at best be delayed and at worst not occur if an expatriate manager persists in always rating his own native culture higher than that of the host society in terms of quality of life, values, technology, and how things get done.

Previous international experience

Expatriates with previous international experience often find overall adjustment easier to attain than do first-time expatriates. The great advantage of previous international experience is that it gives a means of predicting what the new foreign assignment is going to involve. As Black et al. (1992) point out, previous experience allows realistic expectations for the new assignment to be formed, thus reducing uncertainty and facilitating adjustment.

However, according to Selmer (2002) the positive effects of previous experience are usually felt strongly early in the assignment but tend to diminish or disappear later in the assignment.

Linguistic factors

Furnham and Bochner (1982) identify acquisition of the dominant language as the single most important aspect of integration in a foreign culture. Ability to speak a country's dominant language enables newcomers to develop friendly, informal contacts with local people, thus facilitating cross-cultural adjustment. Expatriates who, through their language skills, are able to socialize with the local people are less surprised and frustrated by key aspects of the culture – such as the prevailing work practices and standards. Other reasons are that people who cannot speak the main language tend to have greater adjustment problems since they have less access to written and spoken sources, depend on others for much information, and are often restricted in their social relationships to people from their own culture.

It is not only expatriate managers who benefit from learning the dominant language of the new society. Permanent immigrants also need language skills since fluency in the host country language has been found to be a strong predictor of migrants' chances of obtaining and keeping employment (which, for immigrants, is an important facet of cross-cultural adjustment). Syed and Murray (2009) found that women migrants from China, India, Pakistan, Iraq, and Afghanistan who had inadequate English language skills faced far more difficulties in adjusting to the Australian labour market than women migrants who were proficient in English. English proficiency is a prerequisite for most jobs in Australia and, as the researchers point out, well-qualified migrants in Australia who have little English language ability are often regarded as unsuitable for certain jobs – for instance, marketing and sales jobs which involve direct interaction with English-speaking customers.

Ability to speak the local language increases the prestige and effectiveness of expatriate staff by increasing communication opportunities with local employees and reducing the need for interpreters. Inability to speak the local language has the effect of delaying adjustment because it makes it difficult for the expatriate to become socially integrated. A British manager who worked in a Chinese ceramics company commented to a business acquaintance: 'In China, if you want to really know what is going on you have to talk their language.' Language barriers increase the risk of isolation for expatriates in China and prevent interaction with members of the culture (Selmer, 2006).

SMALL-GROUP EXERCISE: Discussion questions

Working in small groups, discuss each of the following questions and write down the group's agreed answer. At the end of the exercise, each group may present its answers to the other groups for comment.

1. *What causes culture shock?*
2. *What are the key features of the Preparation-and-Interaction model of cross-cultural adjustment? What are the weaknesses of the model?*
3. *Identify three personal qualities which would help a newcomer to quickly adjust to living and working in a foreign country. Give reasons for your choice.*
4. *'Cross-cultural adjustment is a multi-dimensional process.' What are the different dimensions involved?*

Continued

5. *Why is the ability to speak the local language widely considered to be an important predictor of successful cross-cultural adjustment?*
6. *Explain how the social and cultural capital possessed by permanent immigrants can help them to adjust to the new society. Give examples of both kinds of capital.*

Social integration

Au and Fukuda's (2002) survey of 232 expatriates found that those who became involved with local businesses and communities as a result of developing local language skills had higher job satisfaction and more influence in the host organisations than those who did not. Other researchers have reached similar conclusions about the importance of expatriates' possessing local language skills.

- Swami (2009) found that proficiency in English was a strong predictor of sociocultural adjustment for Malay and Chinese students in England since it facilitated interactions with English people and decreased feelings of helplessness in social settings.
- Peltokorpi's (2008) study of 110 expatriates in Japan found that language proficiency, together with cultural empathy, contributed to work adjustment, interaction adjustment, and general living adjustment.
- Masgoret and Ward (2006) identify language proficiency and understanding of the norms and values of the culture as essential pre-requisites for successful cross-cultural adaptation.
- Napier and Taylor's (1995) study of female expatriates in Japan found that Japanese language skills was an important aspect of the expatriates' successful work adjustment.

When a senior English police officer was made responsible for liaising with the Sikh community he set about learning the Sikh language and within a few months had acquired a basic understanding of the language and Sikh culture. He mastered a few common phrases and made a point of using them whenever he met Sikh people. As a result of his willingness to learn the culture and the language he became trusted and accepted by the Sikh community and, according to colleagues, was able to perform his job with increased effectiveness.

KEY POINTS

1. Psychological well-being and the ability to function well in a new society depend on the newcomer's cross-cultural adjustment. Adjustment is achieved through communication with members of the host society culture, which

gives opportunities for new cultural learning. Thus cross-cultural communication competence, including willingness to learn the local language, is an important predictor of adjustment. Adjustment comes from communicating with the local people and from the gradual acculturation that then occurs.

2. Entering a new culture can be stressful and disorienting experience. But it is also an opportunity to learn new cross-cultural skills and to develop psychologically – to grow both professionally and emotionally. As people learn how culture moulds the behaviour of members of other cultures, they start to see how aspects of their own behaviour are also culturally determined. Such cultural self-awareness helps the individual to relate to people from other cultures in a more open and accepting way, and frees them from ethnocentric assumptions of superiority that can cripple communication with members of other cultures.

3. For expatriate managers, international project staff, international students, and others who are *temporary* residents in a foreign culture, adjustment is a relatively short-term issue, and well-motivated individuals with positive attitudes towards the new culture and the new job tend to adjust quickly. But adjustment problems can be much greater for *permanent* immigrant. For permanent immigrants adjusting to the new culture may seem to be an endless process. Some fail to adjust because they are oppressed by feelings that they have irretrievably lost their own culture, language, family, and friends. Many of their problems stem from communication difficulties.

4. The classic U-curve model of cross-cultural adjustment is based on the assumption that adjustment is based on recovery from culture shock. However, this model has been largely replaced by a model of adjustment based on adequate preparation and *interaction* with local people. The psychological distress that accompanies culture shock now is less likely to be seen as pathological and more likely to be seen as a normative response that improves with time. Much evidence shows that acceptance into any new cultural group depends to a great extent on the individual's ability to demonstrate competent and appropriate communicative behaviour.

5. Cross-cultural adaptation theory supports the interaction-based model of adjustment. When people arrive in a new culture they struggle to cope with the experience, and as a result of their struggles new learning and growth occurs. The growth consists of cognitive, affective, and behavioural changes which bring about more effective communication with local people and more positive attitudes towards the culture. The theory is therefore based on the assumption that people have an inherent drive to adapt and integrate to their environment.

6. A widely accepted model is based on the concept of adjustment as a multifaceted phenomenon. Three separate dimensions are involved – work adjustment, interaction adjustment, and general living adjustment. People do not adjust to these different aspects of adjustment at the same time or in the same way. Expatriate managers may, for instance, adjust quickly to the work

environment but take longer to make a general living adjustment. Expatriate managers are committed to doing their jobs well and have a particular interest in work adjustment. Achieving that goal requires constant communication with employees and local colleagues so that interaction adjustment is also encouraged.

7. The extent and pace of an individual's cross-cultural adjustment is influenced by various factors including language skills, family situation, and personality factors. The 'Big Five' personality traits are often identified as important contributors to adjustment because of their importance in directing types of social behaviours (e.g. subordination, affiliation) which occur in all cultures. Another reason is that these traits may increase expatriates' ability to tolerate stress and frustration during their assignments.

QUESTIONS FOR DISCUSSION AND WRITTEN ASSIGNMENTS

1. 'Entering a new culture can be a stressful experience but it also gives opportunities for psychological growth and to learn new skills.' Describe the psychological growth that can occur and the skills that are learned as a result of living in a foreign culture. Give examples from your own experience.

2. The classic recovery-from-shock model of cross-cultural adjustment has largely been replaced by a model based on adequate preparation and interaction with local people. Which model do you prefer, and why?

3. To what extent does the concept of culture shock provide an accurate and useful model of what happens when people enter a new culture?

BIBLIOGRAPHY

Alba, R and Nee, V. Rethinking assimilation theory for a new era of immigration. *The International Migration Review*, 31 (4), 1997, 826–874.

Albright, L et al., Cross-cultural consensus in personality judgments. *Journal of Personality and Social Psychology*, 73, 1997, 270–280.

Arthur, W and Bennett, W. The international assignee: the relative importance of factors perceived to contribute to success. *Personnel Psychology*, 48, 1995, 99–114.

Au, KY and Fukuda, J. Boundary spanning behaviours of expatriates. *World Business*, 37 (4), 2002, 285–296.

Aycan, Z. Expatriate adjustment as a multifaceted phenomenon: individual and organisational predictors. *International Journal of Human R Management*, 8 (4), 1997, 434–56.

Benish-Weisman, M. Between trauma and redemption: story form differences in immigrant narratives of successful and nonsuccessful immigration. *Journal of Cross-cultural Psychology*, 40 (6), 2009, 953–968.

Bennett, JM and Bennett, MJ. *Handbook of Intercultural Training*, 3rd ed. Sage, 2004, pp. 337–362.

Berry, J. Psychology of acculturation: understanding individuals moving between cultures. In R Brislin (ed.), *Applied Cross-cultural Psychology*. Sage, 1990, pp. 232–253.

Berry, JW. Acculturation and adaptation in a new society. *International Migration*, 30, 1992, 69–85.

Bhaskar-Shrinivas, P et al., Input-based and time-based models of international adjustment. *Academy of Management Journal*, 48, 2005, 257–281.

Black, J. The relationship of personal characteristics with the adjustment of Japanese expatriate managers. *Management International Review*, 30 (2), 1990, 119–134.

Black, JS and Gregersen, H. Serving two masters: managing dual allegiance. *Sloan Management Review*, Summer, 1992, 66–71.

Black, JS, Gregersen, HB and Mendenhall, ME. *Global Assignments: Successfully Expatriating and Repatriating International Mamnager*. Jossey-Bass, 1992.

Black, JS and Mendenhall, M. The U-curve adjustment hypothesis revisited: a review and theoretical framework. *Journal of International Business Studies*, 22 (2), 1991, 225–247.

Black, JS, Mendenhall, M and Oddou, G. Towards a comprehensive model of international adjustment: an integration of multiple theoretical perspectives. *Academy of Management Review*, 16 (2), 1991, 291–317.

Bond, MH and Smith, PB. Cross-cultural social and organisational psychology. *Annual Review of Psychology*, 47, 1996, 205–235.

Bourdieu, P. Forms of capital. In J Richardson (ed.), *Handbook of Theory and Research for the Sociology of Education*. Greenwood, 1983, 241–258.

Bourdieu, P. *The Logic of Practice*. Polity Press, 1990.

Caligiuri, PM. The big five personality characteristics as predictors of expatriates' desire to terminate the assignment and supervisor-rated performance. *Personnel Psychology*, 53, 2000, 67–88.

Clouse, MA and Watkins, MD. Three keys to getting an overseas assignment right. *HBR*, October 2009, 115–119.

Conference Board of Canada, The voices of visible minorities, 2004.

Dirks, KT and Ferrin, DL. Trust in leadership. *Journal of Applied Psychology*, 87, 2002, 611–628.

Feldman, DC. Repatriate moves as career transition. *Human Resource Management Review*, 1 (3), 1991, 163–178.

Florack, A et al., Perceived intergroup threat and attitudes of host community members toward immigrant acculturation. *Journal of Social Psychology*, 143 (5), 2003, 633–648.

Fukuyama, F. *Trust: The Social Virtues and the Creation of Prosperity*. Free Press, 1995.

Furnham, A and Bochner, S. Social difficulty in a foreign culture: an empirical analysis of culture shock. In S Bochner (ed.), *Cultures in Contact*. Pergamon, 1982.

Grove, C and Torbiorn, I. A new conceptualisation of intercultural adjustment and the goals of training. *International Journal of Intercultural Relations*, 9, 1985, 205–233.

Harrison, GL. Satisfaction, tension and interpersonal relations: a cross-cultural comparison of managers in Singapore and Australia. *Journal of Managerial Psychology*, 10 (8), 1995, 13–19.

Ho, R, Niles, S, Penney, R and Thomas, A. Migrants and multiculturalism: a survey of attitudes in Darwin. *Australian Psychologist*, 29, 1994, 62–70.

Huang, T-J, Chi, S-C and Lawler, JJ. The relationship between expatriates' personality traits and their adjustment to international assignments. *International Journal of Human Resources Management*, 16, 2005, 1667.

Kang, S-M. Measurement of acculturation, scale formats, and language competence: their implications for adjustment. *Journal of Cross-cultural Psychology*, 37 (6), 2006, 669–693.

Kim, YY. Cross-cultural adaptation: an integrative theory. In RL Wiseman (ed.), *Intercultural Communication Theory*. Sage, 1995, pp. 170–193.

Kim, YY. Long-term cross-cultural adaptation: training implications of an integrative theory. In D Landis, JM Bennett, and MJ Bennett (ed.), *Handbook of Intercultural Training*, 3rd ed. Sage, 2004, pp. 337–362.

Korn/Ferry, *Executive Recruiter Index*, 10th ed. Korn/Ferry International, 2009.

Kossoudji, SA. Immigrant worker assimilation: is it a labour market phenomenon? *Journal of Human Resources*, 24 (3), 1989, 494–527.

Laroche, M et al., Test of a nonlinear relationship between linguistic acculturation and ethnic identification. *Journal of Cross-cultural Psychology*, 29 (3), 1998, 418–434.

Lim, S-L. 'Loss of connections is death': transnational family ties among Sudanese refugee families resettling in the United States. *Journal of Cross-cultural Psychology*, 40 (6), 2009, 1028–1040.

Markovizky, G and Samid, Y. The process of immigrant adjustment: the role of time in determining psychological adjustment. *Journal of Cross-cultural Psychology*, 39 (6), 2008, 782–799.

Marx, E. *Breaking through Culture shock*. Nicholas Brealey Publishing, London, 2001.

Masgoret, A-M and Ward, C. Culture learning approach to acculturation. In DL Sam and JW Berry (eds), *The Cambridge Handbook of Acculturation*. CUP, 2006, pp. 58–77.

Mendenhall, M and Oddou, G. The dimensions of expatriate acculturation: a review. *Academy of Management Review*, 10, 1985, 39–48.

Miller, AM et al., Longitudinal changes in acculturation for immigrant women from the former Soviet Union. *Journal of Cross-cultural Psychology*, 40 (3), 2009, 400–415.

Mol, ST et al., Predicting expatriate job performance for selection purposes. *Journal of Cross-cultural Psychology*, 36 (5), 2005, 590–620.

Napier, NK and Taylor, S. *Western Women Working in Japan*. Quorum Books, 1995.

Ng, ESW and Sears, GJ. What women and ethnic minorities want. Work values and labour market confidence: a self-determination perspective. *International Journal of Human Resource Management*, 21 (5), 2010, 676–698.

Oberg, K. Culture shock and the problem of adjustment to new cultural environments. *Practical Anthropology*, 7, 1960, 177–182.

Palumbo-Liu, D. Introduction. In D Palumbo-Liu and HU Gumbrecht (eds), *Streams of Cultural Capital*. Stanford University Press, 1997, p. 6.

Peltokorpi, V. Cross-cultural adjustment of expatriates in Japan. *International Journal of Human Resource Management*, 19 (9), 2008, 1588–1606.

Ritsner, M and Ponizovsky, A. Psychological distress through immigration. *International Journal of Social Psychiatry*, 45, 1999, 125–139.

Searle, W and Ward, C. The prediction of psychological and sociocultural adjustment during cross-cultural transitions. *International Journal of Intercultural Relations*, 14, 1990, 449–464.

Selmer, J. Practice makes perfect: international experience and expatriate adjustment. *Management International Review*, 42, 2002, 71–87.

Selmer, J. Language ability and adjustment: western expatriates in China. *Thunderbird International Business Review*, 48, 2006, 347–368.

Shaffer, MA, Harrison, DA and Gilley, KM. Dimensions, determinants, and differences in the expatriate adjustment process. *Journal of International Business Studies*, 30, 1999, 557–581.

Stahl, GK and Caligiuri, PM. The effectiveness of expatriate coping strategies. *Journal of Applied Psychology*, 90, 2005, 603–615.

Swami, V. Predictors of sociocultural adjustment among sojourning Malaysian students in Britain. *International Journal of Psychology*, 44 (4), 2009, 266–273.

Syed, J and Murray, P. Combating the English language deficit: the labour market experiences of migrant women in Australia. *Human Resource Management Journal*, 19 (4) 2009, 413–432.

Tahir, AHM and Ismail, M. Cross-cultural challenges and adjustment of expatriates: a case study in Malaysia. *Turkish Journal of International Relations*, 6 (3), 2007.

Tan, NN and Chee, D. Understanding interpersonal trust in a Confucian-influenced society. *International Journal of Cross Cultural Management*, 5 (2), 2005, 199.

Thomas, DC and Ravlin, EC. Responses of employees to cultural adaptation by a foreign manager. *Journal of Applied Psychology*, 80, 1995, 133–146.

Torbiorn, I. *Living Abroad*. Wiley, 1982.

Tsang, EWK. Adjustment of mainland Chinese academics and students to Singapore. *International Journal of Intercultural Relations*, 25, 2001, 347–372.

Tung, RL. American expatriates abroad. *Journal of World Business*, 33 (2), 1998, 125–144.

Van Vianen, AEM et al., Fitting in: surface and deep-level cultural differences and expatriate adjustment. *Academy of Management Journal*, 47 (5), 2004, 697–709.

Vermeulen, H. Segmented assimilation and cross-national comparative research on the integration of immigrants and their children. *Ethnic and Racial Studies*, 33 (7), 2010, 1214–1230.

von Bertanlanffy, L. *General Systems Theory: Foundations, Development, Applications.* Penguin, 1973.

Ward, C et al., *The Psychology of Culture Shock*, 2nd ed. Routledge, 2001.

Zak, PJ and Knack, S. Trust & growth. *Economic Journal*, 470 (3), 2001, 295–321.

Developing cross-cultural skills

8

INTRODUCTION

Methods commonly used by organisations to develop cross-cultural skills include joint projects undertaken by managers of organisations based in different countries, one-to-one coaching by an internal or external coach, planned exposure to foreign cultures, the total immersion method, and formal cross-cultural training programmes. Most cross-cultural skills involve verbal and nonverbal communication, the fundamental tools used by people from different cultures to interact.

Formal cross-cultural training programmes are used by companies to provide managers – especially expatriate managers and those who have to manage employees from diverse cultures – with the cross-cultural skills they need to do their jobs. Global managers, for instance, need communication skills that will enable them to move among diverse markets and cultures around the world. Expatriate managers need to acquire the knowledge and skills needed for effective relationships with host nationals, and the specialized skills that will help them to transfer knowledge, technology, and processes to overseas organisations. A key responsibility of most expatriate managers is the training of local employees – for instance, to enable them to operate imported technology (Rosenzweig and Nohria, 1994). Studies show that when expatriate managers have been trained to use instructional methods and approaches that are *adjusted to the culture* this greatly increases their effectiveness and job performance.

Very few cross-cultural training courses have been specifically designed for female expatriates. Female expatriates' special needs include the need to be informed about important aspects of living and working in a foreign culture – such aspects as how local colleagues will expect them to dress at work, or the kind of interactions with men that are acceptable in the culture.

Many cross-cultural training programmes include components aimed at changing behaviour – for instance, the attitudes that business visitors to foreign countries take with them and the way they address foreigners. Training techniques commonly used to bring about behaviour change include behaviour modelling and feedback (Bandura, 1977). *Behaviour modelling*, derived from social learning theory, is often based on a member of a particular culture modelling specific behaviours which are common and desirable in the culture. The trainees then practise carrying out the observed behaviour, and receive feedback from the tutor and others in the group about their performance. *Feedback* is an important part of the behaviour learning process as it can be used to encourage the desired behaviours and discourage undesired behaviours.

Many cross-cultural training programmes have a strong business emphasis and aim to develop cross-cultural business skills by using business games and practical exercises that simulate various cross-cultural business environments. The wide availability of internet programmes makes it easy for business persons worldwide to participate in online training modules aimed at improving their cross-cultural negotiating and other cross-cultural skills.

BUILDING CROSS-CULTURAL COMPETENCE

Range of methods

Cross-cultural competence is a developmental process that evolves over an extended period of time (Martin and Vaughn, 2007). It enables business people, expatriate managers, international project staff, and others to understand and effectively interact with people from other cultures. Cross-cultural competence requires as a minimum:

- awareness of one's own cultural viewpoint;
- knowledge and understanding of cultural differences;
- well-developed cross-cultural communication and related cross-cultural skills.

Most cross-cultural skills involve verbal and nonverbal communication, the fundamental tools used by people from different cultures to interact (Figure 8.1).

The cross-cultural skills that are required can be developed using a variety of different methods and approaches. Methods commonly used by organisations to improve managers' practical cross-cultural skills are:

- Exposure to foreign cultures
- Coaching
- Total immersion in a foreign culture
- Joint projects
- Formal cross-cultural training programmes

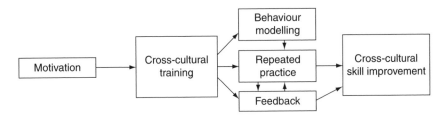

Figure 8.1 Improving cross-cultural skills

Exposure to foreign cultures

A notable trend in international business has been an increase in emerging-market companies buying established Western ones. Examples are: the Indian company Tata Motors' acquisition of Jaguar from Ford; and Mexico-based CEMEX's purchase of RMC, the British cement maker.

When CEMEX acquired RMC British managers were sent to CEMEX plants in Mexico, United States, and Germany to learn CEMEX management methods and business systems (Kanter, 2009). While that was going on CEMEX experts from Mexico, Brazil, Uruguay, and Spain were sent to Britain to learn as much as possible about the way things were done at the RMC plant. The CEMEX experts developed their cross-cultural communication skills as a result of taking classes in English culture and, where necessary, English language. Joint meetings – conducted mainly in English not Spanish – had the same effect.

Colgate–Palmolive is another multinational company which develops cross-cultural skills of professional and management personnel by exposing them to foreign cultures. The company sends management trainees on a series of short-term overseas assignments with the aim of quickly providing the future expatriate managers with varied overseas experience. Each assignment ends with a debriefing interview to capture the lessons learned. Sometimes the foreign exposure is supplemented by formal management training covering specific aspects of the individuals' future jobs, together with wider management skills, such as decision-making or financial control. According to the company's HR staff, the result has been to create a cadre of *culturally flexible managers*, capable of carrying out assignments in virtually any country where the company operates.

Coaching

Multinational companies sometimes select managers for senior expatriate posts on the basis of technical skills alone. But if a technically outstanding individual from the parent company is appointed and only lasts 3 months in the job because he doesn't fit in to the local culture, then his appointment must be considered an expensive mistake. When a multinational firm selected a young manager for a key expatriate post in India it did so mainly because of his technical expertise (Prokesch, 2009). But the company knew that to be successful in India – and to increase the chances of the manager completing his 3-year contract – he would need to demonstrate excellent cross-cultural skills in addition to demonstrating technical competence. Hence the company decided to arrange one-to-one coaching for the manager with an experienced executive coach.

> The coach helped the manager to understand basic cultural differences, and some of the changes he would need to make in his own management style. For instance, he would need to give specific not general instructions to local employees – and then check that the instructions were properly carried out. The coach also explained the importance of developing flexible attitudes towards class and gender, and used impromptu role-plays to help the manager learn how to make appropriate responses when sensitive topics were discussed.

In India the manager consciously applied what he had learned from the coach. His ability to use culturally appropriate behaviour enabled him to relate to his Indian colleagues, and he went on to complete his 3-year assignment.

One-to-one coaching may be an expensive way of developing cross-cultural skills but it is effective. *How* effective depends on the quality and experience of the coach. According to Erickson et al. (2007), a well-informed coach is needed who is capable of giving constructive and, when necessary, painful feedback. Executive coaches are often university experts or retired CEOs and they command high fees. Typically, they are called in by a firm to develop the communication and social skills of managers who have been earmarked for senior management positions at home or abroad, or potentially outstanding individuals who have difficulty working as a team.

Increasing demand for coaches is likely to come from organisations in the big emerging economies of Brazil, China, India, and Russia since managers in those countries tend to be so youthful. As Coutu and Kauffman (2009: 95) point out: 'University graduates are coming into jobs at 23 years old and finding that their bosses are all of 25, with the experience to match.'

Coaching by the manager's boss

In some multinational companies coaching programmes are carried out by senior managers who coach their immediate subordinates. In these cases, business improvements are usually targeted and discussed at the outset, together with aspects of a manager's behaviour that will have to change if the improvements are to be achieved. Gosselin et al. (1997) note that coaching practice draws on the conceptual foundations of feedback and behaviour modelling, and that managers generally prefer to receive feedback from their immediate supervisors rather than from an external coach.

Total immersion in a foreign culture

The total immersion method of developing cross-cultural skills has been proved to be highly effective. Simply by living in a foreign country for an extended period an individual picks up first-hand knowledge of the culture, its people, and its practices. From experience of talking to members of the culture, general principles of cross-cultural communication are distilled that apply not only to that particular culture but also perhaps to many other cultures. An example of cross-cultural competence springing out of basic life experience.

A Spanish engineering company used the total immersion method to develop its managers following a merger with a British firm. The Spanish firm arranged for selected managers to be given 6–12-month work assignments in the head-quarters of the British company. According to one of the managers, total immersion in British culture helped the selected personnel to greatly improve their English, and it also gave them the opportunity to find out how things got done in the company, and how to communicate and cooperate with British colleagues. They learned a lot about the firm's culture and also about the national culture in which the firm was rooted.

Total immersion is a highly effective way of developing cross-cultural skills. But the main problem with the method – like the main problem with raw data – is that it is unorganised, sometimes confusing, and it may take a long time for clear lessons to be learned from it. Moreover, learning a culture by actually living in it is a poor option for international managers, consultants, business people, and others who travel to many countries and who have to communicate with people not just from one culture but from a wide range of cultures.

A well-designed cross-cultural training programme, on the other hand, *accelerates* cultural learning. It arranges in an orderly way the product of many people's first-hand experience of cross-cultural situations; and it gives quick payback by boosting confidence and professionalism in various cross-cultural situations.

Joint projects

When a multinational firm acquires a company in another country cultural issues often get in the way of a fast, effective integration. The poor performance of DaimlerChrysler, for instance, is often blamed on a clash of the German and US cultures that led to major integration problems (Epstein, 2004). After Proctor and Gamble (P&G) acquired Gillette it tackled integration problems head-on by forming nearly a hundred global integration teams to work on joint projects (Kanter, 2009). The teams mostly consisted of matched pairs of managers from the same functional areas in each company. Gillette specialists were allowed – in China they were encouraged – to use their own processes until they had learned P&G's methods.

Sometimes cross-cultural and technical skills are best developed together, and for that to happen people from organisations in different countries have to be given real technical problems to solve. Wilkinson Match has often used multicultural task forces as a mechanism enabling managers to study technical and business problems in tandem. Typically, a task force would be given access to any information required and to any executive's time for the duration of the project. Regular coaching sessions focused on how cross-cultural skills could be strengthened and communication problems between members of the diverse teams could be overcome.

Case study

MINI-CASE: Encouraging cross-cultural collaboration

When a firm purchases a company in another country its managers need to develop the cross-cultural skills that will facilitate effective integration. The necessary skills can sometimes be rapidly developed by the managers participating in joint projects or joint task forces.

When a North American firm launched a programme of joint projects soon after acquiring an electronics company in Japan it aimed to develop cross-cultural management skills that would facilitate the integration. Subsequently, several task forces consisting of managers from the two companies were set up to accomplish precise business goals. Part of the idea was to get quick results that would demonstrate the synergies of the acquisition.

The task forces overcame substantial language and cultural difficulties and achieved good results. One of the task forces, for instance, cut material costs by persuading major suppliers to manage inventory. Another team arranged for written-off receivables to be sold. A third task force found ways to cut scrap rates. These quick results demonstrated the benefits of the acquisition. An important side-effect was that managers in both companies learned *cross-cultural collaboration skills* – skills which would be invaluable in the new company.

Questions:

1. *Apart from establishing joint task forces, what other activities and policies could help the two companies to successfully integrate their operations?*
2. *Identify typical integration problems that occur when two companies based in different countries merge.*

FORMAL CROSS-CULTURAL TRAINING PROGRAMMES
Objectives

Cross-cultural training consists of formal efforts designed to prepare people for more effective interpersonal relations when they interact with individuals from cultures other than their own (Brislin and Yoshida, 1994). According to Brislin (1989), the main objectives of cross-cultural training are:

- To encourage people to see problems from the viewpoint of people from other cultures by using methods such as critical incident situations and discussions.

- To promote a *cultural relativist* approach with the aim of reducing negative stereotyping of members of other cultures and to increase greater awareness of one's own prejudices and assumptions.
- To encourage behaviours appropriate in other cultures – for example, how to greet people, distances that should be maintained while conversing, appropriate nonverbal behaviours, and so on.

Cross-cultural training programmes provide expatriate managers, global managers, and managers of a multicultural workforce – all of whom have to manage people from a wide range of national and cultural backgrounds – with the skills they need to do their jobs. Global managers have jobs with international scope, whether in expatriate assignments or managing multicultural teams (Scullion and Starkey, 2000).

Global management and business education

The need for global management education – as opposed to traditional management education – is great. That need springs from the increasing level of contact and interaction between managers and business people from different cultural backgrounds, creating possible conflicts and subsequent challenges (Funakawa, 1997). Traditional management programmes are not always directly relevant to managers in Asia, Africa, and South America because of the limited cross-cultural transferability of the underpinning models, theories, and assumptions – many of them originating in the West. Global management education needs to challenge culturally bound mindsets and to create opportunities for students to learn from other cultures (Ford, 1998). Global managers need a global perspective, with the emphasis on competent cross-cultural interactions of all kinds. Among the skills needed by global managers are cross-cultural communication skills that will enable them to move among diverse markets and cultures around the world; and assist them in transferring systems, processes, and technologies to different overseas operations of a transnational company.

Among the essential cross-cultural skills needed by expatriate and global managers are:

- 'hard' systems and process skills;
- 'soft' skills needed for building networks and relationships across companies and cultures.

Skill competence

Boyatzis (1982) defines 'skill competence' as the ability to demonstrate a system or sequence of behaviour that is related to achieving a performance goal. *Management competence*, for instance, is the effective use of knowledge and skills in achieving management goals. *Planning competence* is the effective use of skills associated with setting goals, assessing risk, and developing a sequence of planning activities to achieve goals. *Technological competence* – the ability to use new technologies – is an important element in the toolkit of both expatriate managers and managers who remain at home (Pool and Sewell, 2007).

As Jackson (2002) points out, the skill competences required to do a particular management job are used by many multinational companies to recruit, train, and reward managers at home and abroad.

Immediate payback

When an international charity recruited volunteer health workers to work on several projects in Central America it immediately enrolled them on a cross-cultural training programme (O'Brien et al., 1982). The volunteers were trained to understand important features of the particular cultures in which they would be working. They were shown how to use culturally appropriate behaviour in a wide range of social settings.

> The skills they learned enabled them to combine culturally sensitive behaviour, such as respect for elders and consideration for children, with the professional task of giving injections, lancing boils, and dispensing hands-on health care.

The training gave immediate payback by boosting the volunteers' social and professional confidence and increasing the satisfaction of their patients.

Specific cross-cultural *skills* can often be developed remarkably quickly. Cross-cultural *abilities* – aggregates of specific cross-cultural skills – take longer to develop. Essentially, cross-cultural abilities are developed by transferring what has been learnt in acquiring one skill to the next skill – and so on (Thomas and Fitzsimmons, 2008).

Content of cross-cultural training programmes

Cross-cultural training programmes usually focus on developing specific *social and communication skills* needed to negotiate everyday social encounters in foreign cultures. Furnham and Bochner (1982) identify numerous social situations that newcomers find difficult to handle if they lack adequate cross-cultural communication skills. Mendenhall and Oddou (1985) point to skills that expatriate managers need in all cultures, including:

- *cognitive skills* (giving adequate understanding of the host society);
- *practical coping skills* relating to stress-control and relationship-building (e.g. accepting and showing respect for other people's cultural norms);
- *practical communication skills* that facilitate work adjustment and other kinds of cross-cultural adjustment (e.g. competence in conducting multicultural discussions).

According to Yamazaki and Kayes (2004), skills that facilitate expatriate adjustment and job performance include interpersonal skills, information skills, action skills, and analytical skills.

Skills needed in all cultures

The following practical skills are included in many cross-cultural training programmes because the skills are needed in virtually all cultural settings:

- carrying out culturally appropriate greetings, leave-takings, and apologies;
- appropriate nonverbal behaviours, such as distances that should be maintained in conversations;
- expressing ideas and opinions in ways that people from the other culture find acceptable;
- introducing appropriate topics of small talk; moving the conversation away from undesirable topics;
- responding non-judgmentally to the opinions of members of other cultures;
- active listening, paraphrasing, and questioning.

Sometimes a cross-cultural training programme is designed to bring together people from several different cultures so as to give them opportunities to observe and learn from each others' behaviour and values. Thus when Chinese and German participants attended a cross-cultural workshop, the direct way in which the German participants expressed disagreement was seen as very rude and inconsiderate by the Chinese. The Germans, however, explained that they perceived the disagreement as mere argumentative involvement (Gunthner, 2000).

TRAINING METHODS

Linked to training content

Cross-cultural skill development generally requires some combination of cognitive, attitudinal, and behavioural elements (Mendenhall and Oddou, 1985). The underlying rationale is that in order to interact effectively with people from another culture a person must acquire knowledge about the culture (*cognitive learning*), develop positive feelings towards the culture and members of the culture (*attitudinal learning*), and be able to behave appropriately in the culture (*behavioural learning*). Many cross-cultural training programmes include business games and exercises that simulate cross-cultural business environments. The accessibility of internet programmes makes it easy for managers and business persons throughout the world to enhance their negotiating and other cross-cultural skills by participating in online training modules.

As Waxin and Panaccio (2005) point out, the impact of cross-cultural training depends on training content and also the training methods used. Often the content emerges naturally from the training objectives. If, for instance, a key objective is to increase social competence in a given country the content will include demonstration and practice of communication skills needed for confident social performance in the country. In practice, however, most cross-cultural training programmes use *combinations* of different methods and content to develop the required skills (Puck et al., 2008).

Experiential learning

Although there is no clear consensus among cross-cultural training providers about the most effective training methods, according to Brislin et al. (2008) packages with a core of *experiential training* are often found to be the most effective. The strength of experiential learning is that it is tied to the social and political aspects of work and to the dilemmas and problems that occur in jobs in every culture.

Experiential learning theory defines learning as 'the process whereby knowledge is created through the transformation of experience. Knowledge results from the combination of grasping and transforming experience' (Kolb, 1984: 41). The learner touches all the bases – experiencing, reflecting, thinking, and acting – in a recursive process that is responsive to what is being learned, and to the particular cross-cultural or other situation that is involved, such as learning to quickly establish a friendly, cooperative relationship with a foreign business prospect.

Kolb's (1984) experiential learning model consists of four elements:

- concrete experience,
- observation of and reflection on that experience,
- formation of abstract concepts based on the reflection,
- testing the new concepts through experience.

Management training programmes based on experiential learning principles can be very effective in terms of the insights gained and the results achieved, although, as Reynolds (2009) cautions, experiential learning is too lacking in theoretical foundation for it to be established as an accepted methodology.

When Boyatzis and Mainemelis (2000) studied the skill development of full-time MBA students they found a pluralism of learning styles. While 38 per cent of the students had a preference for learning by conceptualizing (e.g. lectures, case studies, readings), 32 per cent had a preference for learning through experience (e.g. internships).

Methods used to change behaviour

Behaviour change is an important learning objective of many cross-cultural training programmes. According to social learning theory (Bandura, 1977), for people to learn new behaviour there must be attention, retention (remembering the new behaviour), and reproduction (ability to reproduce the behaviour learnt in the training sessions). Behaviour change usually occurs in several linked stages:

- *Awareness.* Becoming aware of a problem (e.g. prejudiced feelings towards a particular ethnic group) and the need to change.
- *Motivation.* Becoming motivated to make the change (e.g. by feelings of guilt).
- *Skill development.* Learning appropriate skills – e.g. learning to give positive, non-judgmental responses to members of other cultures.
- *Behaviour change.* Changing the behaviour and integrating the new behaviour into lifestyle.

In cross-cultural training courses behaviour modelling and feedback techniques, based on social learning theory, are widely used to engineer the required changes:

Behaviour modelling is based on social learning theory which explains how people learn from observing others' behaviour. In cross-cultural training programmes members of a particular culture ('live' or on video) model specific behaviours which are common and desirable in the culture. The trainees then practise carrying out the observed behaviour. Repeated practice of the modelled behaviour allows the trainee to approximate to the modelled behaviour.

Feedback. The trainees then receive feedback from the tutor and others in the group about their efforts to perform the modelled behaviour. Feedback can be defined as 'information about the effects of one's actions or efforts relative to some criterion or interest' (Herold and Greller, 1977). In cross-cultural training courses feedback is used to encourage desired behaviour in a particular culture and to discourage undesired behaviour. The type of feedback received – particularly whether a group receives feedback about individual or group performance – affects whether individual or collective improvement will result (Hinsz et al., 1997).

More generally, feedback provides the mechanism by which an individual assesses past efforts and identifies areas of needed improvement. The feedback principle is also used to support cognitive learning. For instance, software might be used to test trainees' knowledge of a particular culture, penalizing trainees for giving the wrong answers and rewarding them for right answers. The concept of feedback was originally used to describe the process by which a system (human or machine) will self-regulate. Feedback about system performance allows the system to reflect, adapt, and self-correct until desired performance standards are achieved. Feedback has long played a central role in theories of learning, continuous improvement, and performance achievement (Van der Vegt et al., 2010).

Other popular training methods

Role-plays are often used to sensitize people to the feelings of people from other cultures. For instance, when the trainee plays the role of a recent immigrant who feels humiliated because of the way an immigration officer talks to her, she begins to experience what many immigrants actually feel and think.

Case studies are used to describe and analyse problems experienced by people who live and work in a foreign country. Typical problems which are highlighted are feelings of isolation, relationship difficulties, and the various symptoms of culture shock.

Culture assimilators are used to give understanding of the values and behaviours of another culture. Several critical incidents are presented that led to misunderstanding or conflict between members of the trainees' culture and the target culture. Alternative explanations of the incident are given. The trainee chooses an explanation. A member of the target culture then reveals the 'correct' explanation and explains why it is correct.

Videos and discussion. One way in which cultural self-awareness can be encouraged is by making videos of conversations between trainees and members of the target culture. The videos are played back and the cultural values and assumptions which are being projected by the trainees are identified and discussed. Generally, as trainees become more aware of their own cultural identities, their understanding and appreciation of other people's cultural identities increases. As they become aware of how culture has moulded their own values and behaviour they see how other people's values and behaviour are also culturally determined. Such insights help them to relate to people from other cultures in a more accepting and open-minded way.

TRAINING DESIGN

Culture-general programmes

Cross-cultural training programmes tend to be *culture-general* or *culture-specific* in approach (although in practice most programmes contain elements of both approaches). Culture-general programmes are designed to give insight into the practices and communicative behaviours exhibited in diverse cultures, together with opportunities to practise some of the behaviours. An example of such behaviours is the avoidance of patronizing or critical comments about members of any other culture.

According to Mendenhall and Oddou (1985), skills needed in all cultures include:

- *skills facilitating relationship-building* (e.g. being non-judgmental and displaying respect for other people's cultural norms);
- *practical communication skills* that facilitate cross-cultural adjustment (e.g. ability to engage in cross-cultural interactions);
- *practical coping skills* relating to mental health and stress-reduction.

Graf (2004) argues that training expatriates on cultural differences *in general* prepares them for the wide range of specific cultural differences they will have to deal with during assignments in various countries. However, a common criticism of culture-general courses is that they tend to be overgeneralized and that it is difficult to apply the learning in any given culture.

Culture-specific programmes

The rationale of culture-specific programmes is that cross-cultural skills are often specific to a particular country and a particular social context, and that the skills required are unlikely to be learned by attending a generalized programme. For instance, the cross-cultural skills needed by an expatriate underground manager employed by a Zambian copper mine are very specific, and the training needs to be geared to meeting those specific needs. An important advantage of culture-specific training is that by focusing on a particular culture the training has the effect of reducing anxiety about working and communicating with members of the culture (Hammer and Martin, 1992).

An example of a culture-specific programme was that developed for the water sector of an African country:

> The objective of the training was to build job competence in sector managers and senior technical staff. Skills had to be taught in ways that were easy to learn and remember. Accordingly, complicated behavioural skills such as how to deal with an angry customer, were broken down into a series of steps, each step being demonstrated by the instructor then practised by trainees.

> Manuals were given to the managers and technical specialists for them to use to instruct employees in their own departments when they returned to their jobs. The manuals covered the testing, operation, dismantling and repair of all equipment and plant in the managers' workplaces. Local contractors supplied illustrated manuals in English and Swahili to ensure that all managers and technical staff would clearly understand the points covered.

> In view of the geographical dispersion of water utilities and the huge distances to be covered, short skill-based workshops were held in different regional centres around the country. One-to-one coaching sessions were arranged to meet certain high-priority needs of top-level managers.

Training evaluation

A commonly used method of planning a cross-cultural training programme is to determine:

- topics that will be covered;
- skills that will be developed;
- training methods that will be used to deliver the learning;
- evaluation techniques that will be used to assess training effectiveness.

Evaluation techniques are used to assess the effectiveness of the overall training programme – that is the extent to which the programme achieved the stated training objectives; or its effect on performance or efficiency. Appropriate evaluation techniques can also be used to measure the success of specific components of a programme or even a particular training session.

Tools that can be used for evaluation include the Intercultural Development Inventory which measures a person's cross-cultural strengths and weaknesses (Hammer and Bennett, 2001), the Cross-cultural Adaptability Inventory which measures personal characteristics facilitating cross-cultural adaptation (Kelley and Meyers, 1995), the Intercultural Sensitivity Inventory which can be used to guide intercultural skills development (Bhawuk and Brislin, 1992), and the Behavioural Assessment Scale for Intercultural Communication Effectiveness, which assesses overall cross-cultural competence (Koester and Olebe, 1988). These measures can be used before and after the training so that it is known what difference the training made.

Long-term behaviour changes brought about by cross-cultural training typically include:

- demonstrating more tact and tolerance during cross-cultural conversations and discussions;
- less willingness to make snap judgments about members of the culture during cross-cultural conversations;
- more effort to understand, listen to, and communicate with members of the culture.

SMALL-GROUP EXERCISE: Discussion questions

Working in small groups, discuss each of the following questions and write down the group's agreed answer. At the end of the exercise, each group may present its answers to the other groups for comment.

1. *What are the main disadvantages of the total immersion method of acquiring cross-cultural competence?*
2. *What are the main objectives of formal cross-cultural training? What do global managers gain from cross-cultural training?*
3. *What is the difference between cross-cultural skills and cross cultural abilities? Give examples of each.*
4. *What different kinds of learning are usually developed in cross-cultural training programmes?*
5. *Describe how behaviour modelling and feedback are used by trainers to teach culturally appropriate behaviour.*
6. *What is the difference between culture-specific and culture-general training programmes? Which of the two approaches gets the best results and why?*

EXPATRIATE TRAINING

Training and expatriate performance

Studies by Mendenhall et al. (2004) and other researchers have shown that cross-cultural training is linked to successful expatriate performance and cross-cultural adjustment, and can have the effect of reducing the number of early returns. An important benefit of appropriate cross-cultural training is that it equips expatriates with the knowledge and skills needed for effective relationships with host nationals. It encourages positive attitudes towards the host culture, and increases awareness of differences of values and practices between cultures.

Much evidence exists to show that expatriate adjustment and job performance can be raised by giving expatriate managers the opportunity to attend appropriate cross-cultural training courses. Yamazaki and Kayes (2004), for instance, identify 73 different skills that influence successful expatriate adjustment and job performance, including cross-cultural communication skills, information skills, and analytical skills.

An example of an appropriate expatriate training course is one dealing with effective techniques for *training local employees* – which is a key responsibility of many expatriate managers. A study of New Zealand expatriate managers in China, for instance, found that the training of local employees was a key responsibility of most of them, and that when they learned to use instructional methods and approaches that were *adjusted to the culture* this greatly increased their overall job performance (Seak and Enderwick, 2008).

But in spite of the high failure rates of expatriate assignments which one estimate puts at 16–40 per cent (Sims and Schraeder, 2005), many organisations fail to provide any cross-cultural training for staff assigned to overseas postings. A possible reason for the neglect is lack of acceptance by top-level managers in many companies that there is a link between expatriate training and expatriate performance. A senior executive in a London-based multinational company admitted to a business visitor:

> We send dozens of excellent people to work on our overseas projects but we never seem to learn from them. Head office people never go out at the end of a successful project to talk to expatriate staff to identify the cross-cultural skills that enabled them to produce the results. Cross-cultural training can be a blunt instrument unless the precise skills required are known.

Cross-cultural interviewing skills

Expatriate managers and managers of any multicultural work force need to learn how to carry out cross-cultural interviews and multicultural meetings in ways that people from diverse cultures will find acceptable. Appropriate skills have to be learnt and appropriate training has to be provided.

Conducting an effective cross-cultural interview is more challenging than conducting a same-culture interview. When interviewer and interviewee come from different national or ethnic backgrounds, relying on traditional interviewing techniques is insufficient and standard techniques may have to be adapted and extended. For instance, standard techniques to encourage interviewees to talk freely – 'reflecting', non-judgmental responses, open questions, and so on – may not work with people who have been raised, say, in a restrictive, authoritarian culture. Accordingly, a different approach and alternative techniques have to be used. The skills required for effective cross-cultural interviewing are examined in Chapter 12.

Performance appraisal skills

Those expatriate managers who are often responsible for appraising the performance of local employees will need to be trained to use *culturally appropriate* appraisal methods, as imported appraisal techniques will not be accepted when they run counter to local customs and values. That was the lesson learned by a Western expatriate manager in a manufacturing company in China. The manager introduced employee appraisal interviews as a basis for awarding bonuses to individual employees.

> But in China team working is the norm and the new system had a disastrous effect on morale, absenteeism and labour turnover and had to be dropped after a few months. The manager was left wondering what kind of bonus arrangement would have been more acceptable – or even whether a bonus scheme was necessary.

The example points up the importance of expatriate managers using culturally appropriate methods and techniques. But some expatriate managers may first have to be trained to identify the culturally appropriate techniques that are required.

Timing of training

Cross-cultural training for expatriates is sometimes found to be more effective if it takes place in-country, after arrival, since this allows for fast feedback in critical situations – for instance, after relationship problems have flared up or initial adjustment problems have occurred (Puck et al., 2008). On the other hand, some kinds of cross-cultural expatriate training can be effective even if they take place months in advance of an expatriate posting. For example, cross-cultural awareness among young Peace Corps volunteers was developed by sending them, months in advance of their first overseas postings, to spend time in a tough ethnic neighbourhood in the United States.

The volunteers would wander round the neighbourhood, chat to vendors or homeless people or people met in the street about day-to-day living problems, violence, drugs, and other topics. The aim was for the volunteers to learn as much as possible about the prevailing culture in the neighbourhood as this would mentally prepare them for the unfavourable conditions waiting for them in Africa or Asia. The experience taught the volunteers the big difference that exists between book-based cultural learning and cultural learning that comes from contact with real people.

Some multinational companies provide structured cross-cultural orientation programmes for managers selected for expatriate assignments. Usually these consist of pre-departure training courses since a clear relationship exists between expatriates' pre-departure knowledge of a foreign culture and all facets of expatriate adjustment (Black and Mendenhall, 1990). In some cases, initial courses are reinforced by further training sessions soon after the expatriates arrive in the country.

Training for female expatriates

Very few cross-cultural training courses have been designed to meet the special needs of female expatriates. Yet in many countries in Asia and the Middle East, women expatriates often complain that they should have been informed, before arrival, about such important aspects as how local colleagues and employees will expect them to dress or to behave in their jobs.

When a young female expatriate manager in Malaysia appeared at work in a sleeveless dress she was aware of the hostile nonverbal signals of her Malaysian colleagues – but she had no idea what she was doing wrong because relevant training and information had not been provided (Tahir and Ismail, 2007). Attending a cross-cultural training course designed for female expatriates would have increased her awareness of dress codes for women in Malaysia, and shown how women expatriates might avoid giving the wrong signals when communicating with men.

DIVERSITY TRAINING

Need to change attitudes

Many large organisations run diversity training courses. 69 per cent of British organisations, for instance, have a diversity policy and 60 per cent offer diversity training with the main aim of facilitating the integration of minority groups into the workforce (Brewer et al., 1999). Diversity training courses usually begin by explaining the benefits to the organisation of having a diverse workforce, and go on to describe the organisation's legal responsibilities under anti-discrimination laws.

However, as Nishii and Mayer (2009) caution, factual information alone rarely brings about attitude change and the elimination of prejudice and discrimination. Prejudice has a strong affective, emotional component and is linked to biased interpretations of information and former experience (Dovidio et al., 2004). Thus entrenched, prejudiced beliefs may be maintained even when employees are confronted with contrary evidence. Alternative, more effective methods may need to be incorporated in diversity training courses which are capable of changing prejudiced attitudes towards minority-group employees.

Training exercises to weaken prejudice

Rather than limiting diversity training to providing employees with lots of factual information, the training has been found to be more effective when it is expanded to increase employees' sense of a *common social identity*. Pendry et al. (2007) describe a training exercise with this objective. Trainees from different racial groups in a multicultural workplace listed the groups they belonged to. They then selected the groups that were most important to them and ranked these in terms of relative importance and discussed the rankings. The discussions revealed the importance that trainees of all races on the course attached to membership of workplace groups. In this way a common social identity was established. For the first time in their lives, perhaps, the trainees started to think of co-workers from another racial group as *in-group* members – an insight which, according to the researchers, could lead to enhanced respect and more cooperative behaviour in the workplace.

Another way of weakening prejudiced attitudes in the workplace is to equip managers with the *practical skills* needed to support a pro-diversity stance. In training sessions, managers could, for instance, be encouraged to:

- personally get to know each member of the diverse workforce in their departments;
- refrain from using language or behaviours that have the effect of excluding some employees and not others.

Nishii and Mayer (2009) found that employees of managers with an inclusive, pro-diversity management style tend to respond positively through increased productivity, loyalty, and job satisfaction.

Motives for introducing pro-diversity policies

Anecdotal evidence suggests that training courses aimed at encouraging managers in the multicultural workplace to adopt a pro-diversity stance have the greatest impact when the training is supported by initiatives taken by top-level management. Relevant actions include the publication and implementation of diversity policies, positive employment policies, the introduction of supervisory guidelines, and the drawing up and publishing of workplace codes of conduct.

However, the pronouncements by top-level management about their reasons for promoting pro-diversity policies cannot always be taken at face value. For example, Soltani (2010) found that minimization of labour costs and other economic factors were the major driving forces behind adopting equal opportunity and diversity practices in employment. Viewed from this perspective, diversity policies and practices emerge in response to increasing labour costs.

For Iranian managers in some sectors in Iran, foreign workers are recruited not in response to pro-diversity policies but because they offer Iranian bosses managerial flexibility. As Soltani (2010) points out, with a predominantly foreign workforce HR-related policies, such as workers' compensation claims, fringe benefits, and tax compliance, working hours and termination of contract remain firmly under the managers' control and are not contested. The managers benefit because they have greater freedom to hire and fire, adjust wages, and negotiate terms of employment.

DEVELOPING CULTURAL AWARENESS

Awareness of cultural acceptability

Cultural awareness gives understanding of the way that other cultures see the world. However, if the level of understanding is inadequate the results can be embarrassing. Consider the case of the reality TV show *Big Brother*. The show, where contestants are locked in the same house until viewers' votes leaves a winner, was launched in the United Kingdom in 2001. In 2004 an Arab TV channel, Lebanese-owned, produced its own version, Al-Ra'is (The Boss), in Bahrain.

According to BBC News Services (1 April 2004), the producers made a few cross-cultural modifications to make the show suitable for Arab viewers:

> For instance, they introduced a prayer area, and the sleeping quarters of male and female contestants were segregated. But these few modifications were not enough. They overlooked the main problem, which was that close interaction between men and women was *culturally unacceptable*.

The producers discovered their mistake when a storm of media criticism erupted and street protests began. After only two showings Al-Ra'is was cancelled. Clearly, a more rigorous assessment of the changes needed should have been made before The Boss was thrown to Bahrain viewers.

Conducting international business

As the fate of Al-Ra'is demonstrates, different countries have different values, different expectations, and different ideas of what is acceptable and what cannot be tolerated. Cultural values and expectations influence how events are judged, how foreign visitors are expected to behave, and how business is expected to be conducted. That is why, before entering a foreign country for the first time, expatriate managers, business visitors, and international travellers need to be aware of cultural values and behaviour in the country that may affect their activities and relationships.

Before visiting a Moslem country, for instance, a Western business visitor needs to be aware of the significance of *Eid*. In the same way Asian business executive who visit the United States needs to be aware of the importance of Thanksgiving to Americans. By demonstrating awareness of important cultural practices and beliefs in the country they are visiting the visitors avoid offending their hosts and embarrassing themselves.

These are some of the reasons why cultural awareness appears as a topic in most cross-cultural training programmes designed for international managers, business executives, and expatriate staff. Cultural awareness is essential for successfully conducting international business. Business executives need cultural awareness so that they can adjust to the communicative preferences of potential business partners in foreign countries. Expatriate staff need cultural awareness to help them communicate with local employees and to help them adjust to the culture where they are carrying out their assignments.

Competitive advantage

Acquiring a basic cultural awareness of a new culture is especially important for foreign business visitors because it gives them competitive advantage over competitors by giving insights into the communicative preferences of the people they will be meeting, such as a preference for formal communication or informal communication. Another advantage of cultural awareness is that it gives the foreign business visitor early warning of any adjustments of personal style that may be needed to make a business visit to the country a commercial success. Basic cultural awareness, for instance, might tell an American sales manager visiting Japan that he needs to adjust his usual chatty, highly informal communication style, and to be more formal and restrained when talking to managers in Japanese companies, more respectful of status differences.

Case study

MINI-CASE: Business trip to Brazil

When a Canadian systems engineer is planning his first business trip to Brazil he makes a point of learning something about the culture from the internet and by talking to colleagues who knew the country well. One piece of information that he acquires strikes him as really important. This is that business people in Brazil prefer to do business with people they like and trust, and who are outgoing and easy to get on with.

In everyday life the Canadian is an unassuming, unassertive person. But he realizes that he will need to make an effort to adjust his personal communication style during his visit to the country. Accordingly, after arriving in Brazil he makes a real effort to be outgoing and friendly to all the people he meets. This change of personal style lays the foundation for what turns out to be a commercially successful business trip.

Basic cultural awareness – acquired in this case largely from the internet – prompted the engineer to adjust his 'natural' communicative style and to relate to his hosts in the way they preferred.

Questions:

1. *Was the engineer right to change his 'natural' communication style during his visit to Brazil? Give reasons for and against.*
2. *Explain why effective cross-cultural communication in a foreign country depends on being aware of the communicative preferences of members of the culture.*

Lack of cultural awareness

The experience of a young British consultant visiting Bangladesh for the first time illustrates how *lack* of cultural awareness can trigger inappropriate behaviour and damage cross-cultural relationships. After arriving in Dhaka the consultant held a meeting with the client – the head of a government department. Soon after the meeting started the official noisily cleared his throat and reached for his spittoon.

The consultant, totally unaware that public throat-clearing and spitting were normal practice in the country, reacted tactlessly and with visible disapproval. The official noticed the reaction and was greatly offended. Relations between the two remained tense for the remaining weeks of the consultant's assignment.

It was only later, when he discussed the incident with a colleague, the consultant realized that a basic cultural awareness would have enabled him to deal tactfully and appropriately with the incident in the conference room. Such awareness could easily have been acquired by talking to colleagues who knew the country well, and who would have briefed him on common social practices in the country. If he had made even a minimal effort to learn something about the culture before his visit, embarrassing blunders could have been avoided and he would have related better to the client and to the local people.

For a business person visiting a country for the first time even a minimal, elementary level of cultural awareness is invaluable.

Levels of cultural awareness

The more people learn about other cultures, the more they become aware of the relative strengths and weaknesses of their own culture. Awareness of their own culture's shortcomings has the great advantage of freeing them from the assumptions of cultural superiority that can cripple communication with people from other countries. The European Union (1997) has identified different levels of cultural awareness that progressively help people to develop a cross-cultural outlook:

1. The first step equates to a minimal level of cultural awareness, awareness only of superficial differences.
2. The second step, acquired through cross-cultural communication and observation, equates to a somewhat higher level of awareness of deeper-level cultural differences.
3. The third step is learning to be tolerant of other cultures, recognizing that they are different from one's own culture and that they have a right to be different.
4. The final step is learning to accept, value, and use cultural differences positively, in the spirit of 'Let's work together in a mutually beneficial manner.'

As Scollon and Scollon (2001) point out, achieving higher levels of cultural awareness brings increased awareness of one's own values, one's own communication, and how people from other cultures might perceive them – thus clearing the ground for necessary adjustments.

Cross-cultural sensitivity training

Multinational project teams are often characterized by distrust and conflict and low levels of group cohesion (Phillips, 1994). That was the situation confronting project management when an international project team was assembled to build a power plant in India. The team consisted of more than 200 expatriate staff from firms in five different countries speaking a total of 20 languages. Not surprisingly, the clash of cultures and tongues generated tensions, stereotyping, and mutual distrust.

> Project management soon realised that the one attribute the experts must have was *cross-cultural sensitivity* as this quality would provide a basis for cooperation and collaboration. Most of the expatriates, however, had been selected for their technical expertise alone and lacked this essential quality.

Cross-cultural sensitivity makes it easier to develop relationships with members of other cultures (Bush et al., 2001). This attribute can be acquired through cross-cultural training which provides opportunities to learn about important cultural values that differentiate cultures. In one training programme, for instance, trainees used a modified version of Kluckhohn and Strodbeck's (1961) Value Orientations instrument to establish their own cultural positions *vis-à-vis* the value positions of other cultures (Maznevski, 1994).

When a person meets someone from another culture, cultural sensitivity helps the individual to see things from the other person's perspective. For example, a culturally sensitive individual is aware of any linguistic or pronunciation difficulties being experienced by the other person. This awareness prompts her to adjust aspects of her own speech to match the speech of her conversational partner. She encourages the other person to continue communicating through using nonverbal behaviours such as smiling, eye contact, head nods, and body orientations which suggest interest and attentiveness.

CULTURAL INTELLIGENCE

Appropriate behaviour

Effective cross-cultural communication requires *behavioural flexibility* – the ability to select appropriate behaviour according to the cultural context (Bhawuk and Brislin, 1992). What is considered appropriate behaviour in a foreign culture can be learned in advance from books, magazine articles, or the internet or, after arrival in the country, by applying cultural intelligence.

Essentially, cultural intelligence is the ability that a person has to adapt across cultures (Lee and Sukoco, 2010). It has cognitive, motivational, and behavioural elements (Sternberg and Grigorenko, 2006), and is a relatively new approach to developing cultural awareness and improving cross-cultural communication ability. Earley and Ang (2003) define 'cultural intelligence' as an expatriate's ability to deal effectively in situations characterized by cultural diversity. Expatriates who are able to recognize and reconcile cultural differences through cultural intelligence are likely to be effective workers in the host country and to have little difficulty interacting with local co-workers (Earley et al., 2006).

Expatriates and international business people with cultural intelligence become adept at picking up cultural differences by listening and observing. They are thus able to behave appropriately and to carry out successful assignments in cultures other than their own. Cultural intelligence involves careful observation of how local people behave, and this may be supplemented by a few perceptive questions. By using such an approach, business visitors quickly discover

- in China, the importance of using both hands to accept somebody's business card and studying it carefully;
- in France or other high power–distance countries, the importance of adopting a courteous, formal manner when communicating with high-status people;
- in Sweden, the importance of not boasting about personal achievements to business contacts.

Simple observation will tell foreign business visitors to the United States that a suit and tie are appropriate for doing business in New York or Chicago, but not in California, where 'smart casual' may be more appropriate. A culturally intelligent factory manager who openly criticises shop floor workers for high scrap rates and poor timekeeping in Detroit would carefully avoid criticism if appointed to an expatriate position in China, where it is taboo to criticise employees in front of others.

Foreign business visitors to a foreign country need to know whether to bow or shake hands when meeting a potential client, they need to know which topics are acceptable to discuss in the small-talk stage of a cross-cultural business discussion. Such knowledge can be acquired through the use of cultural intelligence. Practical exercises to develop cultural intelligence are sometimes included in cross-cultural training courses for business executives.

Improved cross-cultural interaction

The ability to select appropriate behaviour is strengthened by first acquiring the relevant knowledge then practising what has been learned. As Thomas and Inkson (2004) point out cultural intelligence is developed incrementally, with each repeat of the cycle building on the previous one. A person demonstrates cultural intelligence by consciously learning from each cross-cultural interaction. By listening to and observing the other person's reactions during a cross-cultural conversation it is possible to adapt one's own contribution to the conversation and make it more appropriate to the situation. Thus a foreign business visitor to Japan demonstrated cultural intelligence by adopting a 'silent and attentive' strategy in cross-cultural business meetings after learning, by observation, how important it is to become part of the consensus in Japanese business meetings (Zweifel, 2003).

Cultural intelligence works in a somewhat similar way to Mindfulness, a Buddhist concept that implies being fully aware of what is going on within us and around us. During a cross-cultural conversation a culturally intelligent person, like a mindful person, gives careful attention to what is going on communicatively and consciously learns from the experience. He listens carefully to the other person's viewpoint. He is aware of the other person's linguistic problems and therefore, if necessary, simplifies his own language. He encourages the other person to continue communicating by using appropriate nonverbal signals – smiling, head nods, eye contact, and so on. He is attentive to the meanings and feelings underlying the other person's words even when these are imperfectly expressed. In these and other ways a person demonstrates cultural intelligence.

KEY POINTS

1. Most cross-cultural skills involve verbal and nonverbal communication, which are the fundamental tools used by people from different cultures to interact. Cross-cultural skills can be developed using a variety of different methods and approaches, including joint projects, one-to-one coaching, exposure to foreign cultures, and formal cross-cultural training programmes. A well-designed cross-cultural training programme accelerates cultural learning

by arranging in an orderly way the product of many people's first-hand experience of cross-cultural situations.

2. Cross-cultural training helps people to build effective interpersonal relations with individuals from cultures other than their own. It does so by encouraging behaviours appropriate in other cultures, such as culturally appropriate ways of greeting people, and by encouraging trainees to see problems from the viewpoint of people from other cultures. Most cross-cultural programmes promote a cultural relativist approach with the aim of reducing negative stereotyping of members of other cultures and increasing awareness of the trainees' own prejudices and assumptions.

3. Cross-cultural skill development has cognitive, attitudinal, and behavioural elements. To interact effectively with people from another culture a person must acquire knowledge about the culture (*cognitive learning*), develop positive feelings towards the culture (*attitudinal learning*), and be able to behave appropriately in the culture (*behavioural learning*). Expatriate managers need a range of cross-cultural skills to successfully carry out their assignments. These include practical coping skills (relating to stress-control and the management of relationships); practical communication skills; and cognitive skills which give an adequate understanding of the host society.

4. Behaviour modelling and feedback techniques are used in cross-cultural training programmes to bring about behaviour change. According to social learning theory, people learn from observing others' behaviour. Thus in training sessions members of a particular culture ('live' or on video) model behaviours which are common and desirable in a given culture. Trainees then practise carrying out the observed behaviour and receive feedback from the tutor and fellow-trainees. Feedback takes the form of positive and negative reinforcers of aspects of the trainee's performance, the goal being to encourage desired behaviour and discourage undesired behaviour. Repeated practice and feedback allows the trainee to approximate to the modelled behaviour.

5. Training evaluation is used to assess the effectiveness of cross-cultural training programmes. Various evaluation techniques, methods, and instruments are used to measure the extent to which a programme achieved its stated training objectives, or the impact it made on organisational performance or efficiency. Training evaluation techniques are sometimes focused on assessing long-term behaviour changes brought about by the training. Typical behaviour changes are more tact and tolerance during cross-cultural conversations, and less willingness to make snap judgments about members of the culture.

6. Many large organisations – more than two-thirds in the United Kingdom – have a diversity policy. Many multinational and multicultural companies worldwide offer diversity training courses with the aim of facilitating the integration of members of minority groups and members of other cultures into the workforce. Diversity training courses usually explain the benefits of having a diverse workforce and describe the organisation's responsibilities under anti-discrimination laws. But factual information alone rarely brings about

attitude change and the elimination of prejudice and discrimination in the workplace.

QUESTIONS FOR DISCUSSION AND WRITTEN ASSIGNMENTS

1. Identify the practical coping skills needed to help expatriate staff to adjust to living and working in a foreign culture? How can these skills be developed?
2. Typical behaviour changes brought about cross-cultural training are showing more tact and tolerance during cross-cultural conversations, and being less willing to make snap judgments about members of another culture. What training methods can be used to bring about such changes? How can behaviour changes resulting from the training be identified and assessed?
3. Most diversity training courses aim to bring about attitude change and the elimination of prejudice and discrimination in the workplace. Is the provision of factual information alone sufficient to achieve these aims? If not, what other elements are needed?
4. Describe actions that top management could take to make the elimination of prejudice and discrimination in the workplace more likely?

BIBLIOGRAPHY

Bandura, A. *Social Learning Theory*. General learning Press, 1977.

Bhawuk, DPS and Brislin, RW. The measurement of intercultural sensitivity using the concepts of individualism and collectivism. *International Journal of Intercultural Relations*, 16, 1992, 413–436.

Black, JS and Mendenhall, M. Cross-cultural training effectiveness: a review and theoretical framework for further research, *Academy of Management Review*, 15, 1990, 113–136.

Boyatzis, RE. *The Competent Manager*. Wiley, 1982.

Boyatzis, RE and Mainemelis, C. An empirical study of the pluralism of learning and adaptive styles in an MBA Program. Paper presented at a meeting of Academy of Management, Toronto, 2000.

Brewer, MB et al., Diversity and organizational identity. In DA Prentice and DT Miller (eds), *Cultural Divides: Understanding and Overcoming Group Conflict*. Sage, 1999, pp. 337–363.

Brislin, RW. Intercultural communication training. In MK Asante and WB Gudykunst (eds), *Handbook of International and Intercultural Communication*. Sage, 1989, pp. 441–457.

Brislin, RW and Yoshida, T. *Intercultural Communication Training: An Introduction*. Sage, 1994.

Brislin, RW et al., Cross-cultural training: applications and research. PB Smith et al. (eds), *Handbook of Cross-cultural Management Research*. Sage, 2008, pp. 397–410.

Bush, VD et al., Managing culturally diverse buyer-seller relationships. *Journal of the Academy of Marketing Science*, 29, 2001, 391–404.

Coutu, D and Kauffman, C. What can coaches do for you. *HBR*, January 2009, 91–106.

Dovidio, JF et al., From intervention to outcomes: Processes in the reduction of bias. In WG Stephan and P Vogt (eds), *Education Programs for Improving Intergroup Relations: Theory, Research, and Practice.* Teachers College Press, 2004, pp. 243–265.

Earley, C and Ang, S. *Cultural Intelligence: Individual Interactions Across Cultures.* Stanford University Press, 2003.

Earley, PC. Ang, S and Tan, JS. *CQ: Developing Cultural Intelligence at Work.* Stanford University Press, 2006.

Epstein, MJ. The drivers of success in post-merger integration. *Organisational Dynamics,* 33, 2004, 174–189.

Erickson, TJ et al., Eight ways to build collaborative teams. *Harvard Business Review,* November 2007, 100–109.

European Union, Directorate-General for Employment, Industrial Relations and Social Affairs: Developing an intercultural outlook, 1997.

Ford, B. Mediating knowledge: cross-cultural learning. *HR Monthly,* September 1998.

Funakawa, A. *Transcultural Management: A New Approach for Global Organisations.* Jossey-Bass, 1997.

Furnham, A and Bochner, S. Social difficulty in a foreign culture: an empirical analysis of culture shock. In S Bochner (ed.), *Cultures in Contact.* Pergamon, 1982, p. 164.

Gosselin, A et al., Ratee preferences regarding performance management and appraisal. *Human Resource Development Quarterly,* 8, 1997, 315–333.

Graf, A. Screening and training inter-cultural competencies. *International Journal of Human Resource Management,* 15 (6), 2004, 1125, 1142.

Gunthner, S. Argumentation and resultant problems in the negotiation of rapport in a German-Chinese conversation. In H Spencer-Oatey (ed.), *Culturally Speaking.* Continuum, 2000, pp. 218–239.

Hammer, MR and Martin, JN. The effects of cross-cultural training on American managers in a Japanese-American joint venture. *Journal of Applied Communication Research* 20 (2), 1992, 161–182.

Hammer, MR and Bennett, MJ. *The Intercultural Development Inventory.* Intercultural Communication Institute, 2001.

Herold, DM and Greller, MM. Feedback: definition of a construct. *Academy of Management Journal,* 20, 1977, 142–147.

Hinsz, VB et al., The emerging conceptualisation of groups as information processors. *Psychological Bulletin,* 121, 1997, 43–64.

Jackson, T. *International HRM: A Cross-cultural Approach.* Sage, 2002.

Kanter, RM. Mergers that stick. *HBR,* October 2009, 121–125.

Kelley and Meyers, *Cross-cultural Adaptability Inventory.* National Computer Systems, 1995.

Kluckhohn, F and Strodbeck, FL. *Variations in Value Orientations.* Greenwood, 1961.

Koester, J and Olebe, M. The behavioural assessment scale for intercultural communication effectiveness. *International Journal of Intercultural Relations*, 12, 1988, 233–246.

Kolb, DA. *Experiential Learning: Experience as the Source of Learning and Development.* Prentice Hall, 1984.

Lee, L-Y and Sukoco, BM. The effects of cultural intelligence on expatriate performance: the moderating effects of international experience. *International Journal of Human Resource Management*, 21 (7–9), 2010, 963–981.

Martin, M and Vaughn, B. *Strategic Diversity and Inclusion Management.* DTUI Publications Division, 2007, pp. 31–36.

Maznevski, M. Synergy and performance in multi-cultural teams. PhD thesis. University of Western Ontario, 1994.

Mendenhall, M and Oddou, G. The dimensions of expatriate acculturation. *Academy of Management Review*, 10, 1985, 39–47.

Mendenhall, ME et al., Evaluation studies of cross-cultural training programmes. In D Landis et al. (eds), *Handbook of Intercultural Training*, 3rd ed. Sage, 2004, pp. 129–143.

Nishii, LH and Mayer, DM. Do inclusive leaders help to reduce turnover in diverse groups? The moderating role of leader-member exchange in the diversity to turnover relationship. *Journal of Applied Psychology*, 94 (6), 2009, 1412–1426.

O'Brien, G et al., The effects of programmed cultural training upon the performance of volunteer medical teams in Central America. *Human Relations*, 24 (2), 1982, 209–231.

Pendry, LF et al., Diversity training: putting theory into practice. *Journal of Occupational and Organisational Psychology*, 80, 2007, 27–50.

Phillips, N. *Managing International Teams.* Irwin, 1994.

Pool, LD and Sewell, P. The key to employability: developing a practical model of graduate employability. *Education and Training*, 49, 2007, 277–289.

Prokesch, S. How GE teaches teams to lead change. *HBR*, January 2009, 99–106.

Puck, FF et al., Does it really work? Re-assessing the impact of pre-departure cross-cultural training on expatriate adjustment. *International Journal of Human Resource Management*, 19 (12), 2008, 2182–2197.

Reynolds, M. Wild frontiers – reflections on experiential learning. *Management Learning*, 40 (4), 2009, 387–392.

Rosenzweig, PM and Nohria, N. Influences on human resource management practices in multinational corporations. *Journal of International Business Studies*, second quarter, 1994, 229–251.

Scollon, R and Scollon, SW. *Intercultural Communication*, 2nd ed. Blackwell, 2001, p. 151.

Scullion, H and Starkey, K. In search of the changing role of the corporate human resource function in an international firm. *International Journal of Human Resource Management*, 11, 2000, 1061–1081.

Seak, N and Enderwick, P. The management of New Zealand expatriates in China. *International Journal of Human Resource Management*, 19 (7), 2008, 1298–1313.

Sims, R and Schraeder, M. An examination of salient factors affecting expatriate culture shock. *Journal of Business and Management*, 10 (1), 2005, 73–88.

Soltani, E. The overlooked variable in managing human resources of Iranian organisations: workforce diversity – some evidence. *International Journal of Human Resources Management*, 21 (1), 2010, 84–108.

Sternberg, RJ and Grigorenko, EL. Cultural intelligence and successful intelligence. *Group and Organisation Management*, 31, 2006, 27–39.

Tahir, AHM and Ismail, M. Cross-cultural challenges and adjustment of expatriates: a case study in Malaysia. *Turkish Journal of International Relations*, 6 (3), 2007, 72–99.

Thomas, DC and Inkson, K. *Cultural Intelligence: People Skills for Global Business*. Berrett-Koehler, 2004.

Thomas, DC and Fitzsimmons, SR. Cross-cultural skills and abilities. In PB Smith et al. (eds), *Handbook of Cross-cultural Management Research*. Sage, 2008, pp. 201–215.

Van der Vegt, GS et al., Power asymmetry and learning in teams. *Organisation Science*, 21 (2), 2010, 347–361.

Waxin, M-F and Panaccio, A. Cross-cultural training to facilitate expatriate adjustment: it works! *Personnel Review*, 34, 2005, 51–67.

Yamazaki, Y and Kayes, DC. An experiential learning approach to cross-cultural learning. *Academy of Management Learning and Education*, 3, 2004, 362–379.

Zweifel, TD. *Culture Clash: Managing the Global High-performance Team*. Swiss Consulting Group, 2003.

Communicating across cultural distance

9

INTRODUCTION

A country's cultural distance from another country is assessed by comparing important aspects of the culture of each country – for example level of economic development, form of government, religion, language, and ethnic composition (Triandis, 2001). The United States and China, or Russia and Brazil, are examples of countries which are culturally distant from each other.

The concept of cultural distance is widely used in international business, where it is used to assess the extent to which the *business values and practices* in countries differ from each other. As differences increase between any two countries' language, laws, and business practices, cross-cultural communication and cooperation between organisations in the two countries becomes increasingly difficult. Operating a business in a culturally distant country is complicated and expensive. For instance, interpreters and translators often have to be used. Agreements may have to be made with local consultants or agents who know the local business environment and whose services are needed to provide contacts with local suppliers, distributors, and government officials.

The risks as well as the costs of doing business in culturally distant nations can also be high. Potential business difficulties – dealing with local labour laws, for instance – may not be fully understood and may lead to unwise recruitment or redundancy decisions. When great cultural distance separates a company and a foreign business partner, the greater the risk that the practices, procedures, and policies of the two companies will be incompatible, and that effective coordination of the two organisations will be much harder to achieve. Major cross-cultural communication difficulties may be experienced as a result of language problems and different business values.

Cultural distance affects the quality of cross-cultural communication by introducing 'noise' – misunderstandings, misinterpretations, and psychological discomfort – into the communication process. Research evidence consistently shows that communication between people in different cultures tends to be most successful when the participants are culturally close and least successful when they are culturally distant from each other (Fehr, 1996). Communicating with members of culturally distant societies is more difficult than with members of culturally similar societies. Misunderstandings occur because the participants interpret each others' communication and behaviour in terms of their own cultural norms (Barnlund, 1998).

Expatriate managers carrying out assignments in culturally distant countries are constantly at risk of contravening the prevailing communicative norms and expectations, leading to tensions and relationship difficulties with local colleagues and employees. People who live and work in a culturally distant country usually have to go through a very extensive learning and unlearning process before they feel psychologically comfortable in the culture (Kim, 1995).

CULTURAL DISTANCE

What is it?

When we meet people from other cultures we perceive them as very similar to ourselves, very dissimilar, or something in between. There is a continuum from the very similar to the totally foreign. Where we mentally place people on the continuum affects the quality and frequency of our communication with them – even our willingness to communicate. Research shows that cross-cultural communication tends to be more successful in terms of interaction and outcomes when the participants are culturally close (very similar) and less successful when they are culturally distant (totally foreign) from each other (Fehr, 1996).

Furnham and Bochner (1982) classified foreign students from 29 countries attending English universities according to whether their cultures were 'near', 'intermediate', or 'far' from British society. North Europeans were categorized as 'near', South Europeans were 'intermediate', while students from Asia and the Middle East were judged to be 'far' from British culture. Students from 'far' (culturally distant) countries were found to have the greatest difficulty in communicating with British people and in dealing with everyday social situations in Britain. The researchers concluded that cultural distance between home and host countries was a major determinant of stress, and led to failure to communicate and build relationships with local people.

Assessing cultural distance

A country's cultural distance from another country is readily assessed by comparing important aspects of the culture of each country. These include:

- form of government
- level of economic development
- dominant language

- ethnic composition
- dominant religion

Van Vianen et al. (2004) distinguish between surface- and deep-level cultural differences between cultures. *Surface-level differences* include differences relating to general living conditions, food, climate, housing and transport arrangements, leisure possibilities, and so on. *Deep-level differences*, however, include values, beliefs, and ideological ideas that are not immediately visible but which may be expressed in political and religious convictions. Deep-level differences create formidable cultural barriers for expatriate managers, international students, and other foreigners living and working in countries that are culturally distant from their own.

Examples of 'distant' cultures

Australia and Japan or the United States and China are examples of countries that are culturally distant from each other. When Australian and Japanese people meet there are many conspicuous differences and these differences have the effect of complicating cross-cultural communication. Japanese people speak a different language, their verbal and nonverbal behaviour is difficult for an Australian to understand and interpret. Moreover, Japanese people often dress differently, have different eating habits, and do not behave in ways that Australians regard as normal. They are constantly bowing, for instance. If they are given bad news they show no emotion – or they smile. Such behaviour trigger perceptions of strangeness and unpredictability, and the result is that people may be tempted to avoid communicating with them altogether.

In a similar way people are tempted to avoid communicating with hooligans, people who are mentally disturbed people, or physically handicapped people – that is, to escape the anxiety and uncertainty that close contact with them would cause (Gudykunst, 1995).

Rastafari culture is an example of a culture that is 'distant' from virtually all other cultures. Wearing locks, smoking ganja, deification of Haile Selassie, and belief in the apocalypse have been key elements of Rastafari culture. The culture springs from slavery in Jamaica, the French-speaking territories of Martinique and Guadaloupe, and other territories. Campbell (1980) makes the point that in the New World the only authentic religion was deemed to be that of the masters – thinking that led to a massive, sustained onslaught on the religious and cultural practices of the slaves. Every religious expression of the slaves – Voodoo, faith healing, drumming at festivals, and so on – was outlawed. Every cultural expression of the slave was seen as subversive. Today, Rastas assert their own culture, black dignity – for example, in songs such as 'By the rivers of Babylon', which are pregnant with social criticism.

Working in 'distant' cultures

The problems faced by of expatriate managers, international project personnel, exchange students, and other temporary guests in culturally distant countries have been extensively documented. Extreme stress reactions in the form of escapism, neurosis, and psychosis have been noted in individuals whose country of origin is culturally distant from the host country (Krau, 1991). As Kim (1995) notes, people living and working in a 'distant' culture usually have to go through a very extensive learning and unlearning process before they feel psychologically comfortable in the culture.

One of the problems faced by expatriate managers carrying out assignments in culturally distant countries is that they run the risk of contravening the communicative norms and expectations held by members of the culture – either through ignorance of the expectations or rejection of them. This can lead to tensions and relationship difficulties with local colleagues and employees. Their difficulties are compounded when local employees perceive the expatriate managers as a disruptive influence to be endured or resisted – a carrier of concepts, management techniques, and methods of communication that – relative to the culture – are totally alien (Tsui et al., 2002).

Imported management practices

In developing countries employees often respond negatively to imported management practices. For instance, Asian employees may grow cold and distant after receiving feedback from Western managers on their work performance (Guirdham, 2005). If the manager attempts to use a participative management style this may be resisted by the workforce. Employees in these countries may, for instance, shy away from offering suggestions in staff meetings for efficiency improvements because this could be seen as challenging authority. In culturally distant countries such attitudes and responses combine to create formidable communication barriers. Yet ways of surmounting the barriers must be found to enable the expatriate manager to motivate the workforce and to successfully carry out his assignment.

> **Case study**
>
> #### MINI-CASE: New stock control system
>
> An expatriate production manager in a bottling plant in southern Africa plans to introduce a new stock control system based on Total Quality Management (TQM) principles. The manager holds a series of shop floor meetings and explains to employees how TQM works. But after the meetings he can't help feeling that the workers don't really understand the advantages of the system and that he will have problems winning their cooperation.
>
> When union leaders complain to the managing director that they have not been consulted about the production manager's plans, the new system, that is, the plan is put on hold pending the outcome of management–union talks.
>
> The production manager rationalizes his failure by telling himself that the gap separating himself from the workforce was probably too wide to be bridged by

---

Case study

Continued

a few shop floor meetings. After all, he is more educated than the workers, has higher qualifications, greater technical competence, and his income and social status are much higher. These glaring disparities, he tells himself, plus ethnic and cultural differences are what really caused his plan to fail.

Questions:

1. *Why was the manager unable to win the workers' understanding and coopera-tion? List the likely reasons in order of importance.*
2. *What would have been the effect if the manager had first discussed his plan with union leaders?*

Attitudes to visitors from 'distant' cultures

People are often prepared to accept into their communities foreigners who are culturally similar to themselves. But they tend to have a less welcoming attitude towards foreigners from culturally distant societies (Florack, 2003). Swami (2009), for instance, found that Malaysian students in Britain experi-enced prejudice and discrimination from British people on a daily basis. The reason, according to the students, was mainly due to their nationality. But, as the researcher points out, all of the students were Muslim, and religious prejudice may have contributed to the treatment they received.

Attitudes to visitors and immigrants from distant cultures tend to be influ-enced by obvious markers of cultural difference, including skin colour, facial features, hair style, and communication style. These differences can trigger 'us' and 'them' thinking and create suspicion and apprehension, and they help to explain why immigrants from culturally distant nations frequently become the victims of prejudice, discrimination, and hostile stereotyping. Immigrants are often blamed for job shortages, crime, social security fraud, and various other social ills. The immigrants may respond by perceiving culturally distant host cultures as intolerant of strangers, psychologically inaccessible, and extremely difficult to adjust to.

Impact of cultural distance on communication

Abundant evidence exists to show that cultural distance leads to communication difficulties between groups and individuals and may even cause communication to founder. Dwairy (1998) notes, for instance, that Western-trained psychiatrists are trained to keep a professional distance from their clients but that such a strategy does not work with Arab patients.

If an Arab client builds up enough trust to disclose his inner feelings to his psychiatrist, any attempt by the psychiatrist to maintain a professional, non-emotional distance is likely to be interpreted as indifference and coldness. Such misunderstanding leads to communication breakdown and can do a great deal of damage to the development of trust that is essential in treatment.

In medical interviews in Western countries, patients from Middle Eastern countries tend to describe their symptoms very vaguely because their own cultures lack concepts that distinguish mental from physical states (Lipson and Meleis, 1983). For example, vague physical symptoms may substitute for descriptions of anxiety and depression. Similarly, among Chinese expatriates in many countries depression and minor psychiatric disorders are commonly manifested by 'somatising'. This involves focusing on physical symptoms, such as headaches or chest pains, instead of an underlying psychological problem (Kleinman and Good, 1985).

A Chinese student complained to an English doctor about unpleasant itching sensations in the head. Despite close physical inspection and treatment the symptoms persisted. The doctor was puzzled and consulted Chinese medical colleagues in the hospital, who said they thought the student was suffering from depression. A major problem arising from such culturally conditioned communication is that it may lead doctors to make inaccurate diagnoses and to give ineffective treatment.

Typical communication problems

House (2000) identifies typical problems that occur when people from very different cultural backgrounds communicate. They include:

- *Mishearings and mispronunciations.*
- *Comprehension problems*: the linguistic level of the communication presents difficulties for some participants.
- *Insufficient relevant knowledge* on the part of one or more participants regarding the subject of the communication.
- *Emotional responses* (e.g. suspicion, resentment) leading to misinterpretation of the other person's motives and intentions.
- *Awkward, non-cooperative attitudes* by one or more participants.
- '*Production difficulties*'. In the fast-moving discourse the hearer is not able to assemble an appropriate response to points made by others.

An important indicator of cultural distance is variations in pronunciation and usage. For example, Gumperz (1982) observed a group of English-speaking Indian and Pakistani women working in a staff cafeteria in Britain who were perceived as surly and uncooperative by their English customers. They had a good grasp of English grammar and vocabulary but were not familiar with English communicative conventions governing the pronunciation of common English words. For instance, they said 'gravy' with a falling intonation. That sounded rude to English ears.

The example illustrates how communication with members of culturally distant societies tends to be more difficult than with members of culturally similar societies. Scollon and Scollon (2001) point out that when any two people belong to different ethnic or national groups, have different genders, different ages, groups, different educations, different income or occupational groups, or have very different personal histories, each of them will find it difficult to draw accurate inferences about what the other person really means.

APPEAL OF CULTURAL CLOSENESS

Ease of communication

The great majority of people in all cultures prefer to communicate with people who are similar to themselves. They prefer to interact with people who have the same values and beliefs as they themselves have, who belong to the same race, the same social class, who play the same sports and interests, and who are similar to themselves in attitudes, intelligence, and demographic variables (Berscheid and Walster, 1983). As Fehr (1996) points out, any two people will find it relatively easy to communicate with each other if they are similar in ethnic and cultural background, age, gender, social status, education level, and personality factors.

One of the reasons why people prefer to communicate with individuals who are similar to themselves is that similar individuals are likely to reinforce each others' self-images and, in most cases, this is a rewarding experience. One study found that people most preferred to have conversations with individuals whose attitudes duplicated their own exactly, and next chose those who agreed with them on all important issues (Byrne, 1971).

Shared knowledge

Communication between people who are similar to each other in the ways outlined above is relatively effortless. When people communicate in their own cultures, the knowledge, values, and conventional wisdom of the people they speak to mirrors their own and do not need to be explained or challenged. The same cultural system is embedded in their thoughts and words. Similar values and experiences help members of the same culture to achieve effective communication. Moreover, perceptions of the *type* of communication required in a particular context – formal or informal, forceful or restrained, and so on – tend to be shared and accurate.

Research evidence consistently shows that communication tends to be most successful when the participants are culturally close and least successful when they are culturally distant from each other (Scollon and Scollon, 2001). In cross-cultural interactions similar beliefs and assumptions help to create the conditions for successful communication. That is why, for instance, international negotiators tend to make faster concessions when they feel a common bond and identification with persons on the other side (Chen et al., 2003).

In many cross-cultural interactions, however, the cultural backgrounds, beliefs, and experiences of the participants are very different, and the differences can lead to problems of perceptions and attitude and create formidable communication barriers. For example, misunderstandings and miscommunications occur because the participants may interpret each others' communication and behaviour in terms of their own cultural norms (Barnlund, 1998).

RULES OF 'DISTANT' CULTURES

Products of culture

Many aspects of communication are culturally determined. Examples are:

- the type of communication that expatriate managers use to communicate with their local employees;
- numerous aspects of nonverbal communication and how they are interpreted;
- the different ways in which men and women in a particular culture interact in public.

Many nonverbal behaviours are culturally determined, and the greater the distance between cultures, the greater the variations in the behaviours. The baring of chests on hot days is acceptable in Western countries but considered offensive in Japan, South Korea, and some other Asian countries. This particular cultural difference prompted the British government to warn England football fans attending World Cup matches in Japan and South Korea in 2002 to keep their shirts on.

Arab social rules

Business visitors to Arab countries soon become aware of the unspoken rules governing social interactions in these countries. These rules govern everyday behaviours such as men walking down the street hand in hand, and extend to rules governing the way business discussions are conducted. It is important for foreign business visitors to be aware of important rules since ignorance of them can lead to embarrassing conversational gaffes and complicate business relationships.

An important rule in many Arab countries, for instance, forbids strangers to ask about female family members. In some Arab countries, only a woman's father, brothers, husband, or relatives and close friends of the same sex can use her first name (Buda and Elsayed-Elkhouly, 1998). In many countries in the Middle East there are special linguistic forms that men must use when addressing women, and vice versa. Prior knowledge of such important rules is essential for expatriate managers and foreign business visitor who wish to avoid awkwardness and embarrassment during their missions.

The unspoken social rules of Arab cultures are difficult to decipher and can trap the unwary. In countries like the United States, Britain, Germany, and Australia it is rude to turn up late for an appointment or to keep a business visitor waiting. But in some Arab countries it is accepted practice.

Case study

MINI-CASE: Social rules in Arab countries

When a German sales manager makes a business tour of countries in the Middle East he is unaware of local customs and disappointed when reality collides with his expectations. For example, when the German arrives for an appointment with an Arab official he is sometimes kept waiting for an hour or more. But he notices that Arab visitors are always shown straight into the official's office.

Rightly or wrongly, the sales manager assumes that he is kept waiting because of the gross discourtesy of Arab officials. Eventually he becomes so angry and frustrated at what he sees as discourteous and discriminatory treatment that he cancels the rest of his tour and returns to Germany.

What the manager failed to realize was that the true cause of the behaviour lay beyond the individual and was rooted in Arab culture. The Arab visitors who arrived without notice were members of the official's extended family, and they dropped in to discuss such matters as a dispute with a neighbour or some other pressing issue. To refuse to see a cousin or a grandfather who turned up without notice would be a violation of a cardinal social rule in Arab society.

Questions:

1. *Why was the sales manager wrong to cancel the rest of his tour? What other kind of action could he have taken to reduce the problem?*
2. *To what extent should important social rules of a foreign culture always be observed by business visitors?*

Japanese social rules

As foreign business visitors to Japan quickly discover, ignorance of Japanese social rules and conventions can make interactions with Japanese people very difficult to conduct. For instance, Western business people usually feel comfortable discussing their families and personal concerns with casual business contacts. Their Japanese counterparts, however, usually discuss personal or family topics only with people they know very well. Western business visitors who are ignorant of this unwritten rule of Japanese society tend to see this particular kind of Japanese communicative behaviour as a sign of aloofness, of not wishing to be friendly.

Western ignorance of Japanese social rules was demonstrated when an accident nearly became an international incident. When the USS Greenville, an American nuclear submarine, struck and sank a Japanese fishing training vessel nine people on the Japanese ship lost their lives (*Japan Times*, 19 December 2002). After some hesitation, the US government sent a representative to Japan to apologize, and the commander of the submarine was stripped of his rank.

> But Japanese public opinion was outraged. Interviews with a wide range of people, together with media comment, made it clear that in Japanese eyes the US government had not apologised appropriately and that the submarine commander had not been adequately punished.

As the report of the incident made clear, culture moulded the way in which the parties to the incident acted and reacted.

A key rule of Japanese society is that the communication of feelings is more important than the communication of information (Scollon and Scollon, 2001). Thus the apology should have been immediate and deeply felt. For instance, a Japanese business executive who was interviewed said that the person responsible should have bowed to the floor, stayed on the floor for a long time, then come up with tears in his eyes. Others thought the commander should have taken immediate responsibility for what had happened and resigned.

In Japan the apology is the lubricator of the communication and without it further dialogue is difficult if not impossible. By apologizing in the correct manner, an individual demonstrates that he has character and is trustworthy, and wishes to repair the damage. It was the commander's ignorance of these important social rules and conventions in Japanese society that outraged Japanese public opinion and caused cross-cultural communication to founder.

Observing a culture's social rules

Knowledge of important social rules facilitates effective communication in culturally distant countries. But how is that knowledge converted into behaviour? Unconsciously, according to Bourdieu (1977).

Bourdieu contends that people unconsciously acquire a kind of sixth sense ('habitus') in the course of living which helps them to find the sort of communicative behaviour required in first-time social situations. For instance, when a foreign business visitor holds a business discussion with counterparts in a culturally distant society, habitus will help the visitor to unconsciously observe such social essentials as:

- the culturally correct seating position;
- the culturally appropriate spatial distance to be observed during the interaction;
- other important cultural rules relating to the discussion, such as which topics are taboo, or the right time to speak.

Habitus

In short, habitus helps the business visitor to behave in a culturally acceptable way – although, to the individual, it seems that he is simply communicating in a way that is 'natural' (Lovell, 2000). The implication is that many of the skills needed for effective cross-cultural communication are already there, implanted painlessly and unconsciously in the course of living.

Habitus tells the foreign business visitor the kind of verbal and nonverbal communication needed in particular contexts – such as a business meeting with potential business partners, a cross-cultural interview, an official reception, or an informal social event. In each situation it gives the visitor clues about when to speak, who to speak to, the degree of formality needed, the right tone of voice to use, and so on. It helps a foreign business visitor to sense the communicative preferences and expectations of a sales prospect in the host country, to choose appropriate topics for conversation and – when there is a misunderstanding – to decide what to say to put matters right.

To some extent effective cross-cultural communication depends on careful planning and preparation. But not all aspects need to be consciously worked out. Unplanned, impromptu responses to the wide range of communicative behaviours and personalities encountered are, as Bourdieu shows, equally important.

Goodwill

Even when separated by great cultural distance people can successfully communicate with each other provided that they are *motivated* to do so. In particular, the presence of *goodwill* is a factor that can determine the success of a cross-cultural communication event.

When a factory manager in Belarus invited a British consultant to his flat to meet his wife and family the communication problems were daunting. The consultant spoke no Russian, the manager and his family spoke no English. No interpreter was present. The occasion could have been an embarrassing failure, but the hosts communicated a spirit of goodwill by smiling, looking intently at their guest while proposing toasts, and uttering resounding Russian phrases with great earnestness.

> The phrases may have been about life in Minsk, local politicians, or the high quality of local vodka – their guest had no way of knowing. But it didn't matter. No information was communicated, but as an expression of cross-cultural goodwill the occasion was a great success.

MEASURING CULTURAL DISTANCE

Assessing cultural distance

It is possible to measure cultural distance simplistically – for instance, in terms of the extent to which two cultures differ on individualism/collectivism. Using such a crude measure of cultural distance has the advantage of giving an instant answer. But the problem with any crude, single-dimension measure is that it inevitably fails to take into account many important aspects of a culture, such as lifestyle, linguistic closeness, attitudes to women, and so on. Some of these neglected aspects – for instance, lifestyle differences or spending pattern differences – are extremely important for a company to know about, especially if the company is considering extending its operations into the country concerned.

Triandis (2001) argues that cultures are distant from each other to the extent that their *different components* differ. Important components of a culture include economic conditions, languages, politics, religion, and philosophic and aesthetic preferences. Using this approach it is easy to see, for instance, that a democratic society which is characterized by innovation and risk-taking and which has a large entrepreneurial class is culturally distant from a country which is run by a military dictatorship and where most aspects of the economy are owned and controlled by the state.

Kogut and Singh's (1988) index of cultural distance is based on Hofstede's cultural dimensions and measures the relative distance of two given cultures from each other according to the extent of the difference. The index is sometimes used by researchers carrying out cross-cultural research. However, Stahl (2008) points to a disadvantage of using the cultural distance index to measure distance – namely, that two cultures may have very similar cultural distance scores according to the index yet may actually differ on many important cultural aspects – such as attitudes to other cultures, for instance. Thus they may be more 'distant' from each other than the measure suggests.

Estrin et al. (2009) distinguish between two kinds of cultural distance:

- Distance based on Hofstede's four cultural dimensions (the index of cultural distance). This kind of distance is frequently used by researchers conducting cross-cultural studies.
- *Absolute* distance, which reflects the regulations, restrictions, and environmental constraints that together indicate how efficiently a foreign business will be able to operate in the country. This kind of cultural distance is of particular interest to governments and MNEs.

How firms use cultural distance measures

MNEs have a vested interest in measuring cultural distance. If cultural distance is low between the country where a multinational company is based and the country where it intends entering into a strategic alliance with a local company, then cooperation and coordination between the two companies should be relatively trouble-free, with few communication barriers. But when great cultural distance separates a company and a foreign business partner, the greater the risk that the practices, procedures, and policies of the two companies will be incompatible, and that effective coordination of the two organisations will be much harder to achieve.

Multinational companies with subsidiaries in culturally distant countries have to manage the 'distance' between subsidiary and head office locations. Effective management of cultural distance may involve the implementation of:

- appropriate HR and employment practices for use in the subsidiary company;
- appropriate quality management processes;
- new environmental management practices;
- training programmes to support the imported systems and procedures.

TYPES OF CULTURAL DISTANCE

Effects on cross-cultural business

The concept of 'cultural distance' is widely used in the international business world, and refers to wide differences between two countries in language, education, business practices, and economic and cultural development – that is the sum of factors preventing effective communication and the flow of information from and to the market (Johanson and Vahlne, 1977). In international business the term is used especially to assess the extent to which the *business values and practices* in two countries differ from each other. The assumption is that problems confronting organisations which are involved in cross-cultural business or in joint venture projects or strategic alliance operations with companies abroad are likely to expand as differences increase between foreign and home country language, laws, and business environment (Ghemawat, 2007).

Cultural distance creates difficulties for foreign-owned firms in operating in and adapting to the national setting of the host country. For example, as cultural distance increases, it becomes more difficult – and more expensive – to collect and correctly interpret incoming information (Teece, 1982). Pre-existing information – knowledge derived from the home market – is often of limited value in markets located at great cultural distance. Thus cultural distance is a prominent factor hindering international expansion efficiency. Moreover, cultural distance also creates numerous practical problems for expatriate managers. Expatriate managers are responsible for transferring knowledge and developing skills, but Barkema et al. (1996) make the point that the constant presence of cultural factors invariably complicates organisational learning and hinders the development of capabilities in the country.

According to Luo (2004), foreign firms starting operations in culturally distant locations tend to underestimate the risks and overestimate the returns. One reason is that it is more difficult to monitor and manage the foreign operation than they anticipate and more difficult to motivate the indigenous workforce. An equally important reason is that formidable cultural barriers escalate the adaptation costs of resource investments and may cause the parent company to shy away from adequate commitments to the local market.

Cultural distance and cross-cultural communication

A vital aspect of cross-cultural business conduct – effective cross-cultural communication – is much more difficult to achieve with business partners in culturally distant countries. One reason is that cultural distance affects the quality of cross-cultural communication by introducing 'noise' – misunderstandings, misinterpretations, psychological discomfort – into the communication process.

Communicating with organisations in a foreign country and doing business with them is relatively easy if there are common linguistic and cultural features and if the business environment is similar. But when countries differ widely in their values, cultural practices, and business environments the conduct of cross-cultural business is greatly complicated. It also becomes much more expensive. For instance, interpreters and translators may have to be used. Deals may have to be struck with local consultants or agents who are familiar with local business environment and who can provide introductions to local suppliers, distributors, and government officials. (Estrin et al., 2009).

The emerging economies and cultural distance

Most of the major emerging economies – the BRIC countries, for instance – are culturally distant from companies based in the developed countries of North America, Europe, and Australasia. As a result, MNEs which are intending to expand their operations in the major emerging economies will be faced with the challenge of overcoming the many difficulties and constraints associated with cultural distance – such as those described below.

In the emerging economies and other culturally distant markets, the local environment effect often turns out to be stronger than foreign-owned companies anticipate. For instance, local conditions – especially industrial relations and legal arrangements – often stand in the way of companies seeking a free hand to determine working and employment conditions. A foreign company starting to operate in the country will usually have to work within the framework of the national labour laws and collective agreements, where some of the basic conditions for company operations are laid down. Sometimes, however, it is possible for individual companies to modify the basic conditions. For example, Schief (2010) notes that German and American companies operating abroad often make a greater use of overtime to deal with variations in demand than domestically owned companies.

High costs of communication and cooperation

When companies in different countries are separated by great cultural distance, management systems, procedures, and practices of the firms are often incompatible, and this feature makes cross-cultural communication and cooperation much more difficult to achieve. The cost of cooperation between firms is high because cultural and linguistic differences rule out much of the *low-cost, informal communication*, and gossip that normally occur between firms without needing to be planned, arranged, and monitored.

The risks as well as the costs of conducting a business in a culturally distant country can be very high. An important reason is that potential business difficulties – dealing with local labour laws, for instance – may not be fully understood and so may lead to unwise hiring or redundancy decisions. Difficulties in cross-cultural communication and dispute-resolution may be experienced as a result of language and value differences.

Unbudgeted costs tend to occur frequently. For instance, expatriate managers in a culturally distant country may pay too much for local interpreters and local translation services. Firms planning a joint venture with a partner in a culturally distant country often underestimate the costs involved in achieving integration of the two corporate cultures (Cartwright and Cooper, 1996).

Different aspects of distance

Different aspects of cultural distance make a great impact on the way that foreign companies conduct international business with organisations in culturally distant countries. Aspects of cultural distance that most affect foreign firms, expatriate managers, and international business people are:

- Legal distance
- HR distance
- Marketing distance

Legal distance

A firm which plans to begin operating in a country with a very different legal system may have to adapt some of its existing business practices and procedures to suit the new environment. Laws and regulations governing the local labour market, for instance, may rule out the possibility of simply replicating systems and practices that have been developed and successfully used in the parent company at home. This particularly applies to practices and procedures relating to employee contracts, employee pay scale, and staff redundancies. Chang and Rosenzweig (2001) caution that new legal contracts suitable for the country may have to be drawn up, such as new employment contracts, and contracts for employees, distributors, suppliers, subcontractors, agents, and so on.

Moreover, in order to do their jobs effectively in the new business environment, expatriate managers will need to become familiar with relevant local laws (such as laws preventing redundancies or changes in pay scales). In China, changes in the labour market have produced wide divergences in income both at the firm and societal levels as foreign companies quickly discover. The necessary knowledge (for instance, regarding current pay levels for various categories of employee) can always be acquired from local experts – but it comes at a cost. Union Carbide's experience in India shows how important it is for expatriate managers to be thoroughly conversant with the legal constraints before making any agreement with a host organisation which could later have legal repercussions. The agreement that Union Carbide made was to install sophisticated technology and oversee its safe use.

For firms starting operations in China, the problem of dealing with the legal complexities can usually be reduced by the firm's expatriate managers establishing *guanxi* with local and provincial governments (PriceWaterhouseCoopers, 2004).

HR distance

Estrin et al. (2009) assess HR distance between two countries through a comparison of four dimensions in each country:

1. Percentage of economically active population that has attained at least tertiary education.
2. Average schooling years in the total population.
3. Number of computers per 1000 persons.
4. Number of internet hosts per 1000 persons.

When use of these measures reveals that there is wide HR distance between old and new organisations, it is likely that HR policies and practices of the foreign organisation will need to be *adapted* – as opposed to being transferred direct from the parent company at home. Thus the HR practices of subsidiaries of foreign companies operating in the United States tend to have been adapted so as to closely follow US practices (Rosenzweig and Nohria, 1994). Aaker (1990) found that Japanese banking and hotel sector affiliates in the United States had decided, without exception, not to export their Japanese service culture and systems to the United States. Beechler and Yang (1994) studied Japanese service companies in New York City and found that these firms were unable to implement their parent company practices unchanged and were forced to adapt to an American-style HRM system.

Similar constraints are experienced by firms expanding their operations in Europe. When IKEA entered the Spanish market it had to adapt its payment and other HR policies in order to attract and retain competent Spanish employees (Jackson, 2002). In Sweden, IKEA salaries tend to be fixed but the practice is not popular in Spain. Several Japanese companies in China have had to abandon seniority-based pay systems in favour of the market- and performance-based approaches that Chinese employees prefer (Paine, 2010).

The implication is that when there is wide HR distance between a new subsidiary of a company in an overseas country and the parent firm, attempts by expatriate managers to transfer HR practices direct from the parent company to the subsidiary may be unsuccessful. For example, a decentralized organisation structure and structured delegation (as practised in the parent company) will not work in the subsidiary if:

- local staff do not understand how decentralised structures work;
- local managers and supervisors are unwilling to take decisions independently;

- employees' skill and qualification profiles are inadequate for the successful implementation of HR policies;
- local employees are not motivated to achieve high levels of performance and output.

Marketing distance

Marketing expertise is country and region-specific and is based on an intimate understanding of customer preferences, social norms, and the cultural environment of a given market. The implication – as many expatriate managers have discovered – is that in culturally distant countries marketing strategies need to be customized for local consumers. Beamish and Inkpen (1998) note that some multinational companies are relying more on local marketing managers and using fewer expatriates since expatriate marketing managers may not have an intimate understanding of the local market. When this is the case, expatriate managers find it difficult to apply marketing expertise acquired at home in a 'distant' marketing environment.

In almost all cases the local market will turn out to be very different from the home market. For instance, the local market will have different segments of customers to the market at home, and each segment will have its own distinct preferences and buying characteristics. That was what Honda Motors famously discovered when it entered the American market in the 1960s. As a result, Honda had to develop completely new advertising and distribution strategies to match the characteristics of the local market (Pascale, 1984).

To be successful in China expatriate marketing managers find that they need to give attention to governmental relationships in business as well as to the buying characteristics of the market (Cremer and Ramasamy, 2009). An important buying characteristic is that in China buying decisions are influenced by reputation, referrals, and references rather than by price. In many sectors there are a smaller number of potential buyers – but those fewer buyers buy in bulk. Accordingly, pricing policies and advertising budgets may have to be adjusted to take account of these realities.

SMALL-GROUP EXERCISE: Discussion questions

Working in small groups, discuss each of the following questions and write down the group's agreed answer. At the end of the exercise, each group may present its answers to the other groups for comment.

1. *Describe two ways in which cultural distance between two countries can be assessed.*
2. *If a multinational company decides to start operations in a culturally distant country, what communication problems could be anticipated between head office and the subsidiary company?*

3. *Identify typical difficulties facing students studying in a culturally distant country. How can the difficulties be overcome?*
4. *Give examples of surface-level cultural differences and deep-level cultural differences between and two culturally distant countries.*
5. *Give specific examples of communication problems that can arise when people from culturally distant countries interact. What causes the miscommunications that often occur?*
6. *'The greater the distance between cultures, the greater the variations in nonverbal behaviour.' Give examples.*
7. *How does prior knowledge of the unspoken social rules of a 'distant' culture help foreign business visitors to communicate effectively with members of the culture?*

HOW CULTURAL DISTANCE AFFECTS DEPARTMENTS

Using the 'distance' concept

'Distance' between organisational and national contexts is a major concern of multinational companies since each company needs to adjust to the cultural and business environment of each country in which it operates.

The challenges and risks with which firms are confronted increase as difference increases between foreign and home country culture, language, laws, business environment, and human resources (Ghemawat, 2007). Thus the concept of cultural distance makes its impact in various departments and functional areas of multinational firms, especially the following:

- strategic management;
- export management;
- production management;
- HR management;
- marketing management;
- financial management.

Strategic management

The concept of cultural distance helps strategic managers to develop appropriate *performance measures* for foreign subsidiaries, and also allows them to narrow down the options when formulating strategies for global expansion. The expansion strategies of many large companies currently focus on China, which is now the most popular destination for FDI. More than half a million foreign firms now operate in the country (Cremer and Ramasamy, 2009).

When a Western firm is considering expanding into a culturally distant country such as China or India or Russia, strategic management typically needs to decide whether the best way would be to open an overseas branch or to start a joint venture with a local company (Chang and Rosenzweig, 2001). The joint venture option often has important advantages:

- a joint venture with a business partner already established in the country would have the great advantage of giving immediate access to local and regional markets;
- the human resources of the partner company are already fully adjusted to the culture and would be immediately available.

If the overseas branch option is preferred, many important questions would have to be answered, such as which of the parent firm's established systems, processes, and practices would it be possible to transfer directly without expensive adaptation.

Export management

Cultural distance makes a direct impact on export management since it is known to greatly influence the *volume of trade flows* between any two countries. Great cultural difference between, say, the United States and a particular trading partner in Africa, is invariably reflected in very low US exports to that country. On the other hand, if cultural distance decreases in the future as a result, say, of future economic development or improvements in education, exports to the country are likely to increase.

Production management

Production management's interest in cultural distance relates mainly to technology transfer and the installation of systems and procedures in a foreign subsidiary. Much evidence shows that the *speed* of technology transfer within global companies is reduced by cultural distance (Phene et al., 2005).

Installing the best production system in a subsidiary company in a culturally distant country may be impracticable because of basic barriers caused by problems of understanding and communication among local staff. To overcome such basic difficulties local staff may have to be trained at considerable extra cost to ensure that a transfer of knowledge takes place.

HR management

HR managers use the concept of cultural distance to identify those culturally distant countries where, to be successful, expatriate managers will need to be supported through appropriate cross-cultural training and by internal or external support networks. Many HR departments find it difficult to recruit managers for expatriate posts in countries that managers perceive as insular and very different from home. A survey of international recruitment consultants suggests that expatriate managers find it difficult to be successful in culturally distant countries such as China, Japan, the non-Gulf Middle East countries, and in several countries in South America (Korn/Ferry, 2009).

Many HR managers find that transferring HR policies and practices from a parent company to a foreign subsidiary in a culturally distant country is not practicable. For instance, structured delegation procedures as practised in the parent company will not be effective if local managers and supervisors are not sufficiently educated and qualified, or not willing, to take decisions independently.

Marketing management

Expatriate marketing managers, like marketing personnel based in the head office, may have inadequate knowledge and understanding of the market in a culturally distant country. This inadequacy can lead them to make expensive mistakes. For instance, when drawing up plans to penetrate the foreign market they may:

- exaggerate the market potential for the company's products or services;
- commit themselves to excessive – or inadequate – marketing expenditures;
- fail to customize advertising campaigns to match the preferences of local consumers.

Such hazards increase the pressure on MNEs to appoint *local managers* to head the marketing function in foreign subsidiaries.

Financial management

If parent-company accounting practices are transferred to a subsidiary company in a culturally distant country, they may not achieve the same results as in the parent company. Accounting conventions and regulations in culturally distant countries often differ widely from those used at home. This could lead to accounting and bookkeeping practices having to be adapted to the regulatory environment, as well as to the skill profiles that are available locally.

Financial control procedures often need to be simplified to match the capabilities of local staff, and local employees may need to be trained to implement basic new procedures. Depending on the size of the organisation, the cost of designing and running financial training programmes can be very high and may even affect the net profits of the subsidiary.

Case study

MINI-CASE: Visiting a 'distant' culture

The wish to form a realistic picture of Japanese culture is what motivates a consulting engineer, preparing for an extended business trip to Japan, to attend a

Case study

Continued

cultural briefing in London. The engineer hopes the briefing will give him a clear picture of important values, conventions, and practices of Japanese culture, and he is not disappointed.

The presenter, a Japanese professor, begins by talking about aspects of Japanese communication that create problems for foreign visitors, whether the language used is Japanese or English. For example, the Japanese show:

- A tendency to avoid debate, argument, or confrontation. The Japanese are especially careful to avoid embarrassing others by saying no in public.
- A tendency to emphasize sentiment and harmony over logic. The professor mentions the agony aunt columns in Japanese newspapers that repeatedly offer advice on the virtues of social harmony, avoiding confrontation, and not complaining.
- A tendency to choose ambiguous words which, together with vague reactions and controlled facial expressions, can lead to misunderstandings when talking to foreigners.

The professor stresses that such tendencies reflect deep-rooted cultural preferences and so are resistant to change. The best way of dealing with them, he says, is to take them into account when communicating with Japanese people – 'so you don't get the wrong message'.

Conflict avoidance

Participants are warned that 'yes' said by a Japanese person may not mean yes, and that a plain 'no' in Japanese ears sounds intolerably blunt. This explains the Japanese tendency to use ambiguous or misleading phrases such as 'We will give your request careful consideration.' Such words are chosen to show politeness and respect to conversational partners and to avoid unnecessary friction. The professor stresses that Japanese people usually agree with their conversational partners since Japanese place great value on harmony and avoiding open disagreement and conflict. Usually Japanese people are reluctant to debate an issue or to argue or to risk confrontation. He admits that this tendency can be frustrating for Western business visitors who like to get straight down to business without wasting time on small talk.

After arriving in Japan the engineer discovers that the Japanese do indeed communicate in ways mentioned by the professor, including the use of ambiguous or misleading phrases. Such characteristics, he suspects, will make some foreign business visitors perceive their Japanese counterparts as evasive.

The engineer is surprised by some Japanese customs not mentioned in the cultural briefing. When he spends a night at a 'ryokan', a traditional-style inn, he is surprised to find the bathroom set up for group use and that the bath is filled with fresh hot water just once a day. Guests are expected to wash thoroughly and rinse before stepping in, leaving the water clean for others. The manager, who speaks a little English, tells him of the difficulties she has with for-eign guests: 'When something goes wrong they won't accept our explanations. Americans and Europeans argue a lot.'

Question:

1. The professor mentions several aspects of Japanese communication that frus-trate foreigners. How should a foreign business visitor who is looking for straight answers and clear information deal with these traits if they occur in business discussions?

KEY POINTS

1. Most people prefer to communicate with people who are similar to them-selves – who belong to the same country, ethnic group, social class; who have the same interests and values. But cross-cultural encounters bring together people who are often strikingly dissimilar and the result can be tense and awk-ward communication. In such encounters, obvious markers of difference – such as skin colour, facial features, dress, and accent – can lead to 'us' and 'them' thinking and inhibit or distort the communication.

2. When consulting health professionals in Western countries, patients from Arab countries often describe their symptoms very vaguely because their own cultures lack concepts that distinguish mental from physical states. Vague physical symptoms may substitute for descriptions of anxiety and depression. Similarly, among Chinese patients depression and minor psychiatric disorders are commonly manifested by 'somatising'. This involves focusing on phys-ical symptoms, such as headaches or chest pains, instead of an underlying psychological problem.

3. A country's cultural distance from another country can be assessed by com-paring important aspects of the culture of each country, including level of economic development, form of government, dominant religion, and dominant language. A measure of cultural distance, based on Hofstede's cultural dimensions, measures the relative distance of two cultures from each other according to the extent of the differences. Expatriate man-agers carrying out assignments in culturally distant countries may contravene the communicative norms and expectations of the local people, leading to tensions and relationship difficulties with local colleagues.

4. When great cultural distance separates a company and a foreign business partner, the greater the risk that the practices, procedures, and policies of the two companies will be incompatible, and that effective coordination of the two organisations will be much harder to achieve. Collaboration costs are high because cultural and linguistic differences rule out much of the low-cost, informal communication and gossip that normally occurs between firms. Multinational companies with subsidiaries in culturally distant countries often

need to develop *appropriate* management policies and practices for the subsidiaries.

5. Successful marketing practice in culturally distant markets is based on an intimate understanding of customer preferences, social norms, and the cultural environment of a given market. Marketing strategies need to be customized for local consumers. That explains why some multinational companies are relying more on local marketing managers. Expatriate marketing managers may not have an intimate understanding of the local market. This inadequacy leads to expensive mistakes such as exaggerating the market potential for the company's products, or failing to customise advertising campaigns to match the preferences of local consumers.

6. Companies considering expanding into culturally distant countries such as China, India, or Russia, strategic management are often faced with the problem of deciding whether the best way would be to open an overseas branch or to start a joint venture with a local company. A joint venture with a local company would have the advantage of giving immediate access to local and regional markets. Moreover, the management and employees of the partner company are already part of, or fully adjusted to, the culture and would be immediately available.

QUESTIONS FOR DISCUSSION AND WRITTEN ASSIGNMENTS

1. What is cultural distance? How can it be assessed or measured?
2. Explain how the concept of cultural distance is used in the business world.
3. 'Cross-cultural communication is more challenging than same-culture communication and requires greater knowledge and skill.' True or false?
4. To what extent is it possible to create a model of managerial effectiveness that applies across cultures?

BIBLIOGRAPHY

Aaker, DA. How ill the Japanese compete in retail services? *California Management Review*, Fall, 1990, 54–67.

Barkema, HG. et al., Foreign entry, cultural barriers, and learning. *Strategic Management Journal*, 17, 1996, 151–166.

Barnlund, D. Communication in a global village. In MJ Bennett (ed.), *Basic Concepts of Intercultural Communication*. Intercultural Press, 1998, pp. 35–51.

Beamish, PW and Inkpen, AC. Japanese firms and the decline of the Japanese expatriate. *Journal of World Business*, 33, 1998, 35–50.

Beechler, S and Yang, JZ. The transfer of Japanese-style management to American subsidiaries: contingencies, constraints, and competencies. *Journal of International Business Studies*, 25, 1994, 467–491.

Berscheid, E and Walster, E. *Interpersonal Attraction*. Addison Wesley, 1983.

Bourdieu, P. *Outlines of a Theory of Practice*. CUP, 1977, p. 72.

Buda, S and Elsayed-Elkhouly, S. Cultural differences between Arabs and Americans. *Journal of C-c Psychology*, 29 (3), 1998, 487–492.

Byrne, D. *The Attraction Paradigm*. Academic Press, 1971.

Campbell, H. Rastafari: culture of resistance. *Race and Class*, 22 (1), 1980, 1–22.

Cartwright, S and Cooper, CL. *Managing Mergers, Acquisitions, and Strategic Alliances*, 2nd ed. Butterworth-Heinemann, 1996.

Chang, S-J and Rosenzweig, PM. The choice of entry mode in sequential foreign direct investment. *Strategic Management Journal*, 22, 2001, 747–776.

Chen, Y-R, Mannix, EA and Okumura, T. The importance of who you meet: effects of self – versus other – concerns among negotiators in the United States, the People's Republic of China, and Japan. *Journal of Experimental Social Psychology*, 39 (1), 2003, 1–15.

Cremer, RD and Ramasamy, B. Engaging China: strategies for the small internationalising firm. *Journal of Business Strategy*, 30 (6), 2009, 15–26.

Dwairy, MA. *Cross-cultural Counselling*: The Arab-Palestinian Case. Haworth Press, 1998.

Estrin, S. et al., The impact of institutional and human resource distance on international entry strategies. *Journal of Management Studies*, 46 (7), 2009, 1171–1196.

Fehr, B. *Friendship Processes*. Sage, 1996.

Florack, A. et al., Perceived intergroup threat and attitudes of host community members toward immigrant acculturation. *Journal of Social Psychology*, 143 (5), 2003, 633–648.

Furnham, A and Bochner, S. Social difficulty in a foreign culture: an empirical analysis of culture shock. In S Bochner (ed.), *Cultures in Contact*. Pergamon, 1982, p. 190.

Ghemawat, P. *Redefining Global Strategy*. Harvard Business School Press, 2007.

Gudykunst, WB. Anxiety/uncertainty management (AUM) theory: current status. In RL Wiseman (ed.), *Intercultural Communication Theory*. Sage, 1995, pp. 8–58, p. 29.

Guirdham, M. *Communicating Across Cultures at Work*, 2nd ed. Palgrave Macmillan, 2005.

Gumperz, JJ. *Discourse Strategies*. CUP, 1982.

House, J. Understanding misunderstanding: a pragmatic-discourse approach to analysing mismanaged rapport in talk across cultures. In H Spencer-Oatey (ed.), *Culturally Speaking*. Continuum, 2000, pp. 145–164.

Jackson, T. *International HRM: A Cross-cultural Approach*. Sage, 2002.

Johanson, J and Vahlne, J-E. The internationalisation process of the firm – a model of knowledge development and foreign market commitment. *Journal of International Business Studies*, 8, 1977, 23–32.

Kim, YY. Cross-cultural adaptation: an integrative theory. In RL Wiseman (ed.), *Intercultural Communication Theory*. Sage, 1995, 170–193.

Kleinman, A and Good, B. (eds), *Culture and Depression: Studies in the Anthropology and Cross-cultural Psychiatry of Affect and Disorder*. University of California Press, 1985, pp. 429–490.

Kogut, B and Singh, H. The effect of national culture on the choice of entry mode. *Journal of International Business Studies*, 19, 1988, 411–432.

Korn/Ferry, *Executive Recruiter Index*, 10th ed. Korn/Ferry International, 2009.

Krau, E. *The Contradictory Immigrant Problem: A Sociopsychological Analysis.* Peter Lang, 1991.

Lipson, JG and Meleis, AI. Issues in Health Care of Middle Eastern Patients. *Western Journal of Medicine*, 139, 1983, 54.

Lovell, T. Thinking feminism with and against Bourdieu. In B Fowler (ed.), *Reading Bourdieu on Society and Culture*. Blackwell, 2000, p. 27.

Luo, Y. Building a strong foothold in an emerging market. *Journal of Management Studies*, 41 (5), 2004, 749–773.

Paine, LS. The China rule. *HBR*, June 2010, 103–108.

Pascale, RT. Perspectives on strategy: the real story behind Honda's success. *California Management Review*, 26, 1984, 47–72.

Phene, A. et al., Knowledge transfer within the multinational firm. *Management International Review*, 45, 2005, 53–75.

PriceWaterhouseCoopers, Doing Business in China. 2004.

Rosenzweig, PM and Nohria, N. Influences on human resource management practices in multinational corporations. *Journal of International Business Studies*, 25 (2), 1994, 229–251.

Schief, S. Does location matter? An empirical investigation of flexibility patterns in foreign and domestic companies in five European countries. *International Journal of Human Resource Management*, 21 (1), 2010, 1–16.

Scollon, R and Scollon, SW. *Intercultural Communication*, 2nd ed. Blackwell, 2001, p. 151.

Stahl, GK. Cultural dynamics and impact of cultural distance within mergers and acquisitions. PB Smith et al. (eds), *Handbook of Cross-cultural Management Research*. Sage, 2008, 431–448.

Swami, V. Predictors of sociocultural adjustment among sojourning Malaysian students in Britain. *International Journal of Psychology*, 44 (4), 2009, 266–273.

Teece, DJ. Toward an economic theory of the multiproduct firm. *Journal of Economic Behaviour and Organisation*, 3, 1982, 39–63.

Triandis, HC. Individualism and collectivism: past, present, and future. In D Matsumoto (ed.), *The Handbook of Culture and Psychology*. OUP, 2001, p. 45.

Tsui, AS. et al., When both similarities and dissimilarities matter: extending the concept of relational demography. *Human Relations*, 55 (8), 2002, 899–930.

AEM Van Vianen et al., Fitting in: surface and deep-level cultural differences and expatriate adjustment. *Academy of Management Journal*, 47 (5), 2004, 697–709.

Managing and working in multicultural teams

10

INTRODUCTION

Cultural and ethnic diversity can boost the performance of multicultural teams (Adler, 1991). Members bring multiple perspectives to problems and cross-fertilize each others' ideas. On the other hand, fault-lines caused by cultural differences can be a barrier, reducing trust and heightening conflict. Different kinds of diversity in the team make different kinds of impact. Job-related diversity, for instance, gives the team a variety of different perspectives and approaches that helps it to solve complex problems (Hulsheger et al., 2009). Ethnic diversity, by contrast, can create communication difficulties and interpersonal tensions that interfere with innovative efforts and the achievement of team consensus.

Culture-based difficulties of multicultural teams include lack of cooperation between different subgroups; contradictory problem-solving styles; contradictory attitudes towards authority and leadership; and lack of fluency in using the team's working language. Such differences prevent cooperation and coordination between different cultural subgroups, but they can be overcome by the team leader injecting a common focus, a shared sense of purpose. Thus *goal clarity* is essential in multicultural teams because it creates the conditions for effective collaboration among the diverse membership.

Since members of multicultural teams respond to leadership and authority in differing, culturally influenced ways, it follows that different national groups have to be managed and motivated in different ways. Consequently *flexibility* is an essential quality for multicultural team leaders to possess. Another important quality is *cross-cultural communication competence*, a quality that enables a team leader to communicate with the team and adapt messages to the cultural perspectives of individual members. Cross-cultural communication competence also enables diverse specialists to find effective ways of cooperating with each other, thereby reducing levels of stress in the team.

Different beliefs about the relative value of tasks sometimes lead subgroups to spend too much time on low-priority tasks. However, this tendency can be overcome through effective coordination management, with regular progress meetings providing an appropriate tool. Regular progress meetings enable everybody to keep up to date with progress. Key specialists have the opportunity to report on problems that have emerged (such as over-spending, or delays in achieving project milestones) and to obtain members' views about how these problems should be solved. But effective coordination management does not occur automatically. Team leaders *make* it happen – by constantly communicating, socializing, monitoring, and encouraging.

Conflict occurs regularly in multicultural teams. Conflict can be defined as 'the interaction of inter-dependent people who perceive opposition of goals, aims, and values, and who see the other party as potentially interfering with the realisation of these goals' (Putnam and Poole, 1987: 552). Conflict in multicultural teams tends to be either task-based or relationship-based. Task-based conflict is focused on judgmental differences about how best to achieve team goals, and often arises from disagreements about procedures to be followed or from competition among subgroups for limited resources. Such conflict is usually not destructive and can lead to higher levels of performance (Tjosvold, 1998). Relationship-based conflict, on the other hand, is focused on personal or cultural incompatibilities and its effect is usually negative since it can impair decision quality and lower team effectiveness.

PURPOSE OF MULTICULTURAL TEAMS

The diversity factor

Sometimes the only practical way of coordinating the many different competencies required to solve a pressing problem in a multinational organisation is to set up a multicultural team or task force. A multicultural team has been defined as 'a small number of culturally diverse people with complementary skills who are committed to a common purpose and performance goals' (Katzenbach and Smith, 2005). A multicultural *task force* focuses on completing a specific project in a limited time.

Complex products and large-scale complex projects incorporate diverse sub-system technologies, each requiring different forms of expertise. To acquire the wide span of necessary competences a multicultural team sometimes has to be assembled from several countries – for instance, by outsourcing across borders. At other times a multicultural team is formed when a group of experts from an organisation is sent to work in a foreign location alongside foreign counterparts. This happens, for instance, when a firm starts a joint venture with a foreign company.

Corning's joint venture with Siemens to produce fibre-optic cable was an example of a very successful cross-cultural team-effort which was based on the complementary skills and capabilities of the partners. Corning had technological and manufacturing capability: Siemens had worldwide distribution of telecommunications cable.

The complexity factor

Very complex problems seem to demand diversity. At Brown University's brain science programme a diverse team of mathematicians, medical doctors, neuroscientists, and computer scientists from various national and cultural groups was needed to create a system in which a monkey could move a computer cursor with only its thoughts. And when a division of Boeing decided to design a reusable rocket engine, the project was so complex and the competencies required were so wide-ranging that a multicultural team was assembled to carry out the project (Majchrzak et al., 2004). Engineers, IT experts, and rocket scientists from different countries and from various cultural backgrounds found themselves working together. At first members struggled to understand one another. Although all spoke English, there were differences in the way different ethnic and occupational groups used the language. The diverse specialists also had different, culturally derived approaches to problem-solving so that conflict was difficult to avoid. The good news was that disagreement forced the team to thoroughly analyse problems and to avoid over-easy solutions.

To help the team arrive at a common approach to working together the Myers-Briggs Type Indicator (MBTI) was used (Myers and Briggs, 1957). By placing people in one of four personality dimensions, MBTI exposed personality factors underlying the clashing communication and problem-solving styles of team members. Moreover, the team as a whole gained insights into its members' resources and how these could be used to boost performance. At the end of the project team members were reassigned. But their enhanced experience and network of contacts would equip them to participate in many future projects.

PRECONDITIONS OF EFFECTIVENESS

Parent company support

A typical large multinational organisation with overseas subsidiaries may have hundreds of technically competent managers but few with proven ability to manage diversity and a multicultural workforce. At GE Power Generation, one of the world's largest manufacturers of equipment for producing electricity, senior executives openly acknowledge the company's relative lack of cultural diversity at senior levels (Prokesch, 2009). In 2009, for instance, of 25 members of the senior management team 19 were American, four were European, one came from Latin America, and one was Chinese. In an executive meeting called to discuss diversity issues somebody commented: 'Cultural diversity? Look at the lack of Middle Easterners and Chinese – and women – around this table'.

A company's relative lack of experience in managing diversity helps to explain why, once it has assembled a multicultural team for a particular project, the team may be left to fend for itself. Perhaps the team slips from top management's attention (a real risk when the team's activities are not part of the company's everyday operations). Nevertheless, top-level lapses of attention are expensive. For one thing, they may lead to serious delays as requests for information and resources are shunted up and down the communication chain.

Multicultural teams achieve superior performance when they are given the resources they need at the right time. A key resource is the team leader or project manager. Received wisdom teaches that top management in the parent company must put someone in charge of the team who is a good manager then leave him or her to get on with the job. But sometimes top management is unclear about the kind of leader required. A common mistake, for instance, is to overvalue experience at the expense of flexibility and new thinking. But the one quality that a multicultural team leader must have is the ability to *manage diversity* – the ability to work and communicate with people from diverse ethnic, cultural, and functional backgrounds.

Goal clarity

Cultural differences can usually be reduced or overcome by the team leader ensuring that the team has a shared sense of purpose and a common focus. Thus a key task of a newly appointed project manager or team leader is to identify and communicate essential performance goals by translating relevant aspects of the parent company's business strategy into language that team members understand. By that means the leader bridges the communication gap between team members and senior management in the parent company.

Culturally diverse teams tend to be either very effective or very ineffective – as opposed to single-culture teams which are closely centred on average effectiveness (Adler, 1991). Multicultural teams are very effective when everybody understands and accepts the guiding principles for their actions (Vallaster, 2005). Thus *goal clarity* in a multicultural team is essential because it creates the conditions for effective collaboration among the members. Other needed qualities are the same as those required for excellent performance in single-culture teams, notably *communication competence, high task focus*, and *timely information*.

Communication competence

Cross-cultural communication competence accounts for much of the variance in performance of multicultural teams. This quality enables diverse specialists to find effective ways of cooperating, reducing levels of stress in the team (Ulrey and Amason, 2001). Thus when researchers studied the performance of American and Russian managers in multicultural teams, the Americans exhibited higher levels of interpersonal communication and second-language skills (Matveev and Nelson, 2004). These skills enabled them to:

- effectively communicate with team members;
- adapt messages to the cultural perspectives of individuals and sub-groups (see Figure 10.1);
- manage their teams more effectively.

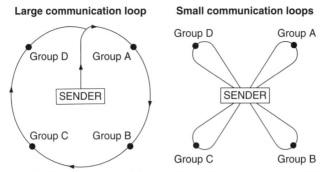

Small communication loops allow quick circulation of the message and rapid feedback. Messages can be translated into the 'languages' preferred by different sub-groups.

Figure 10.1   Intra-team communication

In large multicultural organisations individuals with the most cohesive face-to-face networks are 30 per cent more productive than other employees (Pentland, 2009).

In many companies, supervisors who give time to informal communication with employees tend to have productive teams. A European manufacturer of mobile phones, for instance, puts pressure on supervisors to communicate with new recruits from the outset.

As soon as a new recruit joins the team the supervisor might give her the names and numbers of various people who can provide useful information and whom the newcomer might want to contact. The assumption is that if, through making an effort to communicate, the recruit can acquire a basic understanding of specific job problems she will be better able to contribute to solving them.

Effective team leaders don't always treat people in the way they themselves want to be treated. They tailor communications to the receiver. If some members of the team respond to numbers and statistics that is what they get. Other team members respond to words, or they absorb information more easily if it is presented graphically. Effective team leaders seem to have the ability to communicate with individuals and with national subgroups in the team using their preferred 'language'.

High task focus

When a multicultural team is first set up it consciously seeks orderliness, a clear status-hierarchy, and decisive leadership (Javidan and House, 2001). Members feel the need for direction because the way forward is uncertain. Decisive, task-focused leadership in the early stages enables the team to organise itself and become productive. Several urgent tasks have to be carried out:

- team goals have to be agreed;
- roles and responsibilities have to be allocated;
- appropriate standards and procedures have to be established;
- culturally appropriate performance measures have to be put in place.

Goal ambiguity, stemming from differing views regarding project goals, had a strong negative impact on the projects studied by Levitt et al. (1999).

Without task-focused leadership in the early stages, teams may waste time debating goals and negotiating roles as opposed to doing real work. Task-oriented leadership is therefore needed to make sure that members are clear about what they are supposed to be doing. It is the team leader's job, in the first stages of a multicultural team's life, to provide clarity and orientation by setting *clear goals and priorities*, thereby motivating the diverse membership. Successful multicultural team leaders keep their teams on track by first defining clear priorities then monitoring to check that the team is moving towards them.

At later stages in a team's life a change of approach may be needed. Instead of insisting on conformity and cohesion the leader sometimes needs to encourage nonconformity and divergent thinking so as to exploit the team's creativity. At this mature stage in the team's lifecycle, members will be encouraged to question and to look at options, to discuss errors and to seek feedback – the very process by which teams solve complex problems (Hirst et al., 2009).

Timely information

There are different kinds of diversity. While *values* diversity can decrease job satisfaction in multicultural teams, a study of 92 work groups has shown that *informational* diversity usually has the effect of boosting a team's performance (Jehn et al., 1999). Effective leaders of multicultural teams encourage informational diversity by making sure that relevant project-related information is acquired and communicated to team members, and by establishing ties with other organisations. By establishing communication links with top management in the parent company the team leader ensures that important task-related information is obtained from that source when required.

Majchrzak (2004: 133) describes how team leaders often canvass members of their team for relevant information and opinions about various project-related issues, and then disseminate the information acquired:

I didn't know the team members very well, didn't know how they thought and worked, so I couldn't go directly to the point on an issue. Instead I encouraged a lot of conversation, trying to reach a common view that included all their points. We discussed different alternatives, always asking everyone, 'What do you think about this?'...by surfacing our differences early, we didn't ignore anyone's needs.

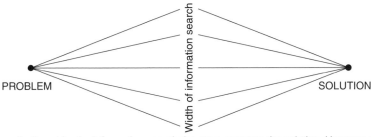

Generally, the wider the information search the more accurate the solution. However, wide searches involve delay, high costs, the emergence of opposed blocks of evidence and also information overload which can confuse the problem-solvers.

Figure 10.2   Information and problem-solving

The strategy is to expose everybody to everybody else's ideas. Task-related knowledge is first acquired then transferred across cultural subgroups. In this way optimum conditions for decision-making are established (Figure 10.2).

Pentland (2009) describes how teams in a German bank were charged with creating new marketing campaigns.

> The teams oscillated between *directive leadership*, required for information collection, and *democratic leadership* which took the form of intense democratic discussions among team members. The dual approach was highly effective in achieving information integration and facilitating decision-making.

Effective team leaders make sure that their teams receive diverse and timely information. However, they avoid *information overload* because of its negative impact on team performance. Today, when copies can be copied and information transmitted costlessly, information may rush at a team faster than they can use it. Fortunately, software tools are available that can reduce the danger – for instance, by sorting and prioritizing incoming emails; or by turning messages into tasks or appointments (Hemp, 2009).

Case study

MINI-CASE: Shared sense of purpose

When a multicultural team is first set up ethnic or national differences often prevent cooperation and collaboration. But that risk is reduced when performance goals are discussed and shared by all members of the team.

Cultural differences can usually be overcome by the project manager injecting a common focus, a shared sense of purpose, from the outset. This truth became evident when ten diverse experts were brought in from branches

---

Case study

Continued

in several countries to form a new team working on a large-scale product development project.

In spite of the varied backgrounds and mix of cultures, cooperation and collaboration between the different national groups was excellent. The main reason for this was that the diverse specialists focused on carrying out responsibilities and achieving performance goals that were discussed and agreed with the project manager immediately after they arrived.

Questions:

1. *'Cooperation and collaboration between the different national groups was excellent.'* To what extent was this due to the initial discussions held between the project manager and team members about performance goals? What other factors may have been involved?
2. If the project team had been much larger – more than a hundred, say – what actions would the project manager have needed to take to ensure that the team had a shared sense of purpose and a common focus?

EFFECTIVE LEADERSHIP OF MULTICULTURAL TEAMS

Varieties of leadership

For newly appointed leaders of multicultural teams, as for newly appointed project managers, the first weeks are difficult. Relationships are undefined, routines not established, team members' expectations unclear. A more basic problem is that members of multicultural teams respond to authority and styles of leadership in differing, culturally influenced ways.

For instance, people from high power–distance countries such as France or Russia usually expect a leader to be decisive and to display much authority. Japanese people, on the other hand, are used to working for managers who take a deep interest in their lives and welfare and who continually consult them as part of the decision-making process. People from individualist countries such as the United States, Canada, and Australia often expect managers to provide opportunities for personal achievement and to reward success.

Faced with so many contradictory expectations and preferences, the one quality that the team leader must possess is flexibility.

Flexibility

As managers of diversity, leaders of multicultural teams must constantly adjust their approach to allow for cultural difference. The style of supervision to which members of one cultural group respond favourably may be different from the kind of supervision which others in the team prefer. Studies show, for instance, that Japanese employees are positively motivated by *failure feedback* from their managers while Canadian employees are motivated by *success feedback* (Heine et al., 2001). Dorfman et al. (1997) found that directive supervision had no impact in the United States, Japan, or South Korea but was effective in Taiwan and Mexico.

Employees in some South American and other countries often respond well to charismatic leadership and are motivated by charismatic leaders. As Shamir et al. (1998) point out charismatic leaders rely largely on *verbal and written communication*. They use communications to display self-confidence, social and physical courage, commitment to the organisation's goals, and total involvement in finding ways to meet them. Such acts by the leader empower employees by motivating them, by inspiring their confidence, and by raising their self-efficacy.

As such examples suggest, different nationalities have to be managed and motivated in different ways – so *flexibility* is an essential quality for multicultural team leaders to possess. A single 'natural' management style does not necessarily equip a manager to become an effective leader of a multicultural team. Fiedler's (1967) contingency model of leadership is based on the assumption that different styles of leadership are needed at different stages in a team's life. The situation – the type of work, the cultural composition of the team, and so on – determines the leadership style required.

Communication ability

Multicultural team leaders need to be good informal communicators. Giving much time and effort to informal communication with members of the team has the effect of encouraging team members to strongly identify with the team or organisation. Individuals who identify with a team or organisation take pride in being a part of it and regard membership as being one of their most important social identities (Shamir et al., 1998).

Moreover, by giving time to informal communication the team leader obtains much valuable information, such as:

- what motivates the various national and cultural subgroups on the team;
- what difficulties individuals and subgroups think the team will have in achieving its goals, and how these difficulties could be overcome;
- what additional resources (people, equipment, information, training, etc.) team members think are needed to improve team performance.

By giving time to informal communication the team leader learns about the interests and abilities of individuals, their areas of expertise, their strengths, and weaknesses. Such knowledge simplifies the important task of allocating appropriate roles and responsibilities to team members.

Management ability

Team leaders need to demonstrate management ability throughout the life cycle of the team. In the early stages of the team's life, for instance, guidelines and decisions are needed about who should be in the team and who should be left out so as to improve the chances of the team doing a good job (Coutu, 2009). Mechanisms have to be established to hold individuals accountable (Sull, 2009). Required resources and reliable information have to be obtained from the parent company at the right time and with the right degree of detail to enable the team to carry out its task. Management ability is also required to overcome goal ambiguity and ensure that the team focuses its efforts on a small number of *priority areas*. Most important of all, team leaders need management ability ensure that the team's tasks are successfully carried out.

Effective multicultural team leaders see collaboration as a holistic challenge and not simply a matter of running seminars urging more collaboration. According to Cross and Parker (2003: 116), effective collaboration 'requires the alignment of unique aspects of formal organisational design, control systems, technology, and human resource practices. And specific cultural values and leadership behaviour can also have a striking effect . . . .'

According to Shamir et al. (1998), the behaviours highlighted by very effective leaders can be clustered into three categories:

1. Emphasizing collective values and ideologies and linking them to a mission and its goals.
2. Emphasizing the collective identity of the group/organisation and linking it to a mission and its goals.
3. Displaying personal commitment to the values, identities, and goals the leader stands for or promotes (Figure 10.3).

Courage

Authority tends to be resisted by members of many teams – a trait which can trigger covert or open attacks on the leader. The risk is greater in multicultural teams because the team leader may meet the expectations of some but not all of the different ethnic and cultural groups. Disruptive individuals often emerge as informal leaders of subgroups. Consider how the Apostles or the Knights of the Round Table were disrupted by the activities of a single disruptive individual. These are some of the reasons why courage is a quality needed by multicultural team leaders. Leaders need the courage to deal with tough interpersonal issues between themselves and team members or between themselves and informal leaders of ethnic and national subgroups.

Rules and strategies may be needed for dealing with potentially disruptive individuals and informal leaders of subgroups. However, a decision to replace an underperforming or a disruptive individual should never be taken in haste – partly because of the negative impact such a decision could have on the team

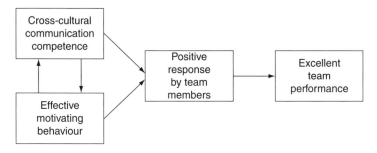

Figure 10.3   Multicultural team leadership

leader's relationship with the rest of the team and with senior management in the parent organisation.

> The project manager of a product development team thought that a programme planner was a disruptive influence and should be reassigned. His report to senior management proposed removing the individual and reallocating his responsibilities among other team members. But he underestimated the degree of support for the programme planner that existed in the company, and his proposal was rejected.

Sizing-up process

Clear structure and procedures need to be introduced soon after a multicultural team is set up to help the team overcome cultural barriers and become productive. If they are imposed at too early a stage, however, they become counterproductive as time must be allowed for the *sizing-up process* to take place.

Maslow's classic experiments with apes and Lorenz's with dogs showed that a sizing-up process goes on when animals first meet, subsequently developing into a dominant-submissive relationship. A somewhat similar process occurs when a multicultural team is first assembled. Conscious and unconscious responses by individual members to cultural differences of communication style, dress, accent, and problem-solving preferences play an important part in this sizing-up process and influence the pattern of future relationships in the team. Only after this sizing-up process has ended will the team be able to turn its full attention to the task for which it was established.

An important aspect of the sizing-up process is the sizing-up by the team of its project manager or allocated leader. Usually, members consciously look for – and are favourably impressed by – signs of decisive leadership. Studies show, for instance, that positive emotional displays by the leader (e.g. expressing strong enthusiasm for team goals, or praising the achievement of an important deadline) are perceived as signs of decisive leadership, and they evoke positive evaluations by the team of the leader's effectiveness (Sy et al., 2005; Van Kleef et al., 2009).

SMALL-GROUP EXERCISE: Qualities of multicultural team leaders

Working in pairs or small groups, discuss each of the following six statements then agree on which of the option (a,b or c) to tick. At the end of the exercise, compare your answers with those of the other teams.

1. *Even when they are swamped by work, successful leaders of multicultural teams take time to relate to team members as people and not just because they want something from them (e.g. weekend work).*

   a. *agree*
   b. *partly agree*
   c. *disagree*

2. *Effective multicultural team leaders always do what they say they will do (e.g. consult team members before taking important decisions).*

   a. *agree*
   b. *partly agree*
   c. *disagree*

3. *Effective leaders of multicultural teams are always fair and impartial in their treatment of team members (e.g. avoiding favouritism, avoiding biased job-performance appraisals).*

   a. *agree*
   b. *partly agree*
   c. *disagree*

4. *During problem-solving discussions effective team leaders focus on possibilities and opportunities, as opposed to emphasizing constraints and difficulties.*

   a. *agree*
   b. *partly agree*
   c. *disagree*

5. *Effective leaders of multicultural teams are good communicators. They give much time and effort to communicating informally with individuals and national subgroups, using their preferred 'language'.*

   a. *agree*
   b. *partly agree*
   c. *disagree*

6. *Effective leaders of multicultural teams establish formal and informal communication links with top managers in the parent company to ensure that project-related information is obtained when required by the team.*

   a. *agree*
   b. *partly agree*
   c. *disagree*

DECISION-MAKING OPTIONS

Expert opinion

Efficient decision-making procedures help a multicultural team to perform well, and there is evidence to show that teams with appointed leaders tend to have more effective decision-making procedures than those without leaders (Vroom and Yetton, 1973). One reason is that appointed leaders have a vested interested in 'getting it right'. As a result, they listen carefully to advice offered by those with relevant knowledge and experience ('expert opinion'), and ensure that the advice is integrated into team decisions.

But some givers of expert opinion are misled by illusions of infallibility. A psychologist serving in the Israeli Defence forces who assessed candidates for officer training has described the powerful sense of getting to know each candidate and the accompanying conviction that he could accurately foretell, without the need for further information, how well the candidate would do in combat (Kahneman and Klein, 2009). But subsequent statistical records proved that his strong conviction that he was right was wrong.

The risks involved in basing team decisions on expert advice were highlighted when Meehl (1954) reviewed some 20 studies comparing forecasts made by experts with predictions made from simple statistical models. In almost all cases, the statistical predictions were found to be more accurate than the experts' forecasts. A possible explanation is that human judgments are 'noisy' – affected by emotional and other factors – to an extent that impairs their validity.

Nevertheless, many leaders of multicultural teams are drawn to expert-based decisions because they are *quick*. Some of them – military commanders or managers of offshore oil installations, for instance – have to make decisions under conditions of great uncertainty and time pressure. The pressures often preclude any orderly effort to generate and evaluate options in the classical manner. A better option is for the managers to use their own judgment and implicit knowledge – their *own* expert opinion, encapsulating experience tried and tested over many years – to make the decision. Klein et al. (1986) investigated fireground commanders and found they had literally no time for orderly decision-making when faced with an inferno. Instead they generated only a single option and that was all they needed.

They identified the option by drawing on their experience of similar situations, and then evaluated the option by *mentally simulating* it to see if it would work in the situation that faced them. If they thought it would, they implemented it. If it had shortcomings, they modified it. If they could not easily modify it, they turned to the next most plausible option – and so on.

Consensus decisions

Decision-making by top-level executives in an organisation is at one end of the decision-making spectrum and consensus decision-making is at the other. The consensus process is especially common in Asia and may even require the agreement of employees at all levels in the organisation. In Japanese companies, for instance, proposals from top management are discussed by junior managers until a consensus view emerges. The developed proposal then goes up to the next level where it is discussed, developed, and again sent up the line. According to Yoshino (1968), Japanese managers will compromise on almost everything until a consensus of some kind is reached.

Consensus decision-making takes up much time as agreement has to be reached on substantive as well as procedural issues. The consensus process takes a long time to play out but the payoff is that implementation is swift and decisive. Because they have been closely involved in developing the plan, all levels of staff are committed to implementing it smoothly. And the company instantly puts all its backing and resources behind it.

Western business visitors often complain that doing business with the Japanese is extremely frustrating because of the great length of time it takes to make even simple decisions. However, consensus decisions have major advantages, including:

- *Reliability*: groups tend to make few gross errors because of the constant feedback created by constant interaction among group members.
- *Accuracy*: decision based on group forecasts and judgments are more likely to be on target than decisions based on the judgments of an individual or a subgroup because of the effect of averaging.
- *Implementation*: the decisions are usually implemented energetically by all members of the group.

Members of multicultural teams who come from collectivist countries are usually comfortable using consensus methods of decision-making, as opposed to majority voting or decisions based on expert advice. *Majority voting* has the advantage of being generally accepted as fair, and it is also a relatively quick method. However, it does little or nothing to satisfy the losers, who are likely to look for ways of reversing the decision at some later stage.

Disadvantages of the consensus method

Some multicultural groups opt to make decisions by consensus as a way of avoiding conflict between national or ethnic subgroups. This leads to options which could trigger conflict not being properly considered. The result is that facile compromise decisions are made.

'Groupthink'

Teams which use group methods of decision-making sometimes fall into the 'groupthink' trap of toeing the line preferred by authority or by the majority (Janis, 1982). Groupthink behaviour has the advantage of protecting group cohesiveness, but only at the cost of overriding a proper assessment of alternatives. It was precisely to counter the possibility of groupthink during the Cuban missile crisis that President Kennedy stayed away from some Cabinet meetings so that those who might be intimidated by his presence would speak out. Robert Kennedy reportedly commented that there was more true give-and-take when the President was not in the room than when he was present.

A simple but effective way of discouraging groupthink in multicultural team meetings is to split the team into subgroups which work simultaneously on the same issue, before jointly preparing a single proposal for presentation to the whole team. Devil's advocacy is an equally simple method. This consists of assigning a particular subgroup to argue against the general view adopted in decision-making meetings of the team. Such an approach has been found to be an effective way of generating more options and improving the quality of decisions (Cosier and Schwenk, 1990).

PERFORMANCE PROBLEMS

Culture-based problems

Multicultural teams bring many advantages to their organisations, including innovation, creativity, and diverse approaches to problem-solving. But they also bring problems that spring from cultural difference. The clash of cultures in the team can lead to stereotyping and mutual distrust which reduces cooperation. Difficulties of verbal and nonverbal communication often complicate relations between different national or ethnic subgroups. Brett et al. (2006) identify typical culture-based difficulties, including:

- contradictory problem-solving styles;
- contradictory attitudes towards authority and leadership;
- lack of cooperation between different subgroups;
- lack of fluency in using the team's working language, or using the language with a cultural 'slant'.

Although English may be the official working language of a team some team members may speak English with an unusual accent or lack of fluency, creating comprehension problems for others on the team.

Cross and Parker (2003: 101) point to the lack of trust that developed between an English and a US member of a multicultural team, based on different meanings attached to the word 'quite'. To the American, quite meant 'a lot of something' so that saying that new software was quite effective meant that it was very effective. To the English person, however, it meant that it was not all that effective. The researchers note that, over time:

> hearing each other use that one word differently in discussions with customers, superiors, and other team members ... created a great deal of distrust in terms of competence ('Is he blind? How could he say that was "quite" effective?')

Such culture-related problems help to explain why, early in their life cycles, culturally diverse groups tend to suffer from lower levels of performance than homogeneous groups (Staples and Zhao, 2006).

Potential for confusion and conflict

Multicultural teams typically experience tensions and conflict stemming from the composition of the team. Individual team members usually have contrasting viewpoints and interpretive frameworks, and often they have different first languages. Such differences typically lead to cultural and linguistic difficulties and to problems stemming from status and power relationships.

> *Cultural difficulties.* Members of multicultural teams tend to have different cultural approaches to such issues as trust and openness. As Mezias et al. (1999) point out, different cultures provide different behavioural scripts for managing relationships within collaborative teams.
>
> *Linguistic difficulties.* During a joint Finnish-British research assignment, British participants needed help in accessing the Finnish language as they needed to translate the Finns' interview records and found this to be an extremely difficult task (Thomas et al., 2009). For instance, the fact that there is no clear linguistic distinction in Nordic languages between 'sex' and 'gender' led to much ambiguity and confusion for the British members of the team.

Power relationships are often an issue during cross-cultural collaborations, reflecting the wider networks and cultures of which the individuals are a part (Thomas et al., 2009). Whose view should prevail about the nature of the problem? Who should decide on the solutions to be adopted? Such questions are not easily answered and often lead to conflict. One way of dealing with such problems is for the team leader to acknowledge that they exist, then to discuss the issue openly and constructively with the whole team.

Process difficulties

When a multicultural team is first established roles and responsibilities are unclear. With their diverse cultural backgrounds, members often disagree about how tasks should be organised and prioritized, how responsibilities should be allocated, which decision-making procedures should be used. Trust and confidence in the project manager/team leader may collapse if information received by the team is inadequate (Ellis and Shockley-Zalabak, 2001). These and other initial process difficulties that are associated with diversity reduce team efficiency.

National and cultural differences among team members create behavioural difficulties which may create *low levels of trust* and undermine team performance (Polzer et al., 2002). Gibb (1964) has described how low trust reduces the performance of teams:

With low trust, people use more strategy, filter information, build interpersonal facades, camouflage attitudes, deliberately or unconsciously hold back relevant feelings and information in the process of interpersonal in-fighting, distort feedback – and thus indirectly sabotage productivity.

Such problems help to explain why diverse workforces tend to have high levels of staff turnover (O'Reilly et al., 1989). One study, for instance, found that in culturally diverse teams in US banks managers were more likely to feel dissatisfied, demoralized, and to leave the team compared with managers in homogeneous teams (Jackson and Schuler, 2003). Effective leadership is needed to counteract the tendency towards high staff turnover (Nishii and Mayer, 2009).

Social loafing

A downward pressure on productivity in multicultural teams may come from *'social loafing'*. This occurs when individuals reduce their efforts and rely on the efforts of other team members when carrying out complex tasks (Earley, 1989). The problem is greater in multicultural teams consisting mainly of people from individualist countries. When working in groups individualists tend to be less motivated and less productive than when they are working alone (Earley, 1993).

Collectivists, by contrast, tend to work efficiently in groups and rarely indulge in social loafing. Japanese students, for instance, have been found to solve problems more efficiently in groups than when working alone (Matsui et al., 1987). When a Japanese psychologist studied problem-solving by Japanese groups, individuals much preferred to go along with the group rather than express their own individual solutions if those solutions would produce disharmony in the group (Scollon and Scollon, 2001).

Clique formation

Halevy and Sagiv (2008) make the important point that it is not the total amount of cultural diversity in a team that determines its particular strengths and effectiveness, but how the team is organised into cultural subgroups. Subgroups which are organised in accordance with rational, task-focused principles can ensure that the team becomes a high-performing unit. But subgroups that form because of emotional, irrational forces may operate as disruptive cliques that reduce overall team performance. This often happens when team members come from national groups holding *negative stereotypes* of each other, bringing the danger that the team will split along cultural fault lines.

Occupational and national subgroups can become insular to the point where cross-functional collaboration is impeded. Encouraging frequent and close interactions between members of these subgroups leads them to get to know one another, to share important information, and to create a common point of view. But when individuals identify more strongly with their national or ethnic subgroup than with the team as a whole cliques may form.

For example, a clique of North American project personnel formed in the early stages of a large international project in an African country. Subsequently, clique members demoralised local staff by openly criticising and ridiculing the Indian project director.

Cliques based on national groupings soon formed when scientists from American, Japanese and German companies assembled in New York to work on the task of developing a revolutionary memory chip (Schneider and Barsoux, 1997). The Japanese group were uncomfortable sitting in small, individual offices and speaking English so they spent most of their time standing in the corridors, comparing notes, and discussing ideas. The American group complained that the Germans did too much planning and that the Japanese failed to make clear-cut decisions. The three groups became increasingly isolated from each other. Overall team performance was the casualty.

Intra-team conflict

Conflict is an ever-present reality in multicultural teams and can greatly affect overall team performance. Team members typically become involved in conflicts over such issues as:

- the distribution of work;
- the allocation of responsibilities;
- the best ways to accomplish the team's goals;
- fair rewards;
- social loafing by particular subgroups.

Certain kinds of conflict – productive conflict – can improve the team's problem-solving. Positive conflict leads team members to question the adequacy of their present thinking, search for better ideas, and consider opposing perspectives (Tjosvold, 1998). The basic steps in productive conflict are for team members to express their ideas and feelings directly, to consciously take the perspective of the other person, to communicate the desire to resolve the conflict for the benefit of the whole team, and to integrate their ideas to produce high-quality solutions (Tjosvold, 1998).

Jehn (1997) distinguishes three types of conflict within teams:

- process conflict;
- task conflict;
- relationship conflict.

Task conflict and process conflict are examples of productive conflict since they generate greater understanding of task-related issues, thus leading to higher levels of team performance. Productive conflict is productive because it obeys the competitive imperative – innovate or fall behind! Productive conflict among team members is focused on judgmental differences about how best to achieve team goals.

Relationship conflict, by contrast, almost always damages team performance. Relationship conflict is usually focused on personal or cultural incompatibilities. Unlike task conflict, relationship conflict causes negative psychological reactions like strain, fear, anger, frustration – feelings which absorb energy, impede communication, and distract team members from their task.

In multicultural teams cultural differences increase the likelihood of relationship conflicts erupting on a regular basis. The effect of relationship conflict is usually negative since it can impair performance and lower team effectiveness (Amason, 1986). Moreover, cultural and communication difficulties impede the team's ability to manage this type of conflict through open discussion.

Examples of productive conflict

Conflict in multicultural teams often arises from disagreements about procedures to be followed in carrying out the task, or from competition among subgroups for limited resources and responsibilities. Conflicts of this kind are task-related and usually not destructive – indeed they often lead to higher levels of performance. This was the outcome when Asian members of an international project team were criticized by European members for consistently failing to observe project deadlines. The Asians, however, saw things differently. They argued that tight deadlines led to poor work – and they gave numerous examples to prove the point. Eventually the two sides agreed to meet to discuss the issue.

> Each group in turn explained its point of view while the other group listened. At the end of the meeting a compromise was reached. Deadlines would stay, but there would be fewer of them.

Sometimes conflict between individuals and subgroups over a particular decision can be resolved by the simple device of inviting the team itself to make the decision.

> When the manager of an international research project tried to find ways of reallocating roles and responsibilities among researchers the team rejected all his proposals as unworkable or unfair. Eventually the manager asked the team itself to solve the problem. The researchers called a meeting and two hours later had worked out new job allocations that were accepted by everybody.

Choice of working language

When a large multicultural team selects a particular language to be its official working language team performance is affected – for better or worse. Some team members may be unable to express themselves clearly in the selected language and lose influence in the team as a result. Native-speakers of the selected language, on the other hand, gain power and influence in the team.

If French, for instance, is the language selected, native French speakers will tend to dominate team discussions and decision-making meetings while native-speakers of other languages may be forced into marginal positions. Thus choice of the official working language is a serious decision and ideally all members of the team should be consulted before a decision is taken.

A study of three foreign firms operating in Hong-Kong reveals the impact made by choice of working language (Vallaster, 2005). The study focused on the performance of multicultural project teams comprising Chinese and European members. English was the second language for everybody and the language in which project issues were discussed.

> It was noticed that the behaviour of all team members changed when they were talking in English, the official working language. They were more inhibited, less fluent; and found it difficult to deal with issues which they would have dealt with easily had they been using their own first languages.

As the example suggests, overall team performance may be affected if some members find it difficult to use the team's official working language.

Size constraints

If a multicultural team is too large or too small performance is affected – although, in any particular case, determining the optimum size is a matter of judgment and experience. As a rough guide, however, the size of a team should be limited by its ability to solve problems of *internal communication and coordination*. Very large teams tend to split into small groups – often along cultural fault-lines – during the group formation stage. When this happens the team subsequently wastes much time sorting out procedural wrangles and interpersonal conflicts. Hulsheger (2009) argues that tendencies to social loafing are greater in larger teams.

Generally speaking, the more members a team has, the longer it takes to become a cohesive and effective unit. As the size of the group goes up, the average contribution by each member declines. Latane et al. (1979) cite Moede's unpublished study, carried out in 1927, which involved members of a group who pulled a rope as hard as possible. At intervals an extra person was added to the team. With each increase in membership there was a decreased average contribution by each member.

PERFORMANCE IMPROVEMENT

Team development

Multicultural teams tend to become increasingly productive over time. The early stages of a team's life are typically characterized by *self-oriented behaviour* (Schein, 1969). Members of the team are unsure about their ability to fit in, they worry about whether they will be able to get on with people from different cultural backgrounds. Time must be allowed for these self-oriented doubts, uncertainties, and conflicts to be acted out and early lapses in team performance must be tolerated.

Emotional, self-oriented behaviour is a natural and necessary part of team development and time is needed to allow emotional growth to occur. Only after a team has gone through this uncomfortable emotional phase of growth and development will it be able to focus on carrying out the task and achieving its goals. As Schein (1969) points out, permitting emotional expression leads to initial discomfort for everybody but eventually leads to higher levels of communication and performance.

Immediately after a multicultural team is set up little appears to be accomplished because of slow progress in carrying out the task. Yet much is accomplished because members are learning about each other. Who is strong and who is weak? What specialized skills do team members have? Which roles on the team are they equipped to fill? Goal-scoring can wait. Emotional expression and growth must first take place.

Stages of growth

Like homogeneous teams, multicultural teams pass through several distinct stages of growth and development. Tuckman (1965) summarizes these stages as:

1. *Forming.* Early in the team's life, members experience anxiety because of uncertainty about future roles and relationships and whether they will be able to meet performance expectations.
2. *Storming.* Overt or suppressed conflict occurs between individuals or cultural subgroups; there is strong disagreement about how work should be done and how decisions should be made.
3. *Norming.* Team norms emerge. Team interactions become more structured, patterned, and team members are more cohesive. Conflict among cultural subgroups gradually subsides.
4. *Performing.* Inter-personal and intercultural difficulties are largely resolved. The team is able to focus on task activities and on achieving team goals.

Multicultural team development does not necessarily proceed sequentially from one stage to the next – indeed, several stages can occur at the same time. Nevertheless, a team must pass through the emotional and conflict-filled stages of team development before achieving effective performance. Interpersonal tensions and conflict between cultural subgroups must be tolerated since the expression of disruptive feelings can expedite the movement towards higher levels of team performance.

Self-examination

Multicultural teams tend to experience initial performance problems because of cultural, procedural, and relational difficulties. But the losses tend to be short-term. Thus the multicultural groups studied by Watson et al. (1993) had low

TEAM DEVELOPMENT

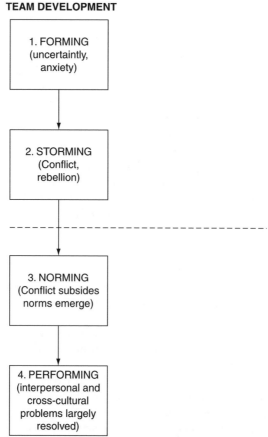

Cross-cultural teams, like individuals, pass through different stages of development. Thus team leaders who tolerate conflict and 'bad' behaviour may expedite team development and ultimately improve team performance.

Figure 10.4   Team development

Source: Based on Tuckman (1965).

levels of performance at first but outperformed single-culture groups by the later stages of their lives.

In practice, an effective way to overcome early performance problems is for team members to discuss them as soon as they arise. Regular *progress meetings* provide the means of doing so. In the meetings team members can identify efficiency blockages and suggest ways in which the blockages could be overcome. Hard and soft problems can be discussed. Hard problems, such as physical resource issues and poor organisation structure. Soft problems, such as or inadequate supervision of team activities or training ideas.

The team development process is shown diagrammatically in Figure 10.4.

Feedback

Feedback has long played a central role in theories of learning, continuous improvement, and performance achievement (Van der Vegt et al., 2010). The concept of feedback was originally used to describe the process by which systems will self-regulate. Feedback about system performance allows a system to reflect, adapt, and self-correct until desired performance standards are achieved. Feedback provides the mechanism by which a multicultural team – a human system – assesses the efficacy of past and present performance and identifies areas where improvement is needed. Whether the team receives feedback about individual or team performance affects a group's orientation to individual or collective improvement (Hinsz et al., 1997)

Arranging for a team to receive feedback on its procedures and communication practices often leads to rapid improvements in team performance. As in a guided missile system, feedback keeps behaviour on target.

> A consultant is invited to sit in on meetings of an international project team in a former Soviet-bloc country. Later he gives feedback to the team. The feedback takes in such issues as poor decision-making procedures and conflict between individuals and sub-groups. The feedback helps the team to make necessary changes and to operate with greater cohesion and efficiency.

Other techniques for improving team efficiency include Drexler's model of team development (Drexler et al., 1988). The model identifies stages that must be passed through to transform a group of culturally disparate individuals into a cohesive team (cohesion referring to the degree to which members desire to remain in the team). The stages include:

- members' becoming clear about team goals (*goal clarity*);
- becoming clear about their roles and responsibilities (*role clarity*);
- demonstrating trust and confidence in each other (*growth of trust*).

By critically examining its own performance, arranging to receive feedback, and using other techniques to facilitate team efficiency, a multicultural team can improve its communication, procedures, and relationships and thus achieve higher levels of performance. Moreover, as a result of using such techniques the team accumulates a body of wisdom and expertise that remains with the team even if individual members leave.

Coordination management

Why do some multicultural teams with similar technical know-how and resources as other multicultural teams consistently perform more efficiently and get better results? Part of the answer lies in the project manager's or team leader's success in coordinating team activities. Thus product development firms with well-managed coordination processes – such as effective communication links between different functional disciplines – are more successful than their competitors in cost, quality, and speed (Hoopes and Postrel, 1999). Coordination management is what makes the difference.

Coordination management is demonstrated when specialists are informed of each others' actions, when technical information is shared across cultural or national subgroups. Such coordination does not occur automatically – the project manager/team leader *makes* it happen by constantly communicating, socializing, monitoring, and encouraging. Effective project managers ensure that information is obtained and shared and that work is not duplicated or wasted. Wasted work is work that is carried out but not used (Hoopes and Postrel, 1999).

Team members' different beliefs about the relative value of tasks can lead subgroups into spending too much time on low priority tasks. Effective coordination management prevents this happening, with regular progress meetings providing a mechanism. Regular meetings ensure that everybody is kept up to date with progress, and key specialists report on problems that have emerged – problems such as overspending or delays in achieving project milestones.

A key aspect of coordination management is to ensure that team activities are coordinated with the activities of other teams and with other organisations. This is usually achieved by establishing inter-team or inter-organisational committees (Rometsch and Sydow, 2007).

CREATIVITY OF MULTICULTURAL TEAMS

Effect of diversity

Leonard and Straus (1997) note that members of different cultures tend to have various thinking styles. They can be analytical, intuitive, logical, experiential, value-driven, and so on. When properly harnessed, this diversity generates dialogue and debate that stimulates creativity and innovation. That is why so many multicultural teams are excellent problem-solvers. The diverse staffing composition of multicultural teams enables them to generate a wider range of high quality ideas than culturally homogeneous groups (Hirst et al., 2009). Novel and useful ideas about products, procedures, and processes. Pragmatic ideas that get results.

The cultural diversity of a multicultural team gives competitive advantage since it brings together varied approaches to problem-solving, allowing the team to use the best from each culture. North American members, for instance, may be able to supply the detailed analysis needed to support a capital expenditure proposal. Asian members, on the other hand, could add a holistic emphasis by showing how different aspects of a proposal balance and relate to each other.

The diverse membership brings wide-ranging knowledge and perspectives to such tasks as:

- deciding how an important project or a key task should be carried out;
- how needed information could be acquired;
- how costs could be reduced.

Moreover, the diversity brings competitive advantage to the parent company. If, for example, some team members have first-hand familiarity with a particular geographical region or a particular product market, the knowledge will enable the company to adjust more briskly than its competitors to market changes in the region concerned.

Different kinds of diversity

Different kinds of diversity in a multicultural team make different kinds of impact. For instance, Hulsheger et al. (2009) distinguish between two distinct kinds of diversity that characterize multicultural teams:

- diversity of cultural background;
- job-related diversity (relating to attributes such as function, education, knowledge, skills, and expertise).

Most innovation initiatives build upon an organisation's existing resources and know-how – its manufacturing and technological expertise and its market knowledge. *Job-related diversity* gives the team a variety of different perspectives and approaches that helps it solve complex problems – such as developing new products or procedures – as well as spotting opportunities for large- and small-scale innovations. Large-scale innovation exploits sudden shifts in markets and technologies with radically new services and products – like Tata's $2500 car for India. Small-scale innovation may involve nothing more than improving a simple administrative procedure in order to save the firm money.

The ability to discuss opposing ideas and integrate divergent viewpoints is vital for this kind of creativity. By contrast, *diversity of cultural background* (e.g. ethnicity or race) may lead to communication difficulties and interpersonal tensions that interfere with creativity and innovative efforts and the achievement of team consensus.

Harrison et al. (1998) distinguish between deep- and surface-level cultural diversity. Surface-level diversity consists of easily observable characteristics of a team such as gender, age, and race. Deep-level diversity relates to differences of beliefs and values among team members (differences which may be decisive for the team's long-term success). Some effects of diversity on the creativity of multicultural teams are difficult to predict and depend on the particular mix of national cultures in the team.

Knowledge diversity

A multicultural team's *social capital* is a resource that can be tapped and used to solve difficult problems in a creative way. Social capital can be defined as 'resources and knowledge derived from the network of relationships possessed by an individual' (Nahapiet and Ghosal, 1998). Since different national groups on the team have access to different knowledge networks, a multicultural team can usually access and exploit an extremely wide and diverse knowledge base.

Knowledge diversity boosts a multicultural team's potential for innovation (Jehn et al., 1999). Knowledge diversity makes it likely that innovations will come not from some brilliant initiative taken by the team leader but from an accumulation of small improvements to existing practices and procedures suggested by individual members of the team; or from impromptu brainstorming sessions where all ideas are welcome and no ideas are barred. Ninety-six per cent of respondents in a Delphi Group (2006) survey identified brainstorming as a primary technique for fostering innovative thinking.

Brainstorming

Brainstorming is a game for any number of players. More important than numbers is that participants should come from as wide a range of disciplines and cultural backgrounds as possible so that the ideas produced cover a very wide spectrum. The aim is to produce as many ideas as possible on a given topic – such as how to double a division's sales within 12 months, or how to improve the image of the organisation among consumers. Every idea is recorded. No criticism is allowed. The players are encouraged to shoot off any ideas that come into their heads, even if they sound stupid or impractical. Often an impractical idea becomes practical after a slight modification.

At this stage the emphasis is on quantity, not quality. Analysis and quality-control will follow, after the session has ended. Later, the recorded discussion is transcribed into a verbatim report which is carefully scrutinized by the brainstorming group or a subgroup for possible leads. The most promising ideas are picked out and developed.

Approaches to problem solving

Some people solve problems systematically, while others solve them intuitively (McKenney and Keen, 1974). While systematic thinkers focus on detail, collect, and analyse all relevant data, intuitive thinkers jump from one approach to another, explore and abandon alternative solutions very quickly until one that feels right emerges. In multicultural teams effective problem-solving often comes from integrating the two styles. This enables the different problem-solving styles of the diverse membership to be deployed with maximum effect.

For instance, a complicated task might be split into discrete work packages which are then allocated to different subgroups. A group of intuitive thinkers, for instance, might work out ideas for improving the public image of the parent company. Simultaneously, a group of systematic thinkers might examine a complicated logistical or resource-allocation task requiring the use of statistical analysis and other quantitative tools.

Systematic problem-solving does not lend itself to open-ended problems that have no correct answer (e.g. how to encourage minority groups to participate in local government). Problems of this kind require 'creative' problem-solving which works by proposing and discarding dozens of ideas in quick succession before a promising idea emerges. With its diverse membership, a multicultural group generates a large number of varied ideas and approaches to a problem, thus increasing the chances of finding the one approach that works.

According to Pelz (1956), optimum problem-solving performance is associated with consulting those who share one's orientation – who support and develop one's ideas – and consulting others who challenge one's views and point out shortcomings. In multicultural teams both kinds of consultation constantly occur because of the wide range of views and approaches represented in a diverse team.

Team v solo

Major breakthroughs in the past have often come from a single genius. But the reality today is that innovations and major breakthroughs usually depend on *teams* of specialists drawn from diverse cultural and ethnic groups – as is the case with multicultural teams.

A diverse team of experts gets better results than a brilliant individual when, for instance, a pooling of ideas increases the chances of successfully solving a problem. On the other hand, a multicultural team may spend too much time examining problems that could be solved much more quickly by an individual problem-solver. The astronomer Johann Kepler spent very little time actually observing stars and planets because of bad eyesight. Instead he studied data accumulated by fellow astronomers. Steiner (1972: 166) notes:

> their observations revealed regularities in the changing character of the firmament. What happened to one star was closely correlated with the movement of another, or with the successive locations of the sun or moon. After lengthy examination of recurrent patterns in the data, Kepler announced his discovery of the solar system.

Other outstanding problem-solving loners are Whittle (jet engine) and Sikorsky (helicopter).

National problem-solving styles

Different cultures have their own distinctive approaches to problem-solving. German managers, for instance, often favour a dialectical approach because it enables them to deal with problems systematically. The dialectical approach consists of examining a thesis then stating the other side of the issue as antithesis.

This polarizes the issue and moves the discussion towards options which can then be systematically assessed. Chinese managers, who are used to Marxist dialectical logic, also see the value of examining and comparing opposing ideas during problem-solving discussions.

Vallaster (2005) notes that managers from Asian countries like to circle round and round a problem before heading towards a solution. An Arab businessman reports that he likes to discuss problems in a holistic way, 'to spend some time discussing everything and nothing, to get the feel of my counterpart, his mood and temperament... I do not like the Western reductionist approach that tries to do one thing at a time' (Mattock, 1999: 111).

A no-nonsense approach to problem-solving with no time-wasting appeals to many American managers, with their 'can-do' approach to most management problems. On international project teams American managers sometimes signal their impatience during discussions which systematically looks at various options for solving a problem, because of the potential for time-wasting. Speedy problem-solving saves time. However, it can also produce suboptimal solutions. If the search ends too soon the best solution is never born. In one study solutions were of higher quality when experimental groups were instructed to find a second solution after they thought they had already solved the problem (Hoffman and Maier, 1961).

VIRTUAL TEAMS

How virtual teams operate

Increasingly, virtual teams are being used by large companies to assemble the breadth of knowledge required to carry out large-scale, complex tasks. In the world of international business virtual teams can be quickly assembled and set up in multiple locations – wherever their members already are. Townsend et al. (1998) found that the advantages of virtual teams include flexibility, high productivity, and high work motivation.

The projects carried out by virtual teams exist as activities, not buildings – team members may never meet face-to-face but only on screens. Effective virtual teams communicate intensely by electronic means. They collaborate online and across national boundaries by using emails, video conferences, intranet–internet systems, collaborative software, fax, instant messaging, and other electronic communication methods. Electronic communication is supplemented, where practicable, by occasional face-to-face contact which develops trust and a shared team identity (Martins et al., 2004).

Team identity can be a problem for virtual teams since high cultural diversity tends to make team identity less important to team members than national identity. As staff turnover rates are often high, there may be doubts about how long the team will continue to exist and this further reduces the tendency to identify with the team (Shapiro et al., 2002). A major disadvantage of virtual teams is that they tend to be unstable due to frequent changes in composition.

Efficiency issues

Virtual teams take time to develop into effective units. Effective collaboration in a virtual team can be more difficult to maintain than in conventional team structures, and some virtual teams experience efficiency problems caused by mistaken allocations of roles and responsibilities (Martins et al., 2004). Resources and training provided by the parent organisation may be inadequate, causing further efficiency problems. Cases are on record of members of virtual teams being unable to operate the electronic tools needed to communicate with other members in other countries. *Language* is often a major source of problems since for some members the team's working language may be a foreign language. These individuals may find it difficult to understand and send messages or to participate effectively in virtual meetings.

Management of virtual teams

A team's performance depends on how well it is managed, but how do you manage people you do not see? The answer is through virtual meetings – the main management tool used by virtual team leaders. Virtual meetings are often the only practical way to find out why a particular communication breakdown happened or why a particular deadline was not hit. But virtual meetings can be difficult to organise as differences in time zones make simultaneous contact with members scattered across the globe difficult to achieve.

A constant problem is that the people attending virtual meetings are just electronic images. This leaves room for uncertainty and misunderstanding. It is not easy for the leader or for other speakers to sense whether their words are being listened to and understood. Thus although traditional face-to-face meetings are time- and travel-intensive and very expensive, they should be held from time to time to discuss important issues, or to allow members of the international team to get to know each other. Coutu (2009) points out that even well-structured virtual teams need to have a launch meeting with everyone present, and a live debriefing at the end of the project.

KEY POINTS

1. Multicultural teams bring many advantages to their organisations, including creativity and new approaches to problem-solving. But they also bring problems that spring from cultural difference. The clash of cultures in the team can lead to stereotyping and mutual distrust which reduces cooperation. Communication difficulties can complicate relations between different national subgroups. Other culture-based difficulties are contradictory problem-solving styles, contradictory attitudes towards authority and leadership, and lack of fluency in using the team's working language.
2. Culturally diverse teams tend to be either very effective or very ineffective (as opposed to single-culture teams which are closely centred on average effectiveness). Multicultural teams become very effective when they are given the

resources they need at the right time, a key resource being the team leader. Essential qualities that the team leader must have are the ability to *manage diversity* and *flexibility*. Flexibility is essential because multicultural team leaders must constantly adjust their management style to allow for cultural difference. Japanese team members, for instance, are likely to be positively motivated by *failure feedback* while Canadian members are more likely to be motivated by *success feedback*.

3. Decisive, task-focused leadership is needed in the early stages of the life of a multicultural team as it enables the team to organise itself and become productive. Task-oriented leaders make sure that members are clear about what they are supposed to be doing. They provide clarity and orientation by setting clear goals and priorities, thereby motivating the diverse membership.

4. Conflict in multicultural teams often arises from disagreements about procedures to be followed or from competition among subgroups for limited resources. Such conflicts are task-related and usually not destructive. *Task-based conflict* is focused on judgmental differences about how best to achieve team goals, but *relationship-based conflict* is focused on personal or cultural incompatibilities and its effect is usually negative since it can impair decision quality and lower team effectiveness. Cultural and communication difficulties impede the team's ability to manage relationship-based conflict through open discussion.

5. Some team leaders – project managers on offshore oil installations, for instance – have to make decisions under conditions of great uncertainty and time pressure. The pressures often preclude any orderly effort to generate and evaluate options in the classical manner. When this is the case, a better option is for the managers to use their own judgment and implicit knowledge – their *own* expert opinion which encapsulates experience tried and tested over many years – to make the decision.

6. Members of multicultural teams who come from collectivist countries are usually comfortable using consensus methods of decision-making, as opposed to majority voting or decisions based on expert advice. *Majority voting* has the advantage of being generally accepted as fair, and it is also a relatively quick method. However, it does little or nothing to satisfy the losers, who are likely to look for ways of reversing the decision at some later stage.

7. Different beliefs about the relative value of tasks can lead subgroups on multicultural teams into spending too much time on low-priority tasks. Effective coordination management by the team leader can prevent this happening, and progress meetings provide the means. Regular progress meetings ensure that everybody is kept up to date with progress, and key specialists can report on overspending and other problems that have emerged. A key aspect of coordination management is ensuring that team activities are coordinated with the activities of other teams and other organisations – perhaps by setting up inter-team or inter-organisational committees.

8. Two distinct kinds of diversity that characterize multicultural teams are diversity of cultural background, and job-related diversity. The two kinds of

diversity make different kinds of impact. Diversity of cultural background (e.g. ethnicity or race) often leads to communication difficulties and interpersonal tensions that interfere with creativity and innovative efforts and the achievement of team consensus. But job-related diversity gives the team a variety of different perspectives and approaches that helps it solve the complex task of developing new products or procedures.

QUESTIONS FOR DISCUSSION AND WRITTEN ASSIGNMENTS

1. Cultural differences in multicultural teams may prevent cooperation and collaboration. How can that risk be reduced? What can be done to ensure that the team's goals are shared by all?
2. Identify factors that allow a multicultural team to achieve high levels of performance. Rank the factors in order of importance.
3. What causes different kinds of conflict to erupt in multicultural teams? What effect does conflict have on team performance?

BIBLIOGRAPHY

Adler, NJ. *International Dimensions of Organisational Behaviour*, 2nd ed. PWS-Kent Publishing, 1991.

Amason, AC. Distinguishing the effects of functional and dysfunctional conflict on strategic decision-making: resolving a paradox for top management teams. *Academy of Management Journal*, 39, 1986, 123–148.

Brett, J. Behfar, K. and Kern, MC. *Managing Multicultural Teams. HBR*, November, 2006, 84–91.

RA Cosier and Schwenk, CR. Agreement and thinking alike: ingredients for poor decisions. *Academy of Management Executive*, 4, 1990, 69–74.

Coutu, D. Why teams don't work. *HBR*, May 2009, 99–105.

R Cross and Parker, A. *The Hidden Power of Social Networks*. Harvard Business School Press, 2003.

Delphi Group, Information survey results – white paper, 2006. Delphi Group.

PW Dorfman et al., Leadership in Western and Asian countries. *Leadership Quarterly*, 8, 1997, 233–274.

Drexler, AB. D Sibbet and Forrester, RH. The team performance model. In WB Reddy and K Jamieson (eds), *Teambuilding: Blueprints for Productivity and Satisfaction*. University Associates, 1988, pp. 45–61.

Earley, PC. Social loafing and collectivism. *Administrative Science Quarterly*, 34, 1989, 565–581.

Earley, PC. East meets west meets Mideast: further explorations of collectivistic and individualistic work groups. *Academy of Management Journal*, 36(2), 1993, 319–348.

K Ellis and P Shockley-Zalabak, Trust in top management and immediate supervisor. *Communication Quarterly*, 49 (4), 2001, 382–398.

Fiedler, FE. *A Theory of Leadership Effectiveness*. McGraw-Hill, 1967.

Gibb, JR. Communication and productivity. *Personnel Administration*, January–February 1964.

N Halevy and Sagiv, L. Teams within and across cultures. In PB Smith et al. (eds), *Handbook of Cross-cultural Management Research*. Sage, 2008, pp. 253–268.

Harrison, DA. Price, KH. and Bell, MP. Beyond relational demography: time and the effects of the surface- and deep-level diversity on work group cohesion. *Academy of Management Journal*, 41, 1998, 96–107.

Heine et al., Divergent consequences of success and failure in Japan and North America. *Journal of Personality and Social Psychology*, 81, 2001, 599–615.

Hemp, P. Death by information overload. *HBR*, September, 2009, 83–89.

VB Hinsz et al., The emerging conceptualisation of groups as information processors. *Psychological Bulletin*, 121, 1997, 43–64.

G Hirst et al., A cross-level perspective on employee creativity. *Academy of Management Journal*, 52 (2), 2009, 280–293.

LR Hoffman and Maier, NRF. Quality and acceptance of problem solutions by members of homogeneous and heterogeneous groups. *Journal of Abnormal and Social Psychology*, March, 1961, 401–407.

D Hoopes and Postrel, S. Shared knowledge 'glitches', and product development performance. *Strategic Management Journal*, 20, 1999, 837–865.

UR Hulsheger et al., Team-level predictors of innovation at work: a comprehensive meta-analysis spanning three decades of research. *Journal of Applied Psychology*, 94 (5), 2009, 1128–1145.

SE Jackson and Schuler, RS. Cultural diversity in cross-border alliances. In D Tjosvold and K Leung (eds), *Cross-cultural Management: Foundations and Future*. Ashgate, 2003, p. 138.

Janis, IL. *Victims of Groupthink: A Psychological Study of Foreign-policy Decisions and Fiascos*, 2nd ed. Houghton Mifflin, 1982.

M Javidan and House, RJ. Cultural acumen for the global manager. *Organisational Dynamics*, 29(4), 2001, 289–305.

Jehn, KA. A qualitative analysis of conflict types and dimensions in organisational groups. *Administrative Science Quarterly*, 42, 1997, 530–557.

KA Jehn et al., Why differences make a difference: a field study of diversity, conflict and performance in workgroups. *Administrative Science Quarterly*, 44, 1999, 741–763.

D Kahneman and Klein, G. Conditions for intuitive expertise: a failure to disagree. *American Psychologist*, 64 (6), 2009, 515–526.

JR Katzenbach and Smith, DK. The discipline of teams. *HBR*, July–August, 2005, 162.

GA Klein et al., Rapid decision making on the fireground. In *Proceedings of the Human Factors and Ergonomics Society 30th Annual Meeting* (Vol. 1). 1986, 576–580.

W Latane et al., Many hands make light work. *Journal of Personality and Social Psychology*, 37 (6), 1979, 822–832.

D Leonard and Straus, S. Putting your company's whole brain to work. *Harvard Business Review*, 75, 1997, 110–119.

R Levitt et al., Simulating project work processes and organisations: towards a micro-contingency theory of organisational design. *Management Science*, 45, 1999, 1479–1495.

A Majchrzak et al., Can absence make a team grow stronger? *HBR*, May, 2004, 133.

LL Martins et al., Virtual teams: what do we know and where do we go from here? *Journal of Management*, 30, 2004, 805–835.

T Matsui et al., Effects of goals and feedback on performance in groups. *Journal of Applied Psychology*, 72, 407–415, 1987.

J Mattock (ed.), *International Management: An Essential Guide to Cross-cultural Business*, 2nd ed. Canning, 1999.

AV Matveev and Nelson, PE. Cross cultural communication competence and multicultural team performance. *International Journal of Cross Cultural Management*, 4(2), 2004, 253–270.

JL McKenney and Keen, PGW. How managers' minds work. *Harvard Business Review*, May–June 1974, 79–90.

Meehl, PE. *Clinical vs. Statistical Prediction: A Theoretical Analysis and A Review of the Evidence*. University of Minnesota Press, 1954.

SJ Mezias et al., Toto, I don't think we're in Kansas anymore. *Journal of Management Inquiry*, 8, 1999, 323–336.

IB Myers and Briggs, KC. *The Myers-Briggs Type Indicator*. Educational Testing Service, 1957.

J Nahapiet and Ghosal, S. Social capital, intellectual capital and the organisational advantage. *Academy of Management Review*, 23, 1998, 242–266.

LH Nishii and Mayer, DM. Do inclusive leaders help to reduce turnover in diverse groups? The moderating role of leader-member exchange in the diversity to turnover relationship. *Journal of Applied Psychology*, 94 (6), 2009, 1412–1426.

LL Putnam and Poole, MS. Conflict and negotiation. In FM Jablin et al. (eds), *Handbook of Organisational Communication*. Sage, 1987, pp. 549–599.

I O'Reilly et al., Work group demography, social integration and turnover. *Administrative Science Quarterly*, 34, 1989, 21–37.

Pelz, C. Some social factors related to performance in a research organisation. *Administrative Science Quarterly*, 1, 1956, 310–325.

Pentland, A. How social networks network best. *HBR*, February, 2009, 37.

JT Polzer et al., Capitalising on diversity: interpersonal congruence in small work groups. *Administrative Science Quarterly*, 47 (2), 2002, 296–324.

Prokesch, S. How GE teaches teams to lead change. *HBR*, January, 2009, 99–106.

M Rometsch and Sydow, J. On identities of networks and organisations. In M Kronberger and S Gudergan (eds), *Only Connect: Neat Words, Networks and Identities*. Liber, 2007, pp. 19–47.

Schein, E. *Process Consultation: Its Role in Organisational Development.* Addison Wesley, 1969.

SC Schneider and J-L Barsoux, *Managing Across Cultures.* FT Prentice Hall, 1997, p. 193.

R Scollon and Scollon, SW. *Intercultural Communication: A Discourse Approach,* 2nd ed. Blackwell, 2001.

B Shamir et al., Correlates of charismatic leadership behaviour in military units. *Academy of Management Journal,* 41 (4), 1998, 387–409.

DL Shapiro et al., Transnational teams in the electronic age: are team performance and high performance at risk? *Journal of Organisational Behaviour,* 23, 2002, 455–467.

DS Staples and Zhao, L. The effect of cultural diversity in virtual teams versus face-to-face teams. *Group Decision and Negotiation,* 15, 2006, 389–406.

Steiner, I. *Group Process and Productivity.* Academic Press, 1972, p. 166.

Sull, D. How to thrive in turbulent markets. *HBR,* February, 2009, 78–88.

T Sy et al., The contagious leader: impact of the leader's mood on the mood of group members, group affective tone, and group processes. *Journal of Applied Psychology,* 90, 2005, 295–305.

R Thomas et al., Let's talk about 'us': a reflexive account of a cross cultural research collaboration. *Journal of Management Inquiry,* 18 (4), 2009, 313–324.

Tjosvold, D. The cooperative and competitive goal approach to conflict: accomplishments and challenges. *Applied Psychology,* 47, 1998, 285–313.

A Townsend et al., Virtual teams: technology and the workplace of the future. *Academy of Management Executive,* 12 (3), 1998, 17–29.

Tuckman, BW. Developmental sequence in small groups. *Psychological Bulletin,* 63 (6), 1965, 384–399.

Vallaster, C. Cultural diversity and its impact on social interactive processes. *International Journal of Cross Cultural Management,* 5(2), 2005, 139–163.

GS Van der Vegt et al., Power asymmetry and learning in teams. *Organisation Science,* 21 (2), 2010, 347–361.

GA Van Kleef et al., Searing sentiment or cold calculation? The effects of leader emotional displays on team performance depend on follower epistemic motivation. *Academy of Management Journal,* 52 (3), 2009, 562–580.

VH Vroom and Yetton, PW. Leadership and Decision-making. University of Pittsburgh Press, 1973.

KL Ulrey and Amason, P. Intercultural communication between patients and health care providers. *Health Communication,* 13 (4), 2001, 449–463.

Watson, WE. K Kumar and Michaelson, LK. Cultural diversity's impact on interaction process and performance: comparing homogeneous and diverse task groups. *Academy of Management Journal,* 36, 1993, 590–602.

Yoshino, MT. *Japan's Managerial System: Tradition and Innovation.* MIT Press, 1968, pp. 254–272.

Cross-cultural meetings and negotiations

11

INTRODUCTION

Participants in cross-cultural meetings come from cultures that differ in power–distance, uncertainty–avoidance, collectivism–individualism, and other cultural dimensions. They therefore have conflicting, culturally influenced views about how meetings should be organised, how decisions should be made, the role of the chair, and other basic matters. National styles and preferences come into play and influence the way the meeting is conducted and sometimes the outcome of the meeting.

Cultural characteristics make an impact in cross-cultural meetings. Managers in Western countries are used to planning and organising their meetings, but find that in meetings held in Arab countries social and business matters rub against each other, sometimes in apparently random order. In countries in Asia, Africa, and South America, business is personal and based on relationships. Western business visitors who attend meetings in these countries have to resist the temptation to get straight down to business and, instead, give time to building relationships before, during, and after the meeting.

Cultural characteristics also play an important role in cross-cultural negotiations. That is why cross-cultural negotiations require a different set of skills and knowledge from domestic negotiations. Cross-cultural negotiators need *cultural awareness* so that they can see the world through the eyes of their negotiating partners and thereby gain insight into the likely tactics and negotiating style of the opposing team. Cross-cultural negotiations have to take into account the laws and policies of two or more nations, and these laws and policies are often inconsistent or directly opposed (Salacuse, 2003).

For most Western negotiators a signed contract represents closure of the deal and if the contract is subsequently broken they often adopt an adversarial or legalistic stance. But since the contract signed at the end of negotiations may be governed by two or more legal systems, settling a post-contract dispute through litigation can be a complicated and costly process. That is one of the reasons why collectivist negotiators usually prefer to settle post-negotiation disputes through bargaining and mediation – methods which allow the all-important business relationship with the other party to be preserved (Chen, 1996).

The choice of a working language for cross-cultural negotiations or cross-cultural business meetings creates winners and losers. The winners are native-speakers of the language (often the home-side) who thereby gain power and influence in the meetings. Non-native speakers of the language (often the away-team) are put at a disadvantage. For instance, they have difficulty presenting their ideas and proposals in what for them is a foreign language and may need to resort to interpreters. If interpreters are needed in cross-cultural negotiations they should ideally have the same cultural background as one of the national teams, together with an excellent knowledge of the other teams' cultural values and practices. This level of experience allows the interpreter to communicate a speaker's intended meaning and to set it in an appropriate cultural context.

The advantage of virtual teams is that they can be quickly assembled and established in multiple locations or wherever their members already are. Team members rarely hold face-to-face meetings. Instead they hold *virtual meetings* using intranet–internet systems, videoconferences, and other methods to collaborate online and across national boundaries. Electronic communication is the norm and virtual meetings are the preferred way for virtual teams to communicate (Handy, 1995).

CROSS-CULTURAL MEETINGS

National styles

Reluctance to disagree is a behavioural trait that can cause uncertainty and frustration in everyday cross-cultural social encounters in Japan – and that may prevent clear decisions being made in cross-cultural meetings. Dodson (2002) describes a meeting of American and Japanese technical staff which had been called to decide whether or not to recall defective intercom units. But putting Americans and Japanese in the same room to reach a decision was like mixing oil and water. Stark differences of approach to decision-making were revealed.

> The Americans worked to surpass and defeat one another. The Japanese avoided disagreeing with the other participants. To the Americans, minimising the expense of recall was important. To the Japanese, the welfare of the infants at risk from the soldering flaw in the intercom unit and the livelihoods of employees of the exposed company were foremost.

A striking aspect of the communication was all the . . . pauses . . . . The Japanese just let them happen, but the Americans were irritated by them and wanted to know what the Japanese were thinking. No doubt psychological factors underlay the behaviour (and no doubt culture underpinned the psychology).

As many business visitors to Japan discover, a core Japanese value is to avoid giving offence gratuitously. In cross-cultural business meetings that trait translates into avoiding saying no. An American salesman later disclosed to business colleagues that during a meeting held in Tokyo he asked a Japanese manager if he would be recommending his board to purchase new paint-spraying equipment that the salesman had just demonstrated. The manager smiled and said: 'That sounds like a good idea.' Weeks later the American learned that a possible purchase proposal had not even been put to the board for discussion.

Brazilian meetings

When Arruda and Hickson (1996) sampled 20 English organisations and 20 Brazilian organisations in both the public and private sectors, strong differences in decision-making approaches and the conduct of business meetings emerged. Brazil is a high power–distance and uncertainty–avoidance country, as opposed to England which is a low power–distance and low uncertainty–avoidance culture. Notable cultural features in Brazil include a strong respect for authority, from the old patriarchal family structure, and 'personalism' from a collectivist rural society. (Personalism means relating to others by means of personal knowledge of them rather than in terms of impersonal rules and duties.)

The researchers found that in Brazilian organisations these national cultural features translate into:

- a need for 'strong' leadership in meetings and other formal communication events;
- many rules and regulations;
- emphasis on direct, informal relationships.

Whereas Brazilian meetings are likely to meander onto other subjects and to leave the agenda unfinished, English meetings are much more likely to stick to the point and finish on time. However, in both Brazilian and English organisations informal communication in corridors and offices was the norm – over and above anything that took place in formal meetings.

In both countries the most difficult and complex decisions were over internal reorganisations, mergers, takeovers, because managers making these decisions were aware that the consequences of such decisions are unquantifiable, indefinable. Other decisions – lesser decisions – are less frightening. At one meeting in Brazil, for instance, a confident, president-only decision was taken to launch a retail chain cross-country. But a somewhat comparable decision by an English company – to move away from doorstep distribution to a franchise form of operation – involved numerous meetings and informal discussions which involved the MD, the operations director, the production director, sales director, marketing director and staff, and finance director and staff.

In spite of the differences, Arruda and Hickson (1996) found a common managerialism in both countries, which consisted of moving decisions through an elite coterie of senior managers who talked the issues over again and again, both inside meetings and outside. The researchers conclude that in both Brazilian and English organisations major decisions are taken above the heads of those below, who are mostly unaware of what is being discussed among the elite. In organisations in both countries middle and junior managers tend to be drawn into the decision-making process only for information inputs.

Culturally influenced views

People who take part in cross-cultural meetings come from various cultures around the world, and these cultures differ – in power distance, uncertainty-avoidance, collectivism/individualism, and other aspects of culture. As a result, they usually have conflicting, culturally influenced views about how a business meeting should be organised, how decisions should be made, the role of the chair, and other basic matters. Some national groups, such as Germans, like to have background information and reports relating to particular agenda items ('working papers') distributed before the meeting (Meyer, 1993).

In Eastern countries meetings tend to be very formal from the viewpoint of an American or an Australian, and interactions tend to be impersonal. In Western countries, by contrast, people tend to use a personal style that puts personal identity above status. Communication tends to be informal – partly because status differences are less important than they are in many Asian organisations.

People from large power–distance countries such as India and Russia, for instance, are used to formal meetings with the chair firmly in control. Australians, on the other hand, seem to have an anti-authoritarian stripe that soon cuts a domineering chairperson down to size. The consequence is that when Australian business people sit round the same table as Russians compromises have to be made on both sides. In the same way, compromises have to be made – or at least special procedures have to be negotiated – when Japanese and Scandinavian managers meet, or when Americans meet Chinese.

Establishing procedures

In cross-cultural meetings the chair or the manager who has organised the meeting will need to deal with the diverse membership in an even-handed way, but will also need to initiate a number of basic procedures to control the meeting and prevent the discussion getting blown off-course. A basic level of formal procedure answers many of the initial questions and uncertainties that the participants have, such as what language will be used, who speaks and in what order, and for how long. Such basic guidelines help a culturally diverse group of people, with their varying norms and expectations, to start working together without delay.

Country similarity theory

A wide range of national styles and preferences come into play in cross-cultural meetings. Business people and managers who attend meetings, not just in their own country but in many countries, need to be aware of the communicative characteristics and preferences of participants from other cultures so that they can adjust their own meeting style according to the norms of the country where the meeting takes place.

Business people who wish to acquire this knowledge of the communicative preferences and characteristics of other cultures need not carry out exhaustive and expensive research on a country-by-country basis. There are short-cuts. *Country similarity theory* is one of them. The theory explains that when countries are similar to each other in language, per capita incomes, extent of industrialization, technology, literacy levels, and other important features, people from those countries will tend to react in similar ways (in meetings and elsewhere) to a given argument or appeal (O'Connell, 1997).

Extending the theory, the communicative characteristics and preferences of a given group of countries – the Baltic countries, say, or the countries of southern Africa – are likely to be very similar because the countries in the group resemble each other in numerous other ways. As a result, knowledge derived from personal experience of how meetings are run in one of the countries of a group (in Botswana, for instance) can be applied, with a reasonable level of confidence, in cross-cultural meetings held in other countries of the same group – in South Africa, Namibia, Swaziland, Zimbabwe, Malawi, and Lesotho.

Incompatible approaches to decision-making

In cross-cultural meetings big value-gaps often separate the participants. Differences of approach and expectation among participants who come from different national cultures quickly appear and have to be dealt with. Procedures have to be agreed that will prevent culture-generated conflict erupting and blowing the meeting off-course. Thus an important first step in most cross-cultural business meetings is to agree on the *procedures* that will be used to control the discussion and to make decisions. Agreement on these points will enable participants, with their conflicting norms and expectations, to start working together productively (Figure 11.1).

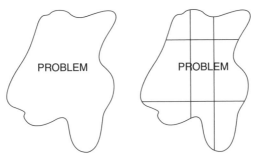

In spite of the cultural and linguistic difficulties, a simple structure can secure systematic coverage of a problem by ensuring that the discussion focuses on one aspect at a time.

Figure 11.1   Structure in cross-cultural meetings

Case study

MINI-CASE: Incompatible approaches to decision-making

Disagreement about decision-making procedures is a feature of many cross-cultural meetings, and incompatible approaches to decision-making emerged as a problem when a British firm acquired a German engineering company.

The new owners asked the German management to develop a new strategic plan and to give this task top priority. However, the Germans were slow to take the numerous decisions needed on production and manpower levels, capital spending plans, and so on.

One reason for the Germans' reluctance was that they were used to making decisions from clear-cut performance targets. But when the Germans asked the new owners to provide targets the Brits responded by advising the Germans to collect their own data and develop their own targets.

A meeting of British and German managers was called to resolve the problem. During the meeting the British team said they could not understand why the Germans wanted all those numbers because what were needed were *fast* decisions. The German team countered by saying that what were needed were *reliable* decisions.

Questions:

1. *Which team was right – and why?*
2. *What kind of compromise solution would have been acceptable to both teams?*

When incompatible approaches to decision-making prevent a cross-cultural meeting making progress the problem can sometimes be overcome by the parties adopting a positive, cooperative stance. The British and German managers attending the meeting might, for instance, have agreed to undertake *joint* data-collection activities.

Culturally determined behaviour

Much of the behaviour observed in cross-cultural meetings is culturally determined. For example, most Americans will confront other participants if they think confrontation is needed to resolve an issue (Keidel, 1996). Chinese participants, like most other Asians, try to avoid confrontational or aggressive behaviour. One study, for instance, found that Chinese, Indian, and Filipino respondents preferred conflict avoidance much more than US respondents (Morris et al., 1998).

In meetings, the Japanese prefer to be good listeners rather than forceful speakers (an approach which helps consensus to be achieved). Japanese participants consider it offensive to press for acceptance of their own ideas and opinions and would much rather use circumlocution and maintain reserve (Stewart, 1985). According to Black and Mendenhall (1993), Japanese delegates avoid conflict because that would mean loss of face for the defeated party. Many foreign business people find that in cross-cultural business meetings Japanese managers consciously maintain harmony by expressing their own ideas in a very restrained manner, or by using circumlocutions. Elashmawi and Harris (1998) note that in some Asian cultures it is common practice in meetings to write down any disagreements with a speaker's argument and to pass it to the chair, or to wait until after the meeting to discuss it.

Maori behaviour in meetings illustrates the impact made by culture. If decisions have to be made, Maoris usually set out to achieve consensus by a process that demands goodwill, patience, and freedom from time constraints – all qualities the Maoris value. Metge (2001) has described the process. First, the Maori delegation pools all the relevant information it possesses. It then identifies a range of different options and scenarios and discusses the advantages, disadvantages, and likely consequences of each of them. As the discussion goes on, individuals group themselves in support of two or three favoured options. But when it becomes obvious that one particular option commands majority support the holders of minority views let go of them and assent to the majority view. The final decision is unanimous.

Size of meeting

The cultural diversity in a cross-cultural business meeting and the clash of views about the procedures to be used can lead to slow progress and cause communication problems. These communication problems are magnified if the meeting is too large. Serious communication and coordination problems can be experienced in large meetings of, say, more than 20 participants. Large meetings generally take much longer than small meetings to reach agreement. They also have to rely on small subgroups or subcommittees to do the detailed work (such as collecting information, drafting statements, planning work schedules, etc.). The link between productivity and size of meeting is shown in Figure 11.2.

A notable feature of very large meetings is that participants tend to address their comments to the chair as opposed to each other, with a consequent loss of pace and spontaneity. Participants in very large meetings sometimes react to what they perceive as being an unfavourable discussion environment by splitting into national subgroups and holding their own unofficial meetings. However, efforts to create a favourable environment for a very large meeting may misfire, as US executives found after arranging a large meeting with a Taiwanese company to discuss a possible joint venture. The Americans thought they had provided the ideal working environment – on board a cruise ship.

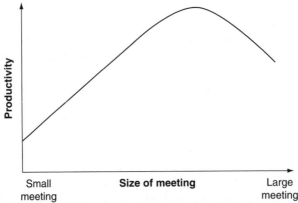

In both cross-cultural and same-culture meetings, size matters. The size of the meeting affects its productivity. At first, as the size of the meeting grows, efficiency grows. But after a certain size has been passed serious 'process' losses occur communication and organisation problems – and productivity dips.

Figure 11.2   Size of meeting and productivity

Security was superb and there were absolutely no distractions. The management teams would be able to really concentrate on the discussions. But after half a day the meetings had to be abandoned because most of the participants were sea-sick.

CULTURAL DIFFERENCES

Factual v expressive cultures

Basic cultural differences affect the interaction and sometimes the outcomes of cross-cultural meetings. Marx (2001) notes the difference between *cool, factual countries* such as Britain, Japan, and China, and *warm, expressive nations* such as Brazil, Italy, and France – the accuracy of the observation is confirmed by the contrasting general ambience of meetings held in these countries. Other basic cultural differences which make an impact in cross-cultural meetings include:

- differences between people from individualist and collectivist societies (e.g. tendencies towards confrontation or conflict–avoidance);
- differences between members of low and high uncertainty–avoidance societies (e.g. differing attitudes regarding the amount of structure and procedure needed in the meeting);
- differences between participants from Eastern and Western societies (e.g. differing attitudes towards attendance times and time required to make decisions);
- differences between members of low power–distance and high power–distance societies (e.g. differences relating to control and hierarchy in the meeting).

In business meetings, participants from collectivist and high power–distance countries are usually very conscious of rank and status. They tend to defer to and side with high-status, powerful individuals, such as the leaders of national delegations. Scollon and Scollon (2001) point out that even if high-status people in the meeting don't contribute to the discussion, their silences are interpreted and participants from high power–distance countries may be reluctant to offer opinions that they feel would be opposed by them. When this 'authority effect' operates it silences low-status participants and leaves the decision-making to those perceived as powerful.

Using a local adviser

When an important meeting is to be held with the representatives of a foreign organisation on the organisation's home ground, participants may need to be briefed about cultural factors which will impinge on the meeting. These include:

- attitudes to time in the culture
- attitudes to relationships
- ideological factors
- typical decision-making methods used in the country

Sometimes a visiting national delegation will make arrangements with a local agent or consultant to act as a cultural adviser. The consultant will be able to advise the visiting team about such aspects as:

- the degree of formality required in meetings;
- methods of decision-making likely to be used;
- whether government officials will have to approve any decisions taken;
- essential points of etiquette that will need to be observed.

Being aware in advance of these and other important cultural features could mean the difference between success and failure in the meeting. Thus Tung (1989) warns that if Western negotiators are ignorant about important Chinese cultural features their negotiations will almost certainly fail.

Differing attitudes to time

Attitudes to time and relationships differ across cultures. In Western countries time spent in business meetings is carefully planned and organised. Decisions are taken with no time wasted. But in South America and much of Asia and Africa business is personal and based on relationships. Thus foreign business people who attend meetings in these countries need to give time to building relationships before, during, and after the meeting. Time spent in informal conversation and small talk at the start of a business meeting in Brazil, for instance, is not time wasted but an opportunity for relationship-building. Western business visitors are used to orderly, agenda-dominated meetings, but they need to resist the urge to get straight down to business in meetings held in a country such as Brazil where building relationships precedes the deal.

International business people are used to attending cross-cultural meetings where little progress seems to be made. In time-oriented cultures such as those of Western Europe and North America meeting times are planned and adhered to. But in cultures with more flexible attitudes to time, starting and finishing times of meetings tend to be approximate. Guirdham (2005) makes the point that participants from cultures with polychronic conceptions of time are likely to process issues simultaneously, to speak simultaneously, with frequent interruptions. They start and end meetings at flexible times, do not take lateness personally, and take breaks when they seem appropriate.

Pacing of business negotiations

In Arab countries, social and business matters often rub against each other in apparently random order. That was the experience of a US export manager who held a meeting with an Egyptian purchasing officer in Cairo (Figure 11.3).

After a late start the two men got down to business, but after ten minutes somebody walked in and began to talk about football. Ten minutes later the man left. But somebody else came in after fifteen minutes and complained about the price of vegetables. The meeting, which should have taken half an hour to complete, lasted two hours.

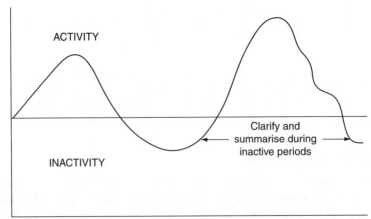

All meetings, whether same-culture or cross-cultural, pass through stages of activity and inactivity in a kind of natural rhythm. The inactive periods provide opportunities for clarifying and summarising.

Figure 11.3   Levels of activity in cross-cultural meetings

Case study

MINI-CASE: Pacing of business meetings

Cross-cultural meetings often have periods of inactivity where nothing seems to be achieved – or where important decisions are made without proper discussion. One reason is that members of different cultures differ in their attitudes towards time and have different ideas about the importance of time-keeping and correct pacing of business negotiations.

When three senior managers from an Indian manufacturing company made a business trip to the United States they were surprised by how quickly things got done. Business negotiations that would take weeks or months in India took just a few days to complete.

Other major differences became obvious to the managers. As they pointed out to their American counterparts, in India many people are usually involved in making important decisions and business deals take a long time to set up. But US managers seem to make decisions quickly. They don't need to consult their colleagues or even their boss.

Questions:

1. *Why is the pacing of business negotiations in the United States faster than in India? What cultural factors are involved?*
2. *If the Indian managers tried to introduce US-style business methods into their own company when they returned to India, what problems would they run into?*

WHICH LANGUAGE TO USE?

Impact on interaction and outcomes

In cross-cultural meetings, irrespective of the country in which they are held, non-native speakers are disadvantaged. For example, they often have difficulty presenting ideas and proposals in what for them is a foreign language. They often find it mentally exhausting to follow the proceedings by listening to a foreign language – regular breaks are needed to address the problem. Regular summaries of the discussion and paraphrases of important contributions have to be provided by the chair or the senior manager who organised the meeting.

In New Zealand, Maori and Pakeha work together on many committees, councils, and boards. But the Maoris are disadvantages since the meetings are almost always conducted in English. One result, according to Metge (2001), is that Maoris often fail to contribute properly to the meeting, and tend to express their frustration through disruptive and aggressive behaviour. An additional problem for Maoris is that meeting procedures – and procedures more generally – are derived from the Pakeha cultural tradition. New Zealand organisations routinely import Western concepts and processes that are then applied to issues of, say, Maori family relations, discounting those that already function effectively in the Maori community.

A French company which is aware of the problems experienced by non-native speakers in cross-cultural meetings has produced guidelines for its managers requiring them to speak slowly and clearly in meetings and, when somebody else is speaking, to ask for clarification at any point in the proceedings.

Language choice

Cross-cultural meetings

The choice of a working language for a cross-cultural business meeting creates winners and losers. The winners are native-speakers of the language who thereby gain power and influence in the meeting. When English, for instance, is the working language Anglophones tend to dominate the discussion and native-speakers of other languages are forced into a marginal position. In Hong Kong, business meetings are usually conducted in Cantonese. Cantonese-speakers are therefore the winners and native-speakers of other languages are the losers.

International conferences

In the same way, selection of a language to be used at an international conference is a major issue because it influences the numbers attending, the interaction, and the kind of conclusions reached or decisions made. Ideally the choice should be made after consulting participants or their organisations. An ill-considered choice of official language may deter people from attending an international conference or symposium. If the best hydro-geologists in a country are unable to speak or understand Spanish there is little point in them attending an international hydro-geology conference where the working language is Spanish.

At an international conference for anthropologists where official sessions were conducted in English, Japanese delegates felt at a disadvantage because although translations were available in French, German, Spanish, and Russian, they were not available in Japanese. According to some of the participants who attended an international chemistry conference in Toronto, North American scientists dominated proceedings and got their viewpoints accepted largely because of their mastery of English.

Sometimes, discussions in a large international conference are conducted in separate small groups mediated by interpreters. For example, the official language of a Snow Engineering conference held in Switzerland was English, but small-group sessions dealing with local snow themes were held in German and French.

Case study

MINI-CASE: Cross-cultural business meetings

When an American sales manager visits Malaysia, the business meetings he attends are conducted in English. Even so, he finds it difficult to follow the discussion due to:

- *Frequent mispronunciations.* The Malaysians do not speak loudly enough and tend to mispronounce words and to run words together.
- *Frequent misunderstandings.* In one meeting the American interprets a long pause as acceptance of his offer to supply a Malaysian company with spare parts for its car fleet. In fact, the pause signalled rejection of his offer.
- *Comprehension difficulties.* The sales manager sometimes fails to understand points made by Malaysian speakers. In one meeting, for instance, a marketing manager describes methods used to estimate future demand. But the marketer is not fluent in English and does not have the knack of being able to express technical points in layman's language.

The sales manager decides that the best way to deal with these difficulties is to admit that he has them and to ask for understanding from his hosts. The Malaysians respond positively. They begin to speak more clearly and distinctly in meetings, and they make sure that he understands important points – for instance, by repeating a point in different words and giving examples.

The Malaysians point out that the American's own pronunciation and explanations are causing problems for them. This feedback prompts the sales manager to improve his own communication by speaking more deliberately, pausing between points, and using simple words and phrases. In one meeting, after using the phrase 'high-viscosity lubricants' the American notices the Malaysians' puzzled expressions and immediately adds: 'That means "thick oil", by the way.'

Questions:

1. *What rules or procedures would have led to better communication in the meetings and enabled all participants to follow the discussion?*
2. *What would have been the advantages and disadvantages of using an interpreter and conducting the meetings in the Malaysians' own language?*

Use of interpreters

Interpreters who are called into cross-cultural meetings should ideally share the same cultural background as one of the national teams, but should also have a very good knowledge of the other teams' cultural values and practices. This level of experience and understanding allows the interpreter to communicate a speaker's intended meaning to the other participants. If, for example, 'fair play' has to be translated into Russian, the interpreter should be able – from her knowledge of Russian culture – to find a Russian phrase that captures the intended meaning. Interpreters should also be capable of clearing up cross-cultural misunderstandings by providing appropriate explanations, such as: 'The speaker's gesture indicates that she thinks the time allowed is unrealistic.'

In cross-cultural negotiations, the interpreter needs to have a grasp of negotiating procedures and vocabulary as well as a good understanding of commonly used technical terminology for the subject being discussed. In scientific conferences the interpreter's ability to accurately translate technical terms is extremely important. Interpreters need to be briefed in advance on the meeting's purpose, agenda, and any specialized vocabulary that may be used. During the meeting the interpreter should not be expected to work non-stop for long periods as the strain of prolonged concentration can lead to translation errors. Most interpreters say that they find it easier to provide accurate translations when contributors speak clearly and slowly and utter only a few phrases before pausing for the translation to be made.

Sometimes a member of one of the teams will act as interpreter during a cross-cultural meeting. There are, however, risks in using a non-professional interpreter. When a Western team conducted a sociological survey of villages in a rural area of India it needed an interpreter. A member of the Brahmin caste who knew the local language offered to help. But the villagers tended to give answers they thought the Brahmin wanted to hear.

Sometimes the Brahmin puts words in the villagers' mouths and gives the answers he thinks they should have made. Such lapses lead to numerous inaccuracies and the fieldwork has to be suspended until a professional interpreter can be brought in from the city.

VIRTUAL MEETINGS

How virtual meetings work

Many multinational companies set up virtual teams, with members located in various countries around the world, to assemble the breadth of knowledge and skill required to carry out an urgent, complex project. In the world of international business virtual teams can be quickly assembled and established in multiple locations or wherever their members already are. The projects carried out by virtual teams are possible because of advances in computer and telecommunication technology. Team members rarely meet face-to-face and collaborate by using email, intranet–internet systems, collaborative software, videoconferences, e-meeting, fax, instant messaging, and other methods to collaborate online and across national boundaries. Electronic communication is the norm and virtual meetings are the preferred way for virtual teams to communicate (Handy, 1995).

A virtual team's performance depends on how well it is managed. But how do you manage people you do not see? By using virtual meetings. Virtual meetings allow the project manager to organise and monitor the activities of the whole team – although a major disadvantage is that the electronic media used reduces the ability to sense the social presence of the other participants. A speaker is unable to see how others are reacting to her words and so cannot assume that they have understood. Traditional face-to-face meetings may also be needed from time to time to communicate important messages, and to provide opportunities for team members to get to know each other as people, not just as images on a screen.

Involving team members

A multipoint videoconference allows many people to meet at one time but, as Zweifel (2003: 69) notes, the medium can become the message:

> I am in charge. I am running the meeting. I am sending the signals and you are forced to receive them .... This leads to a certain recipient mentality on your part. You might feel that I'm doing it to you.

As the example suggests, one of the main challenges in running virtual meetings is to involve members of the team in what is going on. A way of encouraging involvement is to plan a schedule of virtual meetings after discussing possible dates, times, and topics with team members. The meetings need to be held during the working day of as many members as possible. Team members might be invited to propose agenda items for each meeting, and the role of discussion leader could be rotated. The project manager, however, remains responsible for coordinating or monitoring any actions that are agreed during the meetings. Between meetings the geographically dispersed specialists would continue to communicate with other team members through emails and text messaging.

CROSS-CULTURAL NEGOTIATIONS

Different kinds of negotiation

Negotiation, with its potential for conflict and confrontation, has been defined as 'a discussion among conflicting parties with the aim of reaching agreement about a divergence of interest' (Pruitt, 1998: 470). *Cross-cultural* negotiations bring together negotiating parties from organisations in different countries. Examples of cross-cultural negotiations are:

- international sales negotiations;
- business negotiations between firms in different countries seeking a long-term business relationship;
- negotiations to resolve trade disputes between governments or organisations in different countries;
- joint venture negotiations between firms based in different countries.

In cross-cultural negotiations, cultural differences between the parties increase the complexity of the negotiation process; and when many parties are involved in the negotiations the chances of a successful outcome are greatly reduced.

Two-party and multiparty negotiations

Most research on negotiation has focused on the two-party (dyadic) situation. Yet many cross-cultural negotiations involve multiple parties. Two-party negotiations are relatively easy to plan and conduct. The two sides either reach an agreement or not. But in multiparty negotiations the social dynamics and complexity of the negotiations are dramatically increased. An agreement acceptable to all the parties can take a long time to emerge. In Northern Ireland, for instance, multiparty agreement took decades to take shape.

In most cross-cultural negotiations, cultural differences between the parties increase the complexity of the negotiation process. Moreover, when many parties are involved in the negotiation – as often occurs in complex international negotiations – the likelihood of a successful outcome are greatly reduced. Complex cross-cultural negotiations involving *multiple parties* are central to the functioning of the European Union and are an important means of resolving conflict among the member states. Conflict, in the context of the negotiation process, is 'the interaction of inter-dependent people who perceive opposition of goals, aims, and values, and who see the other party as potentially interfering with the realisation of these goals' (Putnam and Poole, 1987: 552).

Groups participating in multiparty negotiations sometimes try to move things along by holding *talks-within-talks* aimed at forming temporary coalitions with other players. In conducting such talks certain strategies have been found to be more effective than others. For instance, Beest et al. (2008) used a computer-mediated coalition game to show that communicating anger in coalition-seeking talks is a very risky strategy. Other participants form negative impressions of the individuals or groups expressing anger in these talks-within-talks and may punish them by excluding them from any coalition agreement that is made.

Where very large groups or entire communities are involved in an international dispute, *public participation mechanisms* sometimes provide the means for the groups concerned to be involved in negotiations aimed at resolving the dispute. Examples of such mechanisms are advisory committees, public hearings, focus groups, and opinion polls.

Joint venture negotiations

Joint venture negotiations usually include discussions about integration issues, about ways in which employees of the companies concerned could overcome the cultural barriers and learn to live together in a collaborative spirit. Joint venture negotiations can be difficult and protracted because the values and mindsets of any two organisations in different countries inevitably differ from each other, and sometimes the differences are very great. That is why a large US-based company allocates a hundred days following an overseas acquisition for the initial integration exercise to unfold (Ashkenas et al., 1998).

Sometimes, slowness and confusion of decision-making at board level in the two joint venture partners complicate the negotiations. For instance, when initial negotiations to establish an American-Egyptian joint venture were held, differences in priorities erupted. Which products? Which markets? What kind of inter-company communications? On one point, however, there was total agreement: the Americans would supply the technology and most of the capital, the Egyptians would supply labour and knowledge of local markets.

How cross-cultural negotiations differ from domestic negotiations

Cross-cultural negotiations are fundamentally different from domestic negotiations and require a different set of skills and knowledge. A major difference is that, irrespective of where they take place, cross-cultural negotiations have to take into account the laws and policies of two or more nations – and these laws and policies are often inconsistent or even directly opposed (Salacuse, 2003).

Another important difference is that successful cross-cultural negotiators need to be able to see the world through their negotiating partners' eyes. This ability (which involves cultural awareness and cultural empathy) gives an insight into the likely tactics and negotiating style of the opposing team.

Thus cross-cultural negotiators need to do more than simply transfer the tactics and methods that they used successfully at home to the international scene. It is essential for the negotiators to understand *cultural differences* and their likely impact on the negotiation process. Other factors that influence success in cross-cultural negotiations are the same as for domestic negotiations and include:

- preparedness of the negotiators;
- negotiating skills of the negotiators;
- quality of information acquired;
- effective management of the negotiation process.

Unless these conditions are met the negotiations may drag on and on or even break down altogether.

NEGOTIATORS' ATTITUDES

Conduct of negotiations

Kirkbride and Tang (1995) argue that the effective conduct of cross-cultural negotiations depends on the negotiators' ability to

- establish general principles early in the negotiation;
- focus on potential areas of agreement;

- avoid confrontation and expressions of anger;
- give the other party something to take home.

Ideally the negotiation should be conducted with these aims in mind.

Cooperative and competitive negotiators

Managers go into cross-cultural negotiations in either a cooperative or competitive spirit. Managers from organisations in Asian countries, for instance, tend to be *cooperative negotiators* (Chen et al., 2003). This implies that they are willing to share information, to compromise, and to make concessions. In China negotiators are highly trained in the art of gaining and offering concessions to the other side (Chen, 1996).

For Japanese managers a negotiating meeting is a place not for conflict but for compromise, and winning or losing is less important than give and take. March (1988) makes the point that very few Japanese know how to negotiate in the Western sense and that the Japanese instinct is for agreements worked out on the basis of give and take, harmony, and building and maintaining long-term relationships.

Managers from organisations in Western countries, on the other hand, tend to be *competitive negotiators* (Pruitt, 1998). These managers are used to competitive, win–lose situations based on the adversarial model. A tactic used by competitive negotiators is to use threats and bluffs and try to maximize outcomes for their own side regardless of the impact on the opposing side. They may, for instance, perceive a negotiating team's willingness to compromise as a sign of weakness. They tend to blame other people – either on their own team or on the other side's team – when problems arise during negotiation and which may affect the outcomes (Putnam, 1994).

Binding contracts

Negotiators from Western countries tend to see a binding contract as the most important outcome of negotiations, but negotiators from other parts of the world often see things differently. Japanese negotiators, for instance, usually see the goal of negotiations with a foreign company being the establishment of a long-term *relationship* with the company (Salacuse, 2003). Any written contract is seen as merely an expression of that relationship. If the foreign company subsequently insists on close adherence to the terms of the contract, the Japanese are likely to perceive such a stance as an expression of distrust that is damaging to the relationship.

Negotiator's mood

Studies suggest that the mood of the negotiators at the time negotiations take place can affect the outcome of negotiations. For instance, Forgas and Vargas (1998) found that during complex negotiations, people in a positive mood tend to have more ambitious goals, higher expectations, and a more cooperative way of negotiating compared to people in a negative mood, and that this positive mood generally leads to a more successful outcome.

Teams v sole negotiators

Two sales negotiators are about to enter into negotiations with the same large state-owned organisation in a Middle Eastern country. They have identical proposals and packages to offer. However, the ways in which they approach the task are very different.

> The first negotiator knows very little about the culture or the organisation, but he is sure his proposal will speak for itself. The second negotiator makes an effort to learn something about the culture and the organisation – including its approach to negotiation. During the meeting the information he has acquired enables him to show that he understands of the organisation's needs. Subsequently, the second negotiator is awarded the contract. *Where did the first negotiator go wrong?*

Negotiating *teams* often achieve better outcomes than sole negotiators in cross-cultural negotiations – especially when the negotiation is about complex issues. In such cases teams, with their wider knowledge and information-gathering resources, are likely to have a deeper understanding of the issues to be negotiated. Moreover, teams generally take pains to prepare adequately for negotiations and to do the necessary research. As a result, they obtain insights into the other team's goals and negotiating strategies. The research and the knowledge acquired usually help the team to present its case strongly.

Japanese negotiating teams speak from a position of strength which comes from the consensus developed in the Japanese organisation about the topic of the negotiation. The consensus process, with its many variations, is common in Japan and other Asian countries (Sebenius, 2002). 'Nemawashi' in Japanese organisations is the process of checking out an idea informally with all those affected by it before it is formally proposed. Formal proposals from top management then follow. These are discussed by junior managers until a consensus view emerges. The developed proposal then goes up to the next level where it is discussed, developed, and again sent up the line. Managers keep compromising until a consensus is reached.

Achieving consensus in a Japanese organisation takes time. But the payoff is that implementation is swift and decisive. The negotiations themselves are simply an opportunity to win approval for an already thoroughly developed proposal.

Leadership

Negotiating teams generally have a nominated leader whose responsibilities include allocating different roles and tasks among team members. A particular team member might, for instance, be allocated the role of steering the discussion towards the issue of pricing, or towards the issue of delivery times. Often the leader gives *himself* the role of presenting key proposals. Brett et al. (2009) suggest that once roles have been allocated, impromptu role-plays can help the individuals concerned to practise playing their roles and anticipating the likely emotional reactions to their contributions from the other side.

People from the collectivist cultures of Asia and the Middle East tend to leave the bargaining to their team leader. The leader is usually the highest-status, most powerful individual on their team. Laroche (2003) observes that when this powerful individual argues in one direction, that usually ends the discussion as far as the rest of the team is concerned.

NEGOTIATION STRATEGIES

Cultural influence

When they participate in cross-cultural negotiations people are influenced by their cultural norms and much of that influence may be unconscious. Negotiators from different countries have different culturally influenced ways of conducting negotiations. According to Sebenius (2002), US negotiators tend to seek agreement on specifics first then build up towards an overall deal. Negotiators from China, on the other hand, tend to first seek agreement on general principles before later working through the details.

Salacuse (1991) identifies some of the specific ways in which negotiating strategies are influenced by culture:

- Some cross-cultural negotiators – the Chinese, for instance – start from agreement on general principles and thus avoid getting bogged down in avoidable disagreement and conflict.
- Some negotiators try to first win agreement on specific minimum proposals and then slowly build up to a comprehensive agreement.
- Other negotiators prefer to begin with a comprehensive opening proposal then look at particular components of the proposal in detail.
- Japanese negotiators often start the negotiating process with early first offers as a way of beginning the essential process of information sharing.

The way that negotiators *react* to a proposal is also culturally influenced. For example, Western negotiators generally react positively to proposals likely to bring innovation and change. Chinese negotiators, on the other hand, react negatively to such proposals if there is any risk of them causing job losses or social instability (Chen, 1996).

Preparations for negotiation need to take into account known cultural and ideological differences between the parties. As Black (1989) points out, negotiations between business people from different cultures frequently fail because of communication and other problems related to cultural differences.

Ideological differences

Brett (2001) argues that a society's social, political, and economic institutions carry the culture's values in their ideologies. Many business people and international managers find that ideological differences can act as a barrier during negotiations – especially with organisations in culturally 'distant' parts of the world. Ideologies tend to be very resistant to change. Accordingly, before negotiations begin, it is important to be aware of important ideological differences which might emerge during the negotiations. Such differences might include, for instance, strong differences of approach to individual as opposed to collective human rights.

Part of the team's preparation should therefore be to determine:

- how they should deal with any ideological points of conflict that may arise;
- how they should present their own proposals in a way that will be ideologically acceptable to the other side.

Common negotiating strategies

Strategies commonly used in cross-cultural negotiations are:

- hard bargaining;
- soft bargaining;
- distributive bargaining;
- principled negotiation.

Hard bargaining

Hard bargaining is highly competitive and sees victory as the goal. Hard bargainers emphasize results over relationships, distrust the other side, and try to gain negotiating advantage – for instance, by demanding one-sided concessions as the price of agreement. When confronted with soft-bargaining opponents hard-bargaining negotiators usually win, but when confronted with other hard bargainers the result may be the failure of negotiations. That was the outcome when hard bargaining by both sides led to the escalation of conflict about the sacking of three employees of Cathay Pacific Airline. The prolonged dispute cost more than $15 m and caused major disruptions of holiday flights during the busiest season of the year (Brett et al., 2010).

Soft bargaining

Soft bargaining aims to preserve a friendly relationship with the negotiation partner, seeks agreement, and offers concessions easily. This strategy reduces the risk of conflict but increases the possibility of one party exploiting the other. Soft bargainers tend to be open and honest about their goals and to share information, and this leaves them vulnerable to hard bargainers, who usually emerge with a better deal.

Distributive bargaining

Distributive bargaining occurs when there is a fixed pie, a limited resource, and when the goal of negotiation is to determine who gets what. It is zero sum strategy – 'I win so you lose.' *or* 'You win so I lose'. Distributive bargaining is essentially competitive and adversarial since each party tries to do better than the others in the negotiation. Even in multi-issue negotiations there is usually a portion of the issues being discussed that concern the distribution of fixed resources.

Principled negotiation

Principled negotiation (Fisher and Ury, 1983) can be an effective strategy when there are reasonable prospects for an agreement which benefits the different parties. The strategy has become synonymous with the phrase 'Win–Win', originally taken from game theory. The principled negotiation approach is to try to find a mutually beneficial outcome from the negotiations.

Information and strategy

When an American and a South Korean team participated in a training exercise to improve their cross-cultural negotiating skills, neither team had information about the other team's goals (Black and Mendenhall, 1993). As a result, each team misinterpreted the other's negotiating strategy and the negotiations get nowhere. However, when the teams obtained information about each other's goals they were able to make correct deductions about the strategies of the other side and the negotiations made good progress.

As the example suggests, effective negotiation strategy depends largely on information. Information relating to the goals and strategies of the negotiating partners is particularly important. Brett et al. (2001) found that in cross-cultural negotiations between US and Japanese negotiators, both sides had little information about the other party's goals and priorities. The negotiators were therefore unable to use information about goals and priorities to generate joint gains.

The effectiveness of a negotiating strategy depends on the quality of information that underpins it. The most valuable kind of information relates to the issue to be negotiated as well as the other team's negotiation goals and likely strategy. Graham (1983) compared Brazilian, Japanese, and American negotiations and found that in American negotiations the outcome depended on the amount of information that had been exchanged. In Japanese negotiations, pre-negotiation communication was important in establishing relationships and clarifying status differences.

Negotiations are more likely to have a successful outcome if the negotiating parties are flexible and prepared to adjust their negotiating strategies in line with what they know about the goals and culturally influenced preferences of the other side. In the absence of reliable information, negotiators have to infer each other's goals indirectly from the pattern of proposals and counterproposals (Adair et al., 2001).

Negotiations are less likely to be successful if both parties are inflexible and focused on beating the other side. When this is the case, conflict is likely to erupt at an early stage in negotiations. Threats trigger counter-threats, one side walks out of negotiations. This pattern of conflict, once started, is difficult to break out of. Even if agreement is eventually reached it is likely to be very one-sided.

Decision-making methods

The content, duration, and outcomes of cross-cultural negotiations are influenced by the decision-making methods used. People from different cultures use different methods, ranging from top-down decision-making at one end of the spectrum to consensus at the other end, with majority-vote methods coming somewhere in between.

> *Majority voting.* Issues are discussed, proposals are made, and the participants then vote on the proposals and the majority wins. This method of resolving issues has the advantage of being generally accepted as fair and quick. However, it does little or nothing to satisfy the losers, who may later try to build influence and reverse the decision.
>
> *Unanimous decision-making.* In multilateral negotiations agreements sometimes have to be agreed to by all parties. This makes it difficult for any one party to get what they want unless they are willing to grant others their wishes. The approach works well except when opposing parties have irreconcilable and contradictory interests.
>
> *Top-down decision-making.* In high power–distance countries with hierarchical organisational structures key decisions are often made by top managers or, in the case of government agencies, by top-level officials such as mayors, governors, and so on. When agreements stemming from a particular cross-cultural negotiation need to be approved by top-level managers or officials on the other side, the leader of the visiting negotiating team should try to arrange at least one meeting with these top-level individuals to convince them of the merits of the team's proposals.

Government and party influence

Salacuse (1991) points to the frequent involvement of government bureaucracies in some cross-cultural negotiations – notably, those held in China – which can delay an agreement. In negotiations with Chinese companies Communist Party officials often play an influential role (even though the companies themselves may be nominally private organisations). Pye (1986) makes the point that in the early stages of a negotiation, the Chinese stress personal interaction and friendship but when serious negotiation begins the Chinese become highly bureaucratized and require coordination with layers of hierarchical committees and senior officials.

Top-level managers in companies, universities, and other public bodies in China often have close relations with the Communist Party. That is why expatriate managers working in China usually need to establish 'guanxi' (connection) with provincial branches of the Communist Party in order to achieve results. Sebenius (2002: 79) points to 'webs of influence' in Asian countries that are more powerful than the negotiating parties themselves.

> In Japan, it may be the keiretsu – industrial groups that are linked by a web of business ties, lending, and cross-shareholdings. In Germany's financial sector, it might be the insurance giant Allianz. In Italy, it may be a set of powerful families. In Russia, it can be the Russian Mafia and other protection rackets. Outsiders need to understand these webs and factor them into their negotiating approach.

STRUCTURE OF NEGOTIATIONS

Distinct stages

Graham's (1987) model of negotiation shows how cross-cultural negotiations tend to move through several distinct stages:

- relationship-building;
- information exchange;
- persuasion;
- concessions;
- agreement.

Relationship-building

Western negotiators usually want to get down to business as soon as possible. Chinese negotiators, on the other hand, will not seriously consider a business deal with foreigners who do not display the all-important behavioural traits of friendship and trust (Breth and Kaiping, 1988). In negotiations with teams from collectivist countries, building mutual trust and understanding before negotiations begin reduces the risk of later conflict. India is an extremely hierarchical society and this is reflected in authoritarian management styles and the adoption of tough negotiating stances in cross-cultural negotiations. But it is also a country where relationships are placed before business. A foreign negotiating team therefore needs to give sufficient time to relationship-building as an important preliminary stage of negotiation.

Information exchange

Are the negotiating partners cooperative or competitive negotiators? Cautious or risk-taking? What is each person's speciality and status in the team? It is important to acquire such information so that appropriate negotiating strategies can be decided. When negotiating with Japanese firms, preliminary information-exchange may last months or years since in Japanese eyes that is the time it takes to build a trusting relationship (Laroche, 2003).

Persuasion

Glenn et al.'s (1977) analysis of UN Security Council speeches made during disarmament negotiations identified three major styles of persuasion: *rational* (United States), *emotional* (Syrians), and *ideological* (Russians). Some Western negotiators combine the rational and the emotional styles. They throw hard facts on the table at the start of negotiations and use them to persuade the other side to take the desired action. But such an approach can backfire. Chinese negotiators would see it as a crude attempt to force them to take up a position prematurely and become involved in avoidable conflict (Chen, 1996). Chinese negotiators' approach to the persuasion stage of negotiations is to outline *general principles* that the other side finds easy to accept (Pye, 1992).

Concessions

Many negotiators start high then make concessions. The tactic is used with the idea of eliciting counter-concessions from the other side and moving the meeting towards an agreement. Chen (1996) shows that Chinese negotiators use concessions in this way. But culture influences concession patterns. Western negotiators, for instance, usually think in terms of short-term tactical concessions. Western negotiators holding trade talks with officials in countries where the commanding heights of the economy are state-controlled often find that their negotiating partners are not authorized to make concessions.

Agreement

What kind of agreement can a negotiating team make without first obtaining the approval of the parent organisation or the government? The team needs to know the answer to this question so that it can make a realistic estimate of the time required to finalise the agreement. Chinese negotiators, for instance, usually need to coordinate with layers of hierarchical committees and officials before an agreement is authorized (Pye, 1986).

Dispute-resolution methods

For Western negotiators a signed contract represents closure of the deal. If the contract is subsequently breached they tend to adopt an adversarial or legalistic stance. But the contract may be governed by two or more legal systems, and settling post-contract disputes through litigation can be complicated and costly. That explains why the Chinese prefer a letter of intent to a contract at the end of talks. A letter of intent maps out *general principles* of the agreement and leaves plenty of scope for compromise and later adjustment (Joy, 1989).

Members of collectivist cultures usually prefer to settle post-negotiation disputes through bargaining and mediation. The assumption is that trusted intermediaries parties will help both sides to confront the issues more effectively. The Chinese assume that compromise and mediation will reduce animosity between the disputants and preserve the business relationship that has been established (Chen, 1996).

Mediation is a form of third-party intervention in which the mediator helps the parties to negotiate an agreement which they then have the option of accepting or rejecting. Mediation is highly appropriate in situations where parties need to cooperate in future and therefore do not wish to damage the business relationship that already exists. Where this is the case, mediation is preferable to *arbitration*, which relies on coercion.

Other ways of resolving post-negotiation disputes include those described by Tinsley (1998), who identifies differences in the way that Japanese, German, and US managers handle disputes. Japanese managers prefer the dispute to be resolved by higher authority, German managers prefer to use pre-existing procedures, rules and regulations to settle the dispute, while US managers focus on addressing the underlying issue.

MEETING THE CHINESE

Overcoming communication problems

Wide cultural differences make communicating with the Chinese difficult for Western business people. Consider what happened when British consultants were asked by the Asian Development Bank to assess plans for a hydroelectric project designed by Chinese experts. The project would provide water and electric power to the rapidly expanding urban population of the coastal plains area of an Eastern province.

Meetings were held with Chinese technical experts to evaluate the project and assess the organisation set up by the Chinese to operate and maintain the dams, generating stations, and water conveyance systems. Communication was potentially a huge problem since none of the consultants spoke Chinese and the Chinese had difficulty understanding and speaking English. However, both teams were composed of technical experts – engineers, geologists, hydrologists, organisation experts, and so on – with similar qualifications and professional interests. There was thus a common understanding of the issues to be discussed which helped to bridge the communication gap.

Just as important, the Chinese provided a team of highly trained interpreters who attended all meetings between the two sides and made sure that all the information required by the consultants was obtained and translated into English. Each interpreter was competent in at least one technical area and so could understand the concepts and technical terminology used in the meetings. Minutes were produced in Chinese and English within a few hours of each meeting, enabling the two sides to confirm or correct details of any decisions taken.

Influence of ideology

But as the meetings went on clashing ideologies were exposed. In one meeting, for instance, the consultants argued that the high staffing levels proposed by the Chinese for the generating stations would lead to high production costs and high tariffs and so needed to be cut. But the Chinese brought their own values to the meeting. They failed to see how eliminating hundreds of jobs could possibly strengthen the project or help the country.

In another meeting, the consultants asked why people were to be moved out of the inundation area to another area hundreds of miles away without consulting the families concerned. For the consultants the issue was one of fundamental human rights for individuals. But the Chinese stressed the overall needs of society. If society benefited then so did the individual.

Gradually the consultants learned that concepts of individual rights and freedoms are not readily understood in a society where authority is deferred to and the collective good is seen as supreme.

KEY POINTS

1. Participants in cross-cultural meetings come from cultures that differ in power–distance, uncertainty–avoidance, collectivism–individualism, and other cultural dimensions. As a result, they usually have conflicting, culturally influenced views about how the meeting should be organised, how decisions should be made, the role of the chair, and other basic matters. The consequence is that when Australians, say, sit round the same conference table as Russians or Indians or Brazilians, compromises have to be made or special procedures negotiated.

2. Irrespective of where a cross-cultural meeting is held, non-native speakers of the language used for communication will be disadvantaged. They often have difficulty presenting ideas and proposals in what for them is a foreign language. They often find it mentally exhausting to follow the proceedings by listening to a foreign language, and need regular breaks. Regular summaries and paraphrases of important contributions have to be provided by the chair or the senior manager who organised the meeting.

3. Virtual teams can be quickly assembled and established in multiple locations, wherever their members already are, and virtual meetings are the preferred way for virtual teams to communicate. The projects carried out by virtual teams are possible because of advances in computer and telecommunication technology. Team members rarely meet face-to-face and collaborate by using

email, intranet–internet systems, collaborative software, videoconferences, e-meeting, fax, instant messaging, and other methods to collaborate online and across national boundaries. Electronic communication is the norm.

4. Being aware in advance of important cultural disparities between the negotiating teams can mean the difference between success and failure in a cross-cultural negotiation. For instance, when holding negotiations with Chinese organisations Western negotiators who are ignorant about important Chinese cultural features will almost certainly fail to achieve their goals. The help of a local consultant may be needed to give advice about such practical aspects as the degree of formality required in meetings, the likely methods of decision-making, and whether government officials will have to approve any decisions taken.

5. Cross-cultural negotiations are fundamentally different from domestic negotiations and require a different set of skills and knowledge. Irrespective of where they take place, cross-cultural negotiations have to take into account the laws and policies of two or more nations. These laws and policies are often inconsistent or even directly opposed. Another difference is that cross-cultural negotiators need to be able to see the world through their negotiating partners' eyes. This ability requires cultural awareness and cultural empathy, but it gives insight into the likely tactics and negotiating style of the opposing team.

6. Managers go into cross-cultural negotiations in either a cooperative or competitive spirit. Managers from Asian countries tend to be *cooperative negotiators*. This implies that they are willing to share information, to compromise, and to make concessions. Managers from organisations in Western countries, on the other hand, tend to be *competitive negotiators*. These managers are used to competitive, win–lose situations based on the adversarial model. They use threats and bluffs and try to maximise outcomes for their own side regardless of the impact on the opposing side.

7. *Hard bargaining* is highly competitive and sees victory as the goal. Hard bargainers emphasize results over relationships, distrust the other side, and try to gain negotiating advantage. *Soft bargaining* aims to preserve a friendly relationship with the negotiation partner, seeks agreement, and offers concessions easily. *Distributive bargaining* occurs when there is a fixed pie, a limited resource, and when the goal of negotiation is to determine who gets what and is essentially competitive and adversarial since each party tries to do better than the others in the negotiation. *Principled negotiation* can be an effective strategy when there are reasonable prospects for an agreement which benefits the different parties.

8. For Western negotiators a signed contract represents closure of the deal. If the contract is breached they tend to adopt an adversarial or legalistic stance. But the contract may be governed by two or more legal systems, and settling post-contract disputes through litigation can be complicated and costly. Members of collectivist cultures usually prefer to settle post-negotiation disputes through bargaining and mediation. The assumption is

that trusted intermediaries parties will help both sides to confront the issues more effectively.

QUESTIONS FOR DISCUSSION AND WRITTEN ASSIGNMENTS

1. Explain how choosing to use a particular language in preference to another language in a cross-cultural meeting can affect the interaction and the outcomes of the meeting.
2. 'Cross-cultural negotiations are fundamentally different from domestic negotiations.' What are the main differences? Why do they occur?
3. Identify the different stages through which cross-cultural negotiations tend to move. Explain how each stage influences the outcome of negotiations.

BIBLIOGRAPHY

Adair, WL, Okumura, T and Brett, JM. Negotiation behaviour when cultures collide: the United States and Japan. *Journal of Applied Psychology*, 86, 2001, 371–385.

Arruda, CA and Hickson, DJ. Sensitivity to societal culture in managerial decision-making: an Anglo-Brazilian comparison. In P Joynt and M Warner (eds), *Managing Across Cultures: Issues and Perspectives*. International Thomson Business Press, 1996, pp. 179–201.

Ashkenas, RN. et al., Making the real deal: how GE Capital integrates acquisitions. *HBR*, January–February 1998, 165–178.

Beest, IV, Van Kleef, GA and Van Dijk, E. Get angry, get out: The interpersonal effects of anger communication in multiparty negotiation. *Journal of Experimental Social Psychology*, 44, 2008, 993–1002.

Black, JS. Japanese/American negotiations: the Japanese perspective. *Business and Economic Review*, 6 (1), 1989, 27–30.

Black, JS and Mendenhall, M. Resolving conflicts with the Japanese: mission impossible. *Sloan Management Review*, Spring 1993, 49–59.

Breth, R and Kaiping, J. Negotiating the contract. In *A Business Guide to China*. Victoria College Press, 1988, p. 163.

Brett, JM. *Negotiating Globally*. Jossey-Bass, 2001.

Brett, JM et al., Negotiating behaviour when cultures collide: the United States and Japan. *Journal of Applied Psychology*, 86, 2001, 371–385.

Brett, JM et al., How to manage your negotiating team. *HBR*, September 2009, 105–117.

Brett, JM et al., Breaking the bonds of reciprocity in negotiations. *Academy of Management Journal*, 41 (4), 2010, 410–424.

Chen, GOH. *Negotiating with the Chinese*. Dartmouth, 1996, p. 86.

Chen, Y-R, Mannix, EA and Okumura, T. The importance of who you meet: effects of self – versus other – concerns among negotiators in the United States, the People's Republic of China, and Japan. *Journal of Experimental Social Psychology*, 39 (1), 2003, 1–15.

Dodson, WR. Bridging the communication gap. *Training Media Review*, 10 (5), 2002.

Elashmawi, F and Harris, PR. *Multicultural Management 2000: Essential Cultural Insights for Global Business Success*. Gulf Publishing, 1998.

Fisher, R and Ury, W. *Getting to Yes: Negotiating Agreement Without Giving In*. Penguin Books, 1983.

Forgas, JP and Vargas, P. Affect and behaviour inhibition: the mediating role of cognitive processing strategies. *Psychological Inquiry*, 9 (3), 1998, 205–210.

Glenn, ES, Witmeyer, D and Stevenson, KA. Cultural styles of persuasion. *International Journal of Intrercultural Relations*, 1, 1977, 52–66.

Graham, JL. Brazilian, Japanese and American negotiations. *Journal of Internatinal Bus Studies*, 14 (1), 1983, 47–61.

Graham, JL. A theory of interorganisational negotiations. *Research in Marketing*, 9, 1987, 163–183.

Guirdham, M. *Communicating Across Cultures at Work*, 2nd ed. Palgrave Macmillan, 2005.

Handy, C. Trust and the virtual organisation. *HBR*, May–June 1995, 40–50.

Joy, RO. Cultural and procedural difficulties that influence business strategies and operations in the People's R of C. *Advanced Management Journal*, 29, 1989, 31.

Keidel, L. *Conflict or Connection: Interpersonal Relationships in Cross-cultural Settings*. EMIS, 1996.

Kirkbride, PS and Tang, SFY. Negotiation: lessons from behind the bamboo curtain. In T Jackson (ed.), *Cross-cultural Management*, Butterworth-Heinemann, 1995, pp. 292–304.

Laroche, L. *Managing Cultural Diversity in Technical Professions*. Butterworth-Heinemann, 2003.

March, RM. *The Japanese Negotiator: Subtlety and Strategy Beyond Western Logic*. Kodansha International, 1988, p. 15.

Marx, E. *Breaking Thro Cult Shock*. Nicholas Brealey Publishing, London, 2001.

Metge, J. *Korero Tahi Talking Together*. Auckland University Press, 2001.

Meyer, H-D. The cultural gap in long-term international work groups: a German-American case study. *European Management Journal*, 11(1), 1993, 93–101.

Morris et al., Conflict management style: accounting for cross-cultural differences. *Journal of International Business Studies*, 29, 1998, 729–747.

O'Connell, J. (ed.), *The Blackwell Encyclopaedic Dictionary of International Management*. Blackwell, 1997, p. 60.

Pruitt, DG. Social conflict. In DT Gilbert et al. (eds), *Handbook of Social Psychology*, 4th ed. Academic Press, 1998, pp. 470–503.

Putnam, LL. Challenging the assumptions of traditional approaches to negotiation. *Negotiation Journal*, 10, 1994, 337–346.

Putnam, LL and Poole, MS. Conflict and negotiation. In FM Jablin et al. (eds), *Handbook of Organisational Communication*. Sage, 1987, pp. 549–599.

Pye, LW. The China trade: making the deal, *HBR*, 64, 1986, 79.

Pye, LW. *Chinese Negotiating Style: Commercial Approaches and Cultural Principles.* Quorum Books, 1992, p. 101.

Salacuse, J. Making deals in strange places: a beginner's guide to International Business Negotiations. In J William Breslin and Jeffery Z Rubin (eds), *Negotiation Theory and Practice.* The Program on Negotiation at Harvard Law School, Cambridge, 1991, pp. 251–260.

Salacuse, J. *The Global Negotiator.* Palgrave Macmillan, 2003.

Scollon, R and Scollon, SW. *Intercultural Communication: A Discourse Approach,* 2nd ed. Blackwell, 2001.

Sebenius, JK. The hidden challenge of cross-border negotiations. *HBR*, March 2002, 76–85.

Stewart, EC. Culture and decision-making. In WB Gudykunst et al. (eds), *Communication, Culture, and Organisational Processes.* Sage, 1985.

Tinsley, C. Models of conflict resolution in Japanese, German, and American cultures. *Journal of Applied Psychology,* 83 (6), 1998, 316–323.

Tung, RL. A longitudinal study of United States-China business negotiations. *China Business Review,* 1, 1989, 57–71.

Zweifel, TD. *Culture Clash: Managing the Global High-performance Team.* Swiss Consulting Group, 2003.

Cross-cultural interviews and selection

12

INTRODUCTION

A diverse workforce can produce competitive advantage for an organisation. But to reap the benefits, the organisation must first ensure that its selection procedures are fair and efficient. However, selection methods vary – those used in some organisations are less fair and efficient than those used in others. There are more differences than similarities in the selection practices used in countries and organisations around the world. The practices actually used usually depend on the conventions and the legislation requirements of each country (Torrington, 1994).

Selection interviews are widely used in North American, European, and Australian organisations. Chinese organisations, on the other hand, tend to put more emphasis on a candidate's company or educational institution (Huo and Glinow, 1995). In Japan, a candidate's relationships and contacts often outweigh other factors in the selection process. Many French organisations use graphology to assess candidates. In developed countries, however, the selection interview is the most widely used selection tool. A fundamental problem with using interviews for cross-cultural selection is that *cultural differences* between interviewer and interviewee may affect perceptions and lead to negative assessments. Another disadvantage is that interviews often fail to distinguish between poor, average, and strong candidates, and that they are poor at predicting candidates' future job performance (Latham and Finnegan, 1993).

Cross-cultural interviews differ from same-culture interviews in several important ways. In cross-cultural interviews, for instance, interviewer and interviewee may have different, culturally influenced expectations of how the interview should be conducted. Moreover, the practice of stereotyping is common in cross-cultural interviews. Stereotyping has the effect of de-individualizing the interviewee, causing resentment in the interviewee and leading to behavioural distortions.

During the interview, standardized, 'off-the-shelf' psychological tests may be used without considering their relevance and validity to culturally diverse candidates – thereby introducing unintentional discrimination into the selection process. In most cross-cultural interviews the language used is the interviewer's native tongue but the interviewee's second or third language. This can have major repercussions for interviewees who have difficulty presenting their ideas and opinions in what for them is a foreign language.

These are some of the reasons why interviewers may need to expand their repertoire of interviewing techniques to enable them to interview candidates from diverse cultures in a fair and professional manner. For example, interviewers may need to be trained to recognize sources of bias in cross-cultural interviews, and to recognize their own tendency to use the assumptions and standards of their own culture to assess candidates from other cultures.

CROSS-CULTURAL SELECTION

Challenge of a diverse workforce

An American bank which carried out a statistical analysis of past and present employees discovered that employees who stayed a long time with the bank had also spent a long time in previous jobs, and that retention rates for ethnic minorities were higher than for whites (Nalbantian and Szostak, 2004). The bank concluded that the best way to retain skilled staff was to recruit more members of ethnic minorities with a record of employment stability. To implement this strategy, however, the bank would first need to improve its selection procedures to ensure they were free from bias and discrimination.

In many organisations biased selection procedures lead to foreigners and members of minority groups (along with women, the disabled, and the elderly) being turned down for jobs which their qualifications and experience would enable them to do well (Leonard, 2001). Indeed, in the United States employment discrimination is so severe that affirmative action programmes have had to be introduced to counter it. In Britain, the Metropolitan Police has had to introduce positive discrimination to make senior posts more accessible to non-white officers.

Organisations worldwide no longer recruit from a homogeneous labour market but increasingly have to recruit from a multiethnic, multicultural workforce. In the global economy organisations are faced with a highly competitive business environment and so need to use the right selection procedures that ensure that the best candidates are appointed, irrespective of cultural or ethnic background. Not all organisations, however, are successful in developing and implementing bias-free selection procedures.

Employee attitudes

The selection process is crucial for organisations to gather information about the qualifications, skills, and motivations of diverse candidates. The selection process is also important for candidates. Organisations may fail to attract and retain excellent people unless they make a positive impression on the candidates at the time of selection. Snape and Redman (2003) point to the negative impact that real or imagined discrimination at the selection stage has on employee attitudes towards the organisation – and also on long-term individual and organisational performance.

Candidates who are well qualified to do the job may choose to go to another organisation if they perceive the selection process to be inefficient or unfair – a problem with which HR managers in organisations in many countries are familiar. A third of respondents in one survey said they would not even consider applying for a job in companies which did not have policies favouring gender and ethnic diversity (Leonard, 2001). The implication is that selection procedures must be *seen* to be fair, unbiased, and pro-diversity.

A diverse workforce can bring competitive advantage to a company (Richard, 2000). According to proponents of the value-in-diversity hypothesis contact between employees from diverse backgrounds leads to the development of novel and creative solutions to an organisation's work problems (Watson et al., 1993). But to realize such benefits, an organisation must first establish a fair and unbiased selection system. That means that it must train its managers and HR professionals to conduct effective cross-cultural interviews.

Case study

MINI-CASE: What candidates expect

When an international consultancy carried out a survey of multicultural candidates who had been selected for jobs in the United States, and others who had been interviewed for employment in the Thailand plant of a large multinational corporation, over 90 per cent of the candidates in both countries were satisfied with the way the interviews had been conducted.

Among the reasons given by both groups were:

1. Candidates were able to speak most of the time during the interview.
2. They found it easy to talk to the interviewer about their accomplishments and experiences.
3. Candidates were able to present themselves accurately during the interview.
4. The interviewer's questions were easy to understand.
5. Interviewers made candidates feel at ease, and effectively managed the time and pace of the interviews.

In both countries the candidates thought they were fairly treated during the interview and that they were given ample opportunities to present themselves.

Most of the candidates in both countries believed that the information elicited would allow the interviewers to make correct selection decisions.

According to the researchers, features that accounted for the positive impressions gained by candidates across two cultures included:

- the tight focus of the interviews;
- skilled cross-cultural interviewers;
- structured interview format and targeted questions.

Source: DDI (1999)

Questions:

1. *The researchers emphasize the importance of 'skilled cross-cultural interviewers'. What are the essential qualities of a skilled cross-cultural interviewer?*
2. *What are the main features of an effective cross-cultural interview? List the identified features in order of importance.*

Examples of interviewer bias

Shih (2002) investigated employers' racial attitudes when the potential labour pool is multiethnic. Interviews that the researcher held with low-skill employers in Los Angeles convinced her that most of the employers viewed African Americans as unmanageable workers who were likely to resist authority and struggle for better working conditions. But the same employers viewed Latino immigrants as manageable workers who were willing to work hard, accept low-status jobs, and obey authority. With regard to higher-skill jobs, employers favoured candidates with stable job behaviours because they saw that as a way of reducing training costs. Shih's (2002) study underlines the extent to which US employers' subjective impressions sometimes shape selection decisions.

As the example suggests, race and ethnicity are potential sources of bias in cross-cultural interviews – as in society more generally. Numerous misunderstandings and misperceptions based on false assumptions can occur when interviewer and interviewee belong to different racial or ethnic groups. Ridley et al. (1994) gives the example of a minority candidate who is turned down for a job because the manager who interviews him notes the candidate's erratic work history and assumes it is a sign of emotional instability. In fact, the candidate has kept moving from one job to another because of racial discrimination.

Much evidence shows that race is an important marker of cultural difference in cross-cultural interviews and can strongly affect the interaction. For instance, in US social survey interviews with blacks, interviewees suppressed critical or hostile attitudes towards white society when the interviewer was white but expressed more militant attitudes to black interviewers (Schuman and Converse, 2003). When asked to say which entertainers they liked, interviewees mentioned black entertainers much more to black interviewers and white entertainers much more to white interviewers.

Researchers and consultants carrying out cross-cultural surveys sometimes find that only local interviewers who belong to the same ethnic group as the respondents are able to collect reliable data. One reason is that 'ethnic' interviewers can conduct interviews in the interviewees' native tongue so that their questions are perfectly clear to the respondents. Moreover, their intimate knowledge of the respondents' ethnic group and the group's values enables them to understand the interviewee's answers and place them in an unbiased cultural context.

Other types of interviewer bias

Gender stereotype bias occurs in both same-culture and cross-cultural interviews. Rumbelow (2003) found that both men and women candidates were penalized if they failed to conform to gender stereotypes held by the interviewer. Focusing on achievements and successes was very important in assessing men but almost ignored in assessing women.

Other common forms of bias are *similarity bias* and *first impression bias*. When Fernandez-Araoz et al. (2009) surveyed 50 CEOs of global companies and executive search consultants they found that many interviewers are subject to various types of psychological bias including the tendency to show a preference for candidates who resemble themselves in some way – such as dressing in a similar way or expressing similar opinions. Earley and Mosakowski (2004) found that interviewees adopting some of the interviewer's nonverbal mannerisms are more likely to be positively assessed.

'First-impression' bias occurs when, within minutes or even seconds, the interviewer reaches a conclusion, pro or con, about the candidate (Fernandez-Araoz et al., 2009). The interviewer then spends the rest of the interview seeking confirmatory evidence for the biased judgment.

Examples of candidate bias

In cross-cultural interviews poor selection decisions may also be made as a result of unreliable assessments stemming from *candidate* bias, stemming mainly from the candidates' distorted or manipulative behaviour during the interview. Examples of candidate bias are:

- social desirability bias;
- courtesy bias;
- reticence bias.

Social desirability bias

Social desirability distortion occurs frequently in cross-cultural interviews. It occurs as a result of interviewees being determined to present themselves in a socially desirable manner (Verardi et al., 2010; Zerbe and Paulhus, 1987). How successful they are depends on their familiarity with the social desirability norms of the country in which the interview takes place.

People from China and most other collectivist societies have a strong need for social approval (Ho, 1993). In an interview this tendency may lead candidates from China and collectivist societies to consciously or unconsciously seek approval – for instance, by agreeing enthusiastically with every comment made by the interviewer.

Courtesy bias

Courtesy distortion is caused when interviewees give only answers that they think the interviewer wants to hear. This leads to unreliable information being collected and an inaccurate assessment of the candidate being made. A way of dealing with courtesy distortion is for interviewers to formulate their questions carefully so that they do not reveal the interviewers' own preferences (Brislin et al., 1973).

Reticence bias

In many Arabic and Asian countries people are expected to be conformist, respectful, and obedient to authority. Arguing with teachers or other authority figures, for instance, is generally not acceptable and forceful expressions of personal opinions and talking about personal achievements are strongly discouraged (Dwairy, 1998). As a result, people brought up in these countries tend to use speech forms expressing uncertainty or modesty – 'I suppose', 'possibly', 'perhaps', and so on (Kress, 1988).

Because of these cultural influences, in job interviews candidates from these countries may make little attempt to demonstrate communication ability or to talk about their accomplishments. Yet this is precisely the kind of behaviour that Western-trained interviewers are looking for.

Unless cross-cultural interviewers are trained to recognize this kind of distorted behaviour candidates may be perceived as being unable to communicate and lacking enthusiasm, and an unfavourable assessment may follow. Impressions of reticence and passivity are particularly likely to be given by female candidates from these cultures. The culturally derived deadpan expression of female interviewees from countries in the Middle East is easily mistaken for lack of interest in the job.

Is the interview a reliable selection tool?

In many countries interviews are the most widely used selection tool (Graves and Karren, 1996). But they are not necessarily the most reliable selection tool. Research findings show, for instance, that interviews are poor at predicting future job performance and often fail to distinguish between poor, average, and strong candidates (Latham and Finnegan, 1993). Anecdotal evidence suggests that many cross-cultural interviewers tend to either overemphasize or underemphasize the importance of a candidate's academic qualifications. When this happens the *best* candidate for a particular job may be turned down.

Employers who have learned through experience that higher degrees don't guarantee skills prefer to hire for attitude then train for skills which will meet the precise needs of the organisation.

Some organisations give less time to assessing the candidate's qualifications than to discovering how the candidate has applied his qualifications in recent projects. A typical approach is for HR staff to make use of a critical-incident technique or a group problem-solving exercise to seek evidence of the candidate's potential for collaborative behaviour in the organisation. According to Cross and Parker (2003), candidate profiles assembled by HR staff in some organisations include each person's three to five most recent projects and the names of the people they had worked with on the projects. This information allows the HR department to contact those listed by the person in order to find out more about how the person performed.

Research by Hubbard et al. (2007) found that not all companies that use selection interviews select the *best* candidate. Successful companies in Australia, for instance, often recruit people who believe in the company's 'mission' – whose values and attitudes fit the company's view of itself – and these people are not necessarily the strongest candidates.

Case study

MINI-CASE: Bias in cross-cultural interviews

Biased cross-cultural interviews can lead to candidates being turned down for jobs which their qualifications and experience would enable them to do well. Consider, for instance, the case of Ibrahim, a 27-year old Egyptian engineer who is interviewed in the same week by two manufacturing companies in Toronto.

The interviewer in the first company notes Ibrahim's strong production experience but suspects that a degree from an Egyptian university is worth less than a Canadian degree. He also notes Ibrahim's foreign accent and unassertive manner and feels that the Egyptian might not get on with other members of the production department. At the end of the interview Ibrahim is turned down for the job.

The interviewer in the second company spends much time discussing Ibrahim's current projects. He is impressed by Ibrahim's positive attitude and thinks he could make a valuable contribution to the company's core competencies. At the end of the interview he offers Ibrahim the job.

Three years later Ibrahim is appointed to a senior management post in the production department.

Questions:

1. *Is the first interviewer right to be concerned about the candidate's qualifications and possible communication problems with colleagues?*
2. *Is the second interviewer right in giving most of the time to discussing Ibrahim's current projects? What are the advantages and disadvantages of adopting this approach?*

Cultural complications

The use of interviews as the principal selection tool can sometimes lead to inaccurate assessments of the candidate. This is the case especially when the interviewer is unconsciously operating from a culturally biased framework. All interviews occur in a particular cultural context; and during cross-cultural interviews the differing cultural backgrounds of interviewer and interviewee greatly influence the interview process, causing entanglements in the interviewer/interviewee relationship and the risk of mutual misunderstanding.

Nonverbal communication

For example, nonverbal behaviours that are often misinterpreted in cross-cultural interviews include gaze behaviour, body posture, and handshake. Western interviewers, for instance, usually approve of a firm handshake at the start of the interview (Stewart et al., 2008). In Western cultures a firm handshake is believed to communicate sociability, friendliness, and dominance, while a less firm handshake (which is common in some Asian and other cultures) is believed to be a sign of introversion, shyness, and neuroticism (Chaplin et al., 2000). From the point of view of a Western interviewer, a *desirable* handshake is a firm and complete grip, vigorous shaking for lasting duration, and eye contact while hands are clasped (Chaplin et al., 2000). Other culturally influenced nonverbal behaviours, such as dress, hair style, smiling, and posture, also influence the way that interviewees are assessed.

Stereotyping

Stereotyping, which frequently occurs in cross-cultural interviews, is a form of unfair treatment that de-individualizes the interviewee and causes resentment (Pedersen et al., 1996). Another kind of unfair treatment associated with cross-cultural interviews is not giving equal amounts of time and attention to interviewees from all ethnic groups. In one study, for instance, white interviewers spent less time, and were less friendly, less outgoing, and more reserved with black candidates than with white candidates (Word et al., 1974).

Group pressures

Individuals in collectivist cultures sometimes give one kind of answer in individual interviews and another kind of answer in group interviews as a result of group pressures coming into play. Consultants and researchers conducting surveys in collectivist countries sometimes arrange for two kinds of interview to collect the required information – individual and group interviews – so that they can compare the two streams of information and identify contradictory answers. These disparities are investigated and, if necessary, eliminated so that the survey findings are not thrown into doubt.

Case study

MINI-CASE: Microfinance application

Poor assessments are made when interviewers use the assumptions and standards of their own culture to assess interviewees from other cultures. This was the case when an Indian business woman who had prepared an excellent proposal for microfinance was turned down by the NGO concerned.

The expatriate manager who conducted the interview recommended that her application should be refused because he was not impressed by her interview performance. But the real reason why the application was unsuccessful may have been that the expatriate manager was insensitive to the communicative expectations of the applicant.

In Indian culture, establishing a personal relationship precedes any business agreement. But the interviewer failed to take into account the cultural context and, during the interview, immediately started to fire questions at the woman. As a result, the woman felt tense and uncomfortable throughout the interview and this was reflected in her rambling and disorganised answers.

Questions:

1. *Why was the woman's application unsuccessful?*
2. *How should the manager have conducted the interview?*

Selection methods used internationally

In Chinese organisations interviews are rarely used – the organisation assesses candidates on the basis of the company or educational institution from which they come (Huo and Glinow, 1995). 'Guanxi' (connections) is also important in China. This brings an element of gender discrimination into play since in China men are more likely to have the right connections (Santoro, 1988).

In Japan, too, a candidate's relationships and contacts often outweigh other factors in the selection process. French companies, often use graphology to assess candidates. British companies tend to put emphasis on references and psychological tests (Shackleton and Newell, 1991). Doubts about the reliability of the interview as a selection tool help to explain why some organisations in Britain prefer to use *assessment centres*. Job offers to private sector posts in Algeria are often based on prior acquaintance or recommendation by a friend (Mellahi and Wood, 2003).

As these examples demonstrate, selection methods vary internationally – indeed, a study carried out in ten countries found more differences than similarities in the selection practices used (Huo et al., 2002). The selection methods used depend largely on the conventions and legislation requirements of the country in which recruitment takes place (Torrington, 1994). In Greece, questions are often asked about family background and origins and marriage – questions which would be technically illegal elsewhere in the European community.

BIAS-REDUCTION STRATEGIES

Structured interview format

The risk of bias in cross-cultural interviews – a constant problem – can be reduced by using a structured interview format. Ryan and Ployhart (2000) found that structured interviews tend to be lower on bias and subjectivity and better at predicting job performance than unstructured interviews. Foreigners and candidates from minority groups have been found to have higher perceptions of the fairness of the selection process when interviews are structured and all questions are job-related (Campion et al., 1997). Moreover, the practice of using structured interviews and job-related questions helps firms to defend themselves against charges of employment discrimination and to win litigation cases.

When managers from a UK utility and from companies in Malaysia, Singapore, and Thailand were asked to rate selection interviews they had conducted, the great majority of both UK and Asian managers thought that a *structured interview format* and *planned questions* helped them to conduct effective interviews (DDI, 1999). A majority of both UK and Asian managers agreed that reaching *consensus decisions* regarding candidates was another helpful component of the interview process.

An important advantage of using structured interviews is that they give greater consistency from interview to interview by producing comparable information from candidate to candidate. Structure can also reduce the risk of bias by standardizing the selection process.

Some organisations attempt to reduce the risk of bias and freak decisions by *diversifying the interview panel*. Others use a combination of methods and rely on a range of selection tools – as opposed to over-relying on the selection interview.

Counselling interviews

However, the positive effect of structuring the interview depends largely on the type of interview. *Counselling interviews,* for example, are more effective when an unstructured format is used. Several decades ago, Western Electric's supervisors used to hold structured counselling interviews with the multicultural workforce to collect their views on working conditions and training effectiveness, but problems arose including insincerity and irrelevant answers. But when the format was changed and unstructured interviews were used, employees were able to talk freely on topics of their own choosing, so that supervisors had to really *listen*. As a result, supervisors became less dogmatic in their ideas, better able to take account of employees' feelings, and their relations with the workforce improved.

Ridley and Lingle (1996) point out that people in some Asian and African countries prefer *directive* counselling interviews and respond positively to 'hands-on', directive counselling approaches. In the United States, too, a preference for directive counselling has been found among Asian American, Japanese American, Native Americans, and black students. Clearly, interviewers need to take these realities into account when conducting counselling interviews with a person from another culture.

Effective counselling depends on taking the *cultural* realities into account. For instance, when a Bangladeshi couple in Bangladesh who were experiencing sexual problems were interviewed by a Western-trained counsellor, they duly arrived with a baby, a grandmother, two uncles, and an aunt.

> During the initial session all the family joined in the discussion. Subsequently, the family helped the couple to solve their problem by providing them with time, privacy and babysitting.

The way in which the couple's problems were dealt with was successful because it reflected Bangladeshi cultural values. The same approach would not work in Australia or Europe or North America, because in those countries the methods used would seem strange or outlandish.

Culturally appropriate psychological and IQ tests

Many multicultural organisations in developed countries use intelligence and psychological tests in recruitment because they wish to provide a fair and objective basis for making selection decisions. However, the practice can have the opposite effect and introduce unintentional bias and discrimination into the recruitment process. This is more likely to be the result when tests developed in Western countries are used without considering their relevance and validity to candidates from other cultural and ethnic backgrounds (Irvine, 1970).

Arguably, psychological and intelligence tests should be included in cross-cultural selection only if the tests take into account aspects of mental functioning considered to be of central importance in the interviewee's own culture. Many authors have warned of the dangers of using assessment instruments that were developed in Western countries with members of other cultures, whose basic assumptions and values are very different from those of the test originators (Verardi, 2010).

Each culture encourages certain abilities and ways of thinking and ignores or represses others. Some collectivist cultures, for instance, stress cooperation and group problem solving, and members of these cultures have long been known to do badly in standardized intelligence and psychological tests which have been developed in Western countries. In a classic study, for instance, very few African mineworkers could understand pictures of their own huts, and none was able to interpret a photograph taken during an assembly task (Biesheuvel, 1969).

Language difficulties

When interviews are conducted in what for the interviewees is a foreign language, candidates may be unable to express themselves clearly or even be unable to understand the interviewer's questions. The interviewer may unintentionally use jargon, acronyms, abbreviations, and idioms of his own language that the interviewee does not fully understand. Candidates may have difficulty talking about certain topics. For instance, the discussion of emotional issues flows much more easily when interviewees are able to use their own native language (D'Ardenne and Mahtan, 1989).

Interviewees may find it mentally exhausting to use a foreign language throughout the interview, and may have difficulty manipulating ideas or presenting arguments using the language of the interviewer, thus increasing the probability of an unfavourable assessment. Thus wherever possible the candidate's own native language should be the language used. If this is not possible, interviewers with a good knowledge of the candidate's culture should conduct the interview so that they can ask culturally appropriate questions and place the answers in an appropriate cultural context.

In cases of serious language difficulty it may be necessary to use an *interpreter* during the interview, although, according to Leigh (1998), doing so transforms the interview group into a triad in which a pairing may develop, leaving one person an outsider.

Choosing one language in preference to another language can make a great impact on the way that participants behave and feel in cross-cultural interviews. When 16 Japanese women living in England were asked if they preferred to be interviewed in English or Japanese all but four of the women opted for English (Burton, 2003). The reason for their preference was that Japanese is a gendered language – male speech is authoritative, female speech is soft and polite. Several of the women thought that if Japanese was used they would be pinned down by its linguistic and cultural values, forced to play a role. In the event, the women who opted to use Japanese during the interview were found to be self-critical and pessimistic. Those who opted to use English, on the other hand, were self-confident and optimistic.

Paralinguistic aspects

Speaking the same language does not mean sharing the same culture. This became apparent when Elias, a Zimbabwean technician, applied for a job in London. The English interviewer used stress as an indirect way of asking for information about former jobs: 'I see you worked for a couple of years in *South Africa* …'

> However, the interviewer's intentions were not clear to the Zimbabwean because in Shona, his native language, stress and intonation are used differently from the way they are used in English. As a result Elias looked puzzled, stayed silent, and was turned down for the job.

The example illustrates how people from different cultural groups are often insensitive to paralinguistic information contained in each others' speech. Bennett (1998: 18) makes the point that blacks in the United States often misinterpret the paralinguistic signals contained in white speech. They may, for instance, fail to correctly interpret 'the fighting cue of "intensity" in the tone of white male talk'.

In same-culture interviews paralinguistic aspects of speech – tone, pitch, pace, rhythm, volume, voice quality – provide a steady stream of clues about the person's meanings and emotional state. Since the participants come from the same cultural background they know which stresses and intonations go with which words. However, when interviewer and interviewee come from different cultural backgrounds such clues are often misinterpreted. Speaking the same language does not mean sharing the same culture.

CULTURAL CLASHES

Stylistic mismatches

Interviewers, like interviewees, tend to use approaches to interviewing that they have learned and practised in their own cultures. Finnish interviewers, for instance, typically use silence to encourage interviewees to take their time and expand their answers. White North American interviewers tend to use an informal, chatty approach as a way of breaking the ice and building rapport at the start of an interview:

> Hi, Phil!
> Hello.
> Have a seat.
> Thanks.
> You got the information pack?
> Yes, here it is.

When interviewer and interviewee come from the same culture this approach works well and rapport is quickly established. But interviewees who come from other cultures may respond in unexpected ways. A Japanese candidate, for instance, would be unsure how to respond to the interviewer's friendly, informal approach since in Japan interviews are very formal and conducted in a range of elaborate, formal styles (Ho, 1993). An African American would also be unhappy with the first-name approach taken by the interviewer – Leigh (1998) points out that African Americans tend to be sensitive about strangers' using their first names.

In the United States a stylistic gap between blacks and whites in interviews has been noted which leads to whites tending to understate their abilities and achievements and blacks tending to overstate theirs (Kochman, 1998). Keidel (1996) describes the stylistic mismatch that occurs when an American communicates with a Finn. When the American asks, 'How are you?' the Finn launches into a five-minute explanation of how he feels – and then expects the American to reciprocate. The American, however, needs a question to trigger a response and the Finn fails to produce one. The American puts an end to the embarrassing silence by asking another question.... And so it goes on. The stylistic gap between the two national cultures remains unbridged. Communication stalls. The discussion stutters to an end.

INTERVIEWER TRAINING

Benefits of cross-cultural training

Interviewers usually have to be trained in cross-cultural interviewing skills in order to get the best out of interviewees whose cultural background differs from their own. Having a good understanding of candidates' cultural values and behaviours helps recruiters to make informed selection decisions. Cross-cultural interviewing programmes equip interviewers with the knowledge, flexibility, and competences required to carry out effective cross-cultural interviews. Ridley and Lingle (1996) found that only a minority of managers and professional selection staff had been trained in the specialized skills required for effective and unbiased cross-cultural selection interviews.

Appropriate cross-cultural training develops the competences required for effective cross-cultural interviewing by:

- adjusting and expanding existing interviewing skills;
- increasing the interviewer's ability to deal with cultural idiosyncrasies;
- increasing the ability to recognize unintentional stereotyping by the interviewer;
- developing cultural empathy;
- coaching and feedback.

Adjusting and expanding existing interviewing skills

A single set of standard interviewing techniques often proves to be inadequate for interviewing people from diverse cultures and may need to be expanded. In traditional interviewing practice, for instance, it is widely accepted that the more two-way interaction that occurs in the interview – the more the interviewee speaks freely and openly – the higher the quality of the information produced (Collins, 2003). Thus virtually all interviewers are trained to use a range of standard techniques to draw out the interviewee.

However, as Draguns (1996) points out, standard techniques for encouraging the candidate to talk – open questions, reflecting, non-judgmental responses, and so on – do not always work with interviewees from other cultures. For example, some candidates may have been raised in restrictive, authoritarian cultures, where people tend to be very guarded in the opinions they utter. In some Asian cultures job interviews are less about self-disclosure than relatively formal situations of *pleading* (Gumperz, 1996), and candidates from such cultures may not respond to the efforts of the interviewer to draw them out because they are simply waiting to be informed about what is required in the job. Cross-cultural interviewers need to be sensitive to such tendencies.

Interviewers need to be trained to deal with such behaviours as courtesy distortion and reticence distortion. An example of *reticence distortion*, for example, is an Asian candidate failing to talk about his personal achievements, or keeping silent for long periods during an interview. An untrained interviewer would be unsure how to interpret the behaviour and might make a biased assessment as a result.

In order to deal with *courtesy distortion*, interviewers have to be trained to ask questions which will not reveal their own views to the interviewee. For instance, the interviewer could ask questions in such a way as to force a choice between statements that are equally weighted for social desirability, such as: 'A lot of respectable people feel that such a decision would be wrong. On the other hand, many responsible citizens think the exact opposite. What do you think?'

Ability to deal with cultural idiosyncrasies

A researcher observed 30 cross-cultural job interviews in large Danish companies and noted that only one of the interviewers had been trained in cross-cultural communication techniques (Jensen, 2003). This one individual was able to deal competently with cultural differences and idiosyncrasies exhibited by the interviewees. The untrained interviewers, however, encountered important communication and other problems. For instance, an untrained interviewer began an interview with a Chinese woman by saying lightly, in a conversational tone: 'I don't know what you know about the organisation?' This was intended as a light, ice-breaking remark, but the Chinese woman misunderstood the interviewer's intention and started to tell the interviewer everything she knew about the organisation.

The way that candidates present themselves or react in cross-cultural interviews often reflects the approach to interviews taken in their home countries. Thus men who come from countries where it is considered inappropriate for interviews to be conducted by women often become embarrassed and tongue-tied when faced with a female interviewer (Saville-Troike, 1982).

Indian candidates tend to stress their qualifications in interviews because in India academic qualifications are very important. American candidates are usually very willing to talk about their personal achievements since the United States is an achievement culture. People from the Middle East, on the other hand, are generally reluctant to talk about their personal achievements because that would go against their cultural values. Guirdham (2005) refers to an Asian woman who collapsed in tears during a job interview, said her father would not approve of her pushing for career advancement, and said she could not go through with the interview.

Cross-cultural interviewers need the ability to recognize such cultural influences. More specifically, they need to be able to accurately interpret the verbal and nonverbal communication of candidates who come from diverse cultural backgrounds – which points to the need for specialized training. Some of the specialized skills required can be developed by studying videos of actual cross-cultural interviews. These generally reveal how easily misunderstandings and misinterpretations occur in cross-cultural interviews. For instance, candidates may not understand what is intended by the interviewer's questions and for that reason give clumsy or irrelevant answers. In many cases it becomes clear that the interviewer has not recognized the extent to which the candidate's disjointed or irrelevant answers are culturally influenced. As a result the interviewer forms a negative impression of the candidate. As Briggs (2002) points out, most interviewers are looking for well formed and coherent answers and when such answers are not forthcoming are liable to make a negative assessment.

The heightened awareness that is gained from observing and discussing videos of actual cross-cultural interviews provides a base for developing practical interview strategies which can be used to avoid misinterpretations and misunderstandings during cross-cultural interviews subsequently conducted by the trainees.

Increasing the ability to recognize unintentional stereotyping

Another reason why videos of actual cross-cultural interviews are used is that they can be used to reveal unintentional stereotyping and bias by interviewers. Trainees learn how a candidates' nonverbal communication can lead to a biased assessment. For instance, non-Chinese interviewers are liable to interpret the general avoidance of eye contact by Chinese candidates as a sign of untrustworthiness, whereas the Chinese themselves consider a general lack of eye contact to be a social courtesy (Joy, 1989). In interviews, African Americans tend to keep eye contact while speaking but not while listening – the reverse of the pattern typical of whites (Dana, 2000). Blacks tend to give listening responses in the 'black cultural' manner of slight, unaccented nods. According to Erickson and Shultz (1982), white interviewers often misinterpret such responses as indicating lack of attention or lack of comprehension and make a negative assessment. In all these cases, learning comes from discussing the attitudes and thinking underlying the responses of the interviewer to the candidate's answers and behaviour.

Attitude training

Attitude training is an important component of cross-cultural interview courses, the aim being to encourage interviewers to understand the perspective of foreigners and minority-group candidates who may present themselves unfavourably in interviews. Participants in one training course were told by an HR manager:

> If you interview somebody for a pipelayer's job and he's got dreadlocks and tatoos and aggressive speech, you shouldn't let your own prejudices get in the way of a rational recruitment decision.

Dublin City Council arranges multicultural training for members of interview boards with the aim of eliminating bias from interviews. The training encourages interviewers take a multicultural perspective in interviews without using the behaviour of white middle class society as the yardstick against which people from other cultures are evaluated. To increase the likelihood that interview boards will treat candidates fairly, irrespective of cultural origin, the Council supplies them with interviewees' career history and qualifications but not with their nationality, age, or religion.

Developing cultural empathy

Empathy is the highest form of communication competence since it enables a person to sense what another person is thinking and feeling (Griffin, 1994) and is essential for effective cross-cultural communication. It is the emotional and psychological sharing of the other person's experience and is widely recognized as an attribute possessed by successful interviewers. Rogers, for instance, advises counsellors to concentrate on being active, empathic listeners with the aim of temporarily entering the private perceptual world of the other and becoming thoroughly at home in it (Rogers, 1980). In Japan the highest form of communication competence is empathy – 'the ability to sense what others are thinking and feeling without their having to spell it out for you' (Griffin, 1994: 418).

An important aim of cross-cultural interviewer training is to develop *cultural empathy,* a general skill or attitude that helps a person feel as a person from another culture feels (Erickson and Shultz, 1982). It enables a person to empathize with the behaviours, feelings, and thoughts of people from other cultures. In cross-cultural interviews, cultural empathy enables the interviewer to understand how the interviewee feels and what the interviewee means (David and Erickson, 1990). It helps an interviewer to relate to interviewees from diverse cultural backgrounds and to make a fair and unbiased assessment (Collins, 2003).

Cultural empathy enables a person to be more sensitive to cultural difference and to relate cross-culturally. Interviewers possessing cultural empathy are more accepting of cultural difference and avoid jumping to conclusions about what the interviewee's physical appearance and unconventional nonverbal behaviour says about him. It enables an interviewer to make an unbiased assessment of a candidate from a different culture. Cultural empathy gives a basic awareness of linguistic and cultural variety among members of other cultures, together with sensitivity towards 'personal and family meaning systems...respectful forms of address...acceptable forms of question and responses...patterns of nonverbal communication' (Pugh, 1996: 122).

Lack of cultural empathy

When a British expatriate manager in Tanzania interviewed a local man for a job on an international development project the manager tried to establish a friendly, cooperative atmosphere from the outset by using a chatty, informal style. The Tanzanian, however, failed to respond as anticipated:

> Come in, John, glad you could make it.
> *Good morning, sir.*
> Have a seat, John – coffee's on the way you'll be pleased to hear.
> *Yes. Good morning, sir.*
> By the way, this is Bill, our IT fundi. You'll be working with Bill if you get the job.
> *Good morning, sir.*
> You've read the job description – yes?
> Yes.
> Anything that's not clear?
> *It is clear.*

The interviewer assumed that a friendly, informal style would encourage John to respond in kind – a signal that any British or American candidate would have recognized. John, however, failed to pick up the signal. It was blocked out by his culturally derived assumptions about the kind of behaviour that a job interview demanded. The interviewer's lack of cultural empathy was further demonstrated by his insensitive use of first-name terms – 'John' and 'Bill'. In Tanzania, even people working for the some organisation tend to address each other more formally, using 'Mr', 'Mrs', or 'Miss'.

Moreover, in Tanzania, deference to managers is the norm, so that when the manager launched straight into the interview, this immediately evoked a deferential and restrained response from the interviewee. A more effective strategy might have been to start with ten minutes' of small talk.

Ideally, the manager should have tried to build a relationship with John in the first ten minutes of the interview and tried to avoid forming any opinion – positive or negative – about the candidate during this time. Chatting about shared interests and experiences, family life, or people and places they both knew would have put the Tanzanian at ease and created the conditions for an effective interview. Once good rapport had been developed, the manager could then have begun to assess the candidate's competencies.

Coaching and feedback

Conducting practice interviews and receiving feedback from the tutor and other trainees is a key part of most cross-cultural interviewing courses. However, interviewers may need more than just a single course to hone their cross-cultural interviewing skills. Sometimes post-training individual feedback on performance and personal follow-up coaching is arranged. Miller and Rose (2009) found that follow-up activities of this kind improve the performance of interviewers by gradually improving their empathic understanding of interviewees.

SMALL-GROUP EXERCISE: Discussion questions

Working in small groups, discuss each of the following questions and write down the group's agreed answer. At the end of the exercise, each group may present its answers to the other groups for comment.

1. From the organisation's point of view why is it important to avoid bias and discrimination in the selection process? What are the negative consequences of failing to do so?
2. Identify the main forms of candidate bias that occur in cross-cultural interviews and explain what can be done to counter them.
3. Explain how a diverse workforce can produce competitive advantage for an organisation.
4. Explain how unintentional discrimination may be introduced into the selection process of a multicultural organisation.
5. List the characteristics of a multicultural interview that create a strong positive impression on candidates. Why does it matter that candidates are impressed?
6. 'Standard interviewing techniques often prove inadequate for interviewing people from diverse cultures.' Explain.
7. What is cultural empathy? Why is cultural empathy an essential quality for cross-cultural interviewers to have?

KEY POINTS

1. A diverse workforce can produce competitive advantage for an organisation. But to reap the benefits the organisation must first ensure that its selection procedures are fair and efficient. This is not always the case. In cross-cultural interviews, cultural differences between interviewer and interviewee sometimes affect perceptions and lead to unfavourable assessments. Standardized, 'off-the-shelf' psychological tests may be used without considering their relevance and validity to culturally diverse candidates, thereby introducing unintentional discrimination into selection.

2. There are more differences than similarities in the selection practices used in countries around the world. The practices used usually depend on the conventions and legislation requirements of each country. Selection interviews are widely used in North America, Europe, and Australia, but not in Chinese organisations, which tend to emphasize the candidate's company or educational institution when making an assessment. In Japan, a candidate's relationships and contacts often outweigh other factors in the selection process, while French companies often use graphology to assess candidates.

3. A major disadvantage of selection interviews is that they are poor at predicting job performance and often fail to distinguish between poor, average, and strong candidates. Another problem is that stereotyping is common in cross-cultural interviews. This practice creates entanglements in the interviewer–interviewee relationship because it de-individualises the interviewee and causes resentment. Another kind of unfair treatment occurs in cross-cultural interviews when interviewers fail to give the same amount of time and attention to candidates from all cultural groups.

4. Structured interviews give greater consistency from interview to interview and produce comparable information from candidate to candidate. Structured interviews are lower on bias and subjectivity and better at predicting job performance than unstructured interviews. Candidates from minority groups have higher perceptions of fairness when interviews are structured and all questions are job-related. Moreover, the practice of using structured interviews and job-related questions helps firms to defend themselves against charges of employment discrimination and to win litigation cases.

5. Interviewees often find it mentally exhausting to have to use a foreign language throughout a cross-cultural interview, and may have difficulty explaining their ideas or presenting arguments. The interviewer may use jargon, acronyms, abbreviations, and idioms of his own language that the interviewee does not fully understand. Thus language becomes a factor working for the interviewer and against the interviewee and increases the probability of an unfavourable assessment. Ideally, interviews should be conducted in the interviewee's own language. Otherwise, interviewers with a good knowledge of the interviewee's culture should conduct the interview so that they are able to place the interviewee's answers in an appropriate cultural context.

6. The interviewing skills of managers and recruitment staff employed by organisations sometimes need to be expanded and enhanced to make them more effective in a cross-cultural interviewing context. A single set of interviewing techniques is inadequate for interviewing candidates from diverse cultural backgrounds. For instance, standard techniques for encouraging people to talk – open questions, reflecting, non-judgmental responses, and so on – may not work with, say, interviewees who have been raised in restrictive, authoritarian cultures.

7. Empathy has long been recognized as an attribute of successful interviewers, but cross-cultural interviewers need to demonstrate cultural empathy. Cultural empathy is a general skill or attitude that helps a person feel as a person from another culture feels. When deployed in a cross-cultural interview it enables the interviewer to make an unbiased assessment of candidates from diverse cultures. Interviewers with cultural empathy are more accepting of cultural difference. For instance, they avoid jumping to conclusions about what an unusual physical appearance or unconventional nonverbal behaviour says about the candidate.

QUESTIONS FOR DISCUSSION AND WRITTEN ASSIGNMENTS

1. Explain the various kinds of bias that can occur in cross-cultural interviews? How can the risk of bias be reduced?
2. What are the most important skills and abilities that are needed by cross-cultural interviewers? Explain how these skills can be developed by means of training.
3. What training methods can be used to help cross-cultural interviewers recognize their own tendencies towards bias and use of stereotypes?

BIBLIOGRAPHY

Adler, NJ. Women in international management: where are they? *California Management Review*, 26, 1984, 78–89.

Barnham, K and Oates, D. *The International Manager*. Business Books, 1991.

Bennett, MJ. (ed.), *Basic Concepts of Intercultural Communication*. Intercultural Press, 1998, p. 18.

Biesheuvel, S. Psychologial tests and their application to non-European peoples. In DR Price-Williams (ed.), *Cross-cultural Studies*. Penguin, 1969.

Black, J. The relationship of personal characteristics with the adjustment of Japanese expatriate managers. *Management International Review*, 30 (2), 1990, 119–134.

Briggs, C. Interviewing, power/knowledge, and social inequality. In J Gubrium and J Holstein (eds), *The Handbook of Interview Research: Context and Method*. Sage, 2002, pp. 911–922.

Brislin, RW et al. (eds), *Cross-cultural Research Methods*. Wiley, 1973, p. 70.

Burton, SK. Issues in cross-cultural interviewing: Japanese women in England. *Oral History*, 31 (1), 2003, 38–46.

Caligiuri, PM and Cascio, WF. Can we send her there? Maximising the success of Western women on global assignments. *Journal of World Business*, 33, 1998, 394–416.

Campion, MA, Palmer, DK and Campion, JE. A review of structure in the selection interview. *Personnel Psychology*, 50, 1997, 655–702.

Chan, CC. Work goals of Bruneian managers: A comparison across gender, age groups, educational levels and managerial levels. *Asia Pacific Journal of Human Resource Management*, 40, 2002, 363–373.

Chaplin, WF et al., Handshaking, gender, personality and first impressions. *Journal of Personality and Social Psychology*, 79, 2000, 110–117.

Collins, M. Interviewer variability: a review of the problem. In N Fielding (ed.), *Interviewing* (Vol. 4). Sage, 2003, p. 89.

Cross, R and Parker, A. *The Hidden Power of Social Networks*. Harvard Business School Press, 2003.

Dana, D. *Managing Cultural Differences*, HR.com internet web site, 2000.

d'Ardenne, P and Mahtani, A. *Transcultural Counselling in Action*. Sage, 1989, p. 24.

Davey, AG. The Tristan da Cunhan children's concepts of equivalence. *British Journal of Educational Psychology*, 38, 1968.

David, AB and Erickson, CA. Ethnicity and the therapist's use of self. *Family Therapy*, 17, 1990, 211–216.

DDI, *Targeted Selection: Cross-Cultural Comparison of Candidate and Interviewer Reactions*. Development Dimensions International, 1999.

Draguns, JG. Humanly universal and culturally distinctive. In PB Pedersen et al. (eds), *Counselling Across Cultures*, 4th ed. Sage, 1996, p. 7.

Dwairy, MA. *Cross-cultural Counselling: The Arab-Palestinian Case*. Haworth Press, 1998, p. 36.

Earley, PC and Mosakowski, E. Cultural intelligence. *Harvard Business Review*, October 2004, 141–142.

Eerdmans, SL. A review of John J Gumperz's current contributions to interactional sociolinguistics. In SL Eerdmans et al. (eds), *Language and Interaction*. Jorn Benjamins Publishing, 2003, p. 91.

Erickson, F and Shultz, J. *The Counsellor as Gatekeeper: Social Interaction in Interviews*. Academic Press, 1982, p. 126.

Fernandez-Araoz, C, Groysberg, B and Nohria, N. The definitive guide to recruiting in good times and bad. *HBR*, May 2009, 74–84.

Gravesand, LM and Karren, RJ. The employee selection interviews: A fresh look at an old problem. *Human Resource Management*, 35, 1996, 163–180.

Greenfield, PM. You can't take it with you: why ability assessments don't cross cultures. *American Psychologist*, 52, 1997, 1115–1124.

Griffin, E. *A First Look at Communication Theory*, 2nd ed. McGraw-Hill, 1994.

Guirdham, M. *Communicating Across Cultures at Work*, 2nd ed. Palgrave Macmillan, 2005.

Gumperz, JJ. *Discourse Strategies*. CUP, 1982, pp. 302–327.

Gumperz, JJ. Interviewing in intercultural situations. In P Drew and J Heritage (eds), *Talk at Work*, CUP, 1992, pp. 302–327.

Gumperz, JJ. The linguistic and cultural relativity of conversational inference. In JJ Gumperz and SC Levinson (eds), *Rethinking Linguistic Relativity*. CUP, 1996, p. 400.

Ho, DYF. Relational orientation in Asian social psychology. In U Kim and JW Berry (eds), *Indigenous Psychologies: Research and Experience in Cultural Context*. Sage, 1993, pp. 240–259.

Hubbard, G et al., *The First XI: Winning Organisations in Australia*. Wiley, 2007.

Huo, YP and Von Glinow, MA. On transplanting human resource practices to China: a culture-driven approach. *International Journal of Manpower*, 16 (9), 3–13, 1995.

Huo, YP. Huang, HJ and Napier, NK. Divergence or convergence: a cross-national comparison of personnel selection practices. *Human Resource Management*, 41 (1), 2002, 31–44.

Irvine, SH. Affect and construct: a cross-cultural check on theories of intelligence. *Journal of Social Psychology*, 80, 1970, 23–30.

Jensen, I. The practice of intercultural communication – reflections for professionals in cultural meetings. *Intercultural Communication*, 6, February 2003–May 2004.

Joy, RO. Cultural and procedural difficulties that influence business strategies and operations in the People's R of C. *Advanced Management Journal*, 29, 1989, 30.

Keidel, L. *Conflict or Connection*. EMIS, 1996, p. 19.

Kochman, T. Black and white cultural styles in pluralistic perspective. In MJ Bennett (ed.), *Basic Concepts of Intercultural Communication*. Intercultural Press, 1998, pp. 131–156.

Korn/Ferry, *Executive Recruiter Index*, 10th ed. Korn/Ferry International, 2009.

Kress, G. (ed.), *Communication and Culture: An Introduction*, New South Wales University Press, 1988, p. 94.

Latham, GP and Finnegan, B. Perceived practicality of unstructured, patterned, and situational interviews. In H Schuler et al. (eds), *Personnel Selection and Assessment: Individual and Organisational Perspectives*. Erlbaum, 1993, pp. 41–55.

Leigh, JW. *Communicating for Cultural Competence*. Allyn & Bacon, 1998.

Leonard, B. Diverse workforce tends to attract more female and minority job applicants. *HR Magazine*, April 2001.

McDonnell, A et al., Learning transfer in multinational companies: explaining inter-organisation variation. *Human Resource Management Journal*, 20 (1), 2010, 23–43.

Mellahi, K and Wood, GT. From kinship to trust: changing recruitment practices in unstable political contexts. *International Journal of Cross-cultural Management*, 3, 2003, 369–381.

Miller, WR and Rose, GS. Toward a theory of motivational interviewing. *American Psychologist*, 64 (6), 2009, 527–537.

Nalbantian, HR and Szostak, A. How Fleet Bank fought employee flight. *Harvard Business Review*, April 2004, p. 124.

Pedersen, PB et al. *Counselling Across Cultures*, 4th ed. Sage, 1996, p. ix.

Pugh, R. *Effective Language in Health and Social Work*. Chapman & Hall, 1996.

Richard, OC. Racial diversity, business strategy, and team performance: A resource-based view. *Academy of Management Journal*, 43, 2000, 164–177.

Ridley, CR and Lingle, DW. Cultural empathy in multicultural counselling. In PB Pederson, JG Draguns, WJ Lonner and J Trimble (eds), *Counselling Across Cultures*, 4th ed. Sage, 1996, p. 36.

Ridley, CR et al., Multicultural training: reexaminatrion, operationalisation, and integration. *Counselling Psychologist*, 22, 1994, 227–289.

Rogers, C. *A Way of Being*. Houghton Mifflin, 1980.

Rumbelow, H. Feminine charm is still a career girl's best friend. *The Times*, 9 January 2003, p. 9.

Ryan, AM and Ployhart, RE. Applicants' perceptions of selection procedures and decisions: a critical review and agenda for the future. *Journal of Management*, 26, 2000, 565–606.

Santoro, MA. Manager's journal: promoting human rights in China is good business. *Wall Street Journal*, 29 June 1988, p. 5.

Saville-Troike, M. *The Ethnography of Communication: An Introduction*. Blackwell, 1982, p. 126.

Schuman, H and Converse, JM. The effects of black and white interviewers on black responses in 1968. In N Fielding (ed.), Interviewing (Vol. 4). Sage, 2003.

Shackleton, V and Newell, S. *Journal of Occupational Psychology*, 64, 1991, 23–36.

Shih, J. Yeah, I could hire this one, but I know it's gonna be a problem. *Ethnic and Racial Studies*, 25 (1), 2002, 99–119.

Sinangil, HK and Ones, DS. Gender differences in expatriate job performance. *Applied Psychology: An International Review*, 52, 2003, 461–475.

Snape, E and Redman, T. Too old or too young? The impact of perceived age discrimination. *Human Resource Management Journal*, 13, 2003, 78–89.

Solomon, CM. Success abroad depends on more than job skills. *Personnel Journal*, 73(4), 1994, 51–54.

Stephan, WG and Stephan, C. Reducing intercultural anxiety through intercultural contact. *International Journal of Intercultural Relations*, 16, 1992, 89–106.

Stewart, GL et al., Exploring the handshake in employment interviews. *Journal of Applied Psychology*, 93 (5), 2008, 1139–1146.

Torrington, D. *International HRM: Think Globally, Act Locally*. Prentice-Hall, 1994.

Verardi, S et al., Psychometric properties of the Marlowe-Crowne Social Desirability Scale in eigth African countries and Switzerland. *Journal of Cross-cultural Psychology*, 41 (1), 2010, 19–34.

Watson, WE, Kumar, K and Michaelsen, LK. Cultural diversity's impact on interaction process and performance. *Academy of Management Journal*, 36, 1993, 590–602.

Word, CO, Zanna, MP and Cooper, J. The nonverbal mediation of self-fulfilling prophecies in interracial interaction. *Journal of Experimental Social Psychology*, 10(2), 1974, 109–120.

Young, R. *Intercultural Communication: Pragmatics, Genealogy, Deconstruction*. Multilingual Matters, 1996, p. 125.

Zerbe, WJ and Paulhus, DL. Socially desirable responding in organisational behaviour: a reconception. *Academy of Management Review*, 12, 1987, 250–264.

Appendix
Power of social networks

HOW SOCIAL NETWORKS STRENGTHEN MANAGERS

Social networking skills are an attribute of successful leaders of multicultural teams, expatriate managers, managers in multicultural workplaces – and indeed of managers at all levels in virtually all sectors. Cross and Parker (2003) worked with organisations in the petrochemicals, pharmaceutical, electronics, and consulting sectors to determine the characteristics of high performers and found that a notable characteristic of high performing managers was that they had larger and more diversified social networks than average and low performers.

The reason why successful managers tend to have wide and diversified social networks is, no doubt, that the managerial tasks (such as hitting output targets or raising quality standards) require *effective collaboration* within and across functional and geographical boundaries, and typically these tasks are successfully carried out through informal social networks.

Social networks help shape common goals and values among an organisation's members. Through social interaction people learn their organisations' languages, codes, values, and practices – a shared vision that is 'a bonding mechanism that helps different parts of an organisation to integrate or to combine resources' (Tsai and Ghosal, 1998: 467).

STRONG AND WEAK TIES

A social network consists of the links of all kinds among a set of individuals (Mitchell, 1973). Links such as friends, friends of friends, professional contacts, internet communities of practice. Links comprising strong and weak ties which together provide privileged information and access to ideas and opportunities. Large social networks consisting of both strong ties and weak ties help managers to find answers to their questions and overcome their difficulties more quickly and easily (Figure A1).

Strong ties consist of interactions occurring at least twice a week (Granovetter, 1973). They give cheap, rich, detailed, and accurate information, and they act as business generators and reputation enhancers. *Weak ties* are usually with people in outside organisations and other countries. According to Cross and Parker (2003), they make a greater contribution to a person's career success, and

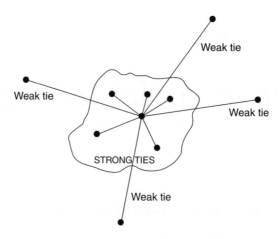

Figure A1   Strong and weak ties

Source: Adapted from Jack (2005).

those who rely on weak ties as sources of ideas are more likely to be innovative than people who rely on strong ties. Figure A2 shows a social network in diagrammatic form.

Personal social networks built up by managers may be supplemented by online communities of practice. As shown by the success of Facebook and the impact of blogs, a sense of community similar to that provided by face-to-face contact can be acquired by electronic means. Facebook was originally developed by students to allow students from different colleges to form social networks.

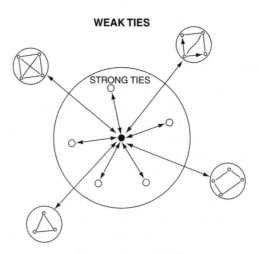

Figure A2   Social networks

Source: Adapted from Jack (2005).

A blog is a website on which items are posted on a regular basis and displayed in reverse chronological order. Since blogs attract responses they provide a means of expanding a manager's social network very quickly.

SOCIAL NETWORKS AND INNOVATION

Innovations in multicultural teams are typically developed through the use of social networks – that is through a collaborative exchange of ideas between people within the team, and between the team and outsiders. Tsai and Ghosal (1998) collected data from 15 business units of a multinational electronics company and found that information exchanged between units had a significant effect on product innovation.

With regard to innovation, multicultural team leaders often find that smaller, tighter social networks (strong ties) are less useful than networks with lots of connections to individuals and organisations outside the main network (weak ties). Weak ties are critical for innovation and the generation of knowledge. They introduce more new ideas than closed networks whose members already share the same knowledge and opportunities. A team leader or project manager with connections to other social networks will, through that, have access to a much wider range of information and so be able to make a greater contribution to innovative projects.

BIBLIOGRAPHY

R Cross and A Parker, *The Hidden Power of Social Networks*. Harvard Business School Press, 2003.

M Granovetter, The strength of weak ties. *American Journal of Sociology*, 78 (6), 1973, 1360–1380.

SL Jack, The role, use and activation of strong and weak network ties: a qualitative analysis. *Journal of Management Studies*, 42 (6), 2005, 1233–1259.

Mitchell, JC. Social Networks. *Annual Review of Anthropology*, 3, 1974, 279–299.

W Tsai and S Ghosal, Social capital and value creation: the role of intrafirm networks. *Academy of Management Journal*, 41 (4), 1998, 464–476.

Books for further study

Adler NJ. *International Dimensions of Organisational Behaviour*. South-Western College Publishing, 1997.

Bartlett CA and Ghosal S. *Managing Across Borders – The Transnational Solution*. Harvard University Press, 1989.

Bennett MJ (ed.). *Basic Concepts of Intercultural Communication*. Intercultural Press, 1998.

Boyd R and Richerson PJ. *The Origin and Evolution of Cultures*. Oxford University Press, 2005.

Brett JM. *Negotiating Globally*. Jossey-Bass, 2001.

Clyne M. *Inter-cultural Communication at Work*. Cambridge University Press, 1994.

Dwairy MA. *Cross-cultural Counselling: The Arab-Palestinian Case*. Haworth Press, 1998.

Earley C and Ang S. *Cultural Intelligence: Individual Interactions Across Cultures*. Stanford University Press, 2003.

Ferraro GP. *The Cultural Dimension of International Business*, 3rd ed. Prentice Hall, 1998.

Fisher G. *Mindsets: The Role of Culture and Perception in International Relations*, 2nd ed. Intercultural Press, 1997.

Fowler SM (ed.). *Intercultural Sourcebook: Cross-cultural Training Methods* (Vol. 2). Intercultural Press, 1999.

Furnham A and Bochner S. *Culture Shock: Psychological Reactions to Unfamiliar Environments*. Methuen, 1986.

Gallois C and Callan VJ. *Communication and Culture*. Wiley, 1997.

Guirdham M. *Communicating Across Cultures at Work*, 2nd ed. Palgrave Macmillan, 2005.

Jackson T. *International HRM: A Cross-cultural Approach*. Sage, 2002.

Kabagarama D. *Breaking the Ice: A Guide to Understanding People from Other Cultures*. Allyn & Bacon, 1993.

Landis D, Bennett JM, and Bennett MJ (eds). *Handbook of Intercultural Training*, 3rd ed. Sage, 2004.

Leigh JW. *Communicating for Cultural Competence*. Allyn & Bacon, 1998.

Lustig MW and Koester J. *Intercultural Competence: Interpersonal Communication Across Cultures*, 3rd ed. Longman, 1999.

Martin MJ and Newman K (eds). *Handbook of Cross-cultural Management*. Blackwell, 2002.

Novinger T. *Intercultural Communication: A Practical Guide*. University of Texas Press, 2001.

Orme MP and Harris TM. *Interracial Communication: Theory into Practice.* Wadsworth, 2001.

Poyatos F (ed.). *Cross-cultural Perspectives in Nonverbal Communication.* Hogrefe, 1988.

Salacuse J. *The Global Negotiator.* Palgrave Macmillan, 2003.

Schirato T and Yell S. *Communication and Culture: An Introduction.* Sage, 2000.

Schneider SC and Barsoux J-L. *Managing Across Cultures.* Prentice Hall, 1997.

Scollon R and Scollon SW. *Intercultural Communication*, 2nd ed. Blackwell, 2001.

Thomas DC. *Cross-cultural Management: Cross-cultural Concepts*, 2nd ed. Sage, 2008.

Thomas DC and Inkson K. *Cultural Intelligence: People Skills for Global Business.* Berrett-Koehler, 2004.

Varner I and Beamer L. *Intercultural Communication in the Global Workplace.* Irwin, 1995.

Wiseman RL (ed.). *Intercultural Communication Theory.* Sage, 1995.

Young S. *Micromessaging: Why Great Leadership Is Beyond Words.* McGraw-Hill, 2006.

Zweifel TD. *Culture Clash: Managing the Global High-performance Team.* Swiss Consulting Group, 2003.

Index